THE LONGMAN COMPANION TO
BRITAIN SINCE 1945

LONGMAN COMPANIONS TO HISTORY

General Editors: Chris Cook and John Stevenson

THE LONGMAN COMPANION TO
BRITAIN SINCE 1945

Chris Cook and John Stevenson

SECOND EDITION

Longman

An imprint of **Pearson Education**

Harlow, England · London · New York · Reading, Massachusetts · San Francisco · Toronto · Don Mills, Ontario · Sydney
Tokyo · Singapore · Hong Kong · Seoul · Taipei · Cape Town · Madrid · Mexico City · Amsterdam · Munich · Paris · Milan

Pearson Education Limited
Edinburgh Gate
Harlow
Essex CM20 2JE
England

and Associated Companies throughout the world

Visit us on the World Wide Web at:
www.pearsoneduc.com

First published 1995
Second edition 2000

© Pearson Education Limited 1995, 2000

The rights of Chris Cook and John Stevenson to be identified as authors
of this Work have been asserted by them in accordance with
the Copyright, Designs and Patents Act 1988.

ISBN 0 582 35674 1 PPR
ISBN 0 582 43729 6 CSD

British Library Cataloguing-in-Publication Data
A catalogue record for this book is available from the British Library

Library of Congress Cataloging-in-Publication Data
Cook, Chris, 1945-
    The Longman companion to Britain since 1945 / Chris Cook and John Stevenson.– 2nd ed.
        p. cm. – (Longman companions to history)
    Includes bibliographical references and index.
    ISBN 0-582-35674-1 (pbk. : alk. paper)
    1. Great Britain–History–George VI, 1936-1952–Handbooks, manuals, etc. 2. Great
Britain–History–Elizabeth II, 1952—Handbooks, manuals, etc. I. Title: Britain since
1945. II. Stevenson, John, 1946- III. Title. IV. Series.

DA592.C628 2000
941.084–dc21   99-087557

Set by 7 in 10/12pt New Baskerville
Produced by Pearson Education Asia Pte Ltd.,
Printed in Singapore

CONTENTS

PREFACE

This second edition of the *Longman Companion to Britain since 1945* has attempted to provide, within a concise and accessible volume, a compendium of essential facts and figures on recent British history. Embracing over 50 years since the end of the Second World War, it covers the major aspects of British history, politics and society from the start of the Attlee administration in 1945 to the final years of the twentieth century. This new edition thus covers the changing politics of the 1990s, with material on the fall of the Major government and the first thousand days of the 'New Labour' administration under Tony Blair.

It provides a detailed chronology together with extensive information on Cabinet appointments, elections and party politics, as well as recent constitutional developments. Britain's changing role in the world, from imperial power to partner in the European Union, is fully covered.

Also included is a wealth of material, presented in easily accessible tabular form, on such topics as population, education, labour and religion. The changing fortunes of the British economy are reflected in key statistics on trade, unemployment and many others.

There are detailed notes on wars and treaties; a biographical section giving brief notes on key careers; a glossary of essential historical and political terms; and an extensive, fully updated bibliography arranged by topic.

Both authors would like to acknowledge the help and advice in the preparation of this new edition of numerous colleagues, in particular Dr Harry Harmer.

Chris Cook
John Stevenson
1 March 2000

LIST OF MAPS

PUBLISHER'S ACKNOWLEDGEMENTS

We are grateful to the following for permission to reproduce copyright
material:

The Economist for a table from *The Economist* 10.6.99, © The Economist,
London, 10.6.99; Office for National Statistics for tables from Central
Statistical Office *Key Data, 1992/3* (HMSO 1993), © Crown Copyright and a
table from General Register Office, Northern Ireland, *Census of Population
1961*, County volumes, Tables XVI (HMSO 1964), © Crown Copyright;
Penguin Books Ltd for a table from *Pears Cyclopaedia*, 103rd edition (Pelham
1994) and tables from *Pears Cyclopaedia*, 108th edition (Penguin 1999).

POLITICAL HISTORY

1 POLITICAL CHRONOLOGY

Coalition government, 1945 (formed May 1940)

1945

Feb. Yalta Conference of Churchill, Stalin and Roosevelt. Representation of the People Act reduces business vote and introduces postal vote for armed forces. Stafford Cripps readmitted to Labour party.

Apr. Death of President Roosevelt (12th); Harry Truman succeeds him. Common Wealth wins by-election at Chelmsford, indicating swing to left. Death of Mussolini (28th); death of Hitler in Berlin (30th).

May Germany surrenders: VE Day (8th). Labour party conference rejects Churchill's call for a continuation of wartime coalition until the defeat of Japan. Labour party leaves coalition and Churchill forms a caretaker administration until the general election called for 5 July.

June Allied Control Commission divides Germany into four occupation zones. Churchill accuses Labour party of having to introduce 'Gestapo' to enforce socialism. Family Allowances Bill enacted.

July General election (5th–26th) gives Labour party a majority of 146 seats. During delay while armed forces votes are counted, Churchill and Attlee attend Potsdam Conference with Truman and Stalin.

Labour government, 1945–50

1945

July Attlee forms first majority Labour government. Principal figures: Attlee (Prime Minister), Ernest Bevin (Foreign Secretary), Hugh Dalton (Chancellor of the Exchequer), Herbert Morrison (Lord President of the Council), Aneurin ('Nye') Bevan (Minister of Health).

Aug. Clement Davies succeeds Sir Archibald Sinclair as Liberal leader. British troops liberate Burma. Atom bombs dropped by US air force on Hiroshima (6th) and Nagasaki (9th); Japan surrenders (13th). USA terminates Lend-Lease to Britain.

Sept. All-India Congress Committee demands that British quit India.

Dec. Britain, USA and USSR agree in Moscow to provisional democratic government in Korea. US loan to Britain agreed of $3.75 billion.

1946

Feb. Bank of England nationalized. Churchill makes 'Iron Curtain' speech at Fulton, Missouri, USA.

Mar. Cabinet mission leaves for India.

May Repeal of Trades Disputes Act 1927.

June Breakdown of negotiations with Congress party in India and Muslim League over a unified India; Cabinet mission leaves India. Bread rationing introduced.

July Nationalization of coal industry. Zionist Irgun terrorist group blow up King David Hotel in Jerusalem, killing 91 people.

Aug. National Insurance Act passed, providing state benefits for unemployment, illness and old age in return for weekly contributions.

Nov. National Health Service Act, providing free medical care for all, including hospital, optician and dental services (to take effect from July 1948).

Dec. Britain and USA arrange economic merger of their zones in Germany. British Medical Association (BMA) opposes arrangements for medical practitioners in the new National Health Service.

1947

Jan. Coal rationing introduced; severest winter weather for half a century.

Feb. British proposals to divide Palestine into Arab and Jewish zones fail to achieve support from either side. Government announces that India will become independent no later than June 1948.

Mar. Truman Doctrine enunciated, offering US support against communist aggression, precipitated by Britain's inability to continue support for royalist forces in Greek Civil War. Mountbatten becomes Viceroy of India to oversee independence. Britain refers Palestine Mandate to the United Nations (UN).

Apr. School leaving age raised to 15.

May Conservatives publish *Industrial Charter*, accepting nationalization and supporting a Workers' Charter. Churchill calls for a 'United States of Europe' at meeting of United Europe Committee. Partition of India agreed in Cabinet, creating Muslim state of East and West Pakistan.

June Mountbatten announces that Indian independence will be brought forward to 15 Aug. 1947. US Secretary of State calls for European Recovery Programme: the 'Marshall Aid Plan'.

July Serious drain of dollar reserves and continued economic problems lead to talk of Attlee's removal.

Aug. Attlee announces austerity plan and takes emergency powers to increase production and restrict home consumption. Indian independence (15th) proclaimed with Nehru as Indian Premier and Ali Khan as Premier of Pakistan. Large-scale communal violence accompanies the decision. Electricity industry nationalized; inland transport nationalized, effective from 1 Jan. 1948.

Sept.	Cripps becomes Minister of Economic Affairs; Harold Wilson becomes President of Board of Trade.
Oct.	Conservative conference adopts *Industrial Charter*; calls for £1 million 'fighting fund' and seeks expansion of Young Conservatives. Cripps introduces major cuts in housing and other construction. Direction of labour introduced by the Control of Engagement Order.
Nov.	Pre-budget leak forces resignation of Dalton as Chancellor of the Exchequer; replaced by Cripps.

1948

Jan.	Burma becomes an independent republic. Bevin calls for a Western European Union to resist Soviet domination.
Feb.	BMA votes against participation in National Health Service.
Mar.	Conservatives greatly increase majority at Croydon by-election. Brussels Treaty signed with France and Benelux countries, a 50-year alliance of economic and military cooperation.
Apr.	Bevan conciliates the doctors by allowing the retention of private beds and independent contracts for general practitioners (GPs) and consultants. US Economic Cooperation Act comes into effect, putting $980 million of Marshall Aid at Britain's disposal.
May	Jews proclaim new state of Israel.
June	State of Emergency declared over dock strike. Beginning of 'emergency' in Malaya with call to arms by Malay Communist party.
July	National Health Service (NHS) comes into being. Beginning of Berlin blockade by USSR and of airlift to supply West Berlin. Representation of the People Act abolishes university and business franchise. Town and Country Planning Act passed.
Nov.	Harold Wilson abolishes a large number of economic regulations: the 'bonfire of controls'. Edmonton by-election sees large fall in Labour support.

1949

Feb.	Clothes rationing ends.
Apr.	North Atlantic Treaty Organization (NATO) created. Ireland declares itself a republic and leaves the Commonwealth.
May	USSR lifts Berlin blockade. Federal Republic of Germany (FRG) established. Gas industry nationalized.
June	Dock strike broken by troops after State of Emergency declared.
July	Serious run on gold and dollar reserves threatens new economic crisis.
Aug.	Cabinet decides on need for devaluation.

Sept.   Cripps announces devaluation of pound from US $4.03 to US $2.88.

Oct.   Beaverbrook via *Daily Express* launches policy of Empire Free Trade.

Nov.   'Groundnuts scheme' comes under attack in the House of Commons. Iron and Steel Nationalization Act is passed.

Dec.   Parliament Act is passed, limiting delaying power of House of Lords to two sessions and one year.

1950

Jan.   Britain recognizes Communist China. General election announced for 23 Feb. State of Emergency declared in Gold Coast after riots in Accra.

Feb.   General election results in Labour majority of five seats.

Labour government, 1950–51

1950

Feb.   Attlee forms government. Principal figures: Attlee (Prime Minister); Cripps (Chancellor of the Exchequer); Bevin (Foreign Secretary).

May   Conservative overtures to the Liberals rebuffed by Clement Davies, the Liberal leader. Petrol rationing ends.

June   Outbreak of Korean War when North Korean troops enter South Korea. UN Security Council authorizes military aid to South Korea.

July   Britain agrees to send troops to Korea.

Sept.   British troops in action in Korea.

Oct.   Chinese troops enter Korean War. Cripps retires. Hugh Gaitskell becomes Chancellor of the Exchequer. Conservatives issue call to build 300,000 houses a year.

1951

Jan.   New rearmament programme of £4,700 million announced.

Feb.   Nationalization of iron and steel takes effect. Bevin resigns from Foreign Office and is replaced by Herbert Morrison.

Apr.   Bevan (along with Harold Wilson and John Freeman) resigns in protest at Cabinet decision to impose NHS prescription charges. 'Bevanite' grouping inaugurated to contest Labour's foreign and defence policies.

May   Iranian Prime Minister, Dr Mussadeq, announces nationalization of British oil assets in Iran, including Abadan oil refinery.

June   Burgess and Maclean, two British diplomats spying for the USSR, flee to Moscow.

Sept.   General election announced for 25 Oct. Conservative election manifesto promises to build 300,000 houses and denationalize the iron and steel industry.

Oct.   General election results in Conservative overall majority of 16 seats.

Conservative government, 1951–55

1951

Oct.   Churchill forms Conservative government. Principal figures: Churchill (Prime Minister); Butler (Chancellor of the Exchequer); Eden (Foreign Secretary). Liberal leader Clement Davies refuses offer of a seat in Conservative Cabinet, asserting the continued independence of the Liberal party.

Nov.   New government commits itself to denationalize iron and steel and road haulage, but introduces severe economies elsewhere in view of balance of payments problems.

Dec.   London Foreign Exchange Market reopens after twelve years.

1952

Jan.   Commonwealth Finance Ministers' Conference in London to coordinate policy of the sterling area. Restrictions imposed on imports and hire-purchase. Sir Gerald Templer becomes High Commissioner in Malaya to deal with communist insurgency.

Feb.   Death of George VI. Elizabeth II ascends throne.

Mar.   Fifty-seven Labour MPs dissent from 'party line' and vote against government defence motion.

July   European Coal and Steel Community established without British participation.

Oct.   Britain's first atom bomb exploded off Monte Bellow Islands, Western Australia. State of Emergency declared in Kenya over Mau Mau revolt.

1953

Feb.   Amnesty for wartime deserters declared.

Mar.   Steel denationalized.

Apr.   Road transport denationalized.

June   Coronation of Elizabeth II. Britain gives *de facto* recognition to the Republic of Egypt.

July   Korean armistice signed at Panmunjon.

Sept.   End of sugar rationing after fourteen years.

Nov.   National Service Act maintains conscription for another five years.

Dec.   Eden announces suspension of negotiations with Egypt on the future of the Canal Zone.

7

1954

Feb.   Nasser seizes power in Egypt.

Mar.   London Gold Market reopens after fifteen years.

Apr.   Geneva Conference on Indo-China opens. Bevan resigns from Labour party shadow cabinet over the party's Far Eastern policy.

July   All food rationing ends. Anglo-Egyptian agreement in Cairo to withdraw British troops from Suez Canal Zone approved by Parliament. Television Act approves setting up of commercial television under the Independent Broadcasting Authority.

Aug.   End of hire-purchase controls.

Sept.   Gaitskell elected treasurer of Labour party, emerging as favourite to succeed Attlee. Bevan bitterly attacks Labour leadership.

Oct.   Macmillan becomes Minister of Defence. Final agreement on British withdrawal of troops from the Canal Zone.

1955

Feb.   Decision to proceed with manufacture of hydrogen bomb announced.

Mar.   Attlee supports government decision on hydrogen bomb; Bevan criticizes lack of leadership and leads 62 MPs in abstaining from vote. Labour Whip withdrawn from Bevan (restored on 28 Apr.).

Apr.   Paris Agreement ratified: FRG to join NATO and Britain to maintain four divisions and tactical air force in mainland Europe. USSR denounces 1942 treaty with Britain and France. Churchill resigns premiership on grounds of ill-health (5th); Eden becomes Prime Minister; Macmillan succeeds him as Foreign Secretary. General election called (15th) for 26 May.

May   General election gives Conservatives an overall majority of 60 seats.

Conservative government, 1955–59

1955

May   Eden forms Conservative government. Principal figures: Eden (Prime Minister); Butler (Chancellor of the Exchequer); Macmillan (Foreign Secretary); Selwyn Lloyd (Minister of Defence).

July   Summit Conference of Britain, France, USA and USSR at Geneva fails to achieve decisive breakthrough in Cold War.

Nov.   State of Emergency declared in Cyprus as a result of EOKA terrorism.

Dec.   Attlee resigns as leader of Labour party (7th); Gaitskell becomes leader on first ballot of Labour MPs with 157 votes to Bevan's 70 and 40 for Morrison (14th). Government reshuffle (20th): Macmillan becomes Chancellor; Selwyn Lloyd, Foreign Secretary; Butler, Lord Privy Seal and Leader of the House.

1956

Feb.   Khrushchev denounces Stalinism at 20th Communist Party Congress in Moscow. Movement for abolition of capital punishment endorsed by Eden. Eden and Eisenhower produce Declaration of Washington, affirming joint Anglo-American policy in Middle East.

Mar.   Archbishop Makarios of Cyprus deported to Seychelles; Bevan, as Labour colonial spokesman, denounces government policy in Cyprus.

June   Egypt announces it will end the Suez Canal Company's concessions on expiry in 1968. Last British troops leave Canal Zone. Bill abolishing capital punishment passes the Commons.

July   House of Lords rejects abolition of capital punishment. Britain and USA withdraw funding from Aswan High Dam (19th); Nasser announces nationalization of the Suez Canal (26th).

Aug.   Eden announces in Commons that military precautions are being taken over the Suez Canal; Gaitskell warns against the use of force, though condemning Nasser. 'Egypt Committee' of the Cabinet discusses use of force against Nasser.

Sept.   Nasser rejects eighteen-nation proposal to resolve Suez dispute. Eden, in Commons debate, warns against 'abject appeasement'; Gaitskell urges referral to UN Security Council (12th–13th). Britain and France refer Suez issue to Security Council on 23rd. Clement Davies resigns as Liberal leader; succeeded by Jo Grimond (5th Nov.).

Oct.   Conservative party conference endorses Eden's policy in the Middle East. Eden and Selwyn Lloyd meet French government in Paris where they discuss military intervention in Suez in collusion with Israel (16th). Outbreak of Hungarian uprising (23rd). Israel invades Egypt via the Sinai Peninsula (29th); as prearranged, British and French governments deliver an ultimatum to Egypt and Israel calling for a withdrawal of both sides to ten miles from Suez; Israel agrees, but Egypt refuses. The RAF and French air force bomb Egyptian airfields (31st).

Nov.   The government defeats a Labour motion of censure amid growing uproar about Britain's role in Suez (1st). Soviet forces retake Budapest after a week of bitter fighting (4th). Large exodus from the British Communist party. British and French troops land at Port Said (5th). Macmillan warns Cabinet that international reaction is threatening the security of sterling (6th). Britain and France accept a ceasefire in Egypt and agree to a UN peacekeeping role (7th). British government denies any collusion with Israel over Suez (22nd); Eden leaves London for Jamaica to recover from exhaustion (23rd), leaving Butler as acting Prime Minister.

Dec.	Suez group of Conservative MPs condemns 'humiliating withdrawal' from Suez (3rd). Macmillan announces large fall in gold and dollar reserves and need to draw on the International Monetary Fund (IMF) for funds (4th). British and French forces begin their withdrawal from Suez (5th). Eden tells the Commons that he had no foreknowledge of the Israeli attack on Egypt (20th).

1957

Jan.	Eden resigns as Prime Minister (9th); Butler is passed over as successor in favour of Macmillan (10th). Macmillan reshuffles the Cabinet: Peter Thorneycroft (Chancellor of the Exchequer); Butler (Home Secretary); Selwyn Lloyd (Foreign Secretary).
Mar.	Gold Coast given independence as Ghana.
Apr.	Decision to discontinue 'call up' for National Service after 1960. Labour party calls for an end to planned British hydrogen bomb tests.
May	First British hydrogen bomb explosion in the central Pacific.
July	Electricity Bill enacted: Central Electricity Generating Board and Electricity Council replace Central Electricity Authority. Federation of Malaya Independence Act is given royal assent.
Aug.	Council on Prices, Productivity and Incomes established.
Sept.	Disarmament discussions in London end without agreement. Publication of Wolfenden Report on prostitution.

1958

Jan.	Treaties establishing European Economic Community (EEC) and European Atomic Energy Community (Euratom) come into force. Thorneycroft resigns in protest at failure of Cabinet to cut government expenditure. Heathcoat Amory becomes Chancellor of the Exchequer. USSR proposes nineteen-nation summit negotiations.
Feb.	Britain and USA agree on the establishment of US missile bases in Britain. Campaign for Nuclear Disarmament (CND) set up with Earl (Bertrand) Russell as president.
Mar.	Liberals win Torrington by-election; first Liberal by-election win since 1928 and beginning of Liberal revival.
Apr.	First Aldermaston march organized by CND.
June	British plan for Cyprus rejected by Greek government.
July	Government decides to resume British nuclear tests. First life peers created.
Oct.	Hire-purchase restrictions removed.
Nov.	France formally rejects British proposal for a European Free Trade Area.
Dec.	Partial convertibility between sterling and the US dollar announced.

1959

Jan.	Britain recognizes Castro regime in Cuba.
Feb.	London Agreement between Britain, Greece and Turkey on independence for Cyprus. Macmillan visits Moscow.
Mar.	Air services agreement between Britain and the USSR. Aldermaston march attracts 20,000 people.
Apr.	Amory introduces tax reliefs of £350 million.
June	Commons debate on Hola Camp deaths during the suppression of Mau Mau.
June/ July	Major unions vote for unilateralist defence policy.
Sept.	General election called for 8 Oct.
Oct.	At general election, Conservatives increase their majority to 100.

Conservative government, 1959–64

1959

Oct.	Macmillan forms government. Principal figures: Macmillan (Prime Minister); Heathcoat Amory (Chancellor of the Exchequer); Lloyd (Foreign Secretary). Bevan becomes Labour deputy leader.
Nov.	European Free Trade Area (EFTA) comes into being. Labour party conference witnesses bitter debate over Gaitskell's proposal to discard Clause IV of the party constitution.

1960

Feb.	Macmillan addresses South African parliament on African nationalism: 'wind of change' speech. Britain agrees to the establishment of a US ballistic missile early warning system in Britain.
Apr.	Blue Streak rocket abandoned as Britain's nuclear warhead delivery system. Hire-purchase restrictions reintroduced and credit squeeze begins.
Mar.	Sharpeville massacre in South Africa arouses widespread protest.
May	Opening and breakdown of Paris Summit Conference. EFTA treaty comes into effect.
June	Commons rejects Wolfenden Commission's recommendations on homosexuality.
July	Selwyn Lloyd replaces Amory as Chancellor of the Exchequer; Douglas-Home becomes Foreign Secretary. Death of Aneurin ('Nye') Bevan.
Aug.	Cyprus becomes independent.

11

Oct.	Federation of Nigeria becomes independent. Labour party conference votes against existing party defence policy and for unilateralism. Gaitskell's 'fight and fight again' speech. Royal Navy's first nuclear submarine *Dreadnought* launched. Committee of 100 formed to coordinate unilateralist direct action.
Nov.	Gaitskell re-elected leader of the Labour party. Britain announces that it will provide facilities for US Polaris submarines at Holy Loch.

1961

Jan.	Hire-purchase controls relaxed.
Feb.	Government announces an increase in NHS prescription charges.
Mar.	First US nuclear submarine arrives at Holy Loch. Conference on discontinuance of nuclear weapons tests between Britain, USA and USSR begins at Geneva.
July	British troops land in Kuwait following an appeal from Kuwaiti government. Macmillan announces government decision to apply for EEC membership. Anglo-American agreement to establish US Missile Defence Alarm Station in Britain. 'Pay pause' announced by Selwyn Lloyd.
Aug.	IMF places £714 million at Britain's disposal. Failure of Geneva Conference. USSR to resume nuclear weapons tests.
Oct.	Labour party conference votes against Polaris bases and German troops being stationed in Britain.
Nov.	Official opening of negotiations for British entry into EEC at Brussels. Commonwealth Immigrants Bill introduced, ending principle of free entry to Britain of Commonwealth citizens.
Dec.	Tanganyika receives independence. Macmillan meets US President Kennedy in Bermuda.

1962

Feb.	National Economic Development Council (NEDC) set up as tripartite body of government, employers, and the Trades Union Congress (TUC).
Mar.	Liberal wins Orpington by-election.
Apr.	End of government's 'pay pause'.
July	Macmillan asks seven senior ministers for their resignations (Night of the Long Knives). Cabinet reconstructed: Butler (Deputy Prime Minister and First Secretary of State); Henry Brooke (Home Secretary); Reginald Maudling (Chancellor of the Exchequer). Government announces setting up of the National Incomes Commission.
Aug.	Jamaica, Trinidad and Tobago become independent.

Dec.	British troops quell uprising in Brunei. Macmillan meets Kennedy at Nassau. In Nassau agreement USA supplies Polaris missiles for use on British submarines as part of a multilateral NATO force. British Railways Board replaces British Transport Commission under terms of the 1946 Transport Act. Beeching made chairman.

1963

Jan.	Britain refused entry to the EEC by French President de Gaulle's veto. Death of Gaitskell.
Feb.	Harold Wilson elected leader of the Labour party.
Mar.	Publication of Beeching Report on British Railways, advocating wide-spread closures of track.
Apr.	Polaris missile agreement signed by Britain and USA.
June	House of Commons censures John Profumo, former Minister for War, for lying to the House.
July	Peerage Bill receives royal assent. Peers may now renounce titles.
Aug.	Partial nuclear Test Ban Treaty signed by Britain, USA and USSR.
Oct.	Macmillan retires. Sir Alec Douglas-Home unexpectedly becomes Prime Minister against general belief that Butler will succeed. Iain Macleod and Enoch Powell refuse to serve under Home. Butler becomes Foreign Secretary; Lloyd, Leader of the House; Anthony Barber, Minister of Health; Edward Heath, Secretary of State for Industry.
Dec.	Zanzibar and Kenya become independent. Federation of Rhodesia and Nyasaland is dissolved.

1964

Jan.	*Rookes* v *Barnard* decision threatens unions with damages for strike action.
Feb.	Britain records largest ever trade deficit.
Mar.	Resale price maintenance abolished.
Apr.	First elections for the new Greater London Council (GLC) won by Labour.
Aug.	US aircraft attack North Vietnam after Gulf of Tonkin incident.
Sept.	General election announced for 15 Oct.
Oct.	General election results in Labour victory and a majority of four seats.

Labour government, 1964–66

1964

Oct. Wilson forms Labour government. Principal figures: Wilson (Prime Minister); James Callaghan (Chancellor of the Exchequer); George Brown (Deputy Prime Minister and Minister for Economic Affairs); Patrick Gordon-Walker (Foreign Secretary). Callaghan imposes 15 per cent surcharge upon imports.

Nov. Callaghan budget raises pensions and abolishes prescription charges, but increases petrol taxes. Britain is forced to borrow £1,000 million to avoid devaluation.

Dec. Wilson agrees to retain Polaris missiles under NATO control.

1965

Jan. NHS prescription charges abolished. Defeat of Patrick Gordon-Walker in Leyton by-election. Succeeded as Foreign Secretary by Michael Stewart.

Feb. Establishment of National Board for Prices and Incomes.

Apr. Import surcharge cut to 10 per cent. TSR-2 fighter plane development cancelled.

May Britain draws $1,400 million from the IMF.

June Hire-purchase terms stiffened.

July Tightening of exchange controls. Home resigns leadership of Conservative party. Edward Heath elected to replace him. Education Secretary, Anthony Crosland, issues circular requesting local authorities to submit plans for comprehensivization within a year.

Sept. Five-Year National Plan aiming at a 25 per cent increase in Gross National Product (GNP) by 1970 announced by George Brown.

Oct. Parliament passes Bill abolishing death penalty.

Nov. Rhodesia makes a unilateral declaration of independence (UDI). Economic sanctions announced.

1966

Jan. White Paper announces proposed Industrial Reorganization Corporation. British government bans all trade with Rhodesia. Vietnam Solidarity Committee formed.

Feb. Hire-purchase terms stiffened. General election called for 31 Mar.

Mar. Labour wins general election with a majority of 97.

Labour government, 1966–70

1966

Mar. Wilson forms a new government. Principal figures: Wilson (Prime Minister); Callaghan (Chancellor of the Exchequer); Stewart (Foreign Secretary).

Apr. Queen's Speech announces intention to apply to join the EEC.

May Callaghan imposes Selective Employment Tax (SET) to shift employment to manufacturing sector from services. A seamen's strike forces introduction of a State of Emergency. Maud Commission on Local Government set up.

July End of seamen's strike. Minister of Technology, Frank Cousins, resigns in protest against government incomes policy. Prices and Incomes Bill introduced providing for an 'early warning' system on prices and incomes. Six-month wage freeze and deflationary measures announced. George Brown resigns from the DEA, but is persuaded to remain in office.

Aug. George Brown exchanges offices with Foreign Secretary Michael Stewart. Sir Edward Compton named Britain's first Parliamentary Commissioner (ombudsman).

Nov. End of import surcharge.

Dec. Wilson and Rhodesian leader Ian Smith hold negotiations on Rhodesia on board HMS *Tiger*. UN Security Council approves British resolution for mandatory sanctions against Rhodesia.

1967

Jan. Prime Minister and Foreign Secretary in Rome for EEC negotiations. Jeremy Thorpe elected leader of the Liberal party following Jo Grimond's resignation.

Feb. Soviet leader Alexei Kosygin in London; meets Queen at Buckingham Palace. Downing Street–Kremlin 'hot line' agreed upon.

May Wilson announces Britain's formal application to join the EEC.

June Arab–Israeli War. Arab oil embargo on Britain. Relaxation of hire-purchase restrictions.

July Defence cuts announced: withdrawal from East of Suez by mid-1970. Vesting date of British Steel Corporation.

Aug. Douglas Jay sacked in Cabinet reshuffle. Wilson takes over Department of Economic Affairs. Further relaxation of hire-purchase controls.

Sept. Arabs lift oil embargo. Dock strike begins in London and Liverpool.

Oct.   Liverpool dockers return to work. HMS *Resolution*, Britain's first Polaris submarine, is commissioned.

Nov.   Devaluation of pound to US $2.40. Aden becomes independent. Chancellor of the Exchequer, James Callaghan, exchanges offices with Home Secretary, Roy Jenkins.

Dec.   France vetoes British application to join EEC.

1968

Jan.   Public expenditure cuts announced.

Mar.   Rush for gold in leading financial centres. Stock Exchange and banks closed in Britain. Resignation of Foreign Secretary, George Brown. Summit meeting of Western Central Bankers agrees two-tier system for price of gold.

Apr.   Cabinet reshuffle. Barbara Castle becomes Minister for Employment and Productivity. Birmingham immigration speech by Enoch Powell (rivers of blood). Heath sacks him from shadow cabinet.

June   NHS prescription charges reintroduced.

Sept.   Basle arrangement for sterling area agreed. Swaziland becomes independent.

Oct.   Failure of HMS *Fearless* talks on Rhodesia. Massive demonstration in London against US involvement in Vietnam War.

Nov.   Hire-purchase restrictions tightened. Credit squeeze imposed.

1969

May   Voting age reduced to 18.

June   Government drops its plans for legal restraints on unofficial strikes in return for a TUC pledge to deal with such disputes.

Aug.   Three-day street battle in Londonderry following Apprentice Boys' march. Army takes over security and police functions in Northern Ireland.

Oct.   Department of Economic Affairs abolished. Divorce Bill enacted.

Dec.   EEC summit meeting at The Hague agrees to negotiations for British entry by June 1970. Parliament votes for permanent abolition of death penalty.

1970

Jan.   Age of majority reduced to 18. Provisional IRA and Provisional Sinn Fein formed. Heath repudiates Powell's statements on race. Conservative party holds Selsdon Park Hotel meeting which agrees on an election agenda of law and order, free market policies, and trade union legislation.

16

Feb. Bill published to compel local authorities to end the 11-plus examination and develop comprehensive schools.

Mar. Favourable by-election result in South Ayrshire for Labour suggests possibility of a snap election.

Apr. Budget by Jenkins announces a record revenue surplus but offers only modest tax concessions. Alliance party formed in Northern Ireland.

May. Labour makes substantial gains in local elections, reinforcing prospects of election. Election called for June (18th). Equal Pay Act enacted.

June Conservatives secure an overall majority of 31 in surprise election victory.

Conservative government, 1970–74

1970

June Heath forms government. Principal figures: Heath (Prime Minister); Iain Macleod (Chancellor of the Exchequer); Reginald Maudling (Home Secretary); Sir Alec Douglas-Home (Foreign Secretary). Negotiations resumed over entry to the EEC. Margaret Thatcher, as Education Secretary, withdraws Crosland circular of 1965, allowing local authorities to retain existing educational structure.

July Death of Macleod; Anthony Barber appointed Chancellor. IRA begin bombing campaign in Northern Ireland.

Aug. Social Democrat and Labour party (SDLP) founded in Northern Ireland.

Oct. Conservative conference calls for an end to support for 'lame duck' industries. Government establishes new conglomerate ministries, the Department of Trade and Industry and the Department of the Environment. Free school milk ended.

Nov. Prices and Incomes Board ended. Government forced to give aid to Rolls-Royce to stave off bankruptcy.

Dec. Industrial Relations Bill introduced (became law in 1971); providing for registered unions to enjoy legal status, but insisting on pre-strike ballots and compulsory 'cooling-off' periods backed up by legal sanctions.

1971

Jan. 'Angry Brigade' bomb attack on home of Robert Carr, Secretary for Employment.

Feb. Financial collapse of Rolls-Royce Limited. Aero-engine interests nationalized. First British soldier killed in Belfast. Decimal currency introduced. Mass TUC demonstration against Industrial Relations Bill.

Mar.   One-day strike by 1.5 million engineers against Industrial Relations Bill. Chichester-Clark resigns Northern Ireland premiership and is succeeded by Brian Faulkner.

June   EEC negotiations completed. Upper Clyde Shipbuilders strike supported widely in Scotland.

July   Barber cuts taxes and removes hire-purchase restrictions in attempt to reduce unemployment. Occupation and work-in at Upper Clyde Shipbuilders.

Aug.   Internment without trial introduced in Ulster. Industrial Relations Bill enacted.

Sept.   TUC votes against registration under Industrial Relations Act.

Oct.   Labour party conference overwhelmingly carries anti-EEC resolution. Parliament endorses British terms of entry to the EEC by 112 votes.

Nov.   Draft agreement signed between Britain and Rhodesia: Rhodesia to be independent if majority of population agree to negotiated terms. Barber increases public spending.

Dec.   Miners vote for industrial action.

1972

Jan.   Miners' strike begins. Britain signs EEC Accession treaty. 'Bloody Sunday': thirteen civilians killed by paratroopers in Londonderry. Unemployment reaches over 1 million.

Feb.   State of Emergency declared in power crisis: large-scale power cuts begin, with 1.5 million workers laid off at the height of the crisis. Wilberforce Inquiry's terms for settling miners' dispute published. Miners vote to return to work.

Mar.   National Industrial Relations Court (NIRC) fines Transport and General Workers' Union (TGWU) for contempt. 'Direct rule' established for Northern Ireland with William Whitelaw as Secretary of State.

Apr.   'Work-to-rule' on British Rail. NIRC orders 'cooling-off' period. NIRC imposes further fine for contempt on TGWU. Roy Jenkins, George Thompson and Harold Lever resign from Labour shadow cabinet over EEC.

May   Pearce Commission concludes that the Rhodesian people are not generally in favour of the settlement plan: sanctions continue.

June   Government decision to 'float' the pound.

July   Robert Carr replaces Maudling as Home Secretary, when Maudling resigns due to 'Poulson' corruption examination. Start of national dock strike following rejection of Jones-Aldington proposals for modernization of the docks.

Aug.	President Idi Amin orders expulsion of 40,000 British Asians from Uganda. Intervention of official solicitor to release dockers imprisoned under Industrial Relations Act.
Sept.	TUC suspends 32 unions for registering under Industrial Relations Act.
Nov.	Government imposes immediate 90-day freeze on prices, pay, rent and dividend increases. Government defeat on new immigration rules.

1973

Jan.	Britain becomes a member of EEC.
Feb.	Start of foreign exchange crisis. US dollar devalued by 10 per cent.
Mar.	Ulster referendum: overwhelming majority in favour of retaining links with Britain. White Paper proposes a Northern Ireland Assembly, elected by proportional representation.
Apr.	Phase Two of counter-inflation policy comes into operation: £1 plus 4 per cent and a price code supervised by new Price Commission.
July	Northern Ireland Assembly's first sitting ends in chaos.
Oct.	Arab–Israeli War. Arabs cut oil supplies to the west. Fire service begins series of unofficial strikes. Phase Three of counter-inflation policy launched: 7 per cent or £2.25 a week with threshold safeguards.
Nov.	Electrical Power Engineers Association bans out-of-hours work. Miners ban overtime. Major rise in oil prices by the Organization of Petroleum Exporting Countries (OPEC). Eleven-person power-sharing executive proposed for Northern Ireland.
Dec.	Rail drivers' union, the Amalgamated Society of Locomotive Engineers and Firemen (ASLEF), bans overtime. Emergency measures taken to conserve fuel: 50 mph speed limit, temperature control in offices, three-day working week announced from 31 Dec. Power engineers call off ban on out-of-hours working. Tripartite Conference (British government, Northern Ireland executive-designate and Irish government) agree to establish a Council of Ireland – the Sunningdale agreement.

1974

Jan.	End of direct rule in Northern Ireland. New executive takes office. Lord Carrington made secretary of new Energy Department. Parliament recalled for two-day debate on energy crisis. Loyalists expelled from Northern Ireland Assembly after angry scenes.
Feb.	National Union of Miners (NUM) calls an all-out strike after an 81 per cent majority for industrial action. Heath calls an election for 28 Feb. (7th); miners' strike begins (10th). General election results in

no overall majority; after talks between Heath and Liberal leader Jeremy Thorpe fail to reach an agreement, Labour forms a government as the largest overall party (301 seats).

Labour government, 1974

1974

Mar.   Wilson forms a minority government. Principal figures: Wilson (Prime Minister); Denis Healey (Chancellor of the Exchequer); James Callaghan (Foreign Secretary); Michael Foot (Secretary for Employment). Miners accept a £103 million pay settlement; three-day week and other power restrictions end.

Apr.   Britain demands renegotiation of EEC terms of entry.

May   State of Emergency in Northern Ireland due to Protestant general strike in protest at Sunningdale agreement. Plan to establish a Council of Ireland postponed. General strike called off. Northern Ireland Assembly suspended and direct rule from Westminster resumed.

July   Industrial Relations Act 1971 repealed. Pay Board and statutory incomes policy abolished. NIRC abolished. Industry Secretary Tony Benn offers government loans and grants to *Scottish Daily News* and to Meriden motor cycle cooperative.

Sept.   General election called for 10 Oct.

Oct.   Guildford pub bombings by IRA; five people are killed and 70 injured. General election results in a Labour majority of three.

Labour government, 1974–79

1974

Oct.   Wilson forms Labour government. Principal figures: Wilson (Prime Minister); Healey (Chancellor of the Exchequer); Callaghan (Foreign Secretary); Roy Jenkins (Home Secretary).

Nov.   Birmingham pub bombings by Provisionals: 21 people killed and 120 injured. Prevention of Terrorism Act passed, proscribing the IRA and giving police wider powers.

Dec.   Government announces aid to British Leyland.

1975

Jan.   Industry Bill introduced proposing National Enterprise Board and planning agreements. Referendum on EEC membership announced.

Feb.   Heath withdraws as Conservative leader after defeat by Margaret Thatcher in first ballot of leadership election. Thatcher elected leader. Wilson–Brezhnev summit meeting agreement in Moscow.

Mar.   Meriden motor cycle cooperative set up. EEC summit meeting reaches agreement on British renegotiation terms. British Cabinet accepts the terms.

Apr.   Government accepts Ryder plan to invest £1,400 million in British Leyland over eight years.

May   *Scottish Daily News* published by workers' cooperative. Elections for Northern Ireland Convention.

June   Referendum gives two-to-one majority for remaining in the EEC. In Cabinet reshuffle, Benn demoted from Employment to Energy.

July   Government announces anti-inflation policy: £6 a week limit on pay increases until Aug. 1976. TUC supports policy.

Nov.   Chequers meeting of government, TUC, NEDC, and Confederation of British Industry (CBI) on strategy to regenerate British industry. Britain applies to IMF for £975 million loan.

Dec.   End of internment without trial in Northern Ireland. Sex Discrimination and Equal Pay Acts come into force.

1976

Mar.   Northern Ireland Convention dissolved: direct rule from Westminster continued. Wilson resigns as Prime Minister.

Apr.   Callaghan defeats Foot in Parliamentary Labour party ballot for leadership and becomes Prime Minister. Foot becomes Lord President of the Council, Crosland becomes Foreign Secretary.

May   TUC endorses Stage 2 of government incomes policy (minimum £2.50, maximum £4 per week increases). Jeremy Thorpe resigns Liberal leadership; Grimond resumes leadership on a caretaker basis.

June   Britain secures £3 billion standby credit from European and American Central Banks.

July   David Steel elected Liberal leader.

Sept.   Roy Jenkins resigns as Home Secretary to become President of the European Commission (succeeded by Merlyn Rees). Government seeks £2,300 million loan from IMF. Ian Smith accepts Anglo-American proposals for majority rule in Rhodesia in two years.

Dec.   British Letter of Intent to IMF. Public spending cuts of £2,500 million, increased indirect taxation and BP share sale.

1977

Jan.   Ian Smith rejects British proposals for transition to majority rule. Bullock Report on industrial democracy published: recommends worker-directors.

Feb.   Death of Crosland; David Owen made Foreign Secretary; British Leyland toolroom workers' strike. Government defeated on guillotine motion on Devolution Bills for Scotland and Wales.

Mar. Lib–Lab Pact arranged, enabling government to defeat Conservative 'no confidence' motion.

May Eleven-day loyalist general strike in Ulster called by United Ulster Action Council. Collapses through lack of support.

July Trade union demonstrations at Grunwick factory in support of claims for union recognition. Stage 3 of incomes policy announced: 10 per cent limit on earnings increases.

Aug. Violent clashes at National Front march, Lewisham, South London.

Sept. Owen presents Ian Smith with Anglo-American proposals for Rhodesian settlement. National Front march in Manchester banned.

Nov. Fire service strikes for a 30 per cent pay increase.

1978

Jan. End of fire service strike. Special Liberal party assembly votes to continue Lib–Lab pact until July. Government suffers serious defeats in Commons on Scottish Devolution Bill. Amendments carried requiring minimum 'Yes' vote of 40 per cent of the whole electorate.

Mar. 'Internal settlement' agreed in Rhodesia between Ian Smith and three black nationalist leaders. Stricter controls on immigration proposed by House of Commons Select Committee.

May Ban on Zimbabwe African National Union (ZANU) and Zimbabwe African People's Union (ZAPU) lifted in Rhodesia. Labour government suffers several defeats on budget – thresholds for higher tax rates raised to £8,000. Steel announces that Lib–Lab pact will end in Aug.

July Government proposes 5 per cent pay guideline for twelve months beginning 1 Aug. Devolution Bills for Scotland and Wales receive royal assent.

Oct. Labour party conference at Blackpool rejects government's 5 per cent pay guidelines.

Nov. TUC General Council refuses to endorse government's 5 per cent pay limit.

Dec. Government wins vote of confidence following previous day's defeat on imposition of sanctions against private companies giving wage increases above 5 per cent.

1979

Jan. Secondary picketing in road haulage strike creates growing difficulties. About 150,000 laid off due to strike. White Rhodesians vote for limited form of majority rule. Labour government survives Commons vote on its handling of industrial relations.

Feb.   Government–TUC 'concordat' with agreement on 5 per cent inflation within three years.

Mar.   Devolution referendums. Wales votes 'no' overwhelmingly. Scotland has insufficient 'yes' vote (i.e. not 40 per cent of total electorate). Government is defeated in 'no confidence' vote, for first time since 1924. General election called, for May.

May   Conservatives secure victory in general election with majority of 41.

Conservative government, 1979–83

1979

May   Mrs Thatcher forms a government. Principal figures: Thatcher (Prime Minister); Carrington (Foreign Secretary); Whitelaw (Home Secretary); Geoffrey Howe (Chancellor of the Exchequer).

June   First direct elections to European Parliament; Conservatives win 60 of the 78 British seats.

Aug.   Commonwealth Conference in Lusaka clears the ground for Lancaster House conference on Rhodesian settlement, which agrees to free elections.

Dec.   Government introduces Employment Bill on picketing, secret ballot and closed shop. End of UDI in Rhodesia; Lord Soames arrives as Governor to supervise elections.

1980

Mar.   Robert Mugabe invited to form government in Rhodesia/Zimbabwe after winning absolute majority in elections.

Apr.   Rioting in St Paul's district of Bristol. End of steel strike. Zimbabwe gains full independence under Premier Mugabe.

May   Iranian Embassy siege; SAS storm embassy and release hostages.

June   British athletes decide to attend Moscow Olympic Games in spite of government displeasure.

Aug.   Clegg pay commission abolished. Unemployment figures pass 2 million.

Sept.   Large-scale cuts in local authority grants.

Oct.   Labour conference at Blackpool proposes new method of electing leader. James Callaghan announces retirement from leadership of Labour party.

Nov.   Government announces 6 per cent pay ceiling in public sector. Michael Foot elected leader of Labour party.

1981

Jan.   Special Wembley conference of Labour party votes for electoral college to select party leader. 'Gang of Four' – Roy Jenkins, Shirley
Williams, William Rodgers and David Owen – announce launching
of a Council for Social Democracy.

Feb.   National Coal Board announces pit closures (13th); plans withdrawn
after strike threat (18th).

Mar.   Twelve MPs and nine peers resign Labour whip and join the Social
Democrats. Social Democratic party (SDP) launched at public meeting (26th).

Apr.   Brixton riots; appointment of Lord Scarman to inquire into riots.

May   IRA man Robert Sands dies after 66-day hunger strike.

July   Rioting by youths in Toxteth (Liverpool), Moss Side (Manchester),
and several other towns and cities. Prince of Wales marries Lady
Diana Spencer.

Sept.   Formation of Liberal–SDP Alliance. Benn narrowly fails to dislodge
Healey in vote for deputy leadership at Labour party conference.
Party adopts a unilateralist defence policy.

Oct.   CND backs 'peace camps' at Greenham Common and Molesworth;
mass CND demonstration in London attracts 150,000. Gallup poll
shows 40 per cent support for the Alliance.

Nov.   Scarman Report on riots criticizes deprivation in inner cities and
poor relations between police and ethnic minorities. Shirley
Williams wins Crosby by-election for Alliance.

Dec.   Arthur Scargill becomes president of NUM.

1982

Jan.   Number of unemployed in UK passes 3 million. Opinion polls show
Alliance two points ahead of Conservatives.

Apr.   Argentine forces invade and take control of Falkland Islands (2nd)
followed by South Georgia (for Falklands War, see p 211).

June   Surrender of Argentine forces in Falklands.

July   IRA bombs in Hyde Park and Regent's Park kill ten soldiers and
injure 50 others.

Dec.   Estimated 30,000 women demonstrate outside Greenham Common
air base against siting of Cruise missiles.

1983

Apr.   £1 coin introduced.

May   Thatcher announces a general election on 9 June.

June Conservatives win general election with a 144-seat majority. Liberal–SDP Alliance wins 26 per cent of the vote but gains only 23 seats.

Conservative government, 1983–87

1983

June Formation of Conservative government. Principal figures: Thatcher (Prime Minister); Lawson (Chancellor of the Exchequer); Howe (Foreign Secretary); Brittan (Home Secretary). Michael Foot announces he will stand down as Labour leader (12th); Roy Jenkins resigns as SDP leader and is succeeded by David Owen (13th).

July Commons votes against restoration of capital punishment.

Oct. Neil Kinnock elected leader of Labour party and Roy Hattersley deputy leader. Trade and Industry Secretary, Cecil Parkinson, resigns after disclosure of affair with former secretary.

Nov. First Cruise missiles arrive at Greenham Common.

Dec. Bomb in Harrods store kills six people and injures 91.

1984

Jan. Government bans trade unions at GCHQ (Government Communications Headquarters) intelligence-gathering centre in Cheltenham.

Mar. National Coal Board announces plans to close pits and shed 20,000 jobs (6th); NUM gives support for all-out strike. Civil servant Sarah Tisdall jailed for passing secret documents to the *Guardian.*

Apr. WPC Yvonne Fletcher shot from Libyan Embassy in St James's Square; police lay siege to embassy and eventually obtain removal of personnel.

May Serious disturbances outside Orgreave coking plant near Sheffield during mass picketing by striking miners. MP Tam Dalyell accuses Prime Minister of lying over the sinking of the Argentine cruiser *General Belgrano.*

July Breakdown of talks between Britain and Argentina over future of Falklands.

Aug. TUC pledges support to miners' strike.

Sept. Leading 'Wet', James Prior, leaves government. At Labour party conference, Neil Kinnock supports the miners but condemns violence.

Oct. IRA bomb wrecks Grand Hotel, Brighton, where Mrs Thatcher and Conservative party leadership are staying; five people are killed and senior figures Norman Tebbit and John Wakeham injured.

Nov. National Coal Board begins back-to-work drive in coal dispute. Government flotation of British Telecom successful, inaugurating process of 'privatizing' major public corporations.

Dec. NUM funds sequestered and receiver appointed to take control. Britain signs Sino-British declaration on future of Hong Kong, assuring its future as a capitalist state for another 50 years after Britain's departure in 1997.

1985

Jan. Clive Ponting acquitted of breaching the Official Secrets Act over *General Belgrano* affair.

Feb. Teachers begin series of selective pay strikes.

Mar. Miners vote to end strike.

Apr. Riot by Liverpool football fans in Heysel Stadium, Brussels, leaves 38 dead and 150 injured. English clubs banned from European competition.

June Social Services Secretary, Norman Fowler, announces major review of welfare, involving phasing out of SERPS (state earnings-related pensions) and reorganization of other welfare benefits.

Sept. Major Cabinet reshuffle. Norman Tebbit becomes chairman of Conservative party. Serious riots in Handsworth, Birmingham (9th). Riots in Brixton after accidental shooting of a woman by police officers.

Oct. Neil Kinnock attacks stand taken by militant members of Liverpool City Council in rate dispute with government, widely interpreted as attempt to reassert control over the party. Riots in Tottenham lead to death of PC Keith Blakelock.

Nov. Anglo-Irish agreement signed at Hillsborough by Mrs Thatcher and Dr Garret Fitzgerald giving Dublin government a say in Northern Irish affairs in return for recognition of the wishes of the majority population in Ulster.

Dec. Mass resignation by Ulster MPs in protest over Anglo-Irish agreement, forcing fifteen by-elections in Ulster.

1986

Jan. Westland affair leads to resignation of Defence Secretary, Michael Heseltine, and, a fortnight later, the Industry Secretary, Leon Brittan. Beginning of Wapping print dispute after movement of printing of Murdoch newspapers to new plant at Wapping.

Feb. Government plans to sell off Austin Rover to Ford stopped by Commons revolt. Agreement signed to build Channel Tunnel.

Mar. High Court imposes surcharges on 81 members of Labour-controlled Lambeth and Liverpool councils. By end of month all 37 unions with political funds have voted to retain them.

Apr.   Mrs Thatcher sanctions use of bases in Britain for US bombing of Libya (15th). Chernobyl nuclear accident spreads radioactive contamination across Britain, especially the north and west.

June   Dissolution of Northern Ireland Assembly announced.

July   Sir Geoffrey Howe makes journey to South Africa to explore possibilities of reform.

Aug.   Mrs Thatcher stands out from other Commonwealth leaders on issue of economic sanctions against South Africa.

Sept.   Liberal assembly votes for non-nuclear amendment in defiance of party leadership, throwing Alliance defence policy into turmoil. Labour conference votes in favour of expulsion of US nuclear bases from Britain.

Oct.   Jeffrey Archer forced to resign as Conservative party deputy chairman following allegations in a Sunday newspaper. 'Big Bang' in city with deregulation of dealing.

Nov.   Government announces increase in public spending in major reversal of earlier policy. Court in Australia begins hearing to prevent former MI5 officer Peter Wright publishing his memoirs. Government launches £20 million anti-AIDS campaign.

Dec.   Investigations announced into Guinness take-over of Distillers group. Government decides to drop GEC Nimrod early-warning radar plane in favour of Boeing system.

1987

Jan.   BBC programme on Zircon spy satellite banned and raid on Glasgow BBC offices by police. SDP–Liberal Alliance hold relaunch with compromise defence policy.

Feb.   Wapping dispute ends. Greenwich by-election won by SDP's Rosie Barnes.

Mar.   Russian leader Gorbachev announces new offer on intermediate missiles in Europe. Sizewell nuclear power station given go-ahead after marathon public inquiry. Government loses Wright case in Australia but seeks leave to appeal.

May   Government announces June general election following relatively successful performance in local government elections and well-publicized visit by Mrs Thatcher to Moscow.

June   Conservative victory in general election by 102 seats.

Conservative government, 1987–92

1987

June   Conservative administration formed. Principal figures: Thatcher (Prime Minister); Lawson (Chancellor of the Exchequer); Howe

(Foreign Secretary). Government proceeds with plans for major reforms in education, further privatization and trade union reform. David Steel announces desire to press for a merger of SDP and Liberal parties. David Owen announces opposition.

July   Injunctions granted to prevent publication of Wright's allegations and contents of his *Spycatcher* book. Jeffrey Archer awarded £500,000 damages for libel.

Aug.   Ballot of SDP membership votes 57 to 43 per cent for opening merger talks. Owen resigns as leader and is replaced by Robert Maclennan.

Sept.   SDP conference supports opening merger talks with the Liberals. Labour leader, Kinnock, wins conference support for widespread policy review. Government loses appeal in Australia to prevent publication of Peter Wright's *Spycatcher*.

Oct.   'Black Monday' (19th) wipes £50 billion off share values.

Nov.   Government announces plans to replace rates with 'community charge' from April 1990.

Dec.   Intermediate Nuclear Forces Treaty between USA and USSR promises large-scale cuts in medium and short-range nuclear missiles.

1988

Jan.   Mrs Thatcher becomes the longest continuously serving Prime Minister in the twentieth century. David Steel announces he will not stand for leadership of new merged party.

Feb.   MPs vote to televise the House of Commons.

Mar.   Liberals and SDP vote for the creation of a new merged party, the Social and Liberal Democrats (SLD). Gibraltar shootings: three IRA members shot by SAS.

Apr.   Government fails to stop TV documentary on the Gibraltar shootings, *Death on the Rock*.

June   UK trade figures show £1.2 billion deficit, sparking fears of ending of economic growth.

July   Government announces plans to privatize water companies. Government raises interest rates heralding end of 1980s' boom. Paddy Ashdown becomes new leader of the SLD. Education Act comes into force, introducing a national curriculum, regular testing, and possibility of schools opting out of local education authority control.

Aug.   Further rise in interest rates following widening of trade deficit. Chancellor Lawson admits that the economy is in decline.

Oct.   Government announces plans to privatize steel industry. Trade unionists at GCHQ are sacked.

Nov. Government proposes loan scheme for students.

Dec. Junior Health Minister, Edwina Currie, forced to resign after statement on presence of salmonella in eggs.

1989

Feb. Ayatollah Khomeini orders the death of Salman Rushdie for his book *The Satanic Verses*; anti-Rushdie demonstrations.

May Interest rates raised to 14 per cent. British government rejects EC Social Charter.

June Tiananmen Square massacre in Beijing. British government denies right of residency to Hong Kong holders of British passports. Labour secures significant gains in direct elections to European Parliament. Greens secure 15 per cent of vote and push Liberal Democrats into fourth place.

July Following disagreement with Mrs Thatcher over membership of the EMS and attitudes to Europe, Geoffrey Howe is replaced as Foreign Secretary by John Major; Howe becomes Leader of the Commons and Deputy Prime Minister.

Aug. Cruise missiles removed from Greenham Common following Intermediate Nuclear Forces Treaty.

Sept. Water companies privatized.

Oct. Interest rates rise to near record 15 per cent; share values show a major fall. 'Guildford Four' are released after fourteen years in prison for IRA bombing. Nigel Lawson resigns as Chancellor, following public disagreement with Mrs Thatcher's private adviser, Alan Walters. John Major becomes Chancellor; Douglas Hurd Foreign Secretary.

Nov. East Germans allowed to pass freely into West Germany; Berlin Wall begins to be demolished. TV broadcasts of Parliament begin.

Dec. Mrs Thatcher defeats 'stalking horse' challenge by Sir Anthony Meyer for Conservative leadership. Czechs form non-communist government; Romanian revolution topples Ceauşescu.

1990

Feb. South African government removes bans on the Communist party, the African National Congress (ANC), and other anti-apartheid groups; Nelson Mandela is released from prison after 27 years.

Mar. Riots follow anti-poll tax demonstration in Trafalgar Square.

Apr. Strangeways Prison riot and occupation (1st–25th). Parts of Iraqi 'Supergun' impounded by customs officers.

June David Owen's 'continuing SDP' is disbanded.

July   London Declaration by NATO leaders formally ends the Cold War. Nicholas Ridley forced to resign over remarks about Germany. Assassination of Ian Gow MP by IRA.

Aug.   Iraqi forces invade Kuwait; EEC, USA and Japan embargo Iraqi oil. Iraq seizes western hostages as a 'human shield'.

Sept.   Iraq releases British men and women held hostage. Polly Peck chairman, Asil Nadir, questioned on fraud charges; shares in company suspended.

Oct.   Britain joins the ERM; Germany reunited. Liberal Democrats take Eastbourne in by-election. Rome Summit of EEC agrees timetable for monetary union in spite of Thatcher's clear opposition.

Nov.   Howe resigns (1st) from the government over Thatcher's comments on European monetary union in Commons debate of 30 Oct. Ireland elects Mary Robinson as its first woman President. Howe's resignation speech (13th) explicitly attacks Thatcher's policies and invites others 'to consider their own response'. The following day Michael Heseltine announces his challenge for the leadership. In the first ballot Thatcher fails to obtain the required majority by four votes (20th); she withdraws from the contest after consultation with her ministers, who reveal loss of support. John Major and Douglas Hurd enter the contest. In the second ballot (27th) Major secures two votes short of an overall majority, leading the other two candidates to withdraw, and becomes Prime Minister. Norman Lamont appointed Chancellor; Heseltine, Environment Secretary.

Dec.   Heseltine promises far-reaching review of the poll tax. Iraq releases all western hostages.

1991

Jan.   US and Allied air attack begins on Iraq (16th), Operation 'Desert Storm'.

Feb.   IRA mortar attack on Downing Street. Allied land offensive begins in the Gulf War (24th); ceasefire called (28th).

Mar.   Conservatives lose Ribble Valley by-election to the Liberal Democrats, forcing government to rethink its stand on the poll tax. Court of Appeal quashes convictions of the Birmingham Six.

Apr.   Government announces that the poll tax will be replaced by a new tax.

July   Bank of Credit and Commerce International (BCCI) collapses. John Major launches Citizen's Charter.

Aug.   Attempted coup against President Gorbachev fails, heralding break-up of the Soviet Union.

Nov.   Newspaper magnate Robert Maxwell dies at sea; investigation of his companies reveals massive fraud.

Dec.   Maastricht Treaty on political and economic union signed by EEC leaders. Britain secures opt-out from single currency and the social chapter.

1992

Jan.   First meeting of self-appointed Muslim Parliament of Great Britain, prompted by the Salman Rushdie affair. Britain and EC recognize Slovenian and Croatian Republics in former Yugoslavia.

Feb.   Economic statistics show that the recession is the longest since 1945.

Mar.   General election announced for 9 April. Ethnic fighting begins in Bosnia-Herzegovina.

Apr.   Conservatives win 21-seat majority in general election in spite of poll predictions to the contrary.

Conservative government, 1992–97

1992

Apr.   John Major forms a government. Principal figures: Major (Prime Minister); Norman Lamont (Chancellor of the Exchequer); Douglas Hurd (Foreign Secretary); Michael Heseltine (Trade and Industry Secretary). Neil Kinnock and Roy Hattersley resign their positions as leader and deputy leader of the Labour party (13th). Chris Patten, defeated MP for Bath, becomes Governor of Hong Kong.

May   Queen's Speech outlines further privatization and creation of a national lottery. Security service (MI5) to be placed on a statutory basis.

June   Danish referendum rejects Maastricht, causing European Communities (Amendment) Bill to be suspended. Peerages for leading Thatcherites: Thatcher, Howe, Lawson, Parkinson and Tebbit.

July   Details of British Rail privatization revealed (14th). John Smith elected leader of Labour party (18th); Margaret Beckett becomes deputy leader.

Aug.   Bank of England begins defence of sterling amid turbulence on foreign exchanges. Lord Owen succeeds Lord Carrington as EC peacemaker in former Yugoslavia.

Sept.   Continuing pressure on pound. Débâcle of 'Black Wednesday' (16th): membership of ERM suspended when Lamont unable to halt the speculators. Resignation of Heritage Secretary, David Mellor.

Oct.   Serious divisions over Europe at Conservative party conference at Brighton. British Coal announces plans to close 31 pits, effectively decimating the industry and leaving 30,000 miners facing redundancy (13th); Conservative back-benchers revolt on the issue (21st).

Nov. Inquiry announced into Matrix-Churchill affair (10th). Queen to pay tax on her private income (26th).

1993

Jan. Single European Market comes into force. John Major issues writs for libel against *New Statesman* and *Scallywag* (over allegations of relationship with Clare Latimer).

Mar. Government defeated in Commons division on Maastricht Bill (8th). Reform of honours system announced, to give greater reward for merit (4th); budget proposals for VAT on domestic fuel (initially at 8 per cent, then 17.5 per cent from 1995) met with outcry (17th). IRA bombs Warrington, killing two children (20th). Heseltine announces £500 million pit rescue plan.

Apr. Britain and China agree to resume talks on Hong Kong, ending months of stalemate (13th). Huge IRA bomb blast in Bishopsgate, City of London (24th). Recession is officially declared to be at an end (28th).

May Conservatives lose Newbury on swing of 29 per cent to Liberal Democrats (6th). Sweeping Conservative county council losses the same day. Inflation falls to 1.3 per cent, lowest figure for 29 years (21st). Major's first high-level Cabinet reshuffle: Kenneth Clarke replaces Norman Lamont as Chancellor; Michael Howard becomes Home Secretary: other moves include John Gummer (to Environment), Gillian Shephard (to Agriculture), David Hunt (to Employment) and John Redwood (to Welsh Office).

June Gallup polls show John Major least popular Prime Minister since opinion polling began (4th); Norman Lamont's bitter Commons attack on Major (9th); Michael Heseltine suffers heart attack (21st); resignation of Michael Mates as Northern Ireland minister over links with fugitive Asil Nadir (24th).

July Additional defence cuts announced (beyond those proposed in the 1991 document *Options for Change*) (5th); House of Lords rejects referendum on Maastricht by 445 votes to 176, the largest turnout of the century (14th); Commons debate on social chapter opt-out ends in government defeat by 325 to 316 after tie in vote on Labour amendment (Speaker's casting vote given to government) (22nd). Government wins confidence vote clearing way for ratification of Maastricht (23rd); Conservatives lose Christchurch by-election to Liberal Democrats on the largest swing against a Conservative government in modern times (29th).

Aug. Government ratifies Maastricht; the same day ERM totters on brink of complete collapse (2nd).

Sept. John Monks appointed new TUC general secretary (10th); government announces public sector pay freeze (14th); far-right British

National Party (BNP) wins seat in Millwall ward of Tower Hamlets municipal by-election; government plans for post office privatization detailed. Labour party conference passes John Smith's 'one member, one vote' (OMOV) motion (29th).

Oct.   Major defence cuts announced, with privatization of Devonport and Rosyth dockyards (18th); Shankill bombing in Belfast, ten dead (23rd); Greysteel pub bombing (30th).

Nov.   European Union (EU) established as Maastricht Treaty comes into force (1st). Queen's Speech outlines Sunday shopping reforms, coal privatization and reform of criminal justice (18th).

Dec.   Home Secretary proposes 'Citizens' Army' to deter crime (4th). 'Downing Street declaration' by John Major and Irish Prime Minister Albert Reynolds on future of Northern Ireland opening way to all-party talks (15th).

1994

Jan.   Resignation of Environment Minister Tim Yeo after scandal (5th); John Major reaffirms 'Back to Basics' policy (6th); Alan Duncan resigns over irregularities in council house purchase (8th); Earl of Caithness, Minister for Aviation and Shipping, resigns (9th); Westminster Council (a Conservative flagship) accused of 'gerrymandering' (13th); controversy continues over Pergau dam deal in Malaysia (25th).

Feb.   Death of Conservative MP Stephen Milligan in bizarre circumstances (7th). Commons vote to lower homosexual age of consent to 18 (21st); Malaysia bans new UK trade deals in wake of Pergau affair (25th).

Mar.   IRA mortar attack on Heathrow Airport (9th); dispute over voting rights in enlarged European Union (15th), compromise later agreed (23rd).

Apr.   VAT on fuel comes into force (at 8 per cent).

May   Heavy Conservative losses to Labour and Liberal Democrats in local elections (5th). Death of John Smith from heart attack (12th).

June   Fourth direct elections to Europe (9th). Heavy Conservative losses to Labour. Liberal Democrats gain their first two MEPs. Conservatives also lose Eastleigh by-election to Liberal Democrats (third consecutive Liberal Democrat gain of a Conservative seat this parliament), finishing in third place. First in series of protracted strikes by signal workers on railways (15th); loyalist gunmen murder six in bar in Loughinisland, County Down.

July   Jacques Santer, Prime Minister of Luxembourg, chosen to succeed Delors as President of the European Commission (Britain having vetoed the Belgian Jean-Luc Dehaene) (15th); Cabinet reshuffle:

casualties include John Patten, Peter Brooke, John MacGregor and Lord Wakeham. Jeremy Hanley appointed party chairman. Promotion for Jonathan Aitken, Stephen Dorrell and Brian Mawhinney (20th). Tony Blair elected leader of the Labour party; John Prescott elected deputy leader (21st). Neil Kinnock appointed European Commissioner (29th).

Aug.   Lord Archer admits 'grave error' when accused of irregular share dealing. IRA announce 'complete cessation' of military operations (31st).

Sept.   Broadcasting ban on Sinn Fein lifted. Liberal Democrat conference votes to decriminalize cannabis. John Major visits South Africa.

Oct.   Tony Blair commits Labour to new social market economy and proposes reform of party constitution. Loyalist paramilitaries declare ceasefire. Conservative conference overshadowed by 'sleaze' allegations.

Nov.   Nolan Committee established after 'cash for questions' revelations cause resignations of Tim Smith and Neil Hamilton.

Dec.   Government defeat on planned VAT increase on fuel. Swing of 29 per cent to Labour as Dudley West by-election lost by Conservatives. Coal industry privatized.

1995

Jan.   Austria, Sweden and Finland join European Union. Army ends daylight Belfast patrols. Widespread animal welfare demonstrations at Shoreham.

Feb.   Joint Anglo-Irish document on future of Northern Ireland published. Barings Bank collapses (later rescued by Dutch ING group).

Mar.   Norman Lamont votes with Labour against government's European policy.

Apr.   Tony Blair wins victory in reform of Clause IV at special party conference.

May   Worst post-war performance by Conservatives in local elections, losing over 2,000 seats. Report of Nolan Committee urges tough new measures to combat 'sleaze' in public life.

June   Resignation of John Major as Conservative party leader precipitates leadership contest. John Redwood resigns as Welsh Secretary to stand against him.

July   Major wins comfortable victory over Redwood (218 votes to 89). However 111 MPs fail to support Major. Cabinet re-shuffle: Heseltine appointed Deputy Prime Minister, Rifkind to Foreign Office, Mawhinney Party Chairman. Virginia Bottomley moved from Health to National Heritage.

Aug. Resignation of James Molyneaux as Ulster Unionist leader (28th).

Sept. David Trimble elected new leader of Ulster Unionist party (8th).

Oct. Defection of Alan Howarth MP from Conservatives to Labour (7th).

Nov. Nigeria suspended from Commonwealth (11th). All-party peace talks breakthrough in Northern Ireland (28th).

Dec. Government loses Commons fisheries vote by two votes (19th). Defection of Conservative MP Emma Nicholson to Liberal Democrats (29th). Government majority now reduced to three.

1996

Feb. First privatized trains begin to operate (4th). IRA ceasefire ended by bombing of South Quays, east London (9th). Publication of Scott Report on arms to Iraq (15th). Resignation of Conservative whip by MP Peter Thurnham (23rd) (later defects to Liberal Democrats).

Mar. Sinn Fein leader Gerry Adams granted US visa (1st). Dunblane school massacre (13th). Imports of British beef into EU countries suspended (21st).

Apr. Lowest mortgage rates since 1965 (9th). Labour wins Staffordshire South East by election on 22 per cent swing from Conservatives (11th).

May Heavy Conservative council losses (2nd). Britain blocks all EU business until beef ban lifted (21st) (ends 21 June).

June Mary Robinson on first-ever state visit to UK by Irish President (4th).

July Confrontation over Portadown loyalist march (7th). Resignation of David Heathcoat-Amory as Paymaster-General (22nd).

Aug. Divorce granted to Prince and Princess of Wales (28th).

Oct. MP Neil Hamilton admits taking cash for questions (1st). Lord McAlpine defects to Referendum party from Conservatives (6th).

Dec. Conservative MP Sir John Gorst resigns party whip (6th). Paymaster-General David Willetts resigns over cash for questions (11th). Labour victory in Barnsley East by-election (12th). Government now in a minority (although this later changes with death of Labour MPs).

1997

Jan. Deselection of Conservative MP for Reigate, Sir George Gardiner (30th) (later defects to Referendum party).

Feb. Labour win Wirral South by-election on 17 per cent swing (27th). Government once again in a minority.

Mar. John Major calls general election for 1 May. Resignation of Tim Smith, Conservative MP for Beaconsfield, over cash for questions.

Labour government, 1997–

May   General election results in Labour landslide with 419 seats (1st); worst Conservative result of modern times; Liberal Democrats win 46 seats (for details, see p 63). Tony Blair becomes Prime Minister; Gordon Brown Chancellor of the Exchequer; Robin Cook Foreign Secretary; John Prescott Deputy Prime Minister. John Major announces intention to resign as Conservative leader (2nd). Labour announces it will join EU social chapter (4th). Bank of England gains control of interest rates (6th). Trade union ban at GCHQ lifted (15th).

June   William Hague elected new Conservative leader in third round of voting (see p 73) (19th). Youngest Conservative leader of modern times.

July   Hong Kong returned to Chinese rule (1st). Britain rejoins UNESCO (1st). Rioting across Northern Ireland follows Drumcree Orange parade (6th). IRA reinstates ceasefire (20th).

Aug.   Death of Diana, Princess of Wales, in car crash in Paris (30th).

Sept.   Scotland votes Yes-Yes in devolution referendum (11th) (see p 120). Narrow Welsh vote in favour of devolution (18th) (see p 122).

Oct.   Opening of all-party Northern Ireland talks (7th). Chancellor commits UK to EMU after next general election (27th).

Nov.   Resignation of David Curry from shadow cabinet over EU policy (1st). Liberal Democrats retain Winchester by-election after disputed general election result (20th). Peter Temple-Morris MP resigns Conservative whip; sits as Independent.

Dec.   Internal market scrapped in NHS reforms (9th). Back-bench Labour revolt over lone parent benefit cuts (10th). Bill to create Scottish Parliament launched (18th).

1998

Jan.   New cross-border council proposed in Northern Ireland peace initiative (12th). Sweeping changes announced to future Conservative leadership elections (14th).

Feb.   Sinn Fein suspended from Northern Ireland peace talks (20th).

Mar.   Labour's second budget distributes record increase in child benefits (17th).

Apr.   Publication of Mitchell draft settlement on Northern Ireland (6th). Rejected by Ulster Unionists. Peace agreement sealed (Good Friday agreement) (10th).

May   Referendum in London approves creation of Mayor (7th). Loyalist Volunteer Force (LVF) declares ceasefire (15th). Referendum in both parts of Ireland on Good Friday agreement (71 per cent in Northern Ireland, 94 per cent in Republic in favour) (22nd).

June Northern Ireland Assembly elections held under proportional representation (for results, see p 117) (25th).

July David Trimble elected First Minister of Northern Ireland, Seamus Mallon Deputy First Minister (1st). Drumcree stand-off (5th). House of Lords rejects equal gay age of consent (22nd). Cabinet reshuffle promotes Peter Mandelson and Alistair Darling (27th). UK ban on use of anti-personnel mines (31st).

Aug. Omagh terrorist bombing by 'Real IRA' leaves 28 dead (15th).

Sept. 'Real IRA' declares total ceasefire (7th). Hague calls ballot of Conservative party members over EU single currency question (7th). Historic meeting of David Trimble and Gerry Adams (10th). Last routine army patrols in Belfast (12th). Britain resumes diplomatic relations with Iran (24th).

Oct. Conservative ballot supports Hague on EU single currency (5th). Neill Report revolutionizes funding of political parties (13th). Arrest of Chilean former dictator General Pinochet sparks furious political argument (17th). Resignation of Ron Davies, Welsh Secretary, after 'lapse of judgement' (27th). Publication of Jenkins Commission on Electoral Reform (29th).

Nov. Details of proposed closer Labour–Liberal Democrat cooperation revealed (11th).

Dec. Sacking of Lord Cranborne (Conservative leader in the House of Lords) by William Hague (2nd). Nobel Peace Prize presented to David Trimble and John Hume (10th). Sixth defeat of European Elections Bill by House of Lords (15th). Parliament Act invoked. Resignation of Peter Mandelson and Geoffrey Robinson from Cabinet (23rd).

1999

Jan. Resignation of Charlie Whelan, Gordon Brown's Press Secretary (4th). Resignation announced of Paddy Ashdown (effective after June European elections) (20th).

Feb. Mortgage rates at lowest level since 1965 (4th). Lawrence Report published (24th).

Mar. EU Commission resigns *en masse* (16th). NATO forces attack Serbia over Kosovo atrocities (see p 212) (24th).

Apr. Introduction of minimum wage (at £3.60 per hour) (1st).

May Voting for first Scottish Parliament since 1707 and new Welsh Assembly. Labour short of overall majority in both (6th). Donald Dewar becomes First Minister in Scotland; Alun Michael First Secretary in Wales.

June Conservative successes in European elections (fought for first time on a list system (see p 70) (10th).

July   Crisis in Northern Ireland peace talks. Deal rejected by Ulster Unionists because IRA fails to decommission. Subsequent resignation of .Seamus Mallon as Deputy First Minister. Full diplomatic relations with Libya re-established (7th). Very limited Cabinet reshuffle; Paul Murphy becomes Welsh Secretary (dubbed 'Night of the Short Knives') (29th).

Aug.   George Robertson (Defence Minister) nominated as new NATO Secretary-General (4th). Election of Charles Kennedy as new leader of Liberal Democrats (9th).

Sept.   Publication of report of Patten Commission on policing in Northern Ireland (9th). Britain suspends arms sales to Indonesia over violence in East Timor (11th).

Oct.   Return of Peter Mandelson to Cabinet as Northern Ireland Secretary (11th).

Nov.   Michael Portillo returned to Westminster in Kensington and Chelsea by-election (25th). Historic steps towards power-sharing in Northern Ireland as new Executive formed (29th).

Dec.   First day of devolved government in Northern Ireland. The Republic of Ireland abandons its claim to the six counties (2nd). Defection of Conservative MP Shaun Woodward to Labour (18th).

2000

Jan.   Report of Wakeham Commission on reform of House of Lords (20th). Report of General John de Chastelain provokes crisis over decommissioning in Northern Ireland (31st).

Feb.   Michael Portillo appointed Shadow Chancellor of Exchequer (3rd). Resignation of Alun Michael as First Secretary in Wales (9th). Replaced by Rhodri Morgan. Suspension of Northern Ireland Executive (11th).

Mar.   Ken Livingstone announces his candidature as an Independent in the elections for Mayor of London (6th).

2 PRINCIPAL MINISTERS

Prime Ministers

July	1945	Clement Attlee
Oct.	1951	Sir Winston Churchill
Apr.	1955	Sir Anthony Eden
Jan.	1957	Harold Macmillan
Oct.	1963	Sir Alec Douglas-Home
Oct.	1964	Harold Wilson
June	1970	Edward Heath
Mar.	1974	Harold Wilson
Apr.	1976	James Callaghan
May	1979	Margaret Thatcher
Nov.	1990	John Major
May	1997	Anthony (Tony) Blair

Lord Chancellors

July	1945	Lord Jowitt
Oct.	1951	Lord Simonds
Oct.	1954	Viscount Kilmuir
July	1962	Lord Dilhorne
Oct.	1964	Lord Gardiner
June	1970	Lord Hailsham
Mar.	1974	Lord Elwyn-Jones
May	1979	Lord Hailsham
June	1987	Lord Havers
Oct.	1987	Lord Mackay
May	1997	Lord Irvine

Chancellors of the Exchequer

July	1945	Hugh Dalton
Nov.	1947	Sir Stafford Cripps
Oct.	1950	Hugh Gaitskell
Oct.	1951	'Rab' Butler
Dec.	1955	Harold Macmillan
Jan.	1957	Peter Thorneycroft
Jan.	1958	Derick Heathcoat Amory
July	1960	Selwyn Lloyd
July	1962	Reginald Maudling

Oct.	1964	James Callaghan
Nov.	1967	Roy Jenkins
June	1970	Iain Macleod
July	1970	Anthony Barber
Mar.	1974	Denis Healey
May	1979	Sir Geoffrey Howe
June	1983	Nigel Lawson
Oct.	1989	John Major
Nov.	1990	Norman Lamont
May	1993	Kenneth Clarke
May	1997	Gordon Brown

Secretaries of State for Foreign Affairs

July	1945	Ernest Bevin
Mar.	1951	Herbert Morrison
Oct.	1951	(Sir) Anthony Eden
Dec.	1955	Selwyn Lloyd
July	1960	Earl of Home
Oct.	1963	'Rab' Butler
Oct.	1964	Patrick Gordon-Walker
Jan.	1965	Michael Stewart
Aug.	1966	George Brown

Secretaries of State for Foreign and Commonwealth Affairs

Mar.	1968	Michael Stewart
June	1970	Sir Alec Douglas-Home
Mar.	1974	James Callaghan
Apr.	1976	Anthony Crosland
Feb.	1977	David Owen
May	1979	Lord Carrington
Apr.	1982	Francis Pym
June	1983	Sir Geoffrey Howe
June	1989	John Major
Oct.	1989	Douglas Hurd
July	1995	Malcolm Rifkind
May	1997	Robin Cook

Secretaries of State for Home Affairs

Aug.	1945	Chuter Ede
Oct.	1951	Sir David Maxwell Fyfe
Oct.	1954	Gwilym Lloyd-George

Jan.	1957	'Rab' Butler
July	1962	Henry Brooke
Oct.	1964	Sir Frank Soskice
Dec.	1965	Roy Jenkins
Nov.	1967	James Callaghan
June	1970	Reginald Maudling
July	1972	Robert Carr
Mar.	1974	Roy Jenkins
Sept.	1976	Merlyn Rees
May	1979	William Whitelaw
June	1983	Leon Brittan
Sept.	1985	Douglas Hurd
Oct.	1989	David Waddington
Nov.	1990	Kenneth Baker
Apr.	1992	Kenneth Clarke
May	1993	Michael Howard
May	1997	Jack Straw

Secretaries of State for the Colonies*

Aug.	1945	George Hall
Oct.	1946	Arthur Creech Jones
Feb.	1950	James Griffiths
Oct.	1951	Oliver Lyttelton
July	1954	Alan Lennox-Boyd
Oct.	1959	Iain Macleod
Oct.	1961	Reginald Maudling
July	1962	Duncan Sandys
Oct.	1964	Anthony Greenwood
Dec.	1965	Earl of Longford
Apr.	1966	Frank Lee

*The office came under Commonwealth Affairs in August 1966 and was abolished in January 1967.

Secretaries of State for Commmonwealth Relations*

July	1947	Viscount Addison
Oct.	1947	Philip Noel-Baker
Feb.	1950	Patrick Gordon-Walker
Oct.	1951	Lord Ismay
Mar.	1952	Marquess of Salisbury
Nov.	1952	Viscount Swinton
Apr.	1955	Earl of Home
July	1960	Duncan Sandys
Oct.	1964	Arthur Bottomley

Aug.   1966   Herbert Bowden
Aug.   1967   George Thomson

* This office was renamed Secretary of State for Commonwealth Affairs in August 1966 before being merged with the Foreign Office in October 1968.

Secretaries of State for Defence*

July   1945   Clement Attlee
Dec.   1946   Alan Alexander
Feb.   1950   Emanuel Shinwell
Oct.   1951   Sir Winston Churchill
Mar.   1952   Earl Alexander of Tunis
Oct.   1954   Harold Macmillan
Apr.   1955   Selwyn Lloyd
Dec.   1955   Sir Walter Monckton
Oct.   1956   Anthony Head
Jan.   1957   Duncan Sandys
Oct.   1959   Harold Watkinson
July   1962   Peter Thorneycroft
Oct.   1964   Denis Healey
June   1970   Lord Carrington
Jan.   1974   Ian Gilmour
Mar.   1974   Roy Mason
Sept.   1976   Fred Mulley
May   1979   Francis Pym
Jan.   1981   John Nott
Jan.   1983   Michael Heseltine
Jan.   1986   George Younger
July   1989   Tom King
Apr.   1992   Malcolm Rifkind
July   1995   Michael Portillo
May   1997   George Robertson
Oct.   1999   Geoff Hoon

*Until April 1964 the office-holders were Ministers of Defence.

Secretaries of State for Health and Social Services

Ministers of Health

Aug.   1945   Aneurin Bevan
Jan.   1951   Hilary Marquand
Oct.   1951   Harry Crookshank
May   1952   Iain Macleod
Dec.   1955   Robert Turton
Jan.   1957   Denis Vosper
Sept.   1957   Derek Walker-Smith

July	1960	Enoch Powell
Oct.	1963	Anthony Barber
Oct.	1964	Kenneth Robinson

Prior to Nov. 1968, those listed were Ministers of Health. In Nov. 1968 the office was combined with the Ministry of Social Security.

Secretaries of State for Social Services

Oct.	1968	Richard Crossman
June	1970	Sir Keith Joseph
Mar.	1974	Barbara Castle
Apr.	1976	David Ennals
May	1979	Patrick Jenkin
Sept.	1981	Norman Fowler
June	1987	John Moore

In 1988, there was a further change, with the creation of separate Secretaries of State for Health and for Social Security.

Secretaries of State for Health

July	1988	Kenneth Clarke
Nov.	1990	William Waldegrave
Apr.	1992	Virginia Bottomley
July	1995	Stephen Dorrell
May	1997	Frank Dobson
Oct.	1999	Alan Milburn

Secretaries of State for Social Security

July	1988	John Moore
July	1989	Tony Newton
Apr.	1992	Peter Lilley
May	1997	Harriet Harman
July	1998	Alistair Darling

Secretaries of State for Education*

Aug.	1945	Ellen Wilkinson
Feb.	1947	George Tomlinson
Nov.	1951	Florence Horsbrugh
Oct.	1954	Sir David Eccles
Jan.	1957	Viscount Hailsham
Sept.	1957	Geoffrey Lloyd
Oct.	1959	Sir David Eccles
July	1962	Sir Edward Boyle
Apr.	1964	Quintin Hogg
Oct.	1964	Michael Stewart
Jan.	1965	Anthony Crosland

Aug.   1967   Patrick Gordon-Walker
Apr.   1968   Edward Short
June   1970   Margaret Thatcher
Mar.   1974   Reg Prentice
June   1975   Fred Mulley
Sept. 1976   Shirley Williams
May   1979   Mark Carlisle
Sept. 1981   Sir Keith Joseph
May   1986   Kenneth Baker
Oct.   1989   John MacGregor
Nov.   1990   Kenneth Clarke
Apr.   1992   John Patten
July   1994   Gillian Shephard
May   1997   David Blunkett

*Minister of Education until Apr. 1964, thereafter Secretary of State for Education (and Science). Employment was added to the title in July 1995.

Secretaries of State for Employment*

Aug.   1945   George Isaacs
Jan.   1951   Aneurin Bevan
Apr.   1951   Alfred Robens
Oct.   1951   Sir Walter Monckton
Dec.   1955   Iain Macleod
Oct.   1959   Edward Heath
July   1960   John Hare
Oct.   1963   Joseph Godber
Oct.   1964   Ray Gunter
Apr.   1968   Barbara Castle
June   1970   Robert Carr
Apr.   1972   Maurice Macmillan
Dec.   1973   William Whitelaw
Mar.   1974   Michael Foot
Apr.   1976   Albert Booth
May   1979   James Prior
Sept. 1981   Norman Tebbit
Oct.   1983   Tom King
Sept. 1985   Lord Young
June   1987   Sir Norman Fowler
Jan.   1990   Michael Howard
Apr.   1992   Gillian Shephard
May   1993   David Hunt
July   1994   Michael Portillo

*From 1945 to Nov. 1959, the office was Minister of Labour and National Service. From Nov. 1959 the office was simply Minister of Labour. In Apr. 1968, the office was reorganized, with a Secretary of State for Employment and Productivity. Productivity was dropped from the title in Nov. 1970. The office was abolished in July 1995.

Secretaries of State for the Environment

Oct.	1970	Peter Walker
Nov.	1972	Geoffrey Rippon
Mar.	1974	Anthony Crosland
Apr.	1976	Peter Shore
May	1979	Michael Heseltine
Jan.	1983	Tom King
June	1983	Patrick Jenkin
Sept.	1985	Kenneth Baker
May	1986	Nicholas Ridley
Oct.	1989	Chris Patten
Nov.	1990	Michael Heseltine
Apr.	1992	Michael Howard
May	1993	John Selwyn Gummer
May	1997	John Prescott*

*John Prescott was Deputy Prime Minister and Secretary of State for Environment, Transport and the Regions.

Presidents of the Board of Trade

July	1945	Sir Stafford Cripps
Sept.	1947	Harold Wilson
Apr.	1951	Sir Hartley Shawcross
Oct.	1951	Peter Thorneycroft
Jan.	1957	Sir David Eccles
Oct.	1959	Reginald Maudling
Oct.	1961	Frederick Erroll
Oct.	1963	Edward Heath*
Oct.	1964	Douglas Jay
Aug.	1967	Anthony Crosland
Oct.	1969	Roy Mason
June	1970	Michael Noble

*Also Secretary of State for Industry, Trade and Regional Development. This office was abolished on 16 Oct. 1964.

Secretaries of State for Trade and Industry*

Oct.	1970	John Davies
Nov.	1972	Peter Walker
Mar.	1974	Peter Shore
Apr.	1976	Edmund Dell
Nov.	1978	John Smith
May	1979	John Nott
Sept.	1981	John Biffen
Apr.	1982	Lord Cockfield

June	1983	Cecil Parkinson
Oct.	1983	Norman Tebbit
Sept.	1985	Leon Brittan
Jan.	1986	Paul Channon
June	1987	Lord Young
July	1989	Nicholas Ridley
Nov.	1990	Peter Lilley
Apr.	1992	Michael Heseltine[†]
July	1995	Ian Lang
May	1997	Margaret Beckett[†]
July	1998	Peter Mandelson
Dec.	1998	Stephen Byers

*From March 1974 to June 1983, Secretary of State for Trade only.
†Holding post of President of the Board of Trade.

A separate Secretary of State for Industry was created. This office was held by the following:

Mar.	1974	Tony Benn
June	1975	Eric Varley
May	1979	Sir Keith Joseph
Sept.	1981	Patrick Jenkin

In June 1983 the office merged back with Trade.

Secretaries of State for Wales

Oct.	1964	James Griffiths
Apr.	1966	Cledwyn Hughes
Apr.	1968	George Thomas
June	1970	Peter Thomas
Mar.	1974	John Morris
May	1979	Nicholas Edwards
June	1987	Peter Walker
May	1990	David Hunt
May	1993	John Redwood
July	1995	William Hague
May	1997	Ron Davies
Nov.	1998	Alun Michael
July	1999	Paul Murphy

Secretaries of State for Scotland

Aug.	1945	Joseph Westwood
Oct.	1947	Arthur Woodburn
Feb.	1950	Hector McNeil
Oct.	1951	James Stuart

Jan.	1957	John Scott Maclay
July	1962	Michael Noble
Oct.	1964	William Ross
June	1970	Gordon Campbell
Mar.	1974	William Ross
Apr.	1976	Bruce Millan
May	1979	George Younger
Jan.	1986	Malcolm Rifkind
Nov.	1990	Ian Lang
July	1995	Michael Forsyth
May	1997	Donald Dewar
May	1998	John Reid

Secretaries of State for Northern Ireland

Apr.	1972	William Whitelaw
Dec.	1975	Francis Pym
Mar.	1974	Merlyn Rees
Sept.	1976	Roy Mason
May	1979	Humphrey Atkins
Sept.	1981	James Prior
Sept.	1984	Douglas Hurd
Sept.	1985	Tom King
July	1989	Peter Brooke
Apr.	1992	Sir Patrick Mayhew
May	1997	Marjorie (Mo) Mowlam
Oct.	1999	Peter Mandelson

Leaders of the House of Commons

July	1945	Herbert Morrison
Mar.	1951	Chuter Ede
Oct.	1951	Harry Crookshank
Apr.	1955	'Rab' Butler
Oct.	1961	Iain Macleod
Oct.	1963	Selwyn Lloyd
Oct.	1964	Herbert Bowden
Aug.	1966	Richard Crossman
Apr.	1968	Fred Peart
June	1970	William Whitelaw
Apr.	1972	Robert Carr
Nov.	1972	James Prior
Mar.	1974	Edward Short
Apr.	1976	Michael Foot
May	1979	Norman St. John Stevas
Jan.	1981	Francis Pym

Apr.	1982	John Biffen
June	1987	John Wakeham
July	1989	Sir Geoffrey Howe
Nov.	1990	John MacGregor
Apr.	1992	Tony Newton
May	1997	Ann Taylor
July	1998	Margaret Beckett

Government Chief Whips

Aug.	1945	William Whiteley
Oct.	1951	Patrick Buchan-Hepburn
Dec.	1955	Edward Heath
Oct.	1959	Martin Redmayne
Oct.	1964	Edward Short
July	1966	John Silkin
Apr.	1969	Robert Mellish
June	1970	Francis Pym
Dec.	1973	Humphrey Atkins
Mar.	1974	Robert Mellish
Apr.	1976	Michael Cocks
May	1979	Michael Jopling
June	1983	John Wakeham
June	1987	David Waddington
Oct.	1989	Timothy Renton
Nov.	1990	Richard Ryder
July	1995	Alastair Goodlad
May	1997	Nick Brown
July	1998	Ann Taylor

Significant ministerial resignations and dismissals*

1947

Nov. Hugh Dalton (Labour Chancellor of the Exchequer, budget leak).

1951

Apr. Aneurin Bevan, Harold Wilson and John Freeman (left-wing opposition to budget proposals).

1954

July Sir Thomas Dugdale (Crichel Down affair, see p 273).

1956

Oct. Anthony Nutting (opposition to Eden's Suez policy).
Nov. Sir Edward Boyle (opposition to Suez intervention).

1957

Mar. Marquess of Salisbury (right-wing opposition to release of Archbishop Makarios from detention).

1958

Jan. Peter Thorneycroft, Enoch Powell and Nigel Birch (differences over economic policy, dismissed by Harold Macmillan as 'a little local difficulty').

Nov. Ian Harvey (homosexual affair).

1963

June John Profumo (lying to the House of Commons concerning the Profumo affair, see p 299).

1966

Feb. Christopher Mayhew (opposition to defence estimates).

July Frank Cousins (incomes policy not acceptable to his trade union background).

1968

Jan. Earl of Longford (opposition to postponement of raising of the school-leaving age).

Mar. George Brown (conduct of government, but reflecting more deep-down personal dissent).

July Ray Gunter (dissatisfaction with government policy generally).

1971

July Teddy Taylor (opposition to entry into EEC).

Oct. Jasper More (opposition to entry into EEC).

1972

July Reginald Maudling (links to John Poulson, architect in corruption scandal).

1973

May Lord Lambton (sex scandal).

May Earl Jellicoe (sex scandal).

1975

Apr. Eric Heffer (voicing opposition to Europe policy in Commons).

June Judith Hart (disenchantment with Harold Wilson).

1976

Feb. Joan Lestor (cuts in education spending).

Dec. Reg Prentice (disillusion with Labour policies, which eventually led him to join the Conservative ranks).

1977

Nov.   Joe Ashton (disagreement over power dispute).

1981

May   Keith Speed (opposition to defence proposals).

1982

Apr.   Lord Carrington (Foreign Secretary), Humphrey Atkins and Richard Luce (responsibility for Argentine invasion of the Falkland Islands).

May   Nicholas Budgen (Conservative policy over Northern Ireland).

1983

Oct.   Cecil Parkinson (scandal over illegitimate child by Sarah Keays).

1985

Nov.   Ian Gow (opposition to government's Northern Ireland policy).

1986

Jan.   Michael Heseltine and Leon Brittan (furious and much-publicized disagreements over Westland affair, see p 313).

1988

Dec.   Edwina Currie (row over salmonella in eggs).

1989

Oct.   Nigel Lawson (Chancellor of the Exchequer, over economic policy after disagreement with Margaret Thatcher).

1990

July   Nicholas Ridley (article in *Spectator* voicing anti-German views).
Nov.   Geoffrey Howe (disagreement over European policy, a resignation which marked the beginning of the downfall of Margaret Thatcher).

1992

Sept.   David Mellor (Heritage Minister, private scandal).

1993

June   Michael Mates (alleged links with fugitive business tycoon Asil Nadir).

1994

Oct.   Tim Smith and Neil Hamilton (junior Northern Ireland Minister and Corporate Affairs Minister, over 'cash for questions' allegations).

1995

June   John Redwood (Secretary of State for Wales, to contest leadership election against John Major).

July   Jonathan Aitken (Chief Secretary to the Treasury, to defend himself over allegations in the 'arms for Iran' affair).

1996

Dec.   David Willetts (Paymaster-General, over 'cash for questions' allegations).

1998

Oct.   Ron Davies (Welsh Secretary, after a 'lapse of judgement' on Clapham Common).

Dec.   Peter Mandelson and Geoffrey Robinson (revelations of their financial affairs).

For a complete list of resignations, the fullest source is D E Butler and G Butler, *British Political Facts, 1900–94* (London, Macmillan, 1994).

3 ELECTIONS

Chronology of principal events

1948   Representation of the People Act abolishes plural voting – the practice of having one vote in the constituency in place of residence, *and* in the place of business or university where educated. The six months' residence qualification is abolished. Permanent Boundary Commissioners set up to report every three to seven years.

1958   Redistribution of Seats Act modifies rules governing Boundary Commissioners and requests reports every ten to fifteen years.

1969   Representation of the People Act reduces minimum age of voting from 21 to 18 years.

1973   Proportional representation introduced into Northern Ireland for the Northern Irish Assembly.

1979   Euro-constituencies created for direct elections to European Parliament.

1985   Representation of the People Act raises the deposit required of candidates from £150 (since it was first introduced in 1918) to £500, mainly to deter 'joke' candidates. The Act also introduces the concept of overseas voting by opening the franchise (for parliamentary and European elections) to British citizens who have lived abroad for up to five years and intended to return to the United Kingdom. This enfranchises an estimated 500,000 ex-patriates.

1989   Representation of the People Act facilitates the 'expatriate' vote by offering a proxy vote to any British citizen who has left in the last 20 years, to be cast in the constituency in which they were last registered.

1998   Proportional representation used for elections to new Northern Ireland Assembly.

1999   Elections held for new Scottish Parliament and Welsh Assembly. For first time, European elections held under a list system of proportional representation (June). Government outlines proposals for ceiling on party general election expenditure. The measures would put a cap of about £20 million on the spending by each of the main parties in the run-up to general elections. Government announces plans to enfranchise mental patients, install polling booths in supermarkets and introduce electronic voting.

Central party spending on general elections, 1964–97 (£ million)

	Tories	Labour	Lib Dems	Combined
1964	1.23	0.50	n.a.	n.a.
1979	2.30	1.60	0.20	4.10
1983	3.80	2.30	1.90	8.00
1987	9.00	4.70	1.75	15.45
1992	11.20	10.60	1.80	23.60
1997	28.30	26.00	3.20	57.50

Expenditure on central party advertising in elections, 1979–97 (£ thousand)

	Tories		Labour	
	Press	Posters*	Press	Posters
1979	766	591	260	354
1983	1 725	843	878	
1987	4 532	1 834	2 144	309
1992	1 800	4 000	1 500	1 768
1997	3 158	11 091	900	5 000

*including cinema in 1979

Growth of the electorate, 1949–97

1949	34 269 770
1959	35 397 080
1965	36 128 387
1970	39 153 000
1979	41 769 000
1983	42 197 344
1987	43 181 320
1992	43 249 721
1997	44 203 694

Source: D E Butler and G Butler, *British Political Facts, 1900–94* (London, Macmillan, 1994)

Turnout, 1945–97*

5 July 1945	72.7
23 Feb. 1950	84.0
25 Oct. 1951	82.5
25 May 1955	76.7
8 Oct. 1959	78.8
15 Oct. 1964	77.1
31 Mar. 1966	75.9
18 June 1970	72.0
28 Feb. 1974	78.8
10 Oct. 1974	72.8
3 May 1979	76.0
9 June 1983	73.0
11 June 1987	75.0
9 Apr. 1992	78.0
1 May 1997	71.5

Source: Butler and Butler, *British Political Facts*

*The highest turnout at a post-war election in Britain was 84 per cent in Feb. 1950, closely followed by 82.5 per cent in Oct. 1951. The lowest turnout was in May 1997.

General election results, 1945–97

Summary of seats won by major parties

	Con.	Lab.	Lib.*	Comm- unist	Plaid Cymru	SNP	Others (GB)	Others (NI)	Total
1945	213	393	12	2	0	0	16	4	640
1950	299	315	9	0	0	0	0	2	625
1951	321	295	6	0	0	0	0	3	625
1955	345	277	6	0	0	0	0	2	630
1959	365	258	6	0	0	0	1	0	630
1964	304	317	9	0	0	0	0	0	630
1966	253	364	12	0	0	0	0	1	630
1970	330	288	6	0	0	1	1	4	630
1974 (Feb.)	297	301	14	0	2	7	2	12	635
1974 (Oct.)	277	319	13	0	3	11	0	12	635
1979	339	269	11	0	2	2	0	12	635
1983	397	209	23	0	2	2	0	17	650
1987	376	229	22	0	3	3	0	17	650
1992	336	271	20	0	4	3	0	17	651
1997	165	419	46	0	4	6	1	18	659

*1983 and 1987 figures for Liberals include SDP MPs. The 1992 and 1997 figures are for the Liberal Democrats.

Source: *Pears Cyclopaedia* (108th edn, London, Penguin, 1999)

Electoral support for Conservative and Labour parties

	Share of vote obtained by:				
	Con. (%)	Lab. (%)	Con. + Lab. (%)	Other parties (%)	(no. of MPs)
1945	39.8	47.9	87.7	12.4	(30)
1950	43.5	46.1	89.6	10.4	(12)
1951	48.0	48.8	96.8	3.2	(9)
1955	49.7	46.4	96.1	3.9	(8)
1959	49.3	43.9	93.2	6.8	(7)
1964	43.4	44.1	87.5	12.5	(9)
1966	41.9	48.1	90.0	10.0	(13)
1970	46.4	43.1	89.5	10.5	(12)
1974 (Feb.)	37.8	37.1	74.9	25.1	(37)
1974 (Oct.)	35.8	39.2	75.0	25.0	(39)
1979	43.9	37.0	80.9	19.1	(27)
1983	42.4	27.6	70.0	30.0	(44)
1987	42.2	30.8	73.0	27.0	(45)
1992	41.9	34.2	76.1	23.9	(44)
1997	30.7	43.2	73.9	26.1	(76)

Principal source: I Budge and D McKay, *The Developing British Political System: The 1990s* (3rd edn, London, Longman, 1993) p 98

Distribution of seats under proportional representation

	Con.	Lab.	Lib. All.
1945	253	307	58
1950	271	288	57
1951	300	305	16
1955	313	292	17
1959	311	276	37
1964	273	278	71
1966	264	302	54
1970	292	272	47
1974 (Feb.)	241	236	123
1974 (Oct.)	227	249	116
1979	279	234	88
1983	276	179	165
1987	275	200	146
1992	273	224	116
1997	202	285	111

Note: The table assumes the parties would have taken the same share of seats as votes.

Individual general elections, 1945–97

5 July 1945

Parliament having been extended because of the war, Churchill wished to continue the coalition until the defeat of Japan. But with the defeat of Germany the Labour party wished to dissolve the coalition and hold an election in the autumn. Churchill decided that the government could not function efficiently with the prospect of an election hanging over it. He ended the coalition and formed a 'caretaker' government which supervised the election.

	Seats	Total vote	% share of total vote
Conservative	213	9 988 306	39.8
Liberal	12	2 248 226	9.6
Labour	393	11 995 152	47.8
Others	22	854 294	2.8
Total	640	25 085 978	100.0

Main features Labour swept to power, winning 393 seats to secure its first overall majority. The Conservative share of the vote fell 13.9 per cent since 1935. The Liberals won only twelve seats, their casualties including Sir Archibald Sinclair (party leader) and Sir William Beveridge. The Conservatives lost five Cabinet members and 27 other ministers in the largest movement of votes at any election since 1918.

23 Feb. 1950

Their term of office coming to an end, and having carried much important legislation, Labour decided to go to the country.

	Seats	Total vote	% share of total vote
Conservative	298	12 502 567	43.5
Liberal	9	2 621 548	9.1
Labour	315	13 266 592	46.1
Others	3	381 964	1.3
Total	625	28 772 671	100.0

Main features Labour narrowly clung on to power (with a five-seat majority). Redrawing of constituency boundaries worked against Labour. Their share of the vote was down only 2.2 per cent compared to 1945 and they secured 46.1 per cent of the vote, compared to 43.5 per cent for the Conservatives. The Liberals polled only 9.1 per cent of the vote, with 319 of their 475 candidates losing their deposit. Turnout was a remarkably high 84 per cent.

25 Oct. 1951

With a narrow Commons majority constantly harassed by the Opposition, and the government's impetus spent, Attlee decided that to postpone an election would lead only to further deterioration in the government's position.

	Seats	Total vote	% share of total vote
Conservative	321	13 717 538	48.0
Liberal	6	730 556	2.5
Labour	295	13 948 605	48.8
Others	3	198 969	0.7
Total	625	28 595 668	100.0

Main features The Conservatives won a narrow victory, capturing 321 seats to Labour's 295, thus securing an overall majority of seventeen. Labour actually polled a greater share of the vote (48.8 per cent, the highest it has ever achieved) than the Conservatives (on 48 per cent). The Liberals almost disappeared altogether, winning only six seats with 2.5 per cent of the vote.

25 May 1955

Churchill's retirement from the premiership meant a change of party leadership. Eden, the new Prime Minister, with the advantage of a rising standard of living and splits in the Labour party, decided to dissolve after Butler's budget had reduced income tax to 6d (2.5p) in the pound.

	Seats	Total vote	% share of total vote
Conservative	344	13 286 569	49.7
Liberal	6	722 405	2.7
Labour	277	12 404 970	46.4
Others	3	346 554	1.2
Total	630	26 760 498	100.0

Main features The Conservatives increased their overall majority to 54 and their share of the vote to 49.7 per cent (the largest share achieved by any party at a general election since 1945). Relatively few seats changed hands (Labour losing 22 compared to the seats held when Parliament was dissolved). The Liberal tally of votes and seats remained abysmally low.

8 Oct. 1959

Improvement in opinion polls and the economy, plus an easing of foreign problems and a recovery of party morale, persuaded Macmillan to take the opportunity to dissolve.

	Seats	Total vote	% share of total vote
Conservative	365	13 749 830	49.4
Liberal	6	1 638 571	5.9
Labour	258	12 215 538	43.8
Others	1	255 302	0.9
Total	630	27 589 241	100.0

Main features Under Harold Macmillan the Conservatives enjoyed an election triumph, notching up a 100-seat majority and their third successive electoral victory. Labour's vote fell 2.6 per cent to 43.8 per cent; the Liberals enjoyed a mild revival (up from 2.7 to 5.9 per cent). The election is remembered for the Conservative slogan 'You've never had it so good'.

15 Oct. 1964

With Parliament nearing the end of its statutory life, Sir Alec Douglas-Home delayed dissolution for as long as possible in the hope of economic improvement and to let the party recover from the divisions resulting from a change of leadership.

	Seats	Total vote	% share of total vote
Conservative	304	12 001 396	43.4
Liberal	9	3 092 878	11.2
Labour	317	12 205 814	44.1
Others	0	348 914	1.3
Total	630	27 655 374	100.0

Main features   The outcome was perhaps the closest in post-war electoral history with an overall Labour majority of only five. The Conservative share of the vote dropped 6 per cent to 43.4 per cent, but Labour rose only 0.3 per cent (to 44.1 per cent). The Liberal share rose 5.3 per cent to 11.2 per cent, but their number of seats rose only to nine.

31 Mar. 1966

Having only a precarious parliamentary majority, Wilson and his party decided to take the opportunity of an upswing in popularity, reflected in the Hull North by-election, to dissolve and improve their position.

	Seats	Total vote	% share of total vote
Conservative	253	11 418 433	41.9
Liberal	12	2 327 533	8.5
Labour	363	13 064 951	47.9
Others	2	452 689	1.7
Total	630	27 263 606	100.0

Main features   With 48 net gains, Labour's victory was impressive. Its tally of 363 seats was its best result since 1945, its share of the vote up 3.8 per cent since 1964 (the Conservatives slipped 1.5 per cent, the Liberals slipped 2.7 per cent, but gained extra seats in the Scottish Highlands). Conservative casualties included Christopher Soames, Henry Brooke and Peter Thorneycroft. Newcomers included Michael Heseltine and David Owen (as a Labour MP).

18 June 1970

From opinion polls and by-election trends Wilson believed he detected a groundswell of support for Labour and dissolved.

	Seats	Total vote	% share of total vote
Conservative	330	13 145 123	46.4
Labour	287	12 179 341	43.0
Liberal	6	2 117 035	7.5
Others	7	903 299	3.1
Total	630	28 347 798	100.0

Main features   The Conservative victory was achieved with 68 net gains, their share of the vote rising 4.5 per cent (Labour was down 4.9 per cent). The Liberals fell back to six seats. Labour casualties included George Brown. The Nationalists lost their by-election victors (Gwynfor Evans and Winnie Ewing).

28 Feb. 1974

The confrontation between the miners and the Heath government, combined with the three-day week, led Heath to dissolve in order to seek a fresh mandate for his policy.

	Seats	Total vote	% share of total vote
Conservative	297	11 868 906	37.9
Labour	301	11 639 243	37.1
Liberal	14	6 063 470	19.3
Others (Northern Ireland)	12	717 986	2.3
Scottish National Party	7	632 032	2.0
Plaid Cymru	2	171 364	0.6
Others	2	260 665	0.8
Total	635	31 333 226	100.0

Main features   The Conservatives failed to win an overall majority, with a net loss of 8.5 per cent of the vote and three seats compared to 1970. In terms both of seats and votes, the two major parties were neck and neck. The Liberals polled over 6 million votes, but won only fourteen seats. The Scottish Nationalists won seven seats.

10 Oct. 1974

Having made numerous policy statements during the summer, the Labour government decided that the opinion polls signified a Labour victory and dissolved the shortest parliament of the century. This, it was hoped, would gain a new mandate for the numerically weak government.

	Seats	Total vote	% share of total vote
Conservative	277	10 464 817	35.9
Labour	319	11 457 079	39.2
Liberal	13	5 346 754	18.3
Others (Northern Ireland)	12	702 094	2.4
Scottish Nationalists	11	839 617	2.9
Plaid Cymru	3	166 321	0.6
Others (GB)	–	212 496	0.7
Total	635	29 189 178	100.0

Main features The second election within a year (the first occasion since 1910 when this had occurred) produced a slightly better result for Labour, whose share of the vote rose 2.1 per cent. Compared to Feb. 1974, the Conservatives suffered a net loss of 20 seats. The Scottish Nationalist tally rose to 11, while the Liberals slipped. Labour would very soon find itself without a working majority.

3 May 1979

A minority Labour government, towards the end of its term of office, was defeated on a vote of confidence.

	Seats	Total vote	% share of total vote
Conservative	339	13 699 954	43.9
Labour	269	11 532 148	36.9
Liberal	11	4 313 811	13.8
Others (Northern Ireland)	12	695 889	2.2
Scottish Nationalists	2	504 259	1.6
Plaid Cymru	2	132 544	0.4
Others	0	343 674	1.2
Total	635	31 222 279	100.0

Main features The 1979 election was a watershed, opening the path to power of Margaret Thatcher and to an unbroken series of Conservative administrations throughout the 1980s and early 1990s. The Conservatives gained a net 62 seats (compared to Oct. 1974). The Liberal vote declined to 13.8 per cent, the Scottish Nationalists plummeted after the devolution referendum (see p 120). The election saw defeat for Shirley Williams (Labour), Jeremy Thorpe (Liberal), Gwynfor Evans (Plaid Cymru) and Winnie Ewing (SNP).

9 June 1983

With a commanding lead in the opinion polls, following the Falklands War of 1982, Mrs Thatcher waited for confirmation of the government's popularity in the municipal election results in May before calling a snap poll on 9 June.

	Seats	Total vote	% share of total vote
Conservative	397	13 012 592	42.4
Labour	209	8 457 118	27.6
Liberal/SDP	23	7 780 589	25.4
Plaid Cymru	2	125 309	0.4
Scottish Nationalists	2	331 975	1.1
Others (Northern Ireland)	17	764 925	2.6
Others	0	198 387	0.5
Total	650	30 670 895	100.0

Main features The Conservatives swept to victory with an overall majority of 144, reducing Labour to 209 seats, its vote down by 9.3 per cent to a mere 27.6 per cent. The Liberal/SDP Alliance polled a massive 25.4 per cent of votes cast, but returned only 23 MPs. It was Labour's most disastrous performance since the inter-war period. Casualties included Tony Benn for Labour (defeated in Bristol South-East) and Shirley Williams and William Rodgers for the SDP.

11 June 1987

Speculation about the date of the general election grew during the early months of 1987, the government benefiting from a number of favourable economic indicators which allowed it to introduce tax concessions in the budget while remaining within its financial strategy. Favourable local election results led to the announcement of polling day as 11 June.

	Seats	Total vote	% share of total vote
Conservative	375	13 763 747	42.2
Labour	229	10 029 270	30.8
Liberal/SDP	22	7 341 275	22.6
Plaid Cymru	3	123 589	0.3
Scottish Nationalists	3	416 873	1.4
Others (Northern Ireland)	17	730 152	2.3
Others	1*	151 517	0.4
Total	650	32 529 423	100.0

*The Speaker

Main features The Conservatives won their third successive general election victory (the first time they had achieved this feat since 1959) with a very similar share of the vote to 1983 (42.2 per cent, down only 0.2 per cent). Labour's vote rose 3.2 per cent, but its tally of seats rose by only 20 to 229. The Liberal/SDP Alliance again failed to break through, its vote falling 2.8 per cent. Margaret Thatcher's third victory left her with an overall majority of 102. Defeated MPs included (for the Alliance) Roy Jenkins (in Glasgow Hillhead) and Enoch Powell (for the Ulster Unionists).

9 Apr. 1992

John Major, who had succeeded Margaret Thatcher in Nov. 1990, delayed the election until April 1992. Opinion polls still pointed to the likelihood of a Conservative defeat but were proved mistaken by an apparent late swing to the Conservatives from Liberals cautious of 'letting in' a Labour government.

	Seats	Total vote
Conservative	336	14 093 890
Labour	271	11 559 857
Liberal Democrat	20	5 995 712
Scottish Nationalist	3	629 552
Plaid Cymru	4	154 439
Others	17	1 176 692

Main features The surprise victory for the Conservatives (who managed to contain their losses to Labour) was matched by Labour's fourth consecutive election defeat. Labour leader Neil Kinnock resigned shortly after the election. The Liberal Democrats failed to make any real breakthrough (except in parts of the south-west, while in Bath they unseated Conservative party chairman, Chris Patten). Liberals secured second place in 154 seats, but were third in 389.

1 May 1997

John Major's beleaguered administration delayed calling an election until the full five years had elapsed. Despite the delay, the Conservatives saw no real recovery in their fortunes in the opinion polls or by-elections as the election approached.

	Seats	Total vote
Conservative	165	9 600 940
Labour	419	13 517 911
Liberal Democrat	46	5 243 440
Scottish Nationalist	6	622 260
Plaid Cymru	4	161 030
Others	19	2 142 621

Main features The Conservatives suffered a defeat of historic proportions at the hands of a rejuvenated New Labour. With their fewest seats since 1906, the party was wiped out in Scotland and Wales. Labour won seats hitherto considered impregnable (such as Wimbledon). The Liberal Democrats won their highest tally since the days of Lloyd George in 1929. Prominent Conservative casualties included Michael Portillo (Defence Secretary) in Enfield Southgate and Scottish Secretary Michael Forsyth.

Famous by-elections since 1945

Motherwell	12 Apr. 1945	First ever by-election victory by Scottish Nationalists; seat gained from Labour.
Torrington	27 Mar. 1958	First Liberal victory at a by-election since 1929; seat gained from Conservative.
Orpington	14 Mar. 1962	The most sensational Liberal victory of the 1960s. The party swept to victory in a safe Tory seat.
Leyton	21 Jan. 1965	Defeat of Labour's Foreign Secretary Patrick Gordon-Walker in a normally safe East London Labour stronghold.
Roxburgh, Selkirk and Peebles	24 Mar. 1965	David Steel won a safe Conservative seat to become the 'baby of the House' and eventual Liberal party leader.
Carmarthen	14 July 1966	The first ever Welsh Nationalist to win a seat in a by-election; seat gained from Labour.
Hamilton	2 Nov. 1967	The first SNP by-election victory since the party won Motherwell in a wartime

		by-election in April 1945. Hamilton heralded the revival of the SNP; seat gained from Labour.
Dudley	28 Mar. 1968	The by-election which saw the largest swing ever recorded to the Conservatives during the 1966–70 Wilson government; seat gained from Labour.
Rochdale	26 Oct. 1972	First of the famous series of Liberal by-election victories of 1972–73; seat gained from Labour.
Sutton and Cheam	7 Dec. 1972	A sensational Liberal victory in one of the safest Tory areas – the London suburbs.
Lincoln	1 Mar. 1973	Dick Taverne won a personal triumph as a Democratic Labour candidate having previously been the town's Labour MP.
Glasgow Govan	8 Nov. 1973	The first SNP by-election victory since Hamilton in 1967; seat gained from Labour.
Walsall North	4 Nov. 1976	The safe Labour stronghold formerly held by John Stonehouse fell on a swing of 22.6 per cent to the Conservatives – the largest swing of the 1974–79 Parliament to a Conservative.
Liverpool Edge Hill	29 Mar. 1979	A sweeping Liberal victory by 8,133 votes in a hitherto safe Labour seat. The 32 per cent swing from labour to the Liberals was the highest yet.
Warrington	16 July 1981	First major SDP by-election assault, led by Roy Jenkins, narrowly fails. Labour retains seat.
Crosby	26 Nov. 1981	Sensational SDP victory by Shirley Williams in normally safe Conservative seat.
Glasgow Hillhead	25 Mar. 1982	Roy Jenkins victorious for SDP; seat gained from Conservatives.
Ryedale	8 May 1986	Most spectacular Alliance gain from Conservatives of 1983–87 period.
Greenwich	26 Feb. 1987	Rosie Barnes secures first-ever SDP by-election gain from Labour.

Glasgow Govan	19 Nov. 1988	Swing of 33.2 per cent to SNP in sensational defeat for Labour.
Vale of Glamorgan	4 May 1989	Labour gain victory on a swing of 12.4 per cent, the largest swing in a seat *gained* by Labour since Liverpool West Toxteth in July 1935; seat gained from Conservatives.
Mid-Staffordshire	22 Mar. 1990	Labour increases its vote by 24.3 per cent, its best result to date in a post-war by-election; seat gained from Conservatives.
Eastbourne	18 Oct. 1990	First by-election victory for the newly formed Liberal Democrats on a swing of 20.1 per cent; seat gained from Conservatives.
Ribble Valley	7 Mar. 1991	The Liberal Democrats take an ultra-safe Conservative seat on a 24.8 per cent swing in what was seen as a verdict on the poll tax.
Newbury	6 May 1993	A sweeping Liberal Democrat victory, on a swing to them of 29 per cent from the Conservatives, in the first by-election since the 1992 general election.
Christchurch	29 July 1993	Following on from Newbury, the Liberal Democrats took this Conservative stronghold on the biggest swing in a by-election in the twentieth century (35.8 per cent).
Eastleigh	9 June 1994	The third successive Conservative seat to fall to the Liberal Democrats (on a swing of 21.4 per cent). Labour came second, the Conservatives third with 24.7 per cent of the vote.
Dudley West	15 Dec. 1994	Massive 29 per cent swing from Conservative to Labour as Labour sweep to victory.
Perth and Kinross	25 May 1995	SNP win first-ever by-election victory from Conservatives.
Winchester	20 Nov. 1997	Liberal Democrats secure 20,000 majority in a seat whose general election majority of three was disputed.

Seats changing hands at by-elections

Date		Constituency	Held formerly by (party)	Victor of by-election
Mar.	1946	English Universities	Independent	Conservative
June	1946	Down	Independent Unionist	Unionist
Nov.	1946	Scottish Universities	Independent	Conservative
Jan.	1948	Glasgow Camlachie	ILP	Conservative
May	1953	Sunderland South	Labour	Conservative
Mar.	1958	Torrington	Conservative	Liberal
Mar.	1960	Brighouse & Spenborough	Labour	Conservative
May	1961	Bristol South-East	Labour	Conservative*
Mar.	1962	Orpington	Conservative	Liberal
June	1962	Middlesbrough West	Conservative	Labour
Nov.	1962	Glasgow Woodside	Conservative	Labour
Nov.	1962	South Dorset	Conservative	Labour
Aug.	1963	Bristol South-East	Conservative	Labour
Nov.	1963	Luton	Conservative	Labour
May	1964	Rutherglen	Conservative	Labour
Jan.	1965	Leyton	Labour	Conservative
Mar.	1965	Roxburgh, Selkirk and Peebles	Conservative	Liberal
July	1966	Carmarthen	Labour	Plaid Cymru
Mar.	1967	Glasgow Pollok	Labour	Conservative
Sept.	1967	Walthamstow West	Labour	Conservative
Sept.	1967	Cambridge	Labour	Conservative
Nov.	1967	Hamilton	Labour	SNP
Nov.	1967	Leicester South-West	Labour	Conservative
Mar.	1968	Acton	Labour	Conservative
Mar.	1968	Meriden	Labour	Conservative
Mar.	1968	Dudley	Labour	Conservative
June	1968	Oldham West	Labour	Conservative
June	1968	Nelson and Colne	Labour	Conservative
Mar.	1969	Walthamstow East	Labour	Conservative
Apr.	1969	Mid-Ulster	Ulster Unionist	Independent Unity
June	1969	Birmingham Ladywood	Labour	Liberal
Oct.	1969	Swindon	Labour	Conservative
Dec.	1969	Wellingborough	Labour	Conservative
May	1971	Bromsgrove	Conservative	Labour
Apr.	1972	Merthyr Tydfil	Independent Labour	Labour
Oct.	1972	Rochdale	Labour	Liberal
Dec.	1972	Sutton and Cheam	Conservative	Liberal

*Seat went to Conservative on petition

Date		Constituency	Held formerly by (party)	Victor of by-election
Mar.	1973	Lincoln	Labour	Democratic Labour
July	1973	Isle of Ely	Conservative	Liberal
July	1973	Ripon	Conservative	Liberal
Nov.	1973	Glasgow Govan	Labour	SNP
Nov.	1973	Berwick on Tweed	Conservative	Liberal
June	1975	Woolwich West	Labour	Conservative
Nov.	1976	Walsall North	Labour	Conservative
Nov.	1976	Workington	Labour	Conservative
Mar.	1977	Birmingham Stechford	Labour	Conservative
Apr.	1977	Ashfield	Labour	Conservative
Mar.	1978	Ilford North	Labour	Conservative
Mar.	1979	Liverpool Edge Hill	Labour	Liberal
Apr.	1981	Fermanagh and South Tyrone	Independent	Anti-H Block
Oct.	1981	Croydon North-West	Conservative	Liberal
Nov.	1981	Crosby	Conservative	SDP
Mar.	1982	Glasgow Hillhead	Conservative	SDP
June	1982	Mitcham and Morden	Ind SDP	Conservative
Oct.	1982	Birmingham Northfield	Conservative	Labour
Feb.	1983	Bermondsey	Labour	Liberal
June	1984	Portsmouth South	Conservative	SDP
July	1985	Brecon and Radnor	Conservative	Liberal
May	1986	Ryedale	Conservative	Liberal
Feb.	1987	Greenwich	Labour	SDP
Nov.	1988	Glasgow Govan	Labour	SNP
May	1989	Vale of Glamorgan	Conservative	Labour
Mar.	1990	Mid-Staffordshire	Conservative	Labour
Oct.	1990	Eastbourne	Conservative	Liberal Democrat
Mar.	1991	Ribble Valley	Conservative	Liberal Democrat
May	1991	Monmouth	Conservative	Labour
Nov.	1991	Kincardine and Deeside	Conservative	Liberal Democrat
Nov.	1991	Langbaugh	Conservative	Labour
May	1993	Newbury	Conservative	Liberal Democrat
July	1993	Christchurch	Conservative	Liberal Democrat
June	1994	Eastleigh	Conservative	Liberal Democrat
Dec.	1994	Dudley West	Conservative	Labour
May	1995	Perth and Kinross	Conservative	SNP

Date		Constituency	Held formerly by (party)	Victor of by-election
June	1995	Down North	UPU Party	UK Unionist
July	1995	Littleborough and Saddleworth	Conservative	Liberal Democrat
Apr.	1996	Staffordshire South-East	Conservative	Labour
Feb.	1997	Wirral South	Conservative	Labour

Summary of by-election changes, 1945–97

Parliament	Government	No. of by-elections	Changes	Con +	Con −	Lab +	Lab −	Lib/All.* +	Lib/All.* −	Others +	Others −
1945–50	Lab.	52	3	3	–	–	–	–	–	–	3
1950–51	Lab.	16	0	–	–	–	–	–	–	–	–
1951–55	Con.	48	1	1	–	–	1	–	–	–	–
1955–59	Con.	52	6	1	4	4	–	1	1	–	1
1959–64	Con.	62	9	2	7	6	2	1	–	–	–
1964–66	Lab.	13	2	1	1	–	1	1	–	–	–
1966–70	Lab.	38	16	12	1	–	15	1	–	3	–
1970–74	Con.	30	8	–	5	1	3	5	–	2	–
1974	Lab.	1	0	–	–	–	–	–	–	–	–
1974–79	Lab.	30	7	6	–	–	7	1	–	–	–
1979–83	Con.	20	6	1	4	1	1	4	1	–	–
1983–87	Con.	31†	6	–	4	1	1	4	–	1	1
1987–92	Con.	24	8	–	7	4	1	3	–	1	–
1992–97††	Con.	18	9	–	8	3	–	4	–	2	1

*Liberal 1945–79; Alliance (Liberal and SDP) 1979–89, Liberal Democrat after 1990.

†Includes 15 by-elections held in Northern Ireland in January 1986 following Unionist resignations in protest at Anglo-Irish Agreement.

††Since the 1997 general election no seats have changed hands at by-elections (as at 29 February 2000). In fact 1998 was the first year since 1832 when no by-elections at all took place.

Source: *Pears Cyclopaedia* (108th edn, London, Penguin, 1999)

European elections

The first direct elections to the 410-member European Parliament took place in June 1979. In Great Britain the result was as follows:

Party	Votes	Votes (%)	Seats
Conservative	6 504 481	50.6	60
Labour	4 253 218	33.0	17
Liberal	1 690 600	13.1	–
Others	421 553	3.3	1 (SNP)
Total	12 873 852	100.0	78

In Northern Ireland, where proportional representation was used, three MEPs were elected.

The second direct elections to the European Parliament took place in June 1984. Although Labour considerably improved on its poor performance in 1979, the Liberal/SDP Alliance failed to secure any representation. The result was as follows:

Party	Votes	Votes (%)	Seats
Conservative	5 426 866	40.8	45
Labour	4 865 224	36.5	32
Liberal/SDP Alliance	2 591 659	19.5	–
Others	429 149	3.2	1 (SNP)
Total	13 312 898	100.0	78

Northern Ireland again returned three MEPs by proportional representation.

The third direct elections to the European Parliament took place in June 1989. Labour achieved an impressive result, taking 45 seats, compared to the Conservatives on 32. The Liberal Democrats not only failed to win a seat, but also were humiliated by an upsurge in Green party support. The Scottish Nationalists again returned a single MEP.

Party	Votes	Votes (%)	Seats
Conservative	5 331 077	34.6	32
Labour	6 153 640	40.0	45
Liberal Democrats	986 292	6.4	–
SNP	406 686	2.7	1
Plaid Cymru	115 062	0.8	–
Others*	2 409 886	15.5	–
Total	15 402 643	100.0	78

*Including 2 292 705 for the Green party

Northern Ireland again returned three MEPs by proportional representation.

The fourth direct elections to the enlarged European Parliament took place in June 1994. The Conservatives, at their lowest ebb in the opinion polls, suffered heavy losses to Labour, but the Liberal Democrats failed to sweep the south, taking only two seats in the south-west. The Scottish Nationalists polled well north of the border, finishing with two seats and 32.6 per cent of the total Scottish poll.

Party	Votes	Votes (%)	Seats
Conservative	4 268 531	27.9	18
Labour	6 753 863	44.2	62
Liberal Democrat	2 552 730	16.7	2
SNP	487 239	3.2	2
Plaid Cymru	162 478	1.1	–
Others	1 062 709	6.9	–
Total	15 287 550	100.0	84

Northern Ireland again returned three MEPs by proportional representation.

The fifth direct elections to the European Parliament took place in June 1999. Elections were held under a new voting system on the basis of regional lists (eleven regions replaced the 84 single-member constituencies in mainland Britain, each region returning between four and eleven MEPs). Northern Ireland continued to elect its three MEPs by the single transferable vote system. On a low turnout, the result marked New Labour's worst electoral rebuff yet. The UK Independence party and the Greens both secured the election of MEPs for the first time.

Party	% Vote*	Seats*
Conservative	35.8	36
Labour	28.0	29
Liberal Democrat	12.7	10
UK Independence	7.0	3
Green	6.3	2
Nationalist	4.5	4
Others	5.7	–

*Excluding Northern Ireland

Source: *The Economist*, 19 June 1999

Referendum results

European Community

The first nationwide use of the referendum in post-war Britain was on 5 June 1975 when the electorate was asked whether the UK should stay in the European Community.

	Votes cast	Turnout (%)	Yes (%)
England	21 722 222	64.6	68.7
Wales	1 345 545	66.7	64.8
Scotland	2 286 676	61.7	58.4
Northern Ireland	498 751	47.4	52.1
UK	29 453 194	64.5	64.5

In addition, every English and Welsh region voted Yes. The only 'No' majorities were in two relatively isolated areas of low population – the Shetlands and the Western Isles.

Devolution

On 1 March 1979 referenda were held in Scotland and Wales over the question of devolution. In Scotland, although more than 50 per cent of those voting favoured devolution, the total voting 'yes' was only 32.9 per cent of the registered electorate, failing to reach the 40 per cent needed to enact the provision. In Wales the outcome was an emphatic rejection of devolution.

Scotland	Votes	% of valid votes
'Yes' vote	1 230 937	51.6
'No' vote	1 153 502	48.4

Wales	Votes	% of valid votes
'Yes' vote	243 048	20.2
'No' vote	956 330	79.8

Referenda on devolution were again held in 1997. For details, see pp 120 and 122.

4 PARTY POLITICS

Conservative party

Leaders of the party

1940–55	Winston Churchill
1955–57	Anthony Eden
1957–63	Harold Macmillan
1963–65	Alec Douglas-Home
1965–75	Edward Heath
1975–90	Margaret Thatcher
1990–97	John Major
1997–	William Hague

Chairmen of Conservative (Private) Members' Committee (1922 Committee)

1945–51	Arnold Gridley
1951–55	Derek Walker-Smith
1955–64	John Morrison
1964–66	William Anstruther-Gray
1966–70	Andrew Harvey
1970–72	Harry Legge-Bourke
1972–84	Edward du Cann
1984–92	Cranley Onslow
1992–97	Marcus Fox
1997–	Sir Archie Hamilton

Chairmen of the party organization (appointed by the leader of the party)

1944–46	Ralph Assheton
1946–55	Lord Woolton
1955–57	Oliver Poole
1957–59	Viscount Hailsham
1959–61	R A 'Rab' Butler
1961–63	Iain Macleod
1963	Iain Macleod / Lord Poole
1963–65	Viscount Blakenham
1965–67	Edward du Cann
1967–70	Anthony Barber
1970–72	Peter Thomas
1972–74	Lord Carrington
1974–75	William Whitelaw
1975–81	Lord Thorneycroft
1981–83	Cecil Parkinson
1983–85	John Selwyn Gummer
1985–87	Norman Tebbit
1987–89	Peter Brooke
1989–90	Kenneth Baker
1990–92	Chris Patten
1992–94	Norman Fowler
1994–95	Jeremy Hanley
1995–97	Brian Mawhinney
1997–98	Lord Parkinson
1998–	Michael Ancram

Conservative leadership elections since 1975

1975 (4–10 Feb.) Challenge to Heath leadership. 1st ballot (4 Feb.): Margaret Thatcher 130; Edward Heath 119; Hugh Fraser 16 (11 abstentions). 2nd ballot (10 Feb.): Margaret Thatcher 146; William Whitelaw 76; Sir Geoffrey Howe 19; James Prior 19; John Peyton 11.

1989 (5 Dec.) Challenge to Thatcher by 'stalking horse' Sir Anthony Meyer. 1st (only) ballot: Margaret Thatcher 314; Sir Anthony Meyer 33 (3 abstentions, 24 spoiled papers).

1990   (20–27 Nov.) Challenge to Thatcher leadership. 1st ballot (20 Nov.): Margaret Thatcher 204; Michael Heseltine 152. (Under party rules, Thatcher required a majority of votes cast plus 15 per cent more of all eligible votes than her opponent. She failed by four votes to attain this total. In the second round, Thatcher did not stand and John Major and Douglas Hurd entered the contest.) 2nd ballot (27 Nov.): John Major 185; Michael Heseltine 131; Douglas Hurd 56. (Because John Major had received less than 50 per cent of the vote, the rules required a third ballot, but after Heseltine and Hurd had withdrawn, the requirement was waived.)

1995   (4 July) John Major resigned on 22 June as leader to offer himself for re-election. 1st (only) ballot: John Major 218; John Redwood 89 (John Redwood resigned as Welsh Secretary to stand against Major).

1997   (10–19 June) John Major resigned after the May 1997 general election defeat. 1st ballot (10 June): Kenneth Clarke 49; William Hague 41; John Redwood 27; Peter Lilley 24; Michael Howard 23. 2nd ballot (18 June): Kenneth Clarke 64; William Hague 62; John Redwood 38. 3rd ballot (19 June): William Hague 92; Kenneth Clarke 70.

Chronology of principal events

1945   Victory in Europe leads to break-up of the coalition and a general election. Conservatives lose, with 213 seats. R A Butler becomes chairman of the Research Department. Formation of the Conservative Political Centre. Assheton, chairman of party organization, organizes Parliamentary Secretariat.

1946   Woolton becomes chairman of party organization (July).

1947   Woolton–Teviot agreement provides for union of Conservative and Liberal National parties at the constituency level, and the adoption of candidates who might be recommended by either headquarters. Party conference approves the Industrial Charter (Oct.).

1948   Maxwell Fyfe Committee Report is adopted by annual conference. Its proposals are aimed at democratizing the process of selection of candidates and securing more efficient party funding.

1950   Conservatives narrowly lose general election (298 seats), but reduce Labour's majority.

1951   Conservatives win general election (321 seats).

1955   Churchill retires as Prime Minister. Eden succeeds him. Conservatives win general election (344 seats).

1956   Suez crisis. Government unpopularity revealed in Tonbridge by-election (June).

1957   Eden retires due to ill-health. The Queen, following advice from senior Conservatives, chooses Harold Macmillan rather than R A Butler as his successor.

1958 Peter Thorneycroft resigns as Chancellor of the Exchequer and Enoch Powell as Financial Secretary to the Treasury: a 'little local difficulty'.

1959 Conservatives win general election (365 seats).

1962 Macmillan's 'Night of the Long Knives' (see p 294).

1963 Macmillan retires due to ill-health. Sir Alec Douglas-Home emerges as leader, despite the challenge of R A Butler, Quintin Hogg and Reginald Maudling. Iain Macleod and Powell refuse to serve in government.

1964 Conservatives lose general election (304 seats).

1965 Under some pressure from the party, Douglas-Home resigns. Edward Heath becomes the party's first elected leader, defeating Maudling and Powell in the ballot. *Putting Britain Right Ahead* is published and is basis of the Conservative election manifesto.

1966 Conservatives lose general election (257 seats).

1967 Conservatives win GLC elections.

1968 Powell raises the immigration issue in 'rivers of blood' speech and Heath dismisses him from the shadow cabinet.

1969 GLC Young Conservatives publish *Set The Party Free*, urging greater party democracy.

1970 Selsdon Park meeting of shadow cabinet. Manifesto published: *A Better Tomorrow*. Conservatives win general election (330 seats). Heath becomes Prime Minister.

1974 Three-day week. Conservatives win 296 seats in Feb. general election and Wilson forms government. Conservatives lose Oct. election (277 seats). Lord Home's Rules Committee rejects National Union Executive recommendation for an electoral college of area chairmen to select leader.

1975 Heath, under pressure from the party, stands for re-election. In ballot for party leadership Margaret Thatcher defeats Heath in first round, and Hugh Fraser, William Whitelaw, James Prior, Geoffrey Howe and John Peyton in second.

1979 Conservatives win general election (339 seats). Margaret Thatcher becomes first woman Prime Minister. Conservatives win 60 of 78 British seats in first direct elections to the European Parliament (June).

1981 Major reconstruction of Thatcher Cabinet in response to growing criticism of economic policy, dismissing one of the most prominent 'Wets', Sir Ian Gilmour, and switching another, James Prior, from the Department of Employment to the Northern Ireland Office. Shirley Williams takes safe Conservative seat at Crosby (Nov.) for the SDP.

1982 Foreign Secretary Lord Carrington and Defence Secretary John Nott offer resignations following Argentine invasion of the Falkland

Islands, but only the former resigns, although John Nott announces intention to resign at next election.

1983 Michael Heseltine appointed Secretary of State for Defence in Jan. Mrs Thatcher wins a resounding victory by 144 seats in general election (June). Cecil Parkinson, party chairman, takes post as Minister for Trade and Industry but forced to resign after personal scandal in Sept. John Selwyn Gummer becomes party chairman.

1984 James Prior announces his return to the back benches. Bomb at Grand Hotel, Brighton, during Conservative party conference, seriously injures Norman Tebbit and the chief whip, John Wakeham, and kills five other people.

1985 Norman Tebbit replaces John Gummer as party chairman with Jeffrey Archer as his deputy.

1986 Westland affair leads to the resignation of Michael Heseltine, Defence Secretary, and Leon Brittan, Trade and Industry Secretary.

1987 Thatcher wins record third term of office in general election in June with 102-seat majority.

1989 Thatcher becomes longest-serving Prime Minister of the twentieth century.

1990 Fall of Margaret Thatcher. Major becomes Prime Minister.

1991 Poll tax abandoned. Government negotiates Maastricht Treaty.

1992 Conservatives win historic fourth successive election victory, overturning the opinion poll predictions (Apr.). John Major follows his victory with Cabinet reshuffle. New appointments include Kenneth Clarke (Home Secretary), Michael Heseltine (Trade and Industry), Malcolm Rifkind (Defence), Virginia Bottomley (Health), John Patten (Education), Michael Portillo (Chief Secretary to the Treasury) and David Mellor (Heritage). Norman Fowler becomes party chairman, following defeat of Chris Patten in general election. October party conference at Brighton reveals serious divisions over European policy, the ERM and Maastricht. Opposition led by Norman Tebbit. Groundswell of opposition to Major leadership begins.

1993 Year of electoral disasters for Conservatives. Newbury by-election lost to Liberal Democrats on swing of 29 per cent (highest swing since 1972 Sutton and Cheam by-election) (May). Liberal Democrats and Labour make sweeping gains in county council elections (May), only Buckinghamshire left in Conservative control. In limited Cabinet reshuffle, following dismissal of Chancellor Norman Lamont, Major appoints Kenneth Clarke (Chancellor), Michael Howard (Home Secretary), John Gummer (Environment), David Hunt (Employment) and John Redwood (Welsh Secretary) (27 May).

1994 Heavy defeat for Conservatives in European elections. By-election defeats at Eastleigh (to Liberal Democrats) and Dudley West (to Labour).

1995   Sweeping Conservative losses in council elections (May). Major resigns party leadership (June) followed by victory over John Redwood (218–89) in July leadership contest. Extensive Cabinet reshuffle: Heseltine Deputy Prime Minister, Rifkind Foreign Secretary, Mawhinney Party Chairman. Eurosceptics, although rebuffed, remain strong. Defections of disaffected Conservative MPs (Alan Howarth to Labour, in October; Emma Nicholson to Liberal Democrats, in December). Conservative overall majority now reduced to three.

1996   Peter Thurnham MP resigns Conservative whip (Feb.). Staffordshire South-East by-election lost on swing of 22 per cent to Labour (Apr.). Further heavy council losses (May) amid continuing sleaze allegations (and cash for questions allegations). Lord McAlpine defects to Referendum party (Oct.). Government temporarily in a minority from December.

1997   Deselection of Conservative MP Sir George Gardiner in Reigate. Conservatives lose Wirral South by-election to Labour on a swing of 17 per cent (Feb). John Major calls election for 1 May (Mar.). Electoral disaster for Conservatives in general election. Only 165 MPs elected. Worst tally of modern times (for details, see p 63). Conservative representation in Wales and Scotland obliterated. John Major resigns as Conservative leader. William Hague elected leader on third round of voting (June) (for details, see p 73). Lord Parkinson recalled as party chairman. Resignation of David Curry from shadow cabinet over Hague's EU policy (Nov.).

1998   Sweeping internal party reforms proposed in *A Fresh Future* (Jan.): party members to have final say in leadership elections (but annual leadership challenges made more difficult). Central Conservative party organization also to undergo major reforms (including closure of regional offices). All foreign donations banned. National Union replaced by National Conservative Convention. Conservative Future to be launched to replace Young Conservatives and Conservative Student Federation. Hague calls ballot (Sept.) of party members over EU policy. Conservative ballot supports Hague (Oct.). Sacking of Lord Cranborne (Conservative leader in House of Lords) (Dec.). Replaced by Lord Strathclyde.

1999   Conservatives regain some lost ground in elections to new Scottish Parliament (May) and in European elections (June). Both elections fought under new electoral systems. Michael Portillo returns to Westminster in Kensington and Chelsea by-election (Nov.). Michael Portillo appointed Shadow Chancellor of the Exchequer (Feb.).

Conservative party membership (decline since 1953)

Year	Total
1953	3 000 000
1975	1 500 000
1982	1 200 000
1992	600 000
1994	500 000
1999	335 000

Labour party

Leaders of the party

1935–55	Clement Attlee
1955–63	Hugh Gaitskell
1963–76	Harold Wilson
1976–80	James Callaghan
1980–83	Michael Foot
1983–92	Neil Kinnock
1992–94	John Smith
1994–	Tony Blair

General secretaries

1944–62	Morgan Phillips
1962–68	Alan Williams
1968–72	Harry Nicholas
1972–82	Ron Hayward
1982–85	James Mortimer
1985–94	Larry Whitty
1994–98	Tom Sawyer
1998–	Margaret McDonagh

Deputy leaders of the party

1945–56	Herbert Morrison
1956–59	James Griffiths
1959–60	Aneurin Bevan
1960–70	George Brown
1970–72	Roy Jenkins
1972–76	Edward Short
1976–80	Michael Foot
1980–83	Denis Healey
1983–92	Roy Hattersley
1992–94	Margaret Beckett
1994–	John Prescott

Chairmen of the Parliamentary Labour party (since 1970)

1970–74	Douglas Houghton
1974	Ian Mikardo
1974–79	Cledwyn Hughes
1979–81	Fred Willey
1981–87	Jack Dormand
1988–92	Stan Orme
1992–97	Doug Hoyle
1997–	Clive Soley

Labour leadership elections

System of election

Prior to 1981 the Parliamentary Labour Party (PLP) possessed the right to elect the leader and deputy leader annually during periods in opposition, although elections were contested on only six occasions after 1945. The 1981 party conference altered these arrangements. Henceforth the constituency parties and the trade unions also participated in leadership elections (with MPs now possessing 30 per cent of the vote, constituency parties 30 per cent and the unions the remaining 40 per cent). These arrangements were altered again in 1993 with the introduction of OMOV (one member, one vote). This required both unions and constituency Labour parties (CLPs) to conduct individual ballots of members. The outcome of these changes was to leave an electoral college where the CLPs, PLP and trade unions had an equal one-third share of the votes.

Summary of Labour leadership elections, 1955–80

Dec. 1955 Resignation of Attlee. Ballot: Hugh Gaitskell 166; Aneurin Bevan 70.

Nov. 1960 Challenge to Gaitskell. Ballot: Hugh Gaitskell 157; Harold Wilson 81.

Nov. 1961 Challenge to Gaitskell. Ballot: Hugh Gaitskell 171; Anthony Greenwood 59.

Feb. 1963 Death of Gaitskell. 1st ballot: Wilson 115; Brown 88; Callaghan 41. 2nd ballot; Wilson 144; Brown 103.

Apr. 1976 Resignation of Wilson. 1st ballot: Callaghan 84; Foot 90; Jenkins 56; Benn 37; Healey 30; Crosland 17. 2nd ballot: Callaghan 141; Foot 133; Healey 38. 3rd ballot: Callaghan 176; Foot 137.

Nov. 1980 Resignation of Callaghan. 1st ballot: Healey 112; Foot 83; Silkin 38; Shore 32. 2nd ballot: Foot 139; Healey 129.

Labour leadership elections since 1983 (final percentage of votes obtained)

Oct. 1983 Resignation of Foot. Ballot: Kinnock 71.3; Hattersley 19.3; Heffer 6.3; Shore 3.1.

Oct. 1988 Challenge to Kinnock. Ballot: Kinnock 88.6; Benn 11.4.

July 1992 Resignation of Kinnock. Ballot: Smith 91.0; Gould 8.9.

July 1994 Death of Smith. Ballot: Blair 57.0; Prescott 24.1; Becket 18.9.

Note: These lists exclude contests for the deputy leadership.

Principal source: Harry Harmer, *Longman Companion to the Labour Party, 1900–1998* (London, Longman, 1999)

Chronology of principal events

1945 Labour withdraw from coalition which leads to a dissolution of Parliament. A massive Labour victory (393 seats) allows Clement Attlee to form the first majority Labour government. It begins a programme of nationalization and social reform, and establishes the National Health Service.

1950 Labour win election by a narrow majority. Total of Labour seats is 315.

1951 Resignations of Aneurin Bevan, Harold Wilson and John Freeman from the government in protest at the imposition of prescription charges. General election sees Labour defeated with 295 seats, though they gain highest total vote.

1955 Division in party when Bevanites oppose manufacture and use of the hydrogen bomb. General election defeat for Labour, who win 277 seats. Attlee retires and Hugh Gaitskell elected leader.

1956 Publication of *The Future of Socialism,* a major revisionist work which argued for socialism as equality, by Anthony Crosland.

1959 Labour defeated in general election, followed by Gaitskell's attempts to revise Clause IV of the party constitution.

1960 Death of Bevan. Leadership defeated over unilateral nuclear disarmament. Gaitskell makes 'fight and fight again' speech at Scarborough conference.

1961 *Signposts for the Sixties* adopted by annual conference. It plans for economic growth under Labour, upon which the social services and standard of living will depend. Unilateralists are defeated.

1963 Death of Hugh Gaitskell. Wilson defeats George Brown and James Callaghan in ballot to become leader.

1964 Labour win election with 317 seats; Wilson forms government with only a precarious majority.

1966 Wilson dissolves Parliament and Labour return to power with 363 seats.

1969 Struggle with the trade unions over the proposals for reform of trade union law embodied in *In Place of Strife.* Cabinet forced to drop its proposals.

1970 Labour defeated in general election, winning 287 seats.

1972 Formation of a TUC–Labour Party Liaison Committee.

1973 Campaign for Labour Party Democracy (CLPD) established as a pressure group to make the parliamentary party more accountable to constituency activists. It aimed to secure mandatory reselection of MPs.

1974 Wilson forms minority government with 301 seats after a stalemate election (March). Enters a 'social contract' with the trade unions as an alternative to a statutory incomes policy. In October Labour win a second close election, taking 319 seats.

1975 Labour ministers campaign for and against EEC in referendum campaign.

1976 Wilson resigns. Callaghan elected leader.

1977 In March the Labour government face almost certain defeat in a 'no confidence' vote. Callaghan and the Liberal leader, David Steel, conclude the 'Lib–Lab' Pact which secures the government's position. Labour loses GLC to the Conservatives.

1978 End of Lib–Lab Pact.

1979 Labour government defeated on a vote of confidence and loses subsequent general election, gaining only 268 seats with a 5.2 per cent swing to the Conservatives. At the party conference (Oct.), sitting MPs required to submit to reselection during the life of each Parliament and final decisions on the content of the election manifesto given to the National Executive Committee (NEC). Committee of Inquiry set up to examine party organization. James Callaghan re-elected leader. Tony Benn goes to the back benches. Underhill Report to NEC reveals depth of entryism by Trotskyist Militant Tendency.

1980 Committee of Inquiry begins work (Jan.). Party conference confirms decision on reselection but reverses decision on control of manifesto. Decision made to take election of party leader out of sole hands of the Parliamentary Labour Party and replace this with an electoral college of MPs, constituency parties, and trade unions. Special conference called for Jan. 1981 to decide on the precise composition of the electoral college. James Callaghan announces his retirement and Michael Foot elected leader under the old system over Denis Healey, who becomes deputy leader (Nov.).

1981 Special Wembley conference votes for election of party leader by electoral college with 40 per cent votes for unions, 30 per cent Labour MPs and 30 per cent constituencies (Jan.). Following day, 'Gang of Four' announce launching of Council for Social Democracy. In March Social Democratic Party launched and twelve Labour MPs resign the party whip, while in April Tony Benn announces his intention of standing against Denis Healey for deputy leadership. Labour recaptures GLC from the Conservatives. At the October conference Healey wins by the narrowest of margins after the elimination of a third candidate, John Silkin. Benn's candidature widely seen as symbolic of growing left-wing influence in the party. The NEC inaugurates inquiry into the Trotskyite group Militant Tendency. Eric Hobsbawm, the Marxist historian, publishes *Forward March of Labour Halted?*

1982 Report of NEC into Militant Tendency requires groups who operate within the party to register and meet specific conditions. NEC decides Militant fails to satisfy the conditions and begins action to expel leaders. Labour party conference accepts unilateral nuclear disarmament as official policy.

1983 Labour party loses Bermondsey by-election to the Liberals after bitter campaign against its left-wing candidate Peter Tatchell. Labour loses the general election with only 28 per cent of the vote, the lowest share since the 1920s. Foot and Healey announce intention of standing down as leader and deputy leader. Neil Kinnock elected leader and Roy Hattersley deputy leader, dubbed the 'dream ticket'.

1984 Miners' strike embarrasses Labour party and TUC, who seek to distance themselves from the more extreme statements of Arthur Scargill, the miners' leader, and picket-line violence. Tony Benn returns as MP for Chesterfield after losing his seat in 1983.

1985   At Labour conference Kinnock vigorously attacks Arthur Scargill and the behaviour of left-wing councillors, especially in Liverpool. Widely seen as a major attempt to stem leftward drift of the party and restore confidence in moderate Labour supporters. NEC launches inquiry into running of the Liverpool district party.

1986   NEC report recommends expulsion of leading members of Liverpool district party. In response, Liverpool and London councillors facing surcharges demand that Labour indemnify them on the party's return to power. After prolonged legal battle, leading Militant supporters in Liverpool expelled from the party.

1987   At general election, Labour loses heavily in spite of running a vigorous and highly professional campaign, and increasing its share of the vote to 32 per cent. Healey announces resignation from shadow cabinet.

1988   Labour launches policy review. Kinnock comfortably defeats Benn's leadership challenge; Hattersley in turn defeats John Prescott for deputy leadership (Oct.).

1989   Major electoral revival in European elections; Labour wins 45 seats, Conservatives win only 31 (June).

1990   Kinnock (having disowned poll tax 'outlaws' in the party in 1989) attacks 'toy town revolutionaries' after poll tax riots (Mar.).

1991   Kinnock denies he is pressured to stand down as leader (Sept.)

1992   Labour loses fourth successive general election (9 Apr.); Kinnock resigns (13 Apr.), Hattersley to resign as deputy leader. John Smith elected leader with massive majority over Bryan Gould; Margaret Beckett is deputy leader (July). New shadow cabinet appointments include Jack Cunningham (foreign affairs), Gordon Brown (shadow chancellor), Tony Blair (home affairs) and Robin Cook (trade and industry). At party conference, Tony Blair and Gordon Brown elected to NEC (Sept.). Conference also reduces weight of unions' conference vote from 87 to 70 per cent.

1993   John Smith proposes reduced role for unions in electing party leader and candidate selection (Feb.); Plant Committee on the electoral system narrowly favours the supplementary vote method, abandoning first past the post (March). Party conference passes John Smith's 'one member one vote' (OMOV) proposal (Sept.). Black Socialist Society formed as alternative grouping to black sections.

1994   Death of John Smith (12 May); Labour triumph in fourth direct elections to Europe, winning 62 seats to Conservatives' 18 (June). Tony Blair elected leader (July); John Prescott elected deputy leader. Labour win Dudley West by-election (Dec.).

1995   Labour's NEC endorses re-writing of Clause IV (Mar.). Special Party Conference backs modernized Clause IV (Apr.). Brighton Conference supports move to reduce trade union block vote at party conference from 70 to 50 per cent (same as constituency parties) (Oct.).

1996   Consultative document, *The Road to the Manifesto,* promotes the 'stakeholder society' (July). Party conference approves general election manifesto *New Labour, New Life for Britain* (Oct.). Conference also rejects renationalization of private utilities. Parliamentary Labour Party votes 86 to 27 to create new disciplinary offence 'to bring the party into disrepute'.

1997   Labour wins Wirral South by-election from Conservatives with swing of 17 per cent (Feb.). Labour secures sweeping general election victory (43.2 per cent of the vote, 418 MPs; no less than 101 women, a record) (May). Major Cabinet appointments include John Prescott as Deputy Prime Minister, Robin Cook as Foreign Secretary and Gordon Brown as Chancellor of the Exchequer. Brighton party conference adopts *Partnership into Power* proposals to reform party decision-making processes and wide changes to NEC. New National Policy Forum for policy formulation also agreed (Sept.). Back-bench Labour revolt over lone parent benefit cuts (Dec.).

1998   Peter Mandelson promoted to Secretary of State for Trade and Industry in Cabinet reshuffle (July). Resignation of Ron Davies as Welsh Secretary (Oct.). Resignation of Peter Mandelson and Geoffrey Robinson from Cabinet as details of their financial dealings are revealed (Dec.).

1999   Labour largest party but without overall majority in both Scotland and Wales in elections for Parliament and Assembly (see pp 120 and 122). New back-bench revolt; 65 back-bench Labour MPs defy whip over disability welfare changes (20 May). Labour suffers reverse in European elections (albeit on very low turnout) (June).

2000   Resignation of Peter Kilfoyle as junior Defence Minister (Jan.). Resignation of Alun Michael as First Secretary in Wales (replaced by Rhodri Morgan). Frank Dobson narrowly beats Ken Livingstone in selection as candidate for London Mayor (Feb.). Ken Livingstone announces his candidature as an Independent in the elections for Mayor of London (Mar.).

Liberal Democrats

Leaders of the Liberal party

1945–56	Clement Davies
1956–67	Jo Grimond
1967–76	Jeremy Thorpe
1976–88	David Steel

Leaders of the Liberal Democrats (Social and Liberal Democrat party)

1988–99	Paddy Ashdown
1999–	Charles Kennedy

Chronology of principal events

1945 Liberals win twelve seats in general election. Sir Archibald Sinclair loses seat and Clement Davies elected chairman of parliamentary party.

1946 Liberal Council wound up.

1947 Woolton–Teviot agreement for formal union of Conservatives and Liberal Nationals.

1950 Nine Liberal MPs returned in general election. Out of 475 Liberal candidates, 319 lose their deposits.

1951 Six Liberals returned at general election. Churchill offers Clement Davies the Ministry of Education. He declines the offer.

1952 H F P Harris appointed to a new post of general director of the party.

1956 Davies resigns leadership. Jo Grimond elected to succeed him.

1958 Mark Bonham-Carter wins Torrington by-election, first Liberal by-election victory since 1929.

1959 Liberals win six seats at general election.

1962 Eric Lubbock wins Orpington by-election.

1963 Lack of further by-election victories causes Liberal upsurge to begin to decline.

1964 Liberals win nine seats in general election.

1965 David Steel wins Roxburgh, Selkirk and Peebles by-election.

1966 Liberals win twelve seats in general election.

1967 Grimond resigns. Jeremy Thorpe elected chairman of Liberal MPs.

1969 Wallace Lawler wins Birmingham Ladywood by-election for Liberals.

1970 Liberals win six seats in general election.

1972–3 By-election victories in Rochdale, Sutton, Ely, Ripon and Berwick.

1974 Liberals win fourteen seats in general election (Feb.). Heath approaches Thorpe with offer of a coalition, but talks fail when Heath refuses to promise electoral reform. Liberals win thirteen seats in general election (Oct.).

1976 Thorpe resigns after party pressure due to his involvement with Norman Scott. An 'interregnum' leadership by Grimond until David Steel elected leader of the party.

1977   Liberals enter Lib–Lab Pact to sustain minority Callaghan government.

1978   End of Lib–Lab Pact.

1979   Liberals win by-election victory in Liverpool Edge Hill, and win eleven seats in general election.

1981   Limehouse declaration (Jan.) followed by formation of the Social Democratic party (SDP) (Mar.). Liberals and Social Democrats agree at conferences to form Alliance to fight the next general election and to ally with each other in by-elections (Sept.). Roy Jenkins almost overturns safe Labour majority at Warrington by-election (July). Bill Pitt wins Croydon North-West for the Liberals (Sept.). Shirley Williams wins safe Conservative seat of Crosby for the SDP (Nov.). Opinion polls predict an Alliance victory at the next general election.

1982   Launch of SDP 'think tank' (Tawney Society) (Jan.). Roy Jenkins wins Glasgow Hillhead for the SDP/Alliance (Mar.). After some dispute Liberals and SDP agree a 50:50 share of seats in local and national elections. Jenkins defeats David Owen in SDP leadership contest (July).

1983   Liberal Simon Hughes wins safe Labour seat of Bermondsey (Feb.), but Alliance fails to take Darlington. Alliance manifesto *Working Together for Britain* (May). During general election campaign Alliance Prime Minister designate, Jenkins, is replaced by Owen. Election results prove a disappointment for the Alliance with 26 per cent of the vote but only 23 seats. Following the general election Owen is elected unopposed to replace Jenkins as leader of the SDP. A merger of the Liberals and SDP postponed for the time being.

1985   Alliance win Brecon and Radnor by-election (July).

1986   Joint commission of Liberals and SDP prepares proposals on defence policy representing a compromise position between the two parties. David Owen pre-empts publication of the report by announcing his commitment to maintaining the nuclear deterrent. Liberal Assembly (Sept.) rejects leadership's recommendations on replacement of Polaris; Alliance slumps in the polls because of rift over defence policy between Liberals and SDP. Popular Cornish Liberal MP David Penhaligon killed in a road crash (Dec.).

1987   Relaunch of Alliance with compromise defence policy (Jan.). SDP win major by-election victory at Greenwich and Liberals comfortably hold Truro. Joint Alliance manifesto produced for the general election and Owen and Steel agree to campaign as joint Alliance leaders. In election, Alliance vote falls to 23 per cent and they gain only 22 seats. Immediately following the election Steel calls for a formal merger of the two parties, but is opposed by Owen and all but one SDP MP. SDP decide to hold a ballot on whether to hold merger talks with the Liberals; a majority of 57 to 43 per cent is announced in favour (Aug.). Owen resigns as leader of the SDP; Robert Maclennan becomes caretaker leader. Portsmouth SDP Council meeting votes for merger talks with Liberals; Owen, John Cartwright and Rosie Barnes oppose this via Campaign for Social Democracy.

1988   Liberal and SDP special conferences (Jan.) vote for merger of the two parties and formation of the Social and Liberal Democrats (SLD). Launch of the new Social and Liberal Democrats. David Owen forms 'continuing SDP' (Mar.) with himself as leader; David Steel announces he will not stand in forthcoming leadership contest (June). Paddy Ashdown elected leader of Social and Liberal Democrats. Social and Liberal Democrats and 'continuing SDP' have separate conferences (Sept.). Tawney Society (SDP think tank) is disbanded (Nov.).

1989   Rival SLD and SDP candidates split the Alliance share of the vote at the Richmond (Yorks) by-election, allowing Conservative victory; poll of SLD members agrees to adopt short title of Liberal Democrats (Feb.); Liberal Democrats pushed into fourth place (with 6.2 per cent of vote) in the direct elections to the European Parliament following surge in Green party support (with 14.5 per cent) (June).

1990   Liberal Democrats manage to retain credible level of support in local elections. Continuing SDP faces impracticality of maintaining a nationwide presence after fiasco of Bootle by-election (May); SDP decides to cease campaigning as a political party (June). Liberal Democrats secure victory at the Eastbourne by-election in the wake of widespread opposition to the poll tax (Oct.). Replacement of Margaret Thatcher with John Major as Prime Minister and Conservative leader (Nov.).

1991   Liberal Democrats win Ribble Valley by-election, effectively ending Conservative attempts to retain the poll tax (Mar.). Extensive Liberal Democrat gains in local elections (May). Liberal Democrat conference supports Ashdown in programme of extra spending on education, 'green' taxes on fuel and pro-federalism in Europe (Oct.).

1992   Ashdown survives revelation of former affair and his handling of the crisis boosts poll rating (Feb.). Liberal Democrats secure 20 MPs in general election on 18.3 per cent share of the vote, but fail to secure the balance of power in outright Conservative victory (Apr.). Speaking at Chard, Paddy Ashdown calls for cooperation on the centre-left to prevent continuing Conservative hegemony. Labour response is unenthusiastic (May).

1993   Liberal Democrats win safe Conservative seat of Newbury in first by-election of the Parliament (May) on same day as sweeping gains in county council elections remove Conservative control from every council except Buckinghamshire. Liberal Democrats take Christchurch by-election (July) on largest anti-Conservative swing in modern times. Accusations of racism over conduct of local party in Tower Hamlets (London) lead to three expulsions from the party (Dec.).

1994 Liberal Democrats win first seats in direct elections to Europe, capturing Cornwall and Plymouth West together with Somerset and Devon North (June). Liberal Democrats capture Eastleigh by-election on same day. Election of Tony Blair (July) to succeed John Smith causes Liberal Democrats to fall back in opinion poll ratings. Robert Maclennan elected president of SLD (Sept.).

1995 Sweeping Liberal Democrat gains in local elections (May). Liberal gains include Guildford, Salisbury and Mid-Sussex. Ashdown gradually abandons policy of 'equidistance' from Conservatives and Labour (June). Liberal Democrats win bitter Littleborough and Saddleworth by-election (July). *Liberal Democrat Guarantee* (the party's new policy statement) issued (Sept.). Defection of Conservative MP Emma Nicholson to Liberal Democrats (first sitting Conservative in modern times to defect) (Dec.).

1996 Liberal Democrat local election gains include archetypal Conservative stronghold of Royal Tunbridge Wells (May). Announcement of joint talks with Labour on post-election programme of constitutional reform (Oct.). Defection of Peter Thurnham, Conservative MP for Bolton North-East.

1997 Euphoria at May general election gains. Liberal Democrats win 46 seats (best result since 1929 under Lloyd George). For details, see p 63. In post-election reshuffle, Paul Tyler becomes Chief Whip, Charles Kennedy takes Agriculture and Rural Affairs portfolio. Ashdown and senior Liberal Democrats join Cabinet committee on constitutional affairs (22 July). Liberals win Winchester by-election (a re-run of the general election) with majority over 21,500 (Nov.).

1998 Closer cooperation between Liberal Democrats and Labour government announced (Nov.).

1999 Paddy Ashdown announces his retirement as leader, to take effect after the European elections (Jan.). Results of leadership election give Charles Kennedy victory over his closest rival, Simon Hughes (Aug.). Sue Kramer chosen on 62 per cent turnout of 10,000 party members in London to fight for Mayor in May 2000 election (12 Aug.).

Liberal Democrat leadership elections

1988	(result declared 28 July)	(on 72% turnout)	
	Paddy Ashdown	41 401	71.9
	Alan Beith	16 202	28.1
1999	(result declared 9 Aug.)	(on 61.6% turnout)	
	Charles Kennedy	28 425	56.6*
	Simon Hughes	21 833	43.4

*This was the result on the fourth and final ballot. After the first ballot, David Rendel was eliminated, Jacquie Ballard after the second and Malcolm Bruce after the third.

5 OTHER PARTIES

Alliance An Alliance of the Liberal party and Social Democratic party (SDP) was formed in Sept. 1981 following the creation of the SDP in March 1981 and the acceptance by both parties of the principle of an alliance at their conferences. The Alliance agreed to an equal shareout of seats for local and parliamentary elections and campaigned under a joint manifesto in both the 1983 and 1987 general elections. In addition, Alliance groups were formed on many local councils, following local election successes. At one point in 1981 the Alliance had an opinion poll rating of over 40 per cent, but obtained only 26 per cent and 24 per cent respectively in the two general elections of 1983 and 1987 in spite of an impressive string of by-election victories. Calls for a merger of the two parties immediately following the 1987 election and votes in favour of merger by the Liberals and the SDP at special conferences early in 1988 terminated the Alliance and created a new party, the Social and Liberal Democrats (see Liberal Democrats, pp 82–7).

Alliance party of Northern Ireland The Alliance party was founded as a non-sectarian alternative to the existing Catholic and Protestant parties in 1970. Led by Oliver Napier until 1984, then by John Cushnahan, and more recently by Lord Alderdice, the party has failed to obtain any MPs at Westminster. A moderate party, in favour of power-sharing and devolution, it follows the UK government line that the majority in Northern Ireland wants to remain part of the UK: any changes must be made with the consent of the majority. It draws its support from all sides. It is pro-European and an ally of the Liberal Democrats.

British National party (BNP) The British National party had become by the 1990s the largest far-right grouping in Britain. It was formed in 1982 following a split in the National Front (see p 91). Led by John Tyndall (whose leadership has come under challenge), it claims to have over 1,000 members. Main areas of support are in the East Midlands, particularly Leicester, west Yorkshire, and west Scotland, where it has strong links with loyalist groups. It won brief fame by winning a local by-election in the Isle of Dogs in 1993. The BNP has links with extreme right groups in mainland Europe. Its political hero is Jean-Marie Le Pen. In 1992 its dozen candidates polled an average 1.1 per cent in the general election. Some former BNP supporters have drifted into terrorist groups such as Combat 18.

Common Wealth (CW) Common Wealth was founded by Sir Richard Acland (Liberal MP for Barnstaple) in 1942. During the prevailing electoral truce (due to the Second World War and the coalition government) its aim was to contest by-elections against 'reactionary' candidates, and it was not opposed by Labour or 'progressive' candidates. But in 1943 membership of Common Wealth was proscribed by the Labour party. Although it won three by-elections (Eddisbury 1943, Skipton 1944 and Chelmsford 1945) only a single candidate of the 23 who ran in the 1945 general election was successful. This victory was at Chelmsford, where no Labour candidate ran, and the Common Wealth victor, Ernest Millington, subsequently joined the Labour party. So too did Acland when the election results became known. Common Wealth contested no more elections, but survived for a time as an organization.

Communist party of Great Britain (CPGB) The Communist party of Great Britain was founded at a Unity Convention held in London in July–Aug. 1920. After the Nazi invasion of the USSR in June 1941, the communists enjoyed a period of success. Membership rose from 12,000 to 56,000 in a year and a half. By 1945 they had two MPs and 200 councillors. The *Daily Worker* was selling 100,000 copies a day. However, since the 1945 general election the CPGB has failed to return an MP, and there has been a steady decline in the total votes cast for it. In the Oct. 1974 general election all 29 CPGB candidates lost their deposits. This helps explain the reappraisal of the party's position in 1977–78. The party was rent by internal divisions over the revision of its programme, *The British Road to Socialism,* and proposals to adopt a strategy based on building a 'Broad Democratic Alliance', laying emphasis on parliamentary methods and 'Euro-communist' in tone. In 1979 the party's 38 candidates polled 16,858 votes, but only 11,606 in 1983 with 35 candidates. Continuing splits with the Euro-communist wing controlling the party machine and hardliners on the *Morning Star* newspaper were reflected in a split candidature in 1987 of nineteen Communist candidates, thirteen Red Front and ten Workers' Revolutionary Party candidates. In Nov. 1991, delegates to the 43rd and final Congress of the Communist party of Great Britain voted 135:72 to drop their name and the Leninist constitution on which the party had been run for 71 years. A new name, Democratic Left, was chosen with a constitution embracing 'creative Marxism, feminism, anti-racism, ecology and other progressive traditions'.

Democratic Left See Communist party of Great Britain, above.

Democratic party A short-lived party formed in 1969 by the maverick Labour MP Desmond Donnelly. Of its seven parliamentary candidates six lost their deposit. It effectively ceased to exist in 1970.

Democratic Unionist party (DUP) Led by the Revd Ian Paisley, the Democratic Unionist party was formed in 1971 out of the earlier Protestant Unionist party. It represents the more militant and populist wing of the loyalist community and has usually returned three MPs to Westminster. Initially a vehicle for Paisley's distinctive views, its deputy leader, Peter Robinson, also achieved some prominence. The DUP strongly opposed the Anglo-Irish agreement, boycotting Parliament for two years in 1985–87. It remains Ulster's most hardline Unionist party. It is fiercely Eurosceptic and considers formal links with Dublin to be anathema.

Ecology party See Green party below.

Green party Founded in 1973 as the People's party, becoming the Ecology party in 1975, the Green party adopted its current name in Sept. 1985. The party campaigns to raise public consciousness about environmental and peace issues and promote an 'ecological' or 'green' perspective on economic matters. By 1987 the Green party had an estimated 6,000 members and had almost 100 parish or community councillors, plus three district councillors. They fielded 133 candidates in the 1987 general election, compared with 53 in 1979, polling 89,854 votes, but losing their deposit in every seat. The Green party's influence extends much wider than its parliamentary performance, with the activities of the Greenpeace organization to alert public attention to environmental hazards. The party achieved a major breakthrough in the 1989 European elections, when it achieved its best results, with 14.9 per cent of the vote, and took second place in six Euro-constituencies, though obtaining no MEPs. The party benefited from growing environmental concerns aroused by Chernobyl, acid rain, the 'greenhouse effect' and pollution. Its membership also rose rapidly, making it an effective force in local politics. The party retains a loose structure and has no leader, only spokespersons. It consistently achieved over 4 per cent of support in national opinion polls between the summer of 1989 and 1990 but fell thereafter. In the 1992 election it polled only 170,000 votes and was subsequently plagued by a period of infighting. However, under the regional list system, it won two seats in the 1999 European elections (having earlier won a seat in the new Scottish Parliament).

Independent Labour party (ILP) Originally founded in Bradford in 1893, largely at the instigation of Keir Hardie, the Independent Labour party was very much in decline in the post-1945 period. This decline largely dated from 1932, when the Labour party conference disaffiliated the ILP. Accordingly, all seventeen ILP candidates stood against Labour candidates in the 1935 election, and four were returned for various Glasgow divisions. In 1945 the ILP ran five candidates and three were successful, but after the death of the party's leader, James Maxton, in 1946, the ILP MPs joined the Labour party. In the 1950 and 1951 elections the ILP ran three candidates, and two in the 1955 and 1959 elections. All lost their deposits, a tale repeated in the cases of the three ILP candidates who stood at by-elections in the 1960s. There were no ILP candidates at the 1964 and 1966 general elections, and in the 1970 general election, the solitary ILP candidate, fighting Halifax, also lost his deposit. No ILP candidates have contested parliamentary elections since 1970.

League of Empire Loyalists An extreme right-wing party founded by A K Chesterton in April 1954. Only four candidates contested elections between 1957 and 1964 (all losing their deposits). In March 1967 it merged with the National Front.

Liberal National party See National Liberal party, pp 91–2.

Liberal party The party, officially relaunched in March 1989, of those dissident Liberals who refused to merge with the Social Democrats and who have maintained an active independent existence. Its first president was Michael Meadowcroft (former Liberal MP for Leeds West). In the 1992 election, it fielded 73 candidates and in the 1994 European elections polled over 100,000 votes. It still has a few councillors.

National Democratic party See National Front, below.

National Front (NF) The National Front was formed in early 1967 following the merger of the League of Empire Loyalists, the British National party and members of the Racial Preservation Society. Shortly afterwards the Greater Britain Movement merged with the Front. The Front's aims included an end to all 'coloured' immigration, repatriation of immigrants living in Britain, withdrawal from the EEC, support for Ulster Unionists and stronger penalties for criminals. In the 1970 municipal elections the NF won 10 per cent of the poll in some places, but in the general election all ten NF candidates lost their deposits, despite an average NF vote of 3.6 per cent of the poll. That year A K Chesterton resigned from the NF after another internal struggle. J O'Brien became chairman of the national directorate. In 1972 John Tyndall replaced O'Brien. The NF polled 10,000 votes in the Leicester local elections of 1973, and won an average 6.8 per cent of the poll in the GLC elections. At the West Bromwich by-election Martin Webster obtained 10 per cent of the votes cast.

The Front ran 36 candidates in the 1974 GLC elections and 54 in the Feb. general election. In the Oct. general election there were 90 candidates, all losing their deposits. In the same year Kingsley replaced Tyndall as leader. In 1975 membership of the NF began to fall. John Read, again voted head of the directorate, expelled Tyndall, who was reinstated by court action. A split occurred, with Read and others leaving to form the National party.

At the 1979 general election, the Front ran 303 candidates, who polled only 190,747 votes. In the wake of electoral disappointment, the leading National Front figures – John Tyndall and Martin Webster – fell out, with charges of political incompetence and hints of unsavoury sexual scandals. Tyndall was ousted in 1980 and took several thousand Front members into the New National party, renaming it the British National party in 1982. Webster aligned himself with activists favouring confrontational tactics. The National Front sought a following among skinheads and football hooligans. The bad publicity that followed encouraged neither a growth in membership nor electoral success. At the 1983 general election 58 National Front candidates averaged a little over 1 per cent of the vote in the constituencies they fought. It was not surprising, given a continuing failure of political cohesion, that the National Front took no part in the 1987 general election and made no impact in the 1990s.

National Liberal party The successor, from 1948 onwards, of the original Liberal National party, formed in 1931 by 23 Liberal MPs who split from the official party to join the ranks of the National government. In the 1931 general election they were opposed by Liberals, but not by Conservatives. They won 35 of the 41 seats they contested. In 1932 the 'Samuelite' Liberals left the National government in protest at its protectionist policies, but the other Liberal Nationals, the 'Simonites', remained. In 1935, 33 of the 44 Liberal National candidates were returned. Between joining the National government in 1931 and 1945 the Liberal Nationals were opposed only twice by Liberals (Denbigh 1935 and St Ives 1937). They were not opposed by a Conservative until 1946 (Scottish Universities). In 1940 Ernest Brown succeeded Sir John Simon as leader. In the 1945 election Brown was defeated and only 13 of the Liberal Nationals' 51 candidates were returned. The Woolton–Teviot agreement (May 1947) urged the constituency parties of the Conservatives and Liberal Nationals to combine, and in 1948 the party adopted the name National Liberal party. In the 1966 Parliament only two MPs styled themselves Conservative and National Liberals, though two other members of the group were elected as Conservatives by Joint Associations (in the constituency of local Conservatives and National Liberals). These four relinquished the room assigned to them in the House in 1966 and the group became fully integrated into the Conservative party.

Official Unionists See Ulster Unionist party pp 96–7.

Plaid Cymru (Welsh National party) Plaid Cymru was founded in 1925 by John Saunders Lewis with the aim of obtaining independence for Wales. Since 1945 it has run candidates at every general election and numerous by-elections, but without success until its president, Gwynfor Evans, won the 1966 Carmarthen by-election. In 1970 Plaid ran 36 candidates and polled 175,000 votes, although none was elected. The party tended to attract a new influx of working-class support from South Wales to supplement the 'hard core' membership of the Welsh-speaking rural North Wales region. It also broadened its appeal by pursuing economic regeneration for the Welsh economy, encouragement for Welsh cultural activities, and full self-government for Wales. The adverse publicity attracted by the activities of the 'Free Wales Army' may have injured the party's prospects for a time, but in the Feb. 1974 general election it won two seats (Caernarvon and Merioneth) and in Oct. 1974 Gwynfor Evans added a third, by again winning at Carmarthen. The lack of support for devolution (only 20 per cent in favour) in the Welsh referendum in early 1979 was taken as marking some decline in enthusiasm for Welsh nationalism. In the 1979 general election the party fielded 36 candidates, polling 132,000 votes and retaining two seats, with Evans again losing Carmarthen. Its vote in 1983 and 1987 fell back to c. 125,000 votes, but electing three MPs in the latter poll. Prior to the 1987 election, Plaid signed an agreement of cooperation with the Scottish Nationalist party. In the 1997 general election, Plaid again returned four MPs (as it had in 1992), taking 10 per cent of the Welsh vote. In the first elections to the Welsh Assembly in May 1999 the party became the main opposition to Labour.

Pro-European Conservative party A breakaway group of Conservatives opposed to the Eurosceptic policy adopted by William Hague as leader after 1997. It contested the 1999 European elections with singular lack of success and seemed destined to disappear rapidly. It published a pro-single currency manifesto. Its founders were former MEPs John Stevens and Brendan Donnelly.

Pro-Life Alliance A single issue party campaigning to outlaw 'any destruction of human life even at its most embryonic stage'. Established by a wealthy Italian Catholic family, the Quintavalles, it held abortion to be the single most important political issue. Its impact on the 1997 general election was minimal.

Referendum party The political brainchild of maverick millionaire business-man (and French MEP) Sir James Goldsmith who financed the party himself. Its sole objective was a referendum on the Maastricht Treaty, fol-lowed by a renegotiation of UK membership of the EU. Its 554 candidates obtained around 830,000 votes in the 1997 general election (2.7 per cent of the national total). Its star figures included Lord McAlpine, Conservative party treasurer 1975–90; Sir Alan Walters, Margaret Thatcher's personal eco-nomics adviser; and Sir George Gardiner, the deselected Conservative MP for Reigate. Its highest vote in 1997 was only 4,188 in Folkestone and Hythe, but it contributed to the defeat of perhaps a dozen Conservative MPs. Following the death of Sir James Goldsmith, Lord McAlpine became leader.

Scottish National party (SNP) The Scottish National party was formed in 1934 as a merger of two earlier groups, the National Party of Scotland founded in 1928 and the Scottish party in 1930. It was not until 1945, however, that the SNP won its first seat. Robert D McIntyre won the Motherwell by-election, but was defeated at the general election three months later. In 1964 the party contested fifteen seats, and in 1966 23 seats, but with no success. Then in 1967 Winifred Ewing won the Hamilton by-election. This encouraged the SNP to field 65 candidates in the 1970 general election, but of these only Donald Stewart in the Western Isles was elected, and 43 lost their deposits. It appeared that the SNP was again in decline, yet in 1973 Mrs Margot Macdonald won the Glasgow Govan by-election. In Feb. 1974 the party won seven seats in the general election and in Oct. 1974 won eleven seats. Poor performances in the Hamilton by-election and the 1978 local elections signi-fied a wane in Scottish nationalism. In 1979 Scotland voted only narrowly for devolution, thus relinquishing the possibility of devolution under the terms of the Act. In the 1979 general election the SNP won only two seats, the same number in 1983, but three in 1987. In 1987 its vote was 417,000 (14 per cent of the Scottish vote) compared to 840,000 (over 30 per cent of the Scottish vote) at its peak in October 1974. Prior to the 1987 election the SNP signed an agreement to cooperate with Plaid Cymru in the next Parliament. Since the late 1980s the party's fortunes have revived. The party won the Glasgow Govan by-election of Nov. 1988 on a swing of 33 per cent to overturn a 20,000 Labour majority. In the district elections the same year it forced the Conservatives into third place. In the 1992 general election SNP polled 629,564 votes, still winning only three seats. In the 1994 direct elections to Europe the party captured two seats. In the 1997 election, it took 22 per cent of the vote in Scotland, winning six seats. Its greatest success (though disappointing compared to its expectations) was in the first elections to the new Scottish Parliament in May 1999. Winning 35 seats it became the main opposition party to the Labour–Liberal Democrat government in Scotland.

Sinn Fein Gaelic for 'we ourselves'. Irish nationalist party founded in 1902 by Arthur Griffiths (1872–1922) and formed into the Sinn Fein League in 1907–08 when it absorbed other nationalist groups. Its part in the struggle for Irish independence did not end in the 1920s. More recently, Sinn Fein has continued in existence as the 'political wing' of the Irish Republican Army, winning four seats in the 1957 Dáil election and operating as a fund-raising and propaganda body into the 1970s. In 1980 and 1981 Sinn Fein put up hunger strikers as candidates for both Westminster and the Dáil. Bobby Sands was elected in a Westminster by-election in 1981 and two candidates for the Dáil. The seats were not taken up. This success led to the joint politico-military strategy 'The Armalite in one hand, and the ballot box in the other', with Sinn Fein contesting the Northern Irish Assembly seats in 1982, gaining 10 per cent of the vote. Sinn Fein's leader, Gerry Adams, was elected to Westminster in 1983 for Belfast West, but as with other Sinn Fein candidates, refused to take his seat. In 1986 Sinn Fein took the controversial decision to take any seats it won in the Irish Dáil, ending its long-standing boycott of southern Irish politics. In 1983 it appeared that Sinn Fein was challenging the Social Democratic and Labour party (SDLP) for the Catholic vote, taking 15 per cent as opposed to the SDLP's 18 per cent, but its support fell back in 1987. In 1992 Gerry Adams lost his seat. In elections in Northern Ireland after 1992, electoral support for Sinn Fein rose steadily. It participated in all-party talks and in the Good Friday agreement. It secured eighteen seats (17.6 per cent of the vote) in the 1998 Assembly elections.

Social and Liberal Democrats (SLD) See Liberal Democrats, pp 82–7.

Social Democratic and Labour party (SDLP) The Social Democratic and Labour party, formed in 1970, grew out of the civil rights campaign in Northern Ireland during the late 1960s. Its first leader was Gerry Fitt, who sat for Belfast West. He stood down in 1983 and was replaced by John Hume, who was elected for the Londonderry seat of Foyle. The SDLP is the major Catholic party of Ulster and has played an important part in all the attempts to create an acceptable political structure in Ulster, including the power-sharing executive of the early 1970s, the Anglo-Irish agreement (Hillsborough) of 1985 and the Good Friday agreement of 1998. It is pro-European and left-of-centre. Since 1981 the SDLP's electoral position in the Catholic community has been under challenge from Sinn Fein, particularly in the 1990s. In 1992 it returned four MPs. The party favours the unification of Ireland through peaceful means with the consent of the majority in the north. In the 1998 Assembly elections it won 24 seats (22.3 per cent of the vote). Seamus Mallon became Deputy First Minister (resigning in 1999 as the Assembly became deadlocked).

Social Democratic party (SDP) The Social Democratic party originated on 25 Jan. 1981 as the Council for Social Democracy, an organization led by four disillusioned Labour politicians (Shirley Williams, David Owen, William Rodgers and Roy Jenkins). The broad aims of the new party were set out in the Limehouse declaration, followed on 26 Mar. 1981 by the setting up of the Social Democratic party as a separate political party. Although its aims were to be decided by reference to its members, its leading members had expressed support for electoral reform through proportional representation, continued membership of the EEC, multilateral disarmament and a reflationary economic strategy with an incomes policy and inflation tax. In Sept. 1981 the party formed an Alliance with the Liberal party to fight the next general election and to reach mutual agreement on the fighting of by-elections and local government elections. Party membership in Oct. 1981 stood at 66,000. The first SDP MP, Shirley Williams, was elected at the Crosby by-election in Nov. 1981. Roy Jenkins won Glasgow Hillhead in 1982 and was subsequently elected leader of the party. In the 1983 general election, the SDP campaigned in alliance with the Liberals, each fighting approximately half the seats, but it returned only six MPs. In June 1983 David Owen succeeded Roy Jenkins as leader, unopposed. In 1986 serious rifts with the Liberal party developed over defence policy, but the Alliance was relaunched early in 1987 and the SDP and Liberals campaigned under a joint leadership in the subsequent general election. The party returned only five MPs; of the 'Gang of Four' only Owen was returned to Parliament. Liberal calls for a merger in the wake of the election led to fierce controversy within the SDP and a ballot of SDP members about opening merger talks with the Liberals. A vote of 57 to 43 per cent in favour of merger talks led to Owen's resignation as leader (6 Aug. 1987) and a major split within the SDP appeared imminent. Owen was succeeded as leader by Robert Maclennan (29 Aug.). In Jan. 1988 at Sheffield, merger with the Liberals was finally approved (by 273 votes to 28 with 49 abstentions). This merger was approved by a ballot of the SDP membership in March and the Social and Liberal Democratic party (now popularly known as the Liberal Democrats) was launched on 3 Mar. 1988. Shortly afterwards Owen attempted to launch a rump SDP as an independent force but this rapidly became an ignominious failure.

Socialist Labour party Formally constituted as a left-wing socialist party in May 1996 by the president of the National Union of Mineworkers, Arthur Scargill (see p 250). It has earlier taken 5.4 per cent of the vote in the Hemsworth by-election of February 1996. Although the party fielded 64 candidates in the May 1997 general election, its impact was minimal. No candidates saved their deposit. Its policies include common ownership, restoration of union rights, withdrawal from the EU, and abolition of public schools, the House of Lords and the monarchy.

Socialist Workers' party (SWP) The Socialist Workers' party (formerly the International Socialist Group) was formed in 1976 as a Marxist party whose objective was to replace capitalism with socialism through revolution. It emphasized the need to establish universal socialist consciousness before such a revolution could occur. The SWP was uncompromising in its attitude to the Soviet Union. Unlike other Marxist organizations, International Socialists believed that the Soviet Union was not and never had been a socialist society but was a form of capitalist state where a class system operated. They adhered to the view that the October Revolution and subsequent development of the Soviet system failed because the Soviet interpretation of Marxist-Leninist theory was not international in character. The organization, which at its height secured approximately 3,000 members, was the largest of the far left political groups. Its members and supporters traversed a wider range of occupations and social backgrounds than many other left-wing organizations. Prominent members of the party included Paul Foot and Tony Cliff.

UK Independence party The successor to the Anti-Federalist League, founded in Nov. 1991 by Alan Sked, a historian at the London School of Economics, to campaign against the Maastricht Treaty. The League unsuccessfully contested the 1992 election. UK Independence party candidates fought by-elections after 1992 (its 2.9 per cent support at the Tamworth by-election of April 1996 marked the best it could achieve) and contested 24 seats in the 1994 European elections (polling 155,487 votes in all). Although it polled over 100,000 votes in the 1997 general election, it paled beside the Referendum party (see p 93). After its abject showing in the Uxbridge by-election (37 votes), its leader Alan Sked resigned. In the 1999 European elections it fielded a full slate of candidates under a new leader, Michael Holmes. It won three seats in the European Parliament.

Ulster Unionist party (UUP) The Protestant Unionists dominated parliamentary and local representation in Ulster from 1921 until the 1970s, taking the Conservative whip at Westminster, and representing Protestant interests in Ulster. The Unionist hegemony was broken in 1970–71 with the Sunningdale agreement and the proposed Council of Ireland, which bitterly divided the Unionist party. The Ulster Unionists (or the Official Unionists as they are also known) are the inheritors of the old Unionist organization, although they are now a less aristocratic and landed party. After a period of rivalry, the Official Unionists increasingly made common cause with the breakaway Democratic Unionist party led by the Revd Ian Paisley in opposition to the Anglo-Irish agreement of 1985. All Unionist MPs boycotted Westminster from 1985 until early in 1987. More recently the Unionists have reacted to the Downing Street declaration (see p 276) with a mixture of caution and anger. Their leader from 1979 to 1995 was James Molyneaux. After 1995, David Trimble became leader. He was part of the Good Friday agreement, becoming First Minister in 1998 in the new Northern Ireland Assembly.

Union Movement The successor, for a brief period after the Second World War, to Sir Oswald Mosley's blackshirts (British Union of Fascists). In 1948 Mosley, from his exile in France, formed the extreme-right Union Movement. Fascism gradually resurfaced in such old stomping-grounds as the East End of London. Mosley returned to fight North Kensington in the 1959 general election but lost his deposit. In 1966 he and three other Union Movement candidates stood again but gained an average 3.7 per cent of the vote. Most of his supporters found a home for their racist and anti-immigrant views in the National Front (see p 91).

United Kingdom Unionist party A recent Northern Ireland based unionist party organized around the winner of the 1995 Down North by-election, Robert McCartney. It offered a home for pro-unionist voters put off by the sectarian links of other parties. It aimed to see Ulster better integrated within the United Kingdom. In January 1999 all four of McCartney's colleagues in the Northern Ireland Assembly resigned from the party in protest at his leadership.

Welsh National party See Plaid Cymru, p 92.

Workers' Revolutionary party (WRP) Originally formed as the Socialist Labour League, the Workers' Revolutionary party became the most orthodox Trotskyist organization in Britain. Its members generally took the view that other Marxist groups were Stalinist and maintained that it was impossible to attain socialism by reforming capitalism. It prophesied the imminent downfall of capitalism with more regularity than socialists in other organizations. Between 1974 and 1983 it fielded 101 candidates at parliamentary elections. All lost their deposits.

6 MACHINERY OF GOVERNMENT

Central government: chronology of principal events

1945   Ministry of Economic Warfare wound up (23 May), Office of Minister of State in Middle East abolished (27 July) along with similar posts in North West Africa, West Africa and Washington, DC.

1946   Wartime Ministry of Information abolished (31 Mar.). Wartime Ministry of Aircraft Production abolished (1 Apr.).

1947   The titles of the Secretary of State for Dominion Affairs and of the Dominions Office are altered to Secretary of State for Commonwealth Relations and Commonwealth Relations Office.

1948   On the independence of India and Pakistan, the India Office ceases to exist and the staff are transferred to the Commonwealth Relations Office, which then becomes responsible for relations with India and Pakistan.

1951   Minister for Welsh Affairs appointed (28 Oct.).

1953   Ministry of National Insurance merged with Ministry of Pensions (3 Sept.).

1954   Ministry of Materials abolished (16 Aug.). Ministry of Agriculture and Fisheries becomes Ministry of Agriculture, Fisheries and Food (18 Oct.). Separate Ministry of Food abolished.

1957   Ministry of Fuel and Power becomes Ministry of Power (13 Jan.).

1959   Viscount Hailsham appointed first Minister for Science (14 Oct.). The office was merged with the Department of Education on 1 Apr. 1964. Ministry of Supply abolished (22 Oct.); Ministry of Labour and National Service becomes Ministry of Labour (12 Nov.).

1962   R A 'Rab' Butler appointed First Secretary of State (effectively Deputy Prime Minister) (13 July). Office not continuously used, but subsequent occupants have included George Brown (1964–66), Michael Stewart (1966–68) and Barbara Castle (1968–70).

1962   Ministry of Works restyled as Public Building and Works (16 July). Becomes part of Environment 15 Oct. 1970.

1963   Secretary of State for Industry, Trade and Regional Development (Edward Heath) appointed (20 Oct.). Office abolished Oct. 1964.

1964   Minister of Education becomes Secretary of State for Education and Science (1 Apr.). War Office abolished (1 Apr.). Secretary of State for Wales created (18 Oct.). Ministry of Land and Natural Resources set up (17 Oct.). Office wound up 17 Feb. 1967. Ministry of Overseas Development created, with Barbara Castle as first minister (18 Oct.).

1966 Colonial Office merged with the Commonwealth Relations Office to form the Commonwealth Office, and the post of Secretary of State for Commonwealth Relations becomes Secretary of State for Commonwealth Affairs (1 Aug.). Post of Secretary of State for the Colonies is retained until 6 Jan. 1967. Ministry of Pensions becomes part of Social Security (6 Aug.). Minister of Social Security appointed (6 Aug.).

1967 Separate Ministry of Defence posts for Air Force, Army and Navy abolished (7 Jan.). Post of Minister of Defence for Equipment abolished 19 June 1970. Ministry of Aviation absorbed into Ministry of Technology (15 Feb.).

1968 Ministry of Labour reconstructed as Ministry of Employment and Productivity (6 Apr.). Secretary of State for Employment and Productivity (Barbara Castle) appointed (6 Apr.). 'Productivity' dropped from title 12 Nov. 1970. Ministry of Health combined with Ministry of Social Security as Secretaryship of State for Social Services; Richard Crossman appointed first Secretary of State (17 Oct.). Commonwealth Office merged with the Foreign Office (17 Oct.).

1969 Office of Postmaster-General ceases when Post Office becomes a Public Corporation (1 Oct. 1969). Ministry of Posts and Telecommunications created (abolished 29 Mar. 1974). Ministry of Power absorbed into Ministry of Technology (6 Oct.). Office of Secretary of State for Economic Affairs abolished (8 Oct.) (established 1964).

1970 Secretary of State for the Environment (Peter Walker) appointed (15 Oct.). Secretary of State for Trade and Industry (John Davies) appointed (15 Oct.). Ministry of Housing and Local Government reorganized under Department of the Environment (15 Oct.).

1972 New Minister for Industrial Development appointed (7 Apr.). Office abolished 5 Mar. 1974. Secretary of State for Northern Ireland (William Whitelaw) appointed (24 Apr.). Ministry for Trade and Consumer Affairs established (5 Nov.) under Sir Geoffrey Howe. Office abolished 5 Mar. 1974.

1974 Secretary of State for Energy (Lord Carrington) appointed (8 Jan.). Shirley Williams becomes first Secretary of State for Prices and Consumer Protection (5 Mar.). Ministry of Aerospace and Shipping abolished (5 Mar.), established in 1971.

1976 Ministry of Transport upgraded to Secretaryship of State (10 Sept.). Reverted to Ministry 1979–81, then became Secretaryship again.

1979 Office of Secretary of State for Prices and Consumer Protection ends.

1983 Office of Minister of Consumer Affairs ended (13 June).

1988 Secretary of State for Health appointed (Secretary of State for Social Services abolished).

1989 Minister for Corporate Affairs appointed (under Trade).

1992 Secretary of State for the National Heritage appointed. Education and Science reverts to Education.

1994 Minister for the Citizen's Charter appointed.

1995 Department of Employment abolished (5 July). Many functions transferred to Education.

1997 Departments of Environment and Transport merged.

1999 Devolution of powers concerning Wales and Scotland to Welsh Assembly and Scottish Parliament.

The Civil Service

Number of civil servants

	Total	Industrial	Non-industrial
1938	581 000	204 000	377 000
1950	972 000	397 000	575 000
1960	996 000	359 000	637 000
1970	702 000	209 000	493 000
1979	732 000	166 000	566 000
1990	567 000	68 000	499 000

Source: *Pears Cyclopaedia* (103rd edn, London, Pelham, 1994)

Heads of the Home Civil Service

1945–56	Sir Edward Bridges
1956–63	Sir Norman Brook
1963–68	Sir Lawrence Helsby
1968–74	Sir William Armstrong
1974–78	Sir Douglas Allen
1978–81	Sir Ian Bancroft
1981–83	Sir Robert Armstrong / Sir Douglas Wass
1983–88	Sir Robert Armstrong
1988–98	Sir Robin Butler
1998–	Sir Richard Wilson

Heads of the Diplomatic Service

1945–46	Sir Alexander Cadogan
1946–49	Sir Orme Sargent
1949–53	Sir William Strang
1953–57	Sir Ivone Kirkpatrick
1957–62	Sir Frank Hoyer Miller
1962–65	Sir Harold Caccia
1965–68	Sir Saville Garner
1968–69	Sir Paul Gore-Booth
1969–73	Sir Denis Greenhill
1973–75	Sir Thomas Brimelow
1975–82	Sir Michael Palliser
1982–86	Sir Antony Acland
1986–94	Sir Paul Wright
1994–97	Sir John Coles
1997–	Sir John Kerr

Permanent Secretaries to the Treasury	
1945–56	Sir Edward Bridges
1956–60	Sir Norman Brook Sir Roger Makins
1960–62	Sir Norman Brook Sir Frank Lee
1962–63	Sir Norman Brook Sir William Armstrong
1963–68	Sir Lawrence Helsby Sir William Armstrong
1968	Sir William Armstrong Sir Douglas Allen
1968–74	Sir Douglas Allen
1974–83	Sir Douglas Wass
1983–91	Sir Peter Middleton
1991–98	Sir Terence Burns
1998–	Sir Nigel Wicks

Secretaries to the Cabinet	
1938–47	Sir Edward Bridges
1947–63	Sir Norman Brook
1963–73	Sir Burke Trend
1973–79	Sir John Hunt
1979–88	Sir Robert Armstrong
1988–98	Sir Robin Butler
1998–	Sir Richard Wilson

Parliament: chronology of principal events

1946 Salary of MPs increased to £1,000 per year; free travel for MPs between their constituencies and Westminster (and their homes and Westminster) introduced.

1949 Delaying powers of the House of Lords reduced to two sessions and one year by the Parliament Act.

1958 Under the Life Peerages Act, life peerages were introduced, to be created by the Queen on the advice of the Prime Minister. These were purely nominated: there was no elective element. Women were able to enter the House of Lords for the first time.

1963 Under the Peerage Act, peers could disclaim their peerages for life (a measure largely the result of the efforts of Tony Benn, otherwise Viscount Stansgate). The Act also abolished the system of elections for Scottish Representative Peers, made certain changes to the status of Irish peers, and allowed for the admission of all female holders of hereditary peerages to the Lords.

1964 Salary of MPs increased to £3,250 per year.

1967 The Labour government established an all-party committee to prepare legislation to reform the House of Lords. Its proposed legislation defeated by the unlikely alliance of Enoch Powell and Michael Foot (see below).

1969 Opposition from both left-wing Labour MPs and the Conservatives forced the abandonment of proposals to reform the House of Lords. Secretarial allowance for MPs (up to £500) introduced as well as free telephone calls within Britain.

1972	MPs' pay increased to £3,500; subsequent increases brought salary to £12,000 per year in 1981.
1974	MPs pass resolution agreeing to declare any financial interest in the proceedings before the House.
1975	First publication of the Register of Members' Interests.
1976	Permanent sound broadcasting of Parliament approved.
1977	Labour party conference calls for total abolition of House of Lords and sweeping modernization of Parliament.
1979	New structure of Select Committees established (to cover the work of each major government department).
1983	MPs' pay linked to Civil Service rates.
1985	Experimental televising of House of Lords recommended by Select Committee.
1988	MPs vote to allow televising of Commons (Feb.).
1995	Report of the Nolan Committee tightens rules to combat 'sleaze'. MPs react angrily. Peers begin to discuss possible self-reform (cross-bencher Earl of Carnarvon publishes booklet *The Second Chamber*). Followed by informal cross-party discussions in 1996 by Lord Weatherill, Lord Marsh etc.
1997	Early abolition of hereditary voting rights promised in Labour election manifesto.
1998	Parliament Act invoked after House of Lords continues to defeat government on European Elections Bill. Compromise over Lords reform: limited number of hereditary peers to remain on temporary basis (the Weatherill Amendment approved by the Lords on 26 October 1999).
2000	The Wakeham Commission proposals on the second stage were announced on 20 January 2000. Wakeham proposed a chamber of approximately 550 members, with the majority chosen by an independent commission and a minority elected from 12 United Kingdom regions.

Speakers of the House of Commons

1943	Douglas Clifton Brown
1951	William Shepherd Morrison
1959	Harry Hylton-Foster
1965	Horace King
1971	Selwyn Lloyd
1976	George Thomas
1983	Bernard Weatherill
1992	Betty Boothroyd

7 LOCAL GOVERNMENT

Chronology of legislation and principal events

1945   Representation of the People Act extended franchise in local government to all those registered for parliamentary elections.

1965   Two-tier system of local government established in London. Greater London Council (GLC) set up, to be responsible for general services; 85 borough councils are amalgamated to form 32 larger units.

1972   Local government reorganization in England and Wales creates six metropolitan counties to run services in the major conurbations, while 39 county councils with new boundaries are established to run major services. A second tier of 375 district councils is to provide local services and amenities. Abolition of 1,200 councils, including the old county borough councils, but 7,000 smaller parish councils retained as a third tier of local government. Subsequent legislation introduced to reform local government along similar lines in Scotland.

1977   GLC lost by Labour to Conservatives.

1980   Councils forced to invite private sector bids for services (e.g. refuse collection).

1981   House of Lords overturns Labour-controlled GLC's cheap fares policy (Dec.).

1985   Local Government Act abolishes Greater London Council and six metropolitan county councils and transfers functions to London boroughs and to metropolitan district councils; some services are transferred to joint authorities, such as police, fire, and waste disposal.

1986   Restrictions placed upon local authority entitlement to block grants from central government with penalties for exceeding set limits. Government takes power to 'ratecap', fix a ceiling on rates set by selected authorities. Lambeth and Liverpool councillors lose appeals against surcharge for failing to set legal rate.

1987   In Liverpool 45 city councillors are surcharged and barred from their council seats for setting an illegal rate in defiance of the government. The government confirms plans to replace domestic rates with a flat-rate community charge ('poll tax'), in Scotland from 1989 and in England from 1991. Business rates are to be set by central government rather than local authorities.

1988 Local Government Finance Act introduces poll tax or community charge. It aimed to abolish the inequalities of the rating system.

1989 Poll tax comes into force in Scotland (1 Apr.). Local Government and Housing Act restrains political activity of local government and stops councils subsidizing rent and rates.

1990 Poll tax comes into force in England and Wales (1 Apr.) and meets widespread protests including riots in London and elsewhere.

1991 Michael Heseltine (Secretary of State for the Environment) announces introduction of new council tax to replace poll tax. As interim measure Chancellor Norman Lamont's budget announces a £140-a-head cut in poll tax for 1991–92.

1992 Local Government Finance Act formally abolishes poll tax. Local Government Act sets up Local Government Commission for England (also Scotland and Wales) to recommend changes in structure, including more unitary authorities.

1994 Local Government Commission recommends abolition of Humberside and Avon counties and recommends changes to structure of several English counties.

1995 Elections held to new unitary authorities in Scotland (Apr.) and Wales (May). These authorities effective from 1996.

1998 Labour introduces 'Best Value' concept of new standards in local government services. Cases of corruption in Labour-controlled local authorities (e.g. Doncaster and Monklands) prompt attack on municipal sleaze.

2000 Elections to be held for new Greater London Authority (GLA) with directly-elected Mayor. See p 282.

8 TRADE UNIONS

Chronology of legislation and principal events

1939–45 Much legislation by government in industrial sphere. Ernest Bevin becomes Minister of Labour. Control of Employment Act gives government power to direct labour. Order 1305 legally restricts strikes and lock-outs and imposes compulsory arbitration. The Bridlington Agreement 1939 between unions affiliated to the Trades Union Congress (TUC) restricts 'poaching' members from each other. Increase in memberships of most unions during war years.

1944 National Union of Mineworkers (NUM) formed to replace Miners' Federation of Great Britain (MFGB) with more centralized organization.

1946 Repeal of Trades Disputes and Trade Union Act 1927.

1948 TUC agreement on wage restraint after government White Paper on Incomes, Costs and Prices.

1951 Order 1305 withdrawn after unsuccessful prosecution of dock strikers. Monckton appointed Minister of Labour (with brief to conciliate the unions) as Conservatives return to power.

1956 Frank Cousins becomes general secretary of Transport and General Workers' Union (TGWU). *Bonsor* v. *Musicians' Union* case decides that a member was wrongfully expelled from trade union and was entitled to damages for breach of contract.

1958 National Arbitration Tribunal, remnant of Order 1305 and valued by unions, goes out of existence. London bus workers' strike.

1956–62 Struggle in Electrical Trades Union over alleged malpractices of communist leadership. Moderates led by Les Cannon and Frank Chapple defeat communists, but only after litigation and expulsion of the union from the TUC and Labour party.

1962 National Economic Development Council formed with TUC participation.

1964 Department of Economic Affairs set up under George Brown, Prices and Incomes Board under Aubrey Jones. *Rookes* v. *Barnard* case makes threat to strike to injure a third party illegal, even if in furtherance of a trade dispute; *Stratford* v. *Lindley* case determines that strike action not in furtherance of a trade dispute is not protected by 1906 Trades Disputes Act.

1965 Trades Disputes Act reverses *Rookes* v. *Barnard* judgment and gives trade unions further legal immunities.

1966   National seamen's strike defeated. Prices and Incomes Bill passes into law. Cousins resigns from Cabinet.

1968   One-day (15 May) national stoppage by Amalgamated Union of Engineering and Foundry Workers against government's prices and incomes policy. Report of Donovan Commission on Industrial Relations (June); led by George Woodcock, Hugh Clegg and Otto Kahn-Freund it argues against legal intervention and for improved voluntary agreements in industrial relations.

1969   Government White Paper *In Place of Strife* contemplates state intervention in industrial relations and legal sanctions against 'wildcat' strikes. Dropped after opposition from the TUC.

1970–71 Conservative government, committed to new legal framework for industrial relations, passes Industrial Relations Act (Aug. 1971), which gives the government wide-ranging and unique powers, and sets up a National Industrial Relations Court and system of registration for unions. Schemes provoke massive TUC opposition and most unions refuse to register or cooperate with it in any way.

1972   Miners' strike begins with widespread power cuts and industrial disruption (Jan.). State of Emergency declared as power crisis worsens and 1.5 million workers laid off (Feb.). Wilberforce Committee reports and grants many of miners' demands; strike called off. *Heaton* v. *TGWU*: first test for the National Industrial Relations Court (NIRC) set up under the Industrial Relations Act. It decides against the union in a blacking dispute, fining them £5,000 and a further £50,000 for contempt, the TGWU refusing to acknowledge the court (Mar.). Further fine in April for contempt. Attempt by railway unions to start industrial action leads to government initiating its 'cooling-off' period and compulsory ballot allowed under the Act. Ballot votes six to one in favour of action and not used by government again (Apr.). Union action over decasualization of labour in docks leads to the imprisonment of the 'Pentonville Five' when they ignore an order from the NIRC to stop blacking containers; leads to national dock strike. *Goad* v. *AUEW* (Amalgamated Union of Engineering Workers): James Goad excluded from union, and appeals to NIRC. Union refuses to acknowledge the court and is fined £5,000, with £50,000 for contempt. Highest number of days lost in strikes since 1926.

1974   Miners strike again, following 81 per cent poll in favour of strike (Jan.). Heath defeated in general election called on the union issue (Feb.). Labour government's Trade Union and Labour Relations Act (Feb.) repeals most of the Industrial Relations Act, although the NIRC survives for a short while, sequestering £280,000 of the Amalgamated Engineering Union (AEU) funds for non-payment of fines. Fines paid anonymously when AEU threaten a national stoppage. Court abolished in July. 'Social contract' initiated between trade unions and government: attempt to achieve industrial peace by agreement and without legal intervention.

1975 TUC accept flat-rate pay increase norm (July). Employment Protection Act gives statutory authority to the Advisory, Conciliation and Arbitration Service (ACAS) to arbitrate, if requested, in industrial disputes, and extends the rights of individual employees and trade unions (Nov.).

1976 Stage 2 4.5 per cent pay limit agreed with TUC. Employment Protection Act comes into force.

1977 Stage 3 sets earnings increase limit at 10 per cent. Fire service strike; soldiers called in to deal with fires.

1978 Unions reject 5 per cent wage norm (Oct.). Beginning of widespread industrial action during winter months by lorry drivers, water workers, hospital and municipal workers, the so-called 'winter of discontent'.

1979 Conservative government wins general election pledged to reform various aspects of trade union law, including the 'closed shop', secondary picketing and introduce use of secret ballot before strikes (May). All-time union membership peak of over 13 million (55 per cent of employed workforce).

1980 First national steel strike since 1926 gains 16 per cent wage increase but leaves way open to massive rationalization of the industry (Jan.–Apr.). 'Day of Action' (14 May), a one-day strike against government trade union legislation, receives only limited support. Employment Act restricts picketing to employees involved in a dispute and their place of work; expands exemptions from closed shop, and offers funds for secret ballots before strikes and for election of trade union officials.

1981 Three railwaymen dismissed for failing to join a union win compensation from British Rail following a decision by the European Court of Human Rights. The decision strengthens determination of the government to reform closed shop legislation further.

1982 Employment Act bans pre-entry closed shop and permits closed shops to exist only where a ballot shows 85 per cent support. Retiring miners' president urges moderation on NUM and miners vote by a small majority against a strike. Arthur Scargill succeeds Joe Gormley as national president of the NUM. Special Wembley conference of the TUC plans campaign against Conservative Employment Acts (Apr.).

1983 Conservative election manifesto promises further legislation to force trade unions to hold ballots on strikes and over payment of the political levy (June). National Graphical Association fined and has assets sequestered in *Stockport Messenger* dispute following its attempts to enforce a closed shop at Warrington printing plant (Nov.–Jan. 1984) and is forced to concede. Overtime ban imposed by NUM (Oct.), following NUM conference decision to oppose pit closures in July – 'rule 41'.

1984   Government bans trade unions at Government Communications Headquarters (GCHQ), Cheltenham. TUC calls 'Day of Action' (28 Feb.), but House of Lords rules in favour of the government's action. Chairman of Coal Board, Ian MacGregor, announces pit closures and loss of 20,000 jobs, without compulsory dismissals; NUM executive sanctions strikes in Yorkshire and Scotland and calls on other areas to support under 'rule 41' without recourse to a national ballot (Mar.). Flying pickets enforce national stoppage and beginning of a series of confrontations between police and pickets. NUM secures only patchy support from other unions and a national dock strike (July) breaks down. South Wales mineworkers have funds sequestered for failure to pay fines over picketing (Sept.) and NUM has assets seized by order of High Court (Oct.). Coal Board begins pre-Christmas 'back to work' drive and 15,000 miners return to work. Violent incidents at Orgreave (May–June) lead to many arrests; a taxi driver is killed by miners when driving a working miner to work in South Wales (Dec.).

1985   Following failure of negotiations, a special delegate conference of the NUM decides on a return to work without agreement (Mar.). Union of Democratic Mineworkers set up, largely composed of Nottinghamshire miners who opposed and worked through the coal strike (Aug.). The new *Today* newspaper breaks with tradition in Fleet Street by securing a one-union deal with the electricians and the use of new print technology.

1986   Wapping dispute between Rupert Murdoch and the print unions when, following a strike, he sacks 5,500 workers and transfers printing to a newly constructed plant at Wapping using members of the electricians' union. Picketing of the plant fails to stop the movement of papers, and fines and sequestrations force the print unions to accept defeat. Widespread disruption in schools as a result of selective strikes by teachers in support of pay claim. Government imposition of a pay settlement and termination of existing negotiating machinery, the Burnham Committee, leads to further action. Trade unions complete ballots on retention of political funds. All 37 unions vote to retain them.

1987   Some teachers' unions call off industrial action, but others continue. Miners agree to industrial action against new Coal Board disciplinary procedures.

1988   Employment Act gives trade union members the right to ignore a union ballot on industrial action. Outlaws industrial action to establish or preserve closed shops and introduces new restrictions on industrial action and election ballots. Manufacturing, Science and

Finance Union formed from the Association of Scientific, Technical and Managerial Staff and the Transport Salaried Staffs' Association.

1989 Employment Act limits cases going to full industrial tribunals; removes restrictions on employment of women and children; abolishes Training Commission. Shadow employment spokesman Tony Blair announces that the Labour party will no longer support the trade union closed shop (Dec.).

1990 Employment Act constrains closed shop by making it unlawful to refuse to employ non-union members; makes all secondary action other than picketing unlawful; forces unions to repudiate unofficial action. The National Union of Railwaymen and the National Union of Seamen form the National Union of Rail, Maritime and Transport Workers.

1992 The Trade Union and Labour Relations (Consolidation) Act brings together all collective employment rights, including trade union finances, elections, dismissal and time off. Strength of trade union delegate votes reduced to 70 per cent at Labour party conference (Oct.). Trade unions still participate in leadership elections and candidate selection. The Amalgamated Engineering and Electrical Union is formed from the AEU and the Electrical, Electronic, Telecommunications and Plumbing Union.

1993 Government abolishes 26 wages councils. John Major refuses to reconsider ban on trade unions at GCHQ at Cheltenham. Michael Howard, Home Secretary, announces legislation to ban strikes by prison officers. Labour leader John Smith secures union backing for changes in Labour party constitution. Formation of Unison.

1994 National Union of Rail, Maritime and Transport Workers calls series of one-day and two-day strikes against Railtrack. TUC invites two Conservative ministers to speak at TUC headquarters.

1995 Unions divided over 'modernizing' changes to Clause IV of Labour party constitution. TGWU, NUM and Unison among those opposing changes. Unions eventually vote 54.6 to 46.4 per cent in favour of revision of Clause IV of Labour party constitution (Apr.). TUC conference calls for £4.26 an hour minimum wage (Sept.). Labour party conference reduces block vote at party conferences from 70 to 50 per cent (Oct.).

1996 Merger of civil service unions to form Public and Commercial Services Union.

1997 Newly elected Labour government restores right of trade union membership for staff at GCHQ Cheltenham (removed under Thatcher administration in 1984) (May). Government signs up to European social chapter on workers' rights (June). Blair calls on TUC to modernize (Sept.).

1998 Labour announces its opposition to EU legislation compelling employers to extend worker's councils (Mar.).

1999   Minimum wage introduced at £3.60 an hour (well below union demands) (Apr.).

Trade union membership and trade disputes, 1945–90

	Total number of trade unions	Total number of union members	Total number of trade union members affiliated to TUC	Number of stoppages beginning in year	Aggregate duration in working days of stoppages in progress in year
1945	781	7 875 000	6 671 120	2 293	2 835 000
1946	757	8 803 000	7 540 397	2 205	2 158 000
1947	734	9 145 000	7 791 470	1 721	2 433 000
1948	735	9 319 000	7 937 091	1 759	1 944 000
1949	726	9 274 000	7 883 355	1 426	1 807 000
1950	732	9 289 000	7 827 945	1 339	1 389 000
1951	735	9 535 000	8 202 079	1 719	1 694 000
1952	719	9 583 000	8 088 450	1 714	1 792 000
1953	717	9 523 000	8 093 837	1 746	2 184 000
1954	703	9 556 000	8 106 958	1 989	2 457 000
1955	694	9 726 000	8 263 741	2 419	3 781 000
1956	674	9 762 000	8 304 709	2 648	2 083 000
1957	674	9 813 000	8 337 325	2 859	8 412 000
1958	665	9 626 000	8 176 252	2 629	3 462 000
1959	658	9 610 000	8 128 251	2 093	527 000
1960	654	9 821 000	8 299 393	2 849	3 024 000
1961	635	9 883 000	8 312 875	2 701	3 046 000
1962	626	9 887 000	8 315 332	2 449	5 798 000
1963	607	9 934 000	8 325 790	2 068	1 755 000
1964	641	10 218 000	8 771 012	2 524	2 277 000
1965	628	10 325 000	8 867 522	2 354	2 925 000
1966	621	10 262 000	8 787 282	1 937	2 398 000
1967	602	10 190 000	8 725 604	2 116	2 787 000
1968	582	10 193 000	8 875 381	2 378	469 000
1969	561	10 472 000	9 402 170	3 116	6 846 000
1970	538	11 179 000	10 002 204	3 906	1 098 000
1971	520	11 127 000	9 894 881	2 228	13 551 000
1972	479	11 349 000	10 001 419	2 497	23 909 000
1973	519	11 456 000	10 022 224	2 873	7 197 000
1974	507	11 764 000	10 363 724	2 922	1 475 000
1975	501	12 193 000	11 036 326	2 282	6 012 000
1976	473	12 386 000	11 515 920	2 016	3 284 000
1977	481	12 846 000	11 865 390	2 703	10 142 000
1978	462	13 112 000	12 128 078	2 471	9 405 000
1979	454	13 498 000	12 172 508	2 080	29 474 000

	Total number of trade unions	Total number of union members	Total number of trade union members affiliated to TUC	Number of stoppages beginning in year	Aggregate duration in working days of stoppages in progress in year
1980	438	12 947 000	11 601 413	1 330	11 964 000
1981	414	12 106 000	11 005 984	1 328	4 266 000
1982	408	11 593 000	10 510 157	1 528	5 313 000
1983	394	11 337 000	10 087 144	1 352	3 754 000
1984	413	11 086 000	9 855 204	1221	27 135 000
1985	409	10 774 000	9 580 502	887	6 402, 000
1986	335	10 500 000	n/a	1053	1 920 000
1987	330	10 500 000	n/a	1004	3 546 000
1988	315	10 400 000	n/a	770	3 702 000
1989	309	10 200 000	n/a	693	4 128 000
1990	287	9 900 000	n/a	620	1 903 000

Sources: H Pelling, *A History of British Trade Unionism* (4th edn, Harmondsworth, Penguin, 1987) pp 297–300; G S Bain and R Price, *Profiles of Union Growth: A Comparative Statistical Portrait of Eight Countries* (Oxford, Blackwell, 1980) pp 37–8; Department of Employment Gazette (London, HMSO). Figures for the total number of trade union members affiliated to the TUC in 1986–90 are not available.

Trends in the 1990s

From its high point in 1979, trade union membership declined rapidly in the Thatcher years. This decline (and a marked decline in industrial militancy) continued in the 1990s. By 1998 TUC affiliated membership had declined to 6.7 million (compared to over 12 million in 1979). The proportion of trade unionists in the workforce had fallen from 39 to 31 per cent since 1989. The number of stoppages hit lows of 203 in 1994 and 206 in 1997. Amalgamations of unions resulted in a reduction of one-third in the number of unions in the two decades after 1979.

9 NORTHERN IRELAND

Chronology of principal events

1945 End of war in Europe; Southern Ireland (Eire) retains strict neutrality in the conflict to the end.

1946 Agreement that future Northern Irish budgets to be arranged in consultation with British government and that parity in services and taxation to be maintained with Britain.

1949 Southern Ireland (Eire) leaves the Commonwealth and becomes the Irish Republic. Social Services Agreement arranges for Britain to pay four-fifths of the excess cost of Northern Irish social services.

1951 National Insurance funds of Britain and Ulster merged and agreement reached for transfer of funds in case of need.

1956 Beginning of renewed IRA campaign against Ulster.

1962 Campaign against Ulster called off by IRA.

1963 Prime Minister Terence O'Neill begins attempt to develop amicable relations with the South.

1965 Exchange of visits between Prime Minister Terence O'Neill and Irish Premier, Sean Lemass.

1966 Revd Ian Paisley imprisoned for militant anti-Catholic activities. Secret Protestant Ulster Volunteer Force declared illegal after spate of attacks on Catholics.

1967 Northern Ireland Civil Rights Association set up.

1968 Civil rights march in Dungannon. Rioting in Londonderry following civil rights march (Oct.). Cameron Commission set up to investigate disturbances.

1969 People's Democracy march from Belfast to Londonderry broken up (Jan.). General election weakens O'Neill's position at Stormont. Further rioting leads to call-up of 'B-specials'. O'Neill resigns and replaced by James Chichester-Clark (Apr.). British Army sent into Belfast and Londonderry following sectarian fighting. IRA splits into 'Official' and 'Provisional' wings. Following report of Hunt Advisory Committee, Royal Ulster Constabulary disarmed and B-specials disbanded, the latter replaced by non-sectarian Ulster Defence Regiment. Housing allocation transferred from local government to Stormont.

1970 Growing violence leads to ban on parades. Army uses rubber bullets and CS gas to combat rioters.

1971 First British soldier killed in Northern Ireland (Feb.). Chichester-Clark resigns as Northern Ireland Premier and replaced by Brian Faulkner (Mar.). Bombing campaign of IRA intensifies, followed by introduction of internment without trial.

1972 'Bloody Sunday' (30 Jan.): holding of banned civil rights march in Londonderry leads to thirteen people being shot by British soldiers. Stormont suspended and direct rule introduced (Mar.).

1973 Northern Ireland Assembly, elected by proportional representation, set up to replace Stormont. 'Bloody Friday' (21 July): bomb explosions in Belfast. Operation Motorman: troops occupy Catholic 'no-go' areas in Belfast and Londonderry. Consultative document on 'power-sharing' in Northern Ireland agreed. Sunningdale talks between London and Dublin agree to setting up of a Council of Ireland and to preserve status of Northern Ireland as part of the United Kingdom (Dec.).

1974 Direct rule ended and beginning of 'power-sharing' experiment (Jan.). General strike called by Protestant Ulster Workers' Council leads to resignation of Brian Faulkner and Northern Ireland executive (May). Direct rule reimposed, collapse of Northern Irish Assembly. IRA extend bombing campaign to Great Britain.

1975 Elections held for a Constitutional Convention on Northern Ireland result in landslide victory for United Ulster Unionist Council. Majority report of Constitutional Convention recommends end of direct rule and re-establishment of a Northern Irish Assembly.

1976 Breakdown of talks between British government and Ulster representatives (Mar.). Direct rule continued. British ambassador in Dublin, Christopher Ewart-Biggs, assassinated by IRA. European Commission for Human Rights finds Britain guilty of torture in Northern Ireland. Peace Movement launched by Betty Williams and Mairead Corrigan.

1977 Ten-day strike (May) by Ulster Unionist Action Council in support of tougher action against the IRA and the implementation of the Constitutional Convention's Report ends in failure.

1978 European Court of Human Rights clears Britain of torture in Northern Ireland, but convicts it of 'inhuman and degrading treatment'.

1979 Airey Neave assassinated at the House of Commons by Irish National Liberation Army (Mar.). Earl Mountbatten assassinated by IRA in Irish Republic (Aug.). Devolution Conference of Northern Ireland political parties fails to reach agreement.

1980 Summit meetings held in May and Dec. between Irish Premier Charles Haughey and Margaret Thatcher. A communiqué after the May meeting affirms wish of the Irish government to secure the unity of Ireland 'by agreement and in peace' but only 'with the consent of a majority of the people in Northern Ireland'. December meeting followed by joint studies on new institutional structures, citizenship

113

rights, security, and economic and cultural cooperation. Republican prisoners mount 'dirty protest' for special status and begin hunger strikes in Oct. (called off in Dec.).

1981 Resumption of hunger strikes for special status leads to deaths of Bobby Sands and Francis Hughes (May). Rioting over hunger strikes leads to more than 50 deaths. Dr Garret FitzGerald becomes Irish Premier (June) and announces intention to make the Irish constitution less offensive to the North. Summit meeting with Thatcher (Nov.) leads to establishment of Anglo-Irish Intergovernmental Council to hold regular meetings at ministerial and official levels to discuss matters of common concern.

1982 Secretary of State for Northern Ireland, James Prior, introduces a Bill for Northern Ireland Assembly to resume legislative and executive powers by a process of gradual devolution. Elections for the Assembly result in 59 per cent of votes for Unionist candidates and 32 per cent to Nationalists (including SDLP, 19 per cent and Sinn Fein, 10 per cent). Both the SDLP and Sinn Fein, however, boycott the Assembly.

1983 New Ireland Forum set up in Dublin on the initiative of John Hume, leader of the SDLP, in May, and begins to prepare report on the way in which unity could be achieved with the North by consent. Participants include representatives of southern Irish parties and SDLP from the North.

1984 Report of New Ireland Forum (May) condemns terrorist activity in the North but calls for a unitary state, achieved by agreement and consent, embracing the whole of Ireland and providing guarantees for the protection and preservation of 'both the Unionist and the Nationalist identities'. Northern Ireland Assembly begins work in June on proposals to strengthen the Assembly and move towards devolution. In July James Prior welcomes the Forum report and Official Unionist report 'The Way Forward' and looks forward to further discussions between the parties in Northern Ireland and between the Irish and British governments. Prior succeeded by Douglas Hurd as Northern Ireland Secretary (Sept.). IRA bomb explodes at Grand Hotel, Brighton, killing five people and narrowly missing Thatcher and the Conservative leadership (Oct.). Unofficial Kilbrandon Report in November recommends a number of safeguards for the Catholic community in the North, including a Bill of Rights, the allowing of flags and emblems, and joint police and judicial procedures. FitzGerald and Thatcher meet (Nov.) for second summit of the Anglo-Irish Intergovernmental Council and issue communiqué outlining support for structures which will guarantee the rights of both communities in the North, opposition to violence, and cooperation in security matters. Thatcher, however, rejects co-federation or joint sovereignty as a solution.

1985   Alliance report *What Future for Northern Ireland?* proposes a joint British-Irish Parliamentary Council and Security Commission. In Nov., meeting of Thatcher and FitzGerald at Hillsborough Castle, near Belfast, produces Anglo-Irish agreement setting up a new Intergovernmental Conference concerned with Northern Ireland and with relations between the two parts of Ireland. Joint communiqué states aim of Anglo-Irish agreement is to promote peace and stability in the North and to reconcile the two major traditions in Ireland, Unionist and Nationalist. Unionists denounce the agreement as a 'sell-out', calling for a referendum of the province. At a massive loyalist demonstration in Belfast (23 Nov.), attended by upwards of 20,000 people, Unionist MPs pledge to resign their seats and force province-wide by-elections. First meeting of Anglo-Irish Conference at Stormont (11 Dec.).

1986   Vote in Ulster by-elections in January endorses Unionist opposition to Hillsborough agreement, although Unionists lose a seat to the SDLP. Ulster Clubs emerge to coordinate grass-roots Protestant opposition to the Anglo-Irish agreement. Unionist leaders meet Thatcher (Feb.) but fail to obtain scrapping of Anglo-Irish agreement and 24-hour general strike called for 3 March. Strike accompanied by widespread violence and intimidation, including attacks on the police. Campaign of intimidation mounted by loyalists on police homes. United States grants $250 million worth of aid to Ulster. Because of Unionist boycott, Cabinet decides not to hold further elections to the Northern Ireland Assembly (June). Unionist MPs effectively boycott Westminster. Unionist MP Peter Robinson arrested for leading a mob across the Irish border (Aug.).

1987   Peter Robinson fined £15,000 for cross-border march (Jan.). Ulster Unionist MPs give up boycott of Westminster. Remembrance Day bombing at Enniskillen kills eleven people (Nov.).

1988   Three unarmed IRA members shot in Gilbraltar by SAS while on bombing mission, leading to accusations of 'shoot to kill' policy.

1990   Ian Paisley and James Molyneaux agree to take part in round-table talks with other parties, but fail to reach agreement.

1991   Peter Brooke, Northern Ireland Secretary, suspends Anglo-Irish agreement to allow constitutional talks.

1992   IRA bomb in City of London causes widespread damage (Apr.). Inter-governmental Conference meets in London and announces suspension of meetings to allow talks to take place. Meeting of representatives of Northern Ireland and of Irish government (June); further discussions in London and Dublin (June–Sept.). Death toll in Northern Ireland from the Troubles passes 3,000 (Aug.). Irish Foreign Minister Dick Spring indicates that articles 2 to 3 of the Irish constitution, asserting a claim to the whole of Ireland, are no longer sacrosanct. Sir Patrick Mayhew announces to the Commons that the constitutional talks have been suspended without agreement (Nov.).

1993   Bomb planted by IRA in Warrington kills two children, causing wide-spread expressions of concern for a Northern Ireland settlement (Mar.). Bomb in the City of London causes huge damage (Apr.). Bombings in Northern Ireland at Belfast, Portadown and Magherafelt cause an estimated £28 million damage (May). Exploratory talks between John Hume of the SDLP and Gerry Adams of Sinn Fein. Ulster Unionists save the government from defeat on the Maastricht Bill, leading to allegations of a 'deal' with John Major. Significant 'progress' reported in SDLP–Sinn Fein talks (Sept.). Shankill Road bombing by IRA (Oct.) leads to considerable pressure for a peace initiative; Irish government offers six-point statement for peace which receives welcome from London. British government admits to several months of clandestine contacts with IRA. Downing Street Declaration by John Major and Taoiseach (Irish Premier) Albert Reynolds, opening way to all-party talks (Dec.). Sinn Fein demands release of IRA prisoners as a gesture: refused.

1994   Gerry Adams given visa to visit United States, despite British opposition (Jan.). IRA mortar attacks on Heathrow Airport (Mar.). IRA demands 'clarification' of British position. British insist on cessation of violence. Sinn Fein refuse to make definitive move towards peace at annual conference (July). IRA declare ceasefire, effective from midnight 31 Aug. Followed by ceasefire from Protestant paramilitaries.

1995   Daylight patrols by British Army end in Belfast (Jan.). British and Irish governments publish Framework Document on future of Northern Ireland. First official meeting for 23 years between British government minister and representative of IRA (May). Release of private Lee Clegg provokes widespread disorder (July). Invitation to Gerry Adams to visit White House from President Clinton (Mar.). Three-day stand-off on Garvaghy Road ended when nationalists allowed to march. President Clinton visits Northern Ireland (Nov.). IRA rejects decommissioning (see pp 273–4) as 'ludicrous'.

1996   Canary Wharf bomb in London Docklands ends IRA ceasefire (9 Feb.). Two killed, 100 injured. At Stormont, US Senator George Mitchell chairs preliminary all-party talks (but Sinn Fein excluded). Rioting across Northern Ireland after five-day confrontation on Garvaghy Road.

1997   Sinn Fein win two seats in the general election as Labour landslide brings Blair to power (1 May). IRA ceasefire resumed (19 July). Sinn Fein admitted to peace talks (9 Sept.). Gerry Adams and Martin McGuinness pay first visit to Downing Street. Ulster Defence Association and Ulster Volunteer Force announce ceasefires (14 Oct.).

116

1998   Centre of Portadown devastated by car bomb (Jan.). Good Friday
peace agreement concluded (10 Apr.). Sinn Fein votes to abandon
force (1,400 attending conference overwhelmingly endorse proposal) (10 May.). Loyalist Volunteer Force announces ceasefire (15
May). Referendum on Good Friday agreement (70 per cent of people in Northern Ireland vote in favour) (23 May). Historic elections
for new 108-member Assembly (see below). SDLP becomes first
nationalist party to win most votes in a province-wide election; Ulster
Unionists take lowest percentage poll since 1920 partition. David
Trimble becomes First Minister as Northern Ireland Assembly meets
(1 July); Seamus Mallon Deputy First Minister. Terrorist bombing of
Omagh leaves 28 dead, over 220 injured in worst-ever atrocity in
Northern Ireland (15 Aug.). INLA announces ceasefire (22 Aug.).
Clinton pays second visit to Northern Ireland (Sept.).

1999   Disarray in the United Kingdom Unionist party of Robert McCartney
when all four of his colleagues resign (6 Jan.). Rebels form Northern
Ireland Unionist party. New 'absolute' deadline of 30 June set by
Blair to end decommissioning deadlock (15 May). Failure to end
deadlock; British government issues blueprint (2 July), but Ulster
Unionists reject it (14 July). Resignation of Seamus Mallon as Deputy
First Minister as Unionists boycott power-sharing and peace deal col-
lapses (15 July). Publication of Patten Report on future of policing
in Northern Ireland: RUC to be renamed Northern Ireland Police
Service (9 Sept.). Peter Mandelson appointed Northern Ireland
Secretary (11 Oct.). Historic steps towards power sharing as new
Executive formed (29 Nov.). First day of devolved government in
Northern Ireland; Irish Republic abandons its claim to the six coun-
ties (2 Dec.).

2000   Furious Unionist reaction to plans for RUC reform (19 Jan.). Crisis
over decommissioning when report of General John de Chastelain
finds no evidence of progress (31 Jan.). Crisis causes suspension of
Executive (11 Feb.).

Northern Ireland Assembly elections: 1998

Party	Seats	% (of first preference votes)
Ulster Unionist	28	21.3
SDLP	24	22.3
Democratic Unionist	20	18.1
Sinn Fein	18	17.6
Alliance Party	6	6.5
UK Unionist	5	4.5

Other parties to win seats included Independent Unionists (three),
Progressive Unionists (two) and the Northern Ireland Women's Coalition.
The overall turnout was 64.52 per cent, with 752,391 votes cast in all.

117

10 SCOTLAND AND WALES

Scotland: Chronology of principal events

1945   Scottish Nationalist party (SNP) win wartime by-election in Motherwell (p 63). Labour general election landslide.

1946   Formation of Development and Industry Council in Scotland.

1955   Over 50 per cent of vote in Scotland won by Conservatives (i.e. Scottish Unionist party).

1957   Establishment of Scottish Standing Committee to examine committee stage of Scottish Bills in the House of Commons.

1965   Highlands and Islands Development Board set up. Scottish Unionist party changes name to Scottish Conservative and Unionist party.

1967   Sensational SNP by-election victory by Winnie Ewing in safe Labour seat of Hamilton (see p 63).

1970   North Sea oil discovery aids Scottish Nationalist cause. Conservative Prime Minister Heath favours a devolved assembly for Scotland (against Labour opposition).

1973   Scottish Assembly recommended by Kilbrandon Commission on the Constitution.

1974   Labour win 40 Scottish seats, SNP win seven in February general election. In October election, SNP win eleven seats. Labour now favours devolution.

1975   Scottish Development Agency established. Reversal of Conservative devolution policy after election of Thatcher as party leader.

1976   Labour introduces Devolution Bills for Scotland and Wales. Bill abandoned after failure to guillotine debates in Commons.

1977   Renewed Labour Devolution Bill faces Tory opposition and rebellion in Labour ranks.

1978   Referendum clause inserted into Devolution Bill by rebel Labour MPs (introduces the 40 per cent hurdle of support from total Scottish electorate).

1979   Referendum rejects devolution (52 per cent yes on 64 per cent turnout. See p 120). Margaret Thatcher becomes Prime Minister and devolution no longer on the agenda. SNP win only two seats in the general election.

1983   SNP again wins two seats in general election.

1986   Standing Commission on the Scottish economy set up.

1987   SNP wins three seats in general election.

1988   Scottish Labour Action formed (for home rule, more internal party democracy and increased autonomy for the party in Scotland). SNP candidate, Jim Sillars, wins Govan by-election. The 'Third Claim of Right'.

1989   Bitter opposition to introduction of the poll tax in Scotland. Establishment of Scottish Constitutional Convention. Formation of Scottish Enterprise and Highlands and Islands Enterprise.

1992   SNP wins three seats in general election; Conservative Prime Minister Major campaigns strongly for the Union. Kinnock succeeded as Labour leader by pro-devolutionist John Smith. Edinburgh EU summit sees Democracy March.

1993   Women's Caucus set up by Labour party in Scotland to secure parity of representation in a future Scottish Parliament. More devolved administration promised to Scottish Office by Major. Scottish Constitutional Commission established (for one year).

1994   Labour party in Scotland changes name to Scottish Labour party. Labour narrowly defeat SNP in Monklands East by-election (June), following death of John Smith. Pledge by Tony Blair at party conference that a future Labour government will establish a Scottish Parliament (follows report of Scottish Constitutional Commission to Scottish Constitutional Convention).

1995   SNP wins Perth and Kinross by-election from the Conservatives (first-ever by-election gain from the Conservatives). First elections for new 'shadow' local government authorities. Michael Forsyth appointed Secretary of State for Scotland. Scottish Constitutional Convention publishes *Scotland's Right*.

1996   Labour firmly commits itself to post-election devolution in Wales and Scotland (27 June). A referendum to be held on the tax-raising powers of a Scottish Parliament as well as on principle of devolution. Labour Campaign for a Scottish Parliament launched (July). Return of the Stone of Destiny to Edinburgh Castle (Nov.).

1997   Labour landslide in general election (May). Labour win 56 seats in Scotland, Liberal Democrats ten, SNP six. Conservatives fail to return a single MP. Publication of White Paper *Scotland's Parliament* (July). Referendum in September gives double-yes vote (see p 120). Publication of Scotland Bill (Dec.). Scottish Parliament to have 129 members, 73 directly elected plus 56 'additional members'.

1998   Opening of Scottish Parliament to be brought forward to July 1999.

1999   Historic elections for new Scottish Parliament (May) (see p 120). Donald Dewar becomes First Minister. Liberal Democrat Jim Wallace becomes Deputy First Minister and Minister for Justice in Labour–Liberal Democrat coalition government..

Elections in Scotland

The devolution referenda

1 Mar. 1979

Yes: 1,230,937 (32.9 per cent of total electorate)
No: 1,153,502 (30.8 per cent of total electorate)
(The proposal failed because less than 40 per cent of total electorate in favour.)

11 Sept. 1997

(1) For Parliament Yes: 1,775,045 (74.3 per cent) No: 614,400 (25.7 per cent)
(2) For tax-raising powers Yes: 1,512,889 (63.5 per cent) No: 870,263 (36.5 per cent)

(All 32 of the local authority areas in Scotland voted overwhelmingly for a parliament, and only two areas, Orkney and Dumfries and Galloway, voted against tax-varying powers.)

Scottish Parliament: the first elections, May 1999

Party	Seats	% votes (1st vote)	% votes (2nd vote)
Labour	56	38.8	33.8
SNP	35	28.7	27.0
Conservative	18	15.6	15.4
Lib Dem	17	14.2	12.5
Others*	3	2.7	11.3

*Scottish Socialist party, Independent and Green

Wales: Chronology of principal events

1948 Creation of Council for Wales and Monmouthshire.

1949 Establishment of Welsh Joint Education Committee.

1951 Appointment of Minister for Welsh Affairs. Opening of Port Talbot steelworks.

1953 Establishment of Broadcasting Council for Wales (and first Welsh-language TV programme broadcast).

1955 Cardiff declared capital of Wales.

1956 First bilingual secondary school, Ysgol Glan Clwyd, opened in Flintshire.

1958 TWW (Television Wales and West) begins transmissions of commercial television in Wales.

1961 Establishment of Welsh Book Council.

1963 Hughes Parry Committee on Status of the Welsh Language set up.

1964 First Secretary of State for Wales (James Griffiths) appointed by new Labour government. Establishment of BBC Wales.

1966 Disaster in Aberfan. Cledwyn Hughes becomes Secretary of State for Wales. Sensational by-election victory of Gwynfor Evans for Plaid Cymru in Carmarthen (see p 63).

1967 Welsh Language Act becomes law. Establishment of Welsh Arts Council.

1968 George Thomas becomes Secretary of State for Wales.

1969 Investiture of Prince of Wales.

1970 Peter Thomas appointed Secretary of State for Wales.

1971 Beginning of the Welsh language nursery school movement (Mudiad Ysgolion Meithrin).

1972 Establishment of Sports Council for Wales.

1974 Local government reorganization in Wales.

1979 Wales votes against devolution in referendum (see p 122). Appointment of Nicholas Edwards as Secretary of State for Wales in incoming Thatcher government. Parliamentary Select Committee for Welsh Affairs established.

1987 Peter Walker appointed Secretary of State for Wales. Foundation of Welsh women's press, Honno.

1990 David Hunt becomes Secretary of State for Wales. End of mining in the Rhondda as last coal-mine closes.

1992 John Redwood appointed Secretary of State for Wales.

1993 Statutory basis for Welsh Language Board as Welsh Language Act becomes law.

1997 Labour election landslide: four Plaid Cymru returned; no Conservatives. Government White Paper, *A Voice for Wales* (July), proposes 60-seat Assembly to take over powers of Welsh Office (40 elected MPs by first-past-the-post, 20 by proportional representation). Wales votes 50.3 to 49.7 per cent in favour of Assembly.

1999 Historic elections for new Welsh Assembly. Labour narrowly defeat Plaid Cymru challenge (see p 122). Alun Michael First Minister. Official royal opening of Assembly for Wales (26 May).

2000 Resignation of Alun Michael as First Minister, succeeded by Rhodri Morgan (Feb.).

Elections in Wales

The devolution referenda

1 Mar. 1979

Yes: 243,948 (11.9 per cent of total electorate) No: 956,330 (46.9 per cent of total electorate)

18 Sept. 1997

Yes: 559,419 (50.3 per cent) No: 552,698 (49.7 per cent)
(Majority 6,721 on turnout of 50.12 per cent)

1997 area breakdown

For		Against	
Merthyr Tydfil	58.21	Cardiff	55.63
Anglesey	50.90	Wrexham	54.72
Carmarthenshire	65.28	Flintshire	61.80
Gwynedd	64.08	Denbighshire	59.23
Caerphilly	54.70	Newport	62.56
Rhondda Cynon Taff	58.47	Powys	57.34
Swansea	51.96	Pembrokeshire	57.21
Ceredigion	59.20	Conwy	59.08
Neath Port Talbot	66.55	Vale of Glamorgan	63.26
Bridgend	54.39	Monmouthshire	67.90
Blaenau Gwent	56.09	Torfaen	50.16

Note: Only a massive 'yes' vote in the rural Carmarthenshire area (49,115 to 26,119) produced a final pro-devolution result.

The Welsh Assembly election, May 1999

Party	Seats	% Votes (1st vote)	% Votes (2nd vote)
Labour	28	37.6	35.4
Plaid Cymru	17	28.4	30.5
Conservative	9	15.9	16.5
Lib Dems	6	13.4	12.6
Others	–	4.7	5.0

SOCIAL HISTORY

1 POPULATION AND MIGRATION

United Kingdom population (million)

	England and Wales	Scotland	Northern Ireland
1951	43.8	5.1	1.4
1961	46.1	5.2	1.5
1971	48.7	5.2	1.5
1981	49.1	5.1	1.5
1991	51.1	5.1	1.6
1999*	53.3	5.1	1.7

*Estimated

Source: *Office of Population Censuses and Surveys*

Selected urban populations, 1951 and 1991

	1951	1991
Greater London	8 348 000	6 890 000
Birmingham	1 113 000	1 007 000
Glasgow	1 090 000	689 000
Leeds	505 000	717 000
Sheffield	513 000	529 000
Liverpool	789 000	481 000
Manchester	703 000	439 000
Bradford	292 000	475 000
Edinburgh	467 000	440 000
Bristol	443 000	397 000
Belfast	444 000	287 000
Coventry	258 000	306 000

Sources: derived from B R Mitchell and P Deane, *Abstract of British Historical Statistics* (Cambridge University Press, 1962) pp 24–7; *Britain 1994* (London, HMSO, 1994) p 28

Gain or loss of population (selected dates)

1966	−82 000
1971	−40 000
1976	−19 000
1981	−79 000
1986	+37 000
1988	−21 000
1989	+44 000
1996	+56 000

Migration

	Outflow	Inflow
1940–49	590 000	240 000
1950–59	1 327 000	676 000
1960–69	1 916 000	1 243 000
1970–79	2 554 000	1 900 000
1980–89	1 824 000	1 843 000

Note: Figures between 1940 and 1963 are for UK and Commonwealth citizens migrating for permanent residence; figures from 1964 refer to all migration of UK and Commonwealth citizens, other than to and from Ireland.

Source: derived from *Office of Population Censuses and Surveys: International Passenger Survey*

Age structure of the UK population (millions)

	Under 16	16–39	40–64	65–79	80 and over
1951	n/a	n/a	15.9	4.8	0.7
1961	13.1	16.6	16.9	5.2	1.0
1971	14.3	17.5	16.7	6.1	1.3
1981	12.5	19.7	15.7	6.9	1.6
1991	11.7	20.3	16.5	6.9	2.2
2001	12.6	19.3	18.1	6.7	2.5

Notes: n/a = not available; figures for 2001 are estimated.

Source: derived from *Social Trends, 1992* (London, HMSO, 1993) Table 1.5

2 EDUCATION

Chronology of legislation and principal events

1944 Education Act (Butler's) introduced by R A 'Rab' Butler, Minister of Education. The Act raised the school-leaving age to 15 and provided free secondary education for all children, divided into three types – grammar schools, technical schools and secondary modern schools – selection for which was to be by an '11-plus' examination. Primary education to be reorganized into infant and junior schools. Free school milk, subsidized meals and free medical and dental inspections to be provided in schools. Provisions were made for raising the school-leaving age to 16 (not implemented until 1973).

1951 General Certificate of Education (GCE) replaces School Certificate as principal examination leading to university entrance.

1959 McMeeking Committee reports in favour of improved technical training, including more apprenticeships and greater facilities for day-release schemes.

1960 Robbins Committee on higher education set up.

1963 Crowther Report recommends raising the school-leaving age to 16 and the provision of part-time education after 16. Conservative administration under Sir Alec Douglas-Home accepts the recommendation of the Robbins Committee for a doubling of university places over the next ten years to 218,000, with an expansion in other areas of higher education to provide another 172,000 places. Colleges of Technology to be developed as technological universities and postgraduate business schools to be established. Newsom Committee on secondary education recommends raising of school-leaving age and an alternative examination to GCE Ordinary Level.

1964 Schools Council founded (Oct.). Labour party elected to power on pledge to reorganize secondary education along comprehensive lines. Michael Stewart announces that teacher training colleges will be renamed Colleges of Education with four-year courses.

1965 Certificate of Secondary Education (CSE) introduced. Secretary of State for Education, Anthony Crosland, announces 'binary principle': technical colleges will not be allowed to join universities or become universities, but will be turned into a separate non-university higher education system – the polytechnics (Apr.). Crosland issues circular 10/65 requesting all local authorities to draw up schemes for making all secondary education in their areas comprehensive (July).

1966 Proposals for a 'University of the Air', later the Open University, are announced (Feb.). White Paper outlines plans for the development of 30 polytechnics; some colleges of advanced technology to receive full university status.

1967 Plowden Committee report on primary schools published (Jan.). First major student disturbances, at London School of Economics (Mar.). Students widely involved in anti-Vietnam War demonstration in Grosvenor Square, London, site of US Embassy (Oct.).

1968 Government deflationary package defers from 1970–71 to 1972–73 the raising of the school-leaving age to 16 (Jan.).

1969 'Black Paper' *Fight for Education* published, attacking 'progressive' educational ideas (Mar.). Open University receives its Charter, offering part-time degree studies to students of all ages via correspondence and broadcasting (June).

1970 Bill published to compel local authorities to end the 11-plus examination and develop comprehensive schools (Feb.). Committee of Vice-Chancellors agrees to students seeing their academic records after occupation of Warwick University (Feb.). Following Conservative victory at the general election, Margaret Thatcher, new Education Secretary, withdraws Crosland circular 10/65 on comprehensive education (June). Free school milk ended (Oct.).

1971 Government announces extra £132 million spending on primary schools (June).

1973 School-leaving age raised to 16.

1975 Reg Prentice, Labour Education Secretary, announces phasing out of direct-grant grammar schools from Sept. 1976.

1976 Education Act requires local education authorities to submit proposals for comprehensive reorganization and limits the scope of local authorities taking up places in independent and direct-grant schools. James Callaghan in speech at Ruskin College, Oxford, calls for a 'great debate' into educational standards.

1979 Education Act by newly elected Conservative government removes compulsion from 1976 Education Act to reorganize along comprehensive lines.

1980 Education Act requires schools to have parents on governing body of schools; relaxes obligation to provide milk and school meals, and establishes assisted places scheme for able pupils to attend independent schools.

1981 Conservative government introduces major cuts in higher education.

1984 Confirmation of introduction of GCSE examination to replace O Level and CSE examinations from 1987.

1986 Education Act makes caning illegal in state schools.

1987 AS Levels introduced to broaden A Level curriculum.

1988 Education Reform Act introduces national curriculum with attainment targets at 7, 11, 14 and 16. Control of school budgets passed to school governing bodies and schools allowed to 'opt out' of local education authority (LEA) control and apply for grant-maintained status. Polytechnics and larger colleges of higher education pass out of local authority control. University Funding Council replaces University Grants Committee. City Technology Colleges (CTCs) to be established outside LEA control, funded by local industry and private initiative (July). Higginson Report proposing five-subject A Level studies rejected by government. Government announces freezing of student grants at 1990 levels and a loan scheme. University teachers threaten exam boycott in pursuit of pay claim. Inner London Education Authority (ILEA) abolished.

1989 Education Minister Kenneth Baker calls for doubling of numbers in higher education based on private money rather than state finance (Jan.). University teachers call off exams boycott in return for a pay deal and system of appraisal (Apr.).

1990 Education (Student Loans) Act introduces loans to supplement higher education grants.

1992 Schools Act requires schools to submit annual reports on children's progress. Local authorities required to produce league tables of school performance. A new national schools inspectorate established on a contract basis with representatives from industry and commerce. Further and Higher Education Act moves 450 further education colleges and 113 sixth form colleges out of LEA control with separate Funding Councils. Polytechnics and large higher education colleges now allowed to call themselves universities. Council for National Academic Awards (CNAA) wound up.

1993 All six teaching unions call on Secretary of State John Patten to cancel tests for 14 year olds; widespread boycott of tests occurs (June). Government accepts Dearing Committee recommendation (Aug.) to streamline classroom tests, scrap school league tables of results for 7 and 14 year olds, slim down the core curriculum and concentrate on 'the three Rs', restrict tests for 7 and 11 year olds to English, maths and science, and those for 14 year olds to the three core subjects until 1996. Education Act (July) sets up new funding agency for schools 'opting out' of LEA control; primary schools allowed to form 'clusters' to apply for grant-maintained status. Powers given to secretary of state to intervene in schools deemed to be 'failing' and to close surplus school places; School Curriculum and Assessment Authority set up to replace National Curriculum Council.

1994 John Patten removed as Education Secretary (July) in Cabinet reshuffle following widespread criticism of his handling of opposition to educational changes.

1995   Plans for a voucher scheme for nursery education announced (July).

1996   Government Education White Paper puts selection back at top of education agenda (June).

1997   Labour government announces aim to reduce size of primary school classes for 5–7 year olds to below 30 pupils by September 2001. Dearing Report on Higher Education recommends a 40 per cent expansion in higher education over the next 20 years (July).

1998   Labour government announces extension of specialist schools initiative begun in 1993, providing from September 1998 330 such schools in England, including 227 technology colleges, 58 language colleges, providing 26 sports and 19 arts colleges (June). Government spending review proposes providing an additional £19,000 million for education over three years to 2002 (July). 'Sure Start' programme allocated £540 million funding over three years to coordinate nursery education, childcare and primary healthcare for children under 3 years (July). Teaching and Higher Education Act introduces £1,000 tuition fees and system of maintenance loans to replace maintenance grants for students in higher education (July). Government sets literacy and numeracy targets for 11 year olds to be reached by 2002 (Sept.).

1999   £230 million made available from the National Lottery fund to train teachers in information and communication technology (Jan.). Government opens up education authority services to private contractors (Mar.). Islington School placed under private management (June). School Standards and Framework Act extends ban on caning to independent schools (Sept.). Legislation permits parents to exercise the right to petition for ballots over grammar schools.

2000   Plans for two-year 'Foundation Degrees' announced.

Government expenditure on education in the UK (£ million)

1940	65.0
1950	272.0
1955	410.6
1960	917.3
1965	1 114.9
1970	2 592.0
1975	5 348.3
1980	13 049.0
1985	16 681.0
1990	23 956.0
1995	38 330.0
2000	41 000.0

Number of school pupils by school type in the UK (000)

	1961	1971	1981	1990	1997
Public sector					
Nursery schools	31	50	89	103	130
Primary schools	4 906	5 902	5 171	4 886	5 380
Secondary schools	3 165	3 555	4 606	3 487	3 709
Independent	680	621	619	613	610
Special	77	103	147	109	116
All schools	8 859	10 230	10 632	9 199	9 905

Source: derived from *Social Trends, 1992* (London, HMSO, 1993) Table 3.5; *Britain 1999* (London, HMSO, 1998) p 127

Number of students in higher education in the UK

	Males	Females
1970–71	274 000	183 000
1975–76	302 000	214 000
1980–81	318 000	217 000
1983–84	334 000	246 000
1989–90	369 000	320 000
1991–92	1 200 000	·
1996–97	2 054 000	

Source: Central Statistical Office, *Key Data, 1992/3* (London, HMSO, 1993) p 68; *Britain 1999* (London HMSO, 1998) p 137

Government expenditure on education

	% of GDP
1970–71	5.2
1975–76	6.3
1980–81	5.4
1983–84	5.2
1989–90	4.6
1997–98	5.5

Source derived from *Social Trends, 1992* (London, HMSO, 1993) Table 7.36; *Britain 1999* (London, HMSO, 1998)

3 HEALTH, SOCIAL WELFARE AND POVERTY

Chronology of legislation and principal events

1942   Publication of Beveridge Report on *Social Insurance and Allied Services*, advocating a system of national insurance, comprehensive welfare and the deliberate maintenance of a high level of employment.

1944   Government White Papers *A National Health Service, Employment Policy* and *Social Insurance* accept the major principles of a national health service, full employment and a comprehensive system of social welfare.

1946   National Insurance Act establishes a comprehensive 'Welfare State' on the lines advocated by the Beveridge Report. Compulsory insurance provides for unemployment, sickness and maternity benefits, old age and widows' pensions, and funeral grants. National Health Service Act provides a free medical service for everyone, including free hospital treatment, dental care and opticians' services. The Act comes into force in 1948. Doctors and dentists now work within the National Health Service though they continue to be able to treat private patients as well. Free milk for all schoolchildren introduced.

1948   National Assistance Act. The Act abolishes all the Poor Laws still in existence and provides cash payments for those in need and without any other source of income.

1961   Graduated pension scheme introduced in addition to flat-rate old age pension.

1966   System of earnings-related supplements for unemployment and sickness benefits introduced.

1967   Abortion Act provides for the legal termination of pregnancy if two registered doctors believe that continuation may injure the physical or mental health of the pregnant woman (or members of her family) or where there is substantial risk of mental or physical abnormalities. Family Planning Act allows local health authorities to provide a family-planning service for all who seek it, either directly or through a voluntary body. Advice provided free with graduated charges for contraceptive devices according to the means of the patient.

1971   Abolition of free milk for schoolchildren. Introduction of Family Income Supplement to provide a cash benefit for poorer families with children.

1973   National Health Service Reorganization Act creates Area Health

Authorities to coordinate health services within the new local government boundaries set up in 1972.

1978 Health Services Act provides for the withdrawal of private medicine from National Health Service hospitals.

1985 Conservative White Paper *Reform of Social Security* proposes wide-ranging reform of the structure of social security.

1986 Social Security Act modifies State Earnings-Related Pension Scheme (SERPS) and encourages personal and occupational pension schemes. Income-related benefits introduced to replace family income supplement, supplementary benefit and housing benefit. A Social Fund created to provide extra help for low-income families. Government launches £20 million anti-AIDS campaign.

1988 Social Security Act alters eligibility for income support and pattern of benefit contributions. Benefit withdrawn from school-leavers who do not join youth training scheme (YTS). Cold weather payments for elderly people to meet heating costs enacted.

1989 Children Act. Changes emergency protection orders for children. Children given stronger representation in care proceedings.

1990 National Health Service and Community Care Act provides for hospitals to opt out and become self-governing trusts; allows general practitioners to control own budgets; reorganizes system of local community care giving local authorities responsibility for care of elderly people in the community.

1991 Child Support Act. Sets up Child Support Agency (CSA) to reassess and enforce maintenance payments for children after divorce or separation and to trace errant fathers. Mothers refusing 'unreasonably' to identify fathers face reductions in benefit. Act arouses widespread protest because of financial hardships caused to second families, highlighted by cases of suicide, and concern that the reform is aimed at saving the Treasury money rather than assisting single parents.

1994 Statutory Sick Pay Act. Implements changes to regulations for payment of sick pay by employers following budget announcement of 1993. Social Security (Incapacity for Work) Act reforms benefit system for those too ill to work, replacing Sickness and Invalidity Benefits by new Incapacity Benefits.

1995 Completion of 'internal market' in the National Health Service under the terms of the 1990 Act; all hospital and community care other than in the Scottish Islands provided by Trusts.

1997 Incoming Labour government promises to implement a minimum wage (May). Utting Report recommends government adopt a comprehensive strategy for residential childcare. White Paper on NHS, *The New NHS* proposes abolition of 'internal market', reduction in bureaucracy, and increased spending in specialist areas (Dec.).

1998 £5 billion Welfare-to-Work scheme introduced, aiming to tackle youth and long-term unemployment by providing training or work (Mar.). Reforms to National Insurance to improve incentives to work for low paid and reduce bureaucracy (Mar.). First Health Action Zones set up to improve health in deprived urban areas (Apr.). Report on mental health policy recommends provision of 24-hour crisis intervention and a national framework of minimum standards. Extra £73 million granted for community care (July). Completion of government spending review allocates £20 billion to NHS over the next three years.

1999 Minimum wage introduced of £3.60 per hour for over 21s (Apr.). Government enacts reform of Child Support Agency, outlined in 1998, simplifying assessment of payments and decentralizing the system; mothers now allowed to receive up to £10 per week of any maintenance for their children without reduction of benefit (July). Parental leave scheme proposed by government, allowing parents right to thirteen weeks unpaid leave in the first five years after birth of a child (Aug.).

Life expectancy

Year of birth	Males	Female
1931	58.4	62.4
1961	67.9	73.8
1981	70.8	76.8
1991	73.2	78.8
2002	74.5	79.9

Note: figures for 2002 are projected.

Source: Central Statistical Office, *Key Data, 1992/3* (London, HMSO, 1993) p 71

Medical practitioners and services in the UK

	Number of GPs (000)	Average number of patients per doctor (000)	Number of prescriptions dispensed (000,000)	Number of dentists (000)
1961	23.6	2.25	233.2	11.9
1971	24.0	2.39	304.5	12.5
1981	27.5	2.15	370.0	15.2
1990	31.6	1.89	446.6	18.6
1996	32.2	1.87	500.0	19.1

Source: Central Statistical Office, *Key Data, 1992/3* (London, HMSO, 1992) p 72; *Britain 1999* (London, HMSO, 1998) p 194

National Health Service patients, UK

	Average number of beds available (000)	Patients treated per bed available	Discharges and deaths (000)
1971	526	12.3	6 437
1976	484	13.6	6 525
1981	450	16.0	7 179
1984	429	17.8	7 666
1987	392	20.6	8 088
1990	337	25.7	8 641

Source: derived from Central Statistical Office, *Key Data, 1989/90* (London, HMSO, 1989) p 68; *Key Data, 1992/3* (London, HMSO, 1992) p 71

National Health Service hospital in-patient waiting lists, 1971–97 (000)

1971	591.7
1976	700.8
1981	736.6
1985	802.6
1990	841.2
1993	1 064.8
1997	1 100.0

Source: derived from Central Statistical Office, *Key Data 1986* (London, HMSO, 1986) p 54; D McKie and D Bindman, *The Guardian Political Almanac, 1994/5* (London, 1994) p 100; *Britain 1999* (London, HMSO, 1998) p 198

Government expenditure on health and personal social services

	Total spending (£ billion)	% of GDP
1979–80	9.3	4.5
1980–81	12.0	5.1
1981–82	13.5	5.2
1982–83	14.7	5.2
1983–84	15.5	5.0
1984–85	16.7	5.0
1985–86	17.7	4.9
1986–87	18.9	4.8
1987–88	20.7	4.8
1988–89	22.8	4.7
1989–90	24.7	4.8
1990–91	27.8	5.0
1991–92	31.5	5.4
1992–93	34.7	5.8
1993–94	36.2	5.7
1997–98	36.4	5.8
1999–00	40.0	n/a

Source: derived from D McKie and D Bindman, *The Guardian Political Almanac, 1994/5* (London, 1994) p 99; *Pears Cyclopaedia 1998–1999* (London, 1998)

135

4 HOUSING

Chronology of legislation and principal events

1946   New Towns Act set up a number of development corporations entrusted with the building of new towns in various parts of the country.

1947   Town and Country Planning Act. County councils compelled to prepare plans for the development of their areas and given powers of compulsory purchase. Planning permission required for major alterations to buildings or changes in land use by owners.

1951   Conservative government pledges itself to building 300,000 houses per year. Housing subsidies for local authority housing raised from £22 to £35 per home. Local authorities empowered to license private contractors to build a greater number of council houses and encouragement given to private house-building.

1957   Rent Act of Conservative government abolishes rent control on 810,000 houses and allows rent increases for 4.3 million houses still controlled.

1965   Rent Act of Labour government reintroduces rent control over the great majority of privately owned, unfurnished accommodation with the intention of ending Rachmanist abuses (see p 300).

1968   Collapse of Ronan Point tower block in London, following a gas explosion, leads to widespread review of high-rise developments.

1972   Housing Finance Act forces local councils to charge 'fair rents' for subsidized council houses. Rent rebates and allowances to be given to those unable to afford the new rents.

1974   Housing Act increases aid to housing associations and introduces Housing Action Areas. Rent Act introduces protection for tenants in furnished accommodation; extends rent tribunal powers and tenants' rights.

1975   Community Land Act introduces a plan to bring development land within public control. Repealed 1979.

1976   Agricultural Rent Act. 'Tied' cottages abolished in rural areas.

1980   Housing Act gives council tenants right to buy their houses.

1985   Urban Housing Renewal Unit set up to assist local authorities to improve run-down council estates.

1987   Conservative government announces plans for council estates to opt for private landlords.

1988 Housing Act. Introduces Housing Action Trusts to take over estate management where tenants vote for it.

1993 Government announces rent-to-mortgage scheme, allowing a million tenants to purchase their homes gradually.

1994 Value of mortgage interest relief cut in stages to 15 per cent rate.

1995 Housing Act obliges local authorities to provide advice for homeless.

1997 Council of Mortgage Lenders introduces voluntary mortgage code to set benchmark standards of good lending practice.

1998 In response to an independent report that a further 4.4 million dwellings will be required between 1991 and 2016, the government proposes to raise from 50 to 60 per cent the proportion built on previously developed sites, a database on land use, and task forces to make better use of such sites (Feb.). Local authorities allocated £1,300 million to meet housing needs, including release of capital receipts from house sales. English house condition survey reveals 7.5 per cent of housing stock is unfit (May). Urban Development Corporations (UDCs) set up in 1981 wound up and continuing functions taken over by English Partnership agency, charged with development of vacant, derelict or contaminated land.

Houses built in England and Wales

	Local authority	Private
1945–49	432 098	196 317
1950–54	912 805	228 616
1955–59	688 585	623 024
1960–64	545 729	878 756
1965–69	761 224	994 361
1970–74	524 400	885 300
1975–79	542 292	746 506
1980–85	225 928	736 365
1986–90	155 500*	903 600
1991–95	149 000	708 000

*Includes Housing Association construction

Source: derived from *Annual Abstract of Statistics* (London, HMSO, 1987, 1994, 1997)

Households in bed and breakfast, hostels and temporary accommodation

	Bed and breakfast	Hostels	Other	Families designated homeless by local authorities
1979	1 790	3 850	–	55 530
1980	1 330	3 380	–	–
1981	1 520	3 320	–	–
1982	1 640	3 500	4 200	–
1983	2 700	3 400	3 740	–
1984	3 670	3 990	4 640	–
1985	5 360	4 730	5 830	–
1986	8 990	4 610	7 190	–
1987	10 370	5 150	9 240	–
1988	10 970	6 240	12 890	–
1989	11 480	8 020	18 400	–
1990	11 130	9 010	25 030	140 350
1991	12 150	9 990	37 790	–
1992	7 630	10 840	44 600	–
1993	5 000	10 290	38 720	134 190
1995	–	–	–	117 490
1997	–	–	–	103 340

Source: derived from D McKie (ed.), *The Election: A Voter's Guide* (London, Fourth Estate, 1992) p 147; *Britain 1999* (London, HMSO, 1998) p 352

Types of housing tenure in England and Wales

	Owner-occupiers	Rented from local authority	Rented from private landlords	Others
1914	10.0	1.0	80.0	9.0
1939	31.0	14.0	46.0	9.0
1966	46.7	25.7	22.5	5.1
1970	50.0	30.0	15.0	5.0
1977	54.0	32.0	9.0	5.0
1985	61.9	27.3	8.3	2.5
1990	67.0	24.0	7.0	2.0
1996	73.0	15.0	7.0	5.0

Source: derived from A H Halsey (ed.), *Trends in British Society since 1900* (London, Macmillan, 1971) p 308; *Facts in Focus* (Harmondsworth, Penguin, 1972) p 51; *Annual Abstract of Statistics* (London, HMSO, 1994); *Britain 1999* (London, HMSO, 1998)

5 ENVIRONMENT AND POLLUTION

Chronology of legislation and principal events

1943   Ministry of Town and Country Planning set up.

1946   Simon Report on Domestic Fuel Policy includes measures for preventing domestic smoke. First smokeless zone legislation introduced in the Manchester Corporation Act.

1947   Town and Country Planning Act provides statutory framework for planning procedures.

1949   National Parks and Access to the Countryside Act sets up National Parks with special protection for areas of outstanding beauty.

1951   First smokeless zone established in Coventry.

1952   Ridley Report on use of fuel and power resources recommends measures for smoke prevention. London smog disaster kills more than 4,000 people.

1955   London declared a smokeless zone.

1956   Clean Air Act passed.

1957   Major radioactive leak at Windscale nuclear plant.

1958   National Society for Clean Air established.

1960   Radioactive Substances Act passed.

1962   Further smog in London kills an estimated 750 people. Recognition of effect of Strontium 90.

1966   Aberfan disaster when sludge from coal tip kills 250 people, most of them children.

1967   *Torrey Canyon* oil tanker disaster creates large-scale pollution on coasts of the south-west.

1968   Clean Air Act tightens control over air pollution.

1970   Department of the Environment established by combining several existing ministries. Royal Commission on Environmental Pollution established.

1972   UN Conference on the Human Environment held in Stockholm.

1974   Control of Pollution Act.

1975   Explosion at chemical plant at Flixborough draws attention to dangers of petrochemical plants near urban areas. Founding of Ecology party to campaign on behalf of environmental and conservation issues.

1976   Royal Commission on Environmental Pollution recommends inspectorate for all forms of pollution.

1979   Clean Air Council axed.

1980   First air quality standards established in the United Kingdom in line with EEC directives.

1981   Wildlife and Countryside Act establishes protection for animal and plant species.

1982   White Paper on radioactive waste management.

1983   Report of Royal Commission on Environmental Pollution, recommending adoption of lead-free petrol, accepted by the government. Royal Society agrees to investigate problem of acidification of surface waters in Norway and Sweden.

1984   Government announces plans for new powers controlling pesticides.

1986   Sellafield (Windscale) nuclear plant affected by radioactive leaks. Government announces four sites for possible dumping of low-level radioactive waste. Chernobyl nuclear accident in USSR contaminates upland areas of northern and western Britain; bans imposed on the sale and slaughter of animals. First confirmed case of BSE (bovine spongiform encephalopathy) amongst cattle in the United Kingdom.

1987   Sizewell B power station given go-ahead after marathon public inquiry finds in its favour. Government announces abandonment of search for dumping sites for low-level nuclear waste. Ecology party changes its name to the Green party to contest general election, fielding 133 candidates.

1988   Commission of the European Community issues range of proposals including rules for protecting the ozone layer, for municipal waste incineration, for tighter control of hazardous waste, for protecting wild fauna and flora, and for control of gases relevant to 'greenhouse effect'. BSE made a notifiable disease and infected animals subject to compulsory slaughter.

1989   Government publishes Environmental Protection Bill. EU directives controlling emissions from car exhausts adopted. Green party obtains 15 per cent of vote in UK European elections. Ban on some cattle offal for human consumption as a result of BSE.

1990   Government White Paper *The Common Inheritance* published, committing government to reduce global warming, protect the ozone layer and reduce acid rain. Environmental Protection Act passes into law.

1992   'Earth Summit', UN Conference on Environment and Development, meets at Rio de Janeiro. UK Renewable Energy Advisory Group reports that renewable energy sources should 'make a significant contribution to future energy supply'.

1993   *Braer* oil tanker produces major pollution of the Shetlands.

1994   Report of Royal Commission on Environmental Pollution urges major switch from private to public transport, from roads to railways.

1995   Government White Paper proposes partial sell-off of nuclear power industry. Protests led by Greenpeace force the abandonment of plans to dump oil platform *Brent Spar* in the Atlantic.

1996   Government announces possible link between BSE and new variant of Creutzfeldt-Jacob disease in humans. Immediate EU and world-wide ban on beef and beef product exports from Britain (Mar.). Government sponsors slaughter of male calves likely to have BSE; 1.2 million slaughtered by August 1998. Cattle over 30 months old excluded from food chain by sponsored slaughter scheme involving 2.4 million animals by August 1998 (May–July).

1997   Government orders further material excluded from animal carcases at slaughter and prohibits use in cosmetic and medicinal products (Mar.). Government inquiry announced into link between BSE and new variant CJD (Dec.).

1998   EU adopts labelling rules for genetically modified soya and maize (May).

1999   Genetically modified crop experiments vandalized by protesters; government reaffirms support for regulated tests of GM crops (July). Ban lifted by EU on British beef exports (Aug.).

6 WOMEN

Chronology of legislation and principal events

1945 Family Allowances Act grants allowances for children.

1948 National Health Service provides free health care for women.

1967 Abortion Act provides for legal termination of pregnancy. Family Planning Act allows local health authorities to provide a family planning service.

1969 Divorce Act liberalizes divorce laws by granting divorce on any grounds showing an 'irretrievable breakdown' in a marriage.

1970 Equal Pay Act designed to prevent discrimination in pay between men and women doing equal work; to come into operation by Dec. 1975.

1975 Sex Discrimination Act makes discrimination between men and women unlawful in employment, education, training and the provision of housing, goods, facilities and services. Discriminatory advertisements are made illegal. Sex discrimination defined as treating a person less favourably than another on the grounds of his or her sex. Equal Opportunities Commission set up to assist enforcement of Equal Pay and Sex Discrimination Acts.

1984 Amendment to the Sex Discrimination Act entitles women to equal pay with men when doing work which is the same, broadly similar, or of equal value.

1987 Sex Discrimination Bill prepared to bring 1975 Act in line with EEC directives, including one relating to the right of women to continue working until the same age as men. First women as editors of national newspapers.

1991 Child Support Act sets up Child Support Agency to secure maintenance from errant fathers. House of Lords decision declares that rape within marriage is an offence.

1992 Anglican Synod votes for ordination of women (Nov.). Representation of women in Commons reaches high of 58.

1994 The first 32 women priests are ordained in Bristol Cathedral.

1996 Labour party conference votes to take measures to increase representation of women in the parliamentary party to 50 per cent in ten years.

1997 Record numbers of women elected to Parliament, including 101 Labour MPs, bring total to 121. Five women Cabinet members appointed. Widespread criticism of reduction of single-parent benefits by Labour government as part of Welfare-to-Work scheme.

1998   Government announces that all policy documents, programmes, and plans will include specific assessments of their impact on women. Government announces target of 50 per cent women's representation on quangos and public bodies. Ministry of Defence opens number of posts in armed forces to women.

1999   Introduction of minimum wage of £3.60 an hour widely anticipated to assist many female low-paid workers. Reform of Child Support Agency allows women to retain £10 of maintenance payments per child without loss of benefit.

Representation of women in the House of Commons

1945	24
1950	21
1951	7
1955	24
1959	25
1964	29
1966	26
1970	26
1974 Feb.	23
1974 Oct.	27
1979	19
1983	23
1987	41
1992	58
1997	121

Women as percentage of the labour force, 1951–98 (women over school-leaving age)

1951	32.7
1961	37.5
1966	42.2
1971	42.6
1981	45.5
1988	45.5
1998	44.4

Source: derived from *Census of Population of England and Wales* for the various years

7 THE MEDIA

The press: chronology of principal events

1946 Newsprint restrictions partly removed.

1947 First Royal Commission on the Press set up.

1949 Royal Commission on the Press recommends setting up of Press Council to oversee all aspects of the press and handle complaints.

1950 Total sale of all national daily newspapers reaches all-time peak of 17 million copies per day. *News of the World* achieves circulation of 8.5 million.

1953 Press Council set up according to recommendations of Royal Commission of 1949.

1955 *News Chronicle* absorbs *Daily Dispatch.*

1957 *Picture Post* ceases publication; *Which?* consumer magazine founded.

1960 *News Chronicle, Star, Sunday Graphic* and *Empire News* cease publication.

1961 Second Royal Commission on the Press appointed. *Private Eye* and *Sunday Telegraph* launched.

1962 *Sunday Times* magazine launched; *Reynolds News* merges with *Sunday Citizen. New Society* launched. Shawcross Commission on the Press expresses concern about concentration of the press; criticizes growth of newspaper involvement with television and advises admission of lay members to Press Council.

1964 *Observer* and *Daily Telegraph* launch magazine supplements. *Sun* launched.

1966 *The Times* moves news to front page (replacing classified advertisements).

1968 *Time Out* magazine founded.

1969 *News of the World* and *Sun* change to tabloid format and are bought by Rupert Murdoch's News International.

1971 *Daily Mail* adopts tabloid format.

1972 *Cosmopolitan* magazine founded.

1973 Following the Report of the Committee on Privacy, further lay members appointed to Press Council.

1976 *Evening Post* in Nottingham becomes first newspaper using new technology and direct input from journalists.

1977   McGregor Commission on the Press reveals increased concentration of ownership, growing economic difficulties, and greater division between 'quality' and 'popular' press.

1978   *Daily Star* launched from Manchester. Publication of *The Times* and *Sunday Times* suspended for eleven months.

1980   London *Evening News* closes; *Evening Standard* becomes *Standard*.

1981   *The Times* and *Sunday Times* bought by Murdoch's News International.

1982   *Mail on Sunday* becomes first photocomposed national newspaper.

1984   Robert Maxwell purchases Mirror Group Newspapers. Reuters News Agency floated as public company. Birmingham *Daily News* becomes first free daily.

1986   News International titles (*The Times, Sunday Times, Sun, News of the World*) move to Wapping. Eddie Shah launches *Today*; *Independent* launched; *Sunday Sport* launched.

1987   *Daily Telegraph, Sunday Telegraph, Observer* and *Evening Standard* move out of Fleet Street.

1989   *Financial Times* and Express Newspapers move from central London.

1990   *Independent on Sunday* and *European* launched.

1991   Press Complaints Commission replaces Press Council. Robert Maxwell dies leaving Mirror Group in disarray. Heritage Secretary David Mellor warns press they are 'drinking in the Last Chance Saloon' for invasions of privacy. Calcutt Commission set up to assess effectiveness of press self-regulation.

1993   Calcutt Report *Review of Press Self-Regulation* published and recommends introduction of a statutory complaints tribunal. Government announces intention of bringing forward proposals to deal with intrusion on private property and use of surveillance devices. Press Complaints Commission announces steps to strengthen voluntary regulation by increasing number of independent members, strengthening code of practice and setting up a helpline service for members of public.

1994   Electronic Telegraph launched (the first UK national newspaper to go online).

1998   Press Complaints Commission Code of Practice altered in the aftermath of the death of Diana, Princess of Wales, and concerns about media intrusion; respect for privacy and 'private places' recognized and restrictions placed on 'persistent pursuit' and harassment.

Total national newspaper sales, 1937–98 (millions)

	1937	1947	1957	1979	1993	1998
Total dailies	9.9	15.5	17.0	14.2	12.9	13.0
Total Sundays	15.7	29.3	26.9	18.9	15.7	14.5

Sources: derived from R Williams, *The Long Revolution* (2nd edn, Harmondsworth, Penguin, 1965) p 233; *Britain 1979* (London, HMSO, 1979) pp 406–7; *Britain 1994* (London, HMSO, 1994) pp 452–3; *Britain 1999* (London, HMSO, 1998) p 283

Number of newspapers, 1937–98

	1937	1947	1959	1978	1998
National morning	9	9	9	9	10
London evening	3	3	3	2	1
National Sunday	17	16	15	7	9
Weekly papers	1 303	1 162	900	700	
Provincial evening					} 1 350*
and morning	107	100	98	78	

*Includes free-sheets.

Sources: derived from R Williams, *The Long Revolution* (2nd edn, Harmondsworth, Penguin, 1965) p 233; *Britain 1979* (London, HMSO, 1979) pp 406–7; *Britain 1994* (London, HMSO, 1994) pp 452–3; *Britain 1999* (London, HMSO, 1998) pp 283–4

Newspaper circulations (000)

National daily	1978	1993	1998
Daily Express	2 401	1 489	1 168
Daily Mail	1 933	1 772	2 295
Daily Mirror	3 778	2 670	2 321
The Sun	3 931	3 527	3 713
Daily Telegraph	1 345	1 022	1 073
Financial Times	181	290	353
The Guardian	273	412	402
The Independent	–	343	220
The Times	294	364	787
News of the World	4 935	4 606	4 334
The Sunday People	3 854	2 012	1 745
Sunday Express	3 243	1 717	1 085
Sunday Mirror	3 832	2 662	2 070
The Observer	688	503	412
Sunday Telegraph	845	580	841
The Sunday Times	1 409	1 224	1 354
The Mail on Sunday	–	1 991	2 211

Broadcasting: chronology of principal events

1946 Television transmissions resumed.

1949 Report of the Broadcasting Committee rejected introduction of advertising and any breach in the BBC's monopoly.

1954 Television Act establishes commercial television under the overall control of the Independent Broadcasting Authority (IBA); programmes to be financed by advertising and transmitted by regionally based companies.

1955 First commercial television transmissions.

1962 Report of Pilkington Committee on Broadcasting criticizes 'trivial' nature of many television programmes, especially on the commercial channels. Recommendation that greater powers be given to the IBA over its programme companies rejected by the government.

1964 Partly as a response to the Pilkington Report, only the BBC is permitted to go ahead with a second channel, BBC2, which begins transmission in April.

1966 Colour television introduced.

1972 Sound Broadcasting Act ends BBC monopoly of radio by allowing setting up of commercial radio stations.

1973 First commercial radio stations begin broadcasting.

1978 Government publishes proposals on future of broadcasting following report of Annan Committee. A fourth television channel to be established in which priority to be given to the minority and educational interests not catered for on existing channels, including a Welsh language service for Wales, to be financed by advertising and government grants.

1982 Channel 4 provides national television service under the control of the IBA.

1983 Cable Authority set up to supervise cable television networks.

1986 Peacock Committee rejects introduction of advertising to fund the BBC but recommends the development of wider choice for consumers in television output and an increase in sources of supply.

1987 Government forces BBC to halt programme on Zircon spy satellite.

1988 Government bans live broadcasting of IRA spokesmen. Government protests against Thames Television's *Death on the Rock* documentary about shootings of three IRA members in Gibraltar.

1989 Satellite TV transmissions begun by Rupert Murdoch's Sky TV.

1990 British Satellite Broadcasting (BSB) begins transmission in April but merges (Nov.) to form BSkyB. Broadcasting Act creates Independent Television Commission to replace IBA and Cable Authority and license Channel 3, Channel 4, a new Channel 5, cable and satellite television. At least 25 per cent of all TV output to be bought from independent producers. Independent TV licences to be bought from highest bidders. New Radio Authority set up to allocate up to three national commercial stations, awarded by competitive tender, and supervise all independent radio. Broadcasting Standards Council put on a statutory basis.

1992 Government discussion paper *The Future of the BBC* published, setting out framework for debate on the future of the BBC. BBC publishes own discussion document, *Extending Choice.*

1994 BBC announces plans for a 24-hour news and sports network to replace Radio 5. Heritage Secretary Peter Brooke announces that the BBC has passed vetting by independent consultants and will receive index-linked licence fees for the next three years. Government White Paper proposes a ten-year renewal of the BBC Charter in return for greater cost-effectiveness of BBC.

1995 BBC begins digital radio broadcasts.

1996 Broadcasting Act sets out regulatory framework for new digital ter-restial broadcasting, allowing for the licensing of at least 24 national digital television channels and twelve digital radio services. New BBC Royal Charter comes into effect allowing the BBC to continue as the UK's main public service broadcaster until 2006.

1997 BBC launches 24-hour news channel (News 24). Channel 5 goes on air as fifth terrestrial television channel.

1998 First digital television programmes broadcast.

1999 Digital commercial radio broadcasts begin (Digital One).

8 CRIME AND POLICE

Chronology of legislation and principal events

1946   Police Act abolished or amalgamated 45 of the smaller non-county police forces.

1964   Police Act encourages the setting up of joint crime and traffic squads. In 1966 amalgamation reduced the number of police forces in England and Wales from 117 to 49. Complaints against forces to be handled by an officer from an outside force.

1965   Metropolitan Police set up 'Special Patrol Group' (SPG) of 100 volunteers specially trained for riot control, gun use and intervention to support particular divisions at the command of Scotland Yard. Death penalty abolished.

1969   Police National Computer Unit set up at Hendon to store information and provide direct links with the 800 police stations in England and Wales. Became operational in 1974.

1974   Diplomatic Protection Group of armed constables set up to provide protection for diplomatic premises in London.

1977   Members of Scotland Yard Obscene Publications Squad jailed for corruption. Sir Robert Mark, Commissioner of Metropolitan Police, reveals that almost 400 officers have left or been required to leave the Metropolitan Police since 1972 following investigations of corruption.

1979   Police Act set up a Police Complaints Board to deal with complaints from the public against the police.

1981   Scarman Report, following inner-city riots, criticizes police community relations in urban areas, particularly in regard to ethnic minorities.

1984   Police and Criminal Evidence Act strengthens police powers of arrest for suspected offences. Home Office issues new codes of practice for the detention, treatment and questioning of arrested persons. Independent Police Complaints Authority set up.

1984–5 During the miners' strike the police set up a national system of allocating police resources and mount largest ever peace-time mobilization to police mining areas.

1985   Prosecution of Offences Act establishes independent Crown Prosecution Service for England and Wales.

1986   Public Order Act abolishes the common law offences of riot, rout and unlawful assembly and creates new public disorder offences of riot, violent disorder, affray and disorderly conduct; new regulations on processions and assemblies.

1987   Criminal Justice Act amends regulations relating to investigation and trial for fraud.

1988   Criminal Justice Act strengthens Attorney-General's right to extradite and challenge lenient sentences. Amends rules of evidence for criminal proceedings and allows courts to seize assets of convicted offenders.

1991   Criminal Justice Act aims to ensure greater consistency in sentencing; introducing range of 'community' penalties and new arrangements for early release of prisoners. War Crimes Act allows prosecution of UK residents who were suspected of war crimes during the Second World War.

1993   Criminal Justice Act to combat international fraud, drugs trade and money laundering.

1994   Police and Magistrates' Courts Act reconstitutes police authorities, reducing number of local councillors and increasing Home Office nominees. Home Office recommendations are heavily modified. Criminal Justice and Public Order Act extends sentencing of 10–13 year olds; greater range and duration of custodial sentences for young offenders; unconditional 'right to silence' ended; restrictions placed on bail; police given power to take DNA samples; measures to deal with trespass and limit New Age travellers, also to evict squatters; new anti-terrorist measures; also extends powers against obscenity and pornography.

1996   Cullen Report on Dunblane shooting published; recommends ban on all handguns except the smallest calibre (.22).

1997   Incoming Labour government accepts the Cullen Report; passed into law as the Firearms Act.

1998   Crime and Disorder Act aimed at keeping young offenders out of the criminal justice system; police and local authorities are required to develop partnerships for crime prevention; orders can be applied to prevent anti-social behaviour and restrict sex offenders. Government appoints Anti-Drugs Co-ordinator or 'Drug Czar'.

1999   Metropolitan Police accused of 'institutionalized racism' in report on their handling of the murder of the black teenager Stephen Lawrence.

Major disturbances and demonstrations

1947   Anti-Semitic demonstrations in Liverpool and Manchester following execution of two British soldiers in Palestine.

1958   Race riots in Notting Hill (London) and the Midlands.

1961   'Sit-down' demonstrations in London organized by Campaign for Nuclear Disarmament (CND).

1964–66 'Mods' versus 'Rockers' disturbances at seaside resorts, usually at Bank Holiday weekends.

1967 'Sit-in' at London School of Economics and Political Science begins wave of similar demonstrations in several universities (Mar.). Anti-Vietnam War demonstration mounted by Vietnam Solidarity Campaign leads to disturbances outside US Embassy in Grosvenor Square (London) (Oct.).

1968 Anti-Vietnam War demonstrations in London lead to clashes with police in Grosvenor Square (Mar. and Oct.).

1973 Riot in Parkhurst prison.

1974 Red Lion Square (London) clashes between National Front and opponents; one man killed (June).

1976 Disturbances at West Indian Notting Hill Carnival in London (Sept.). Hull prison riot; an estimated £1 million worth of damage (Aug.–Sept.).

1977 Clashes between police and mass pickets at Grunwick strike (July–Sept.).

1979 Southall disturbances between police and anti-National Front demonstrators; one man killed (April).

1980 Rioting in St Paul's area of Bristol by black youths (Apr.). Clashes in Lewisham between National Front and Anti-Nazi League (Apr.).

1981 Rioting in Brixton (Apr.) leads to setting up of Scarman Inquiry. Serious riots in Toxteth (Liverpool) and Moss Side (Manchester), followed by 'copycat' rioting by youths in many other towns and cities (July).

1983 Serious disturbances outside Warrington printing plant of *Stockport Messenger* as members of National Graphical Association attempt to enforce a closed shop (Nov.–Dec.).

1984–85 Series of disturbances during the miners' strike, principally between pickets and police forces protecting non-strikers. A Yorkshire miner is killed at Ollerton (Mar. 1984) and a taxi-driver carrying a working miner is killed in South Wales (Dec. 1984). The largest confrontations take place outside the Orgreave coke plant, near Sheffield (May–June 1984) when thousands of police and pickets struggle for control of access to the plant. Almost 12,000 miners are arrested during the course of the strike, many for public order offences.

1985 Football supporter killed in riot by Leeds and Birmingham supporters (May). At the Heysel Stadium, Brussels, 38 people killed and 250 injured following the collapse of a wall during rioting between Liverpool and Juventus fans (May). Riots in Handsworth area of Birmingham in which two Asian men die in a fire (Sept.). Violent rioting in Brixton following the police shooting and wounding of

Mrs Cherry Groce (Sept.). Serious rioting at Broadwater Farm estate in Tottenham in which a police constable is killed (Oct.).

1986 Series of disturbances outside the Wapping printing works of Rupert Murdoch after the strike and dismissal of 5,500 print and other workers (May). Most serious night of violence in British gaols, affecting nineteen institutions, during prison officers' dispute (May).

1987 Outside Wapping print works 300 injured in demonstrations on anniversary of strike against Rupert Murdoch; widespread criticism of police behaviour (Jan.). After disturbances at Notting Hill Carnival 97 people arrested (Aug.).

1990 Series of anti-poll tax demonstrations across country (Mar.). Anti-poll tax rally in London, attended by estimated 300,000 people, leads to rioting in Trafalgar Square (31 Mar.). Major riot at Strangeways prison, Manchester (Apr.) leads to almost four-week siege of prison and estimated damage of several million pounds. Anti-poll tax demonstrators battle with police in Brixton (Oct.).

1991 Youths battle with police in series of disturbances in Leeds, Telford, Cardiff and Oxford (July–Aug.). Youths in Newcastle upon Tyne engage in three nights of arson, looting and affray.

1992 Five nights of disorder at estates in Coventry between youths and police (May). Riots in Hartcliffe area of Bristol with arson of shops and library (July). Attacks on police in Burnley and Huddersfield.

1993 Demonstrations against Twyford Down road scheme at Winchester. Beginning of series of protests against A12–M11 link road in London.

1994 Riots in London against Criminal Justice and Public Order Act.

1995 Widespread demonstrations at ports on the south and east coasts against the export of live animals. Disturbances in the Manningham area of Bradford by mainly Muslim youths, partly against widespread prostitution and allegations of police harassment in the district (June). Rioting in Marsh Farm estate in Luton (July).

1997 Protests over road schemes (A30 extension) and Newbury by-pass.

1998 Countryside March in London attracts 250,000 demonstrators.

1999 Anti-capitalist demonstrators in the City of London cause £1 billion of damage. Disturbances in Dover between local residents and asylum-seekers.

Notifiable offences recorded by the police, 1930–97

	England and Wales	Scotland
1930	147 031	36 723
1935	234 372	59 753
1940	305 114	62 266
1945	478 394	86 075
1950	461 435	74 640
1955	438 085	74 773
1960	743 713	102 617
1965	1 133 882	140 141
1970	1 568 400	167 200
1975	2 105 600	232 482
1978	2 395 800	277 213
1980	2 688 200	364 600
1985	3 611 900	462 000
1990	4 543 600	959 100
1992	5 383 487	589 500
1997	4 595 700	420 640

Note: figures relate to indictable, generally more serious offences, reported to or discovered by the police. Figures for Scotland up to 1985 also include minor, non-indictable offences. The Theft Act 1969 altered the categories of indictable offences, and the figures from 1970 are not strictly comparable to those before.

Daily average prison population (England and Wales)

1940	9 300
1950	20 000
1960	27 100
1970	39 000
1977	41 600
1985	46 300
1988	48 600
1993	45 800
1997	61 000

Source: *Annual Reports* of the Prison Commissioners and Prison Department of the Home Office

Drug-related offences in the UK, 1976–90

1976	12 754
1981	17 921
1986	23 905
1990	44 922

Source: Central Statistical Office, *Key Data, 1992/3* (London, HMSO, 1992) p 48

153

9 RELIGION

Chronology of principal events

1942   William Temple becomes Archbishop of Canterbury.

1958   Death of Pius XII; Pope John XXIII elected.

1959   Second Vatican Council convened, the first since 1870; begins reappraisal of Roman Catholic liturgy and policy.

1960   Lord Fisher is first Archbishop of Canterbury to visit the Pope since the Reformation.

1962   Consecration of new Coventry Cathedral. First Hindu temple opened in London.

1963   Controversy aroused by the radical theology of the Bishop of Woolwich's (John Robinson's) *Honest to God.* Sales reach 300,000 copies.

1965   Dr Donald Coggan, Archbishop of York, advocates 'marriage' between Anglican and Methodist churches.

1969   The Sharing of Church Buildings Act enables agreements to be made by two or more churches for the sharing of church buildings.

1970   Translation of the New English Bible completed.

1972   United Reformed Church formed from the merger of the Congregational Church of England and Wales, and the English Presbyterian Church. General Synod of the Church of England fails to approve a scheme for Anglican–Methodist unity, already endorsed by Methodists.

1979   Revised Prayer Book introduced for Anglican services.

1980   Dr Robert Runcie becomes 102nd Archbishop of Canterbury.

1982   Pope John Paul II visits Britain.

1985   Church of England report 'Faith in the City' criticized by the Government for depiction of inner-city problems. Church of England general synod approves ordination of women deacons.

1987   Anonymous attack on Dr Runcie in Preface to *Crockford's Clerical Directory*, accusing him of weakness and indecisiveness. Its author, an Oxford don, Dr Gareth Bennett, commits suicide.

1988   First Jain temple opened in Leicester.

1989   Dr Runcie visits Pope John Paul II in Rome to discuss growing tension over ordination of women.

1990   First two women Anglican priests ordained in United Kingdom in Belfast.

1990   George Carey enthroned as 103rd Archbishop of Canterbury (Apr.).

1992   Anglican Synod votes decisively for ordination of women (Nov.). A number of Anglicans secede to Church of Rome.

1993   Church of England announces massive losses of Ecclesiastical Commissioners in property deals.

1994   The first 32 women priests ordained in England in Bristol Cathedral (12 Mar.). Confidential preliminary discussions revealed on new attempt to join Anglican and Methodist churches. First women priests ordained in Scottish Episcopal Church (Dec.).

1997   Muslim Council of Britain formed to represent national and regional bodies, mosques, and other organizations. Council of Churches for Britain and Ireland presents major report on *Unemployment and the Future of Work*.

1998   General Synod of the Church of England announces changes in central structure of the Church; Church Commissioners to be reduced by two-thirds and powers transferred to a new Archbishops Council, chaired by the Archbishops of Canterbury and York, which would, from 1999, become the Church's central governing body. Formal conversations between the Anglican and Methodist Churches about unity scheduled for 1999; also informal trilateral talks between Anglicans, Methodists and the United Reform Church will begin.

Archbishops of Canterbury

1945	G Fisher
1961	M Ramsey
1974	D Coggan
1980	R Runcie
1991	G Carey

Source: *Crockfords*, 1945–

Roman Catholic Archbishops of Westminster

1943	B Griffin	(Cardinal, 1946)
1956	W Godfrey	(Cardinal, 1958)
1963	J Heenan	(Cardinal, 1965)
1976	B Hume	(Cardinal, 1976)
2000	C Murphy-O'Connor	

Source: *The Catholic Directory*, 1900–

Adult churchgoers in England, 1975–89

	1975 (%)	1979 (%)	1985 (%)	1989 (%)
Free Church	30	31	33	34
Anglican	32	31	31	31
Roman Catholic	38	38	36	35
	(m)	(m)	(m)	(m)
Total (100%)	4.1	4.0	3.8	3.7

Religious affiliations in Ulster, 1961

	Protestant	%	Catholic	%
Belfast	301 520	72.5	114 336	27.5
Co. Antrim	206 976	75.6	66 929	24.4
Co. Armagh	61 977	52.7	55 617	47.3
Derry City	17 689	32.9	36 073	67.1
Derry County	64 027	57.4	47 509	42.6
Co. Down	190 676	71.4	76 263	28.6
Co. Fermanagh	24 109	46.8	27 422	53.2
Co. Tyrone	60 521	45.2	73 398	54.8

Source: General Register Office, Northern Ireland, *Census of Population 1961*, County volumes, Tables XVI (Belfast, HMSO, 1964)

Buddhists, Hindus, Muslims and Sikhs in Britain (000)

	1970	1975	1997
Buddhists	6	21	25
Hindus	50	100	400–550
Muslims	250	400	1 000–1 500
Sikhs	75	115	400–500
Jews	410	410	285

Note: figures are estimated

Sources: derived from HMSO, *Social Trends*, No. 8 (London, HMSO, 1977); *Britain 1999* (London, HMSO, 1998) pp 246–7

10 IMMIGRATION AND RACE RELATIONS

Chronology of legislation and principal events

1947 Anti-Semitic demonstrations in Liverpool and Manchester after the execution of two British sergeants in Palestine.

1948 British Nationality Act confers the status of British Subject on all Commonwealth citizens. At Tilbury Docks (east London) 491 Jamaican immigrants arrive on SS *Empire Windrush*, beginning postwar influx of Commonwealth immigrants.

1957 First Notting Hill West Indian Carnival in west London.

1958 Anti-immigrant riots in Notting Hill and Nottingham. Coloured People's Progressive Association founded in Notting Hill by Claudia Jones and Frances Ezzrecco.

1959 Standing Conference of West Indian Organizations in the UK formed. *West Indian Gazette* launches first Caribbean carnival in St Pancras's Town Hall.

1962 Commonwealth Immigrants Act ends the 'open door' policy for former British colonial subjects. In future most immigrants are required to have a work permit (employment voucher) to enter the UK. Defeat of Patrick Gordon-Walker at Smethwick as a result of anti-immigration vote.

1964 Campaign against Racial Discrimination founded (collapsed in 1968).

1965 Race Relations Act makes racial discrimination unlawful in places of public resort (but not in housing and employment). Race Relations Board is created to investigate complaints of racial discrimination.

1967 Formation of the National Front, seeking an end to all 'coloured' immigration and repatriation of immigrants living in Britain. Foundation of Universal Coloured Peoples' Association (UCPA), Britain's first avowedly black power group, by Obi Egbuna.

1968 Commonwealth Immigrants Act: East African Asians holding British passports lose their automatic right to stay in the UK. Passed as a direct response to the expected wave of expulsions of Asian settlers from East Africa. Race Relations Act extends areas of unlawful discrimination to employment, housing, education and services. A Community Relations Commission is set up to promote 'harmonious community relations'. Enoch Powell's 'rivers of blood' speech on immigration, calling for voluntary repatriation of immigrants, causes major controversy and leads to his expulsion from the shadow cabinet by Edward Heath.

1969   Sir Learie Constantine, the West Indian cricketer, becomes a life peer.

1971   Immigration Act tightens controls on immigration to UK: it allows 'patrial' entry, that is entry only to those born in the UK or whose parents or grandparents were of British origin.

1972   30,000 Ugandan Asians expelled by Idi Amin are forced to resettle in Britain. Muslim Ladies Circle formed in Nottingham (later renamed Muslim Women's Organization).

1973   National Front candidates win their highest vote in local elections in Leicester. Formation of Manchester Black Women's Cooperative and Brixton Black Women's Group.

1974   Strike at Imperial Typewriters in Leicester of Asian women.

1975   First *Who's Who of Asians in Britain*. David Pitt, black chairman of the GLC, becomes Lord Pitt.

1976   Race Relations Act replaces the Race Relations Board and Community Relations Commission with the Commission for Racial Equality (CRE), responsible for both dealing with discrimination and promoting equality of opportunity and good race relations. Disturbances at Notting Hill Carnival.

1978   Formation of Women of Africa and African Descent (OWAAD). OWAAD becomes Organization of Women of African and Asian Descent.

1979   Immigration rules remove the automatic right of husbands or fiancés of women settled in the UK to join them. Further restrictions on entry of parents, grandparents and children over 18; permanent settlement no longer possible for those staying temporarily. Viv Anderson becomes first black footballer to play for England. Southall disturbances between Asian youths and National Front demonstrators. National Front puts up 303 candidates in the general election but all lose their deposits. Front begins to break up. First Black Women's Centre opens in Stockwell Road, South London.

1980   Rioting in St Paul's area of Bristol by black and Asian youths.

1981   British Nationality Act supersedes the Nationality Act 1948 by replacing the status of UK and colonial citizen with three categories: British citizen, citizen of British dependent territories, and British overseas citizen. It revokes the automatic right to British citizenship of any child, including those born in the UK, unless at least one of his or her parents is a British citizen by birth. Children born overseas to parents of patrial or naturalized British citizenship could be refused entry to the UK. The Act is widely denounced as 'racist' for its restrictions on non-white entry. Inner-city riots in Brixton

(London), Moss Side (Manchester) and Toxteth (Liverpool) are the most serious civil disturbances for decades. Scarman Commission appointed to investigate their causes. The report blames the widespread deprivation of inner-city areas and sense of discrimination among black and Asian youths.

1982 First Asian judge appointed.

1985 Further serious clashes between police and black youths in Handsworth (Birmingham), Brixton (London), and at the Broadwater Farm Estate (north London), where a policeman is killed.

1987 Four MPs from ethnic minority backgrounds are elected at the general election.

1988 Immigration Act further tightens controls on immigration: it removes concession previously given to men who settled in the UK before 1973 whose wives and children had been able to enter without marriage tests or financial and accommodation tests. Claims to British citizenship now have to be established before travelling.

1989 Britain refuses residency to 3.25 million Hong Kong Chinese who currently hold British passports. Ayatollah Khomeini issues *fatwa* calling for the death of British writer Salman Rushdie, author of allegedly 'blasphemous' *The Satanic Verses*. Widespread demonstrations by Muslims against Rushdie's book.

1990 British Nationality (Hong Kong) Act extends British citizenship to up to 50, 000 Hong Kong residents in four categories: professionals, key entrepreneurs, police services, and also sensitive services. Assessments are to be made on a points system with scores for age, education, training and fluency in English. A survey records 50 Asian millionaires in Britain.

1992 Asian *Who's Who* lists over 300 Asian millionaires; first meeting of Muslim 'Parliament'.

1993 Asylum and Immigration Appeals Act reduces number of asylum-seekers admitted to Britain by restricting those allowed 'Exceptional Leave to Remain'.

1995 Muslim youths involved in disturbances in Manningham district of Bradford.

1997 Labour government proposes inquiry into the investigation of the death of Stephen Lawrence.

1999 Report of Lawrence inquiry blames 'institutionalized racism' in the Metropolitan Police for failure of prosecution over the death of Stephen Lawrence. Formation of National Civil Rights Movement. Bishop of Rochester (Michael Nazir-Ali) becomes first black bishop to take seat in House of Lords.

Distribution of ethnic minorities, 1991

Districts with largest ethnic minorities	%	Total
London boroughs		
Brent	44.9	1 091 000
Tower Hamlets	42.4	899 000
Hackney	35.4	571 000
Ealing	32.4	610 000
Lambeth	30.1	738 000
Haringey	29.0	587 000
Harrow	26.3	526 000
Waltham Forest	25.6	543 000
Southwark	24.4	534 000
Hounslow	24.3	497 000
Lewisham	22.0	508 000
Redbridge	21.4	484 000
Westminster	21.4	374 000
Wandsworth	20.2	509 000
Islington	18.9	311 000
Barnet	18.3	537 000
Camden	17.8	303 000
Croydon	17.6	557 000
Outside London		
Leicester	28.5	771 000
Slough	27.7	280 000
Birmingham	21.5	2 066 000
Luton	19.7	339 000
Wolverhampton	18.5	447 000

Source: Census returns 1991

11 CIVIL LIBERTIES AND CENSORSHIP

Chronology of legislation and principal events

1948 National Assistance Act allows unmarried mother to apply for state support for herself and child.

1959 Obscene Publications Act makes tendency to 'deprave and corrupt' main test of obscenity, allowing literary or other experts to be called in defence.

1960 Wolfenden Commission recommends relaxation of laws against homosexual acts in private.

1965 Death penalty abolished. Ombudsman introduced to remedy cases of maladministration.

1966 Sexual Offences Bill makes homosexual acts between consenting adults legal.

1967 Abortion legalized. Sexual Offences Bill becomes law.

1969 Censorship of plays by Lord Chamberlain abolished. Age of voting reduced to 18.

1970 Age of majority reduced from 21 to 18.

1972 Theatres allowed to open on Sundays.

1974 Prevention of Terrorism Act gives wide powers to the police to hold suspects for five days and to deport them.

1978 Britain convicted by European Court of Human Rights of 'inhuman and degrading conduct' towards IRA prisoners in Northern Ireland.

1984 Data Protection Act establishes data protection agency to control information stored on computer. Sarah Tisdall, employee at Ministry of Defence, imprisoned for six months for disclosing a document to the *Guardian*.

1987 Family Law Reform Act gives full legal rights to children born outside marriage. Government forces BBC to halt programme on Zircon spy satellite.

1988 Government protests against Thames Television programme *Death on the Rock* about Gibraltar shootings. Ban on live broadcast of IRA spokesmen.

1989 Children Act defines 'rights' of children. New Official Secrets Act replaces Official Secrets Act 1911 with ban on disclosure by all present or former members of the security services and ban on government servants or contractors disclosing information on work of security services or on international relations prejudicial to British interests. Security Services Act places security services on statutory basis with a Commissioner to oversee.

1993   Director of MI5 named publicly.

1994   Sunday Trading Act deregulates shopping. Sunday racing and betting also allowed. Criminal Justice and Public Order Act criminalizes protests in the form of trespass. Broadcast ban on IRA lifted.

1995   First horse racing on Sunday (May).

1999   Government proposes major restriction on crimes which can be tried by jury.

12 GAY AND LESBIAN RIGHTS

Chronology of legislation and principal events

1958   Homosexual Law Reform Society set up to campaign for legislation to implement the recommendations of the 1957 Wolfenden Report.

1960   Kenneth Robinson, MP, urges early action on Wolfenden, but defeated in the Commons (June).

1962   Leo Abse, MP, proposes a mild Bill to alleviate the worst excesses of the existing law; defeated (Mar.).

1964   New Director of Public Prosecutions issues instructions that all cases are to be referred to him before prosecution, but number of prosecutions increases.

1965   Lord Arran introduces issue of homosexual law reform in the Lords; a Bill to decriminalize adult homosexual relations is introduced (May); Lord Arran's Bill passes the Lords.

1966   Humphry Berkeley introduces Bill in the Commons to decriminalize adult homosexual acts; passes first and second readings, but falls because of general election in March. After the election, Arran reintroduces his Bill in the Lords, where it passes (June); Abse introduces identical Bill in the Commons where it is approved on first reading (June). Abse's Bill passes second reading (Dec.) by 194 votes to 84.

1967   Abse's Bill passes third reading (July); receives Royal Assent (July). Committee for Homosexual Law Reform founded.

1970   Homosexual Law Reform Committee changes name to Campaign for Homosexual Equality. Gay Liberation Front launched at the London School of Economics.

1972   Launch of *Gay News*. First Gay Pride March held in London.

1975   Gay Left launched.

1976   Gay Christian Movement founded.

1977   Prosecution of *Gay News* on blasphemy charges.

1979   Opening (6 Dec.) of most celebrated gay club in London (Heaven).

1981   AIDS identified amongst homosexual community on West Coast of America. Launch of *Capital Gay* (June); later becomes pioneer of the 'free' gay press.

1983   Terence Higgins Trust founded to assist AIDS victims.

1985   Opening of first Lesbian and Gay Centre in London. Labour party conference passes gay and lesbian rights resolutions.

1987 Gay Christian Movement becomes Lesbian and Gay Christian Movement. *The Pink Paper* launched as national free news-based paper.

1988 Under Section 28 of the Local Government Act local authorities are barred from 'promoting' homosexuality by teaching in schools.

1990 OutRage formed to campaign against discrimination and anti-gay activities. *All Points North*, gay paper for northern England, is founded.

1992 Homosexuality legalized on the Isle of Man.

1994 Protests by OutRage activists at enthronement of the Bishop of Durham. Twelve Anglican bishops named as gay by OutRage in protest aimed at exposing the hypocrisy of the Church over gay rights. Age of consent for gay sex lowered to 18.

1995 Labour pledge to lift homosexual ban in the armed forces. High Court upholds ban on homosexuality in the armed forces. Judge concedes 'tide of history' will end this discrimination.

1996 Approval given for a case against the unequal age of consent to go to Europe.

1997 Chris Smith becomes first openly gay Cabinet minister. Foreign nationals in homosexual relationships win right to settle in UK.

1998 Strong anti-homosexual majority at Lambeth Conference. First Professorship of Gay and Lesbian Studies created (at Nottingham Trent University) (June).

1999 Majority in House of Commons (281 to 82 votes) in favour of equalizing the age of consent (Mar.). Rejected again by House of Lords (Apr.); government promises legislation to overturn 'Clause 28'; the House of Lords ruled that homosexual couples in a long-standing relationship have the same tenancy rights as heterosexuals (Oct.).

2000 Ban on gays in armed forces lifted (Jan.). House of Lords defeats government attempt to overturn Clause 28; House of Commons votes overwhelmingly again for equalizing age of consent (263 votes to 102) (Feb.). Department of Education asks Equal Opportunities Commission to draw up a code of practice for companies on how to treat gay employees.

ECONOMIC HISTORY

1 ECONOMIC POLICY

Chronology of legislation and principal events

1945

21 Aug.   End of Lend-Lease; followed by emergency US and Canadian loans to Bank of England.

1946

1 Jan.   Nationalization of Bank of England.

1947

5 June   General Marshall announces proposal to establish Marshall Aid to Europe (to be instituted in 1948).

15 July   Sterling made convertible currency on terms agreed in return for US loans.

20 Aug.   Convertibility suspended.

4 Oct.   Agriculture Act gives permanent force to subsidies and protection employed in wartime.

1948

4 Feb.   'Wage Freeze' and dividend restraint.

Apr.   Organization for European Economic Cooperation (OEEC) established to administer Marshall Aid.

July   Marshall Aid Plan formally instituted.

30 July   Monopolies Commission established by Monopolies and Restrictive Practices Act.

1949

18 Sept.   Devaluation of pound from US \$4.03 to US \$2.80.

1950

13 Dec.   Marshall Aid suspended as no longer necessary.

1951

7 Nov.   Bank rate increased from 2 per cent to 2.5 per cent. Import liberalization suspended to ease drain of dollars.

1955

25 Oct.   Autumn budget following balance of payments crisis.

1956

2 Aug.   Restrictive Trade Practices Act establishes Restrictive Trade Practices Court.

Nov.   Suez Crisis threatens run on British gold reserves.

11 Dec.   Stand-by credits arranged to meet balance of payments crisis caused by Suez Crisis.

1957

12 Aug.   Council on Prices and Productivity set up.

19 Sept.   Bank rate raised to 7 per cent to meet sterling crisis.

27 Dec.   Further convertibility reforms.

1959

20 Nov.   European Free Trade Association (EFTA) Treaty signed.

1960

4 Dec.   OEEC extended and reconstituted to include USA and Canada; retitled Organization for Economic Cooperation and Development (OECD).

1961

20 July   Plowden Report on Control of Public Expenditure.

25 July   'Pay Pause' announced by Chancellor Selwyn Lloyd following balance-of-payments crisis. National Economic Development Council established with representatives of the government, business and the trade unions.

10 Aug.   Britain applies to join the European Economic Community (EEC).

1963

Jan.   Negotiations on entry to EEC terminated.

1964

16 July   Resale Prices Act greatly limits resale price maintenance.

26 Oct.   Incoming Wilson government meets balance-of-payments crisis by imposing 15 per cent import surcharge and export rebates of £70 million a year.

Nov.   Callaghan's autumn budget announces 6*d* (= 2½p) increase in income tax and petrol duty and rise in National Insurance; prescription charges abolished; old age pensions raised. Major selling of sterling begins and bank rate raised to 7 per cent. Central banks provide US $3,000 million in support of sterling.

Dec.   International Monetary Fund (IMF) lends US $1,000 million to Britain.

1965

Mar.   Prices and Incomes Board set up.

Apr.   Import surcharge reduced to 10 per cent. Credit squeeze tightened.

May   Further IMF drawing of US $1,400 million.

Aug.   Monopolies and Mergers Act extended to services.

13 Sept.   Publication of first National Economic Plan by George Brown's Department of Economic Affairs.

1966

25 Jan.   Industrial Reorganization Corporation established to encourage rationalization of British industry.

6 Mar.   Announcement of adoption of decimal currency from 1971.

20 July   Bank rate raised to 7 per cent to meet sterling crisis; taxes increased, credit restricted, and prices and incomes 'standstill' announced.

12 Aug.   Prices and Incomes Act enforces standstill.

Nov.   Import surcharge abolished.

1967

11 May   Britain makes second application to join EEC.

18 Nov.   Sharp wave of selling of sterling forces devaluation of pound from US $2.80 to US $2.40; bank rate increased to 8 per cent.

27 Nov.   British application to EEC vetoed by French President De Gaulle.

1968

19 Jan.   Large cuts in government expenditure announced, including reintroduction of prescription charges.

19 Mar.   Chancellor Roy Jenkins imposes higher taxes and duties in major deflationary package.

Nov.   Trade gap worsens; Jenkins introduces crisis package of consumer tax increases and credit squeeze.

1970

Feb.   Jenkins announces that first priority for the economy is investment.

June   Jenkins introduces neutral budget to secure balance of payments surplus instead of pre-election budget widely expected.

27 Oct.   Heath government announces expenditure cuts of £330 million with tax cuts to stimulate the economy.

1971

15 Feb.   Changeover to decimal currency.

30 Mar. Budget replaces surtax with graduated tax; adoption of Value Added Tax (VAT) announced for 1973.

15 Aug. USA ends dollar–gold convertibility, ending the Bretton Woods system in operation since 1945.

23 Aug. Sterling is floated to conform to new system.

19 Dec. General currency realignment agreed.

1972

18 Feb. Wilberforce Court of Inquiry recommends 22 per cent pay increase to end miners' strike.

26 Sept. Anti-inflation programme announced to include pay and prices freeze and establishment of Prices Commission and Pay Board.

1973

1 Jan. Britain joins the EEC.

4 Mar. European currencies floated against the pound.

1 Apr. Value Added Tax replaces excise duties and Selective Employment Tax.

6 Oct. Yom Kippur War leads to Arab oil boycott, followed by quadrupling of oil prices.

8 Oct. Announcement of 'Phase Three' anti-inflation proposals.

13 Dec. Miners' overtime ban leads government to introduce three-day week from January to conserve energy supplies.

1974

11 Feb. Full-scale miners' strike begins.

8 Mar. Incoming Wilson government ends three-day week.

11 Mar. Miners' strike concluded.

31 Dec. Retail prices show yearly rise of 19 per cent and wage rates of 29 per cent and fall in industrial production of 3 per cent.

1975

18 June First landing of North Sea oil.

11 July Universal pay rise limit of £6 per week announced from 1 Aug. in White Paper *The Attack on Inflation*.

12 Aug. Monthly price index shows twelve-month increase of record 26.9 per cent.

20 Nov. Announcement of cash limits to public expenditure in next financial year.

1976

19 Feb. Public expenditure White Paper published, showing cuts in spending of £1.0 billion in 1977/78 and £2.4 billion in 1978/79 compared with previous plans.

7 Mar.   Sterling falls below US $2 for first time.

6 Apr.   In budget £1.3 billion tax cuts are announced but made dependent on agreement by the Trades Union Congress (TUC) to a new low pay norm in Stage 2. On 5 May 4.5 per cent pay formula agreed; endorsed at special TUC meeting on 16 June.

22 July   Announcement of further £1,000 million cut in public expenditure in 1977/78.

29 Sept.   Government approaches IMF for a US $3.9 billion stand-by credit.

7 Oct.   Minimum lending rate increased to 15 per cent.

28 Oct.   Sterling closes at US $1.5675 – its lowest yet.

15 Dec.   A further cut in public expenditure of £1,000 million in 1977/78 and £1,500 million in 1978/79 is announced as part of the agreement with the IMF.

1977

11 Aug.   Unemployment reaches new post-war peak of 1,635,800.

7 Sept.   TUC supports twelve-month rule for Stage 3. Government continues to seek voluntary 10 per cent limit on earnings increases.

1978

4 Jan.   UK official reserves rise to US $20.6 billion – the highest ever.

9 Jan.   US Treasury announces it will intervene in foreign exchange markets to halt decline in dollar.

17 Feb.   Inflation (year on year) falls below 10 per cent for first time since 1973.

1979

12 Mar.   European Monetary System (EMS) starts. Britain enters EMS but not Exchange Rate Mechanism (ERM).

12 June   New Conservative government's budget cuts income tax from 33 to 30 per cent and raises VAT from 8 to 15 per cent.

24 Oct.   Abolition of exchange controls.

15 Nov.   Minimum lending rate touches 17 per cent.

1980

26 Mar.   Announcement of Medium Term Financial Strategy (MTFS).

June   Britain becomes net exporter of oil.

2 June   Agreement on reduction of Britain's EEC budget contribution.

Oct.   Sterling reaches peak exchange with $US (2.39).

21 Nov.   Youth Opportunities Programme doubled.

1981

Jan.   Bottom of post-war slump for Britain.

20 Aug.   Minimum lending rate abolished.

1982

27 July   Hire purchase controls abolished.

9 Sept.   Unemployment reaches 3 million.

1984

13 Mar.   Beginning of miners' strike.

26 June   Fontainebleau summit agrees permanent settlement of Britain's EEC contribution.

28 Nov.   Government sells 33 per cent of British Telecom.

3 Dec.   British Telecom shares (sold in Nov.) gain 45 per cent premium in first Stock Exchange dealings.

1985

4 Mar.   End of year-long miners' strike (26.1 million working days lost).

7 Mar.   Sterling touches bottom level of US $1.05.

19 Mar.   Chancellor Nigel Lawson announces increase in mortgage rates and selective tax rises.

1986

Oct.   'Big Bang' at Stock Exchange introduces computerized trading.

Dec.   Sterling allowed to fall sharply following failure of Lawson and Prime Minister to agree on entry into the ERM.

1987

June   Unemployment falls below 3 million.

Oct.   'Black Monday': £50 billion wiped off share values as Dow Jones and world stock markets record largest fall since 1929. Widespread fears of a world slump are gradually eased.

1988

Mar.   Lawson cuts 2p off standard rate of income tax and reduces top rate to 40p.

June   Balance-of-payments crisis looms; widely blamed on tax cuts in previous budget.

July   Interest rates rise to 11.5 per cent, from 7.5 per cent earlier in the year.

Aug.   Further interest rises (to 12 per cent) in face of huge trade gap recorded in July.

Oct.	House price figures show rise of 34 per cent in twelve months.
Dec.	Interest rates reach over 13 per cent.

1989

Feb.	Sterling reaches a new high against European currencies.
Mar.	Lawson introduces low-key budget designed to keep inflation under control.
June	Lawson indicates 1990 as possible date for entry into ERM.
Sept.	Thatcher adviser Alan Walters continues openly to criticize the ERM; split between Thatcher and Lawson evident.
Oct.	Sterling slides and share prices fall steeply. Interest rates rise to 15 per cent. Lawson resigns as Chancellor and is replaced by Major.
Dec.	Sterling falls to low of DM 2.7225 from peak of DM 3.225 in 1988.

1990

May	Thatcher drops opposition to ERM.
June	Major announces alternative of a new European currency to be used alongside other currencies.
Sept.	Major announces commitment to join ERM 'at earliest possible date'.
8 Oct.	ERM entry announced at parity of DM 2.95.
Nov.	Unemployment rises to 1.7 million; the biggest monthly rise since 1986.
28 Nov.	Major succeeds as Prime Minister following resignation of Thatcher: Norman Lamont takes over as Chancellor.
Dec.	Further record rise in unemployment, the largest since 1981.

1991

Mar.	Unemployment reaches over 2 million. VAT raised to 17.5 per cent to finance government's cut of £140 per head in poll tax (community charge).
Apr.	Government announces that poll tax will be replaced by a council tax based on property values.
July	Bank of Credit and Commerce International (BCCI) closes after discovery of fraud.
Oct.	Chancellor Lamont announces at Conservative party conference that he detects 'green shoots' of recovery.
Nov.	Robert Maxwell dies at sea; trading in shares of Maxwell Communications and Mirror Group Newspapers suspended. Widespread fraud discovered (Dec.).
Dec.	At Maastricht, Major negotiates an opt-out on joining a single European banking system.

1992

Mar.   Election called. Unemployment at 2.6 million.

May   Lamont describes unemployment as 'a price worth paying' to defeat inflation. Interest rates fall to 10 per cent.

Sept.   Sterling falls to new low and approaches its ERM floor. Panic rises in interest rates to 15 per cent fail to hold the pound's level. Sterling leaves the ERM (16 Sept.). Base rates return to 9 per cent. £5 billion lost in defence of ERM.

Oct.   £20 billion wiped off share values.

1993

Jan.   Unemployment peaks at 2.99 million; inauguration of Single European Market for goods and services.

Feb.   Unemployment falls for the first time since 1990. Public sector pay ceiling of 1.5 per cent announced.

Mar.   VAT announced on domestic fuel in two-stage plan.

Apr.   Gross Domestic Product shows first rise in eight quarters. Inflation at 1.3 per cent is the lowest since Feb. 1964.

May   Chancellor Lamont resigns in delayed response to ERM débâcle; replaced by Kenneth Clarke.

Nov.   Clarke in November budget raises taxes by record amount to bridge budget deficit and confirms that VAT will be levied on fuel.

1994

Aug.   Government has evidence that the economy is growing at more than 3 per cent per year.

Sept.   Interest rates go up half a per cent in first rise since departure from ERM.

1995

Nov.   1995 budget projects that public spending will be a lower share of GDP than at any time since 1964. A generally cautious budget reduces taxes and cuts public expenditure by *c.* £3 billion to balance. Lowest tax band of 20 per cent widened and Private Finance Initiative, for privately funded public projects, set a target of £14 billion by 1999.

1996

Nov.   Chancellor resists calls for higher interest rates. Standard rate of income tax cut by 1p in budget (to 23p); tax reductions balanced by increases in taxes on tobacco and petrol. PSBR (Public Sector Borrowing Requirement) estimated at 3.5 per cent of GDP and projected to fall steadily.

1997

Feb.   Shadow Chancellor, Gordon Brown, announces that an incoming Labour government would maintain the existing government's spending plans for its first two years and leave basic and higher rates of income tax unchanged.

May   Labour government puts setting of interest rates in the hands of the Bank of England.

June   Chancellor Brown announces proposed privatization of the Tote, the Royal Mint, London Transport, and the Commonwealth Development Corporation.

July   Labour budget announces 'Windfall Tax' on 'excess' profits of public utilities to fund the Welfare-to-Work initiative, raising £5.2 billion in two instalments in December 1997 and December 1998.

Oct.   Chancellor indicates that Britain will join European Monetary Union after the next election subject to appropriate conditions and a referendum.

1998

May   Launch of the 'euro' with eleven participating countries; new European Central Bank in charge of European monetary policy set up.

Aug.   Dow Jones Index suffers second biggest fall in history as a result of rouble crisis and fears of international effects.

Oct.   Interest rates cut, beginning response to lower interest rates in Europe.

1999

Mar.   Budget cuts basic rate of income tax to 22p; new rate of 10p introduced; MIRAS (tax relief on mortgages) scrapped and married couples allowance abolished.

Dec.   FTSE reaches record high (6930.2) (30th).

2000

Jan.   Deal between Vodafone and German rival Mannesmann creates largest company in Britain.

Feb.   National Minimum Wage to rise to £3.70 per hour in October (hourly youth rate to rise to £3.20 in June) (15th).

175

2 TRADE AND FINANCE

UK balance of trade (annual averages, 1930–96)

	Balance of visible trade	Balance of invisible trade	Net balance
1930–34	−328	+301	−27
1935–38	−356	+332	−24
1946–50	−160	+104	−56
1951–55	−345	+326	−19
1956–60	−94	+226	+132
1961–65	−218	+176	−42
1966–70	−297	+441	+144
1971–75	−2 263	+1 219	−1 044
1976–80	−1 969	+2 393	+424
1981–85	−2 397	+3 937	+3 608
1986–90	−17 222	+5 352	−11 870
1991–96	−11 900	+6 166	−5 700

Sources: P Deane and W A Cole, *British Economic Growth, 1688–1959* (2nd edn, Cambridge University Press, 1967) p 36; B R Mitchell and H G Jones, *Second Abstract of British Historical Statistics* (Cambridge University Press, 1971) p 142; Central Statistical Office, *United Kingdom Balance of Payments 1967–78* (London, HMSO, 1978); Central Statistical Office, *Key Data, 1992/3* (London, HMSO, 1994) p 29; *Pears Cyclopaedia 1998–1999* (London, Penguin, 1999)

Gross Domestic Product at 1985 prices

	(£ million)
1971	272 321
1981	319 193
1986	372 042
1991	408 565

Source: Central Statistical Office, *Key Data, 1992/3* (London, HMSO, 1994) p 19

Gross Domestic Product at 1995 prices

	(£ million)
1987	609 023
1992	648 975
1995	712 548
1997	756 144

Source: derived from *United Kingdom National Accounts 1998*

National income at real cost

	(£ million)
1938	4 671
1950	10 784
1955	15 511
1960	20 809
1965	28 807
1970	39 567
1975	82 179
1977	107 990
1980	171 204
1985	264 019
1988	352 954
1991	433 361
1995	713 597
1997	811 535

Sources: B R Mitchell and P Deane, *Abstract of British Historical Statistics* (Cambridge University Press, 1962) pp 367–8; Central Statistical Office, *Key Data, 1992/3* (London, HMSO, 1994) p 29; *Britain 1999* (London, HMSO, 1998) p 383

Public expenditure as percentage of GDP

1947–48	44
1952–53	30
1958–59	25
1963–64	36
1968–69	41
1973–74	43
1978–79	44
1981–82	47
1984–85	46
1987–88	41
1989–90	39
1992–93	44
1997–98	44

Government expenditure by main areas (£ billion)

	1979/80	1983/84	1988/89	1993/94	1998/99
Defence	9.4	15.7	19.2	23.4	22.2
Transport	3.7	5.5	5.9	10.5	9.5
Housing	5.6	4.4	3.2	5.5	n/a
Education	10.5	15.8	22.6	33.7	38.3
Health	11.1	18.3	27.0	36.8	37.2
Social Security	20.1	36.9	50.2	87.1	94.0
Total of all spending	90.4	140.4	179.8	281.0	333.0

Trends in economic performance (annual percentages)

	Inflation	National income growth	Productivity growth	Unemployment rate
1960–73	4.8	3.4	2.9	2.5
1973–79	14.9	2.4	1.8	3.4
1979–89	8.2	2.5	2.0	9.0
1989–96	3.9	1.7	1.6	7.9

3 PRICES AND INCOMES

Prices and wages, 1950–96 (1955 = 100)

	Retail price index	Weekly earnings	Real earnings
1950	77	68	91
1955	100	100	100
1960	114	130	114
1965	136	175	129
1970	170	250	147
1977	407	661	162
1979	499	844	169
1985	865	1 537	178
1990	1 154	2 321	201
1996	1 398	3 055	219

Prices and disposable incomes, 1971–96 (1971 = 100)

	Retail prices	Average earnings	Real average earnings	Real disposable incomes
1971	100.0	100.0	100.0	100.0
1972	107.5	111.7	103.9	108.4
1973	117.3	127.2	108.4	115.4
1974	136.0	150.0	110.3	114.4
1975	168.7	189.7	112.4	114.9
1976	196.7	220.5	112.1	114.5
1977	228.0	240.3	105.4	112.0
1978	246.7	271.2	109.9	120.6
1979	279.9	313.1	111.9	127.6
1980	330.4	378.2	114.5	129.6
1981	369.6	426.5	115.4	128.7
1982	401.4	466.7	116.3	128.0
1983	419.6	506.2	120.6	131.4
1984	440.7	536.5	121.7	134.8
1985	467.3	581.9	124.5	138.5
1986	483.2	627.9	129.9	144.9
1987	503.3	676.7	134.5	150.0
1988	528.0	735.5	139.3	158.6
1989	569.2	802.4	141.0	167.2
1990	622.9	880.4	141.3	172.0
1991	659.5	951.4	144.2	171.9
1992	684.2	1 009.2	147.5	175.2
1993	695.1	1 042.4	150.0	176.2
1994	712.5	1 084.6	152.2	176.8
1995	736.7	1 120.7	152.1	181.9
1996	755.8	1 157.7	153.1	188.4

Comparative rise in consumer prices (per cent per year, annual average)

	1959–87	1987–88	1988–89	1989–90	1990–91	1991–92	1995–96
USA	4.9	4.1	4.8	5.4	4.3	3.0	2.1
Japan	5.8	0.6	2.3	3.0	3.3	1.7	0.2
France	6.7	2.8	3.2	3.0	3.0	3.0	1.9
W Germany*	3.5	1.3	2.8	2.7	3.5	3.6	1.8
Italy	9.3	5.1	6.3	6.4	6.3	5.7	4.4
UK	7.7	4.9	7.8	9.5	5.8	3.7	2.9

*Germany after 1990.

4 INDUSTRY

Coal production, exports and imports, 1940–97 (million tonnes)

	Output	Exports	Imports
1940	224.3	8.8	n
1945	182.2	1.8	n
1950	216.3	6.2	n
1955	221.6	5.5	n
1960	193.6	2.6	n
1965	187.5	2.0	n
1970	133.4	1.0	n
1978	122.0	1.4	n
1988	103.8	1.8	12.0
1993	80.8	0.6	19.8
1997	47.0†	1.0	20.0

n = Negligible

†Opencast and deep-mined

Sources: B R Mitchell and H G Jones, *Second Abstract of British Historical Statistics* (Cambridge University Press, 1971) pp 66, 68; Central Office of Information, *Britain 1990* (London, HMSO, 1990) pp 303–5; *Britain, 1994* (London, HMSO, 1994) pp 217–18; *Britain 1999* (London, HMSO, 1998) p 496

Coal production, employment and collieries (selected years)

	1954/ 55	1967/ 68	1975/ 76	1976/ 77	1977/ 78	1985/ 86	1988/ 89	1992/ 93	1997/ 98
Output (million tonnes)	221.6	170.9	123.8	118.9	119.0	104.5	103.8	80.8	47.0 †
Labour force (000)	695.0	391.9	247.1	242.0	240.5	154.6	87.0	44.0	15.7
Number of collieries	850	376	241	238	231	133	86	50	53 ††

†Opencast and deep-mined

††Plus 79 opencast sites

Oil production, exports and imports, 1978–97 (million tonnes)

	Production	Exports	Imports
1978	53.9	2.8	113.3
1982	102.9	61.7	33.8
1986	126.5	82.1	32.6
1988	113.6	63.8	32.8
1990	91.3	57.0	52.7
1992	94.3	57.6	57.7
1997	120.1	79.0	50.0

Sources: Central Office of Information, *Britain 1990* (London, HMSO, 1990) p 229; *Britain 1994* (London, HMSO, 1994) p 213; *Britain 1999* (London, HMSO, 1998) p 492

Steel production, 1940–97 (million tonnes)

1940	12.0
1950	16.0
1960	24.0
1970	28.0
1980	11.3
1985	15.7
1990	16.7
1992	14.9
1997	18.5

Sources: B R Mitchell and P Deane, *Abstract of British Historical Statistics* (Cambridge University Press, 1962) pp 136–7; Central Office of Information, *Britain 1994* (London, HMSO, 1994) p 158; *Britain 1999* (London, HMSO, 1998) p 477

Motor vehicle production, 1938–97

1938	445 000
1948	500 000
1960	1 353 000
1965	1 722 000
1970	1 641 000
1975	1 648 000
1979	1 479 000
1985	1 311 000
1993	1 621 000
1997	1 700 000

Sources: *The Motor Industry of Great Britain*, annual reports; M Jenkins, *Daily Mail Year Book, 1981* (London, Harmsworth Publications, 1980) p 290; *Britain 1994* (London, HMSO, 1994); *Britain 1999* (London, HMSO, 1998) p 481

Manufacturing employment, 1979–98

1979	7 107 000
1981	6 099 000
1984	5 302 000
1987	5 049 000
1990	5 046 000
1992	4 521 000
1998	4 081 000

Source: HMSO, *Annual Abstract of Statistics, 1979–* (London, HMSO, 1979–)

5 EMPLOYMENT AND UNEMPLOYMENT

Employment, 1979–98 (million)

	Private sector	Self-employed	Public sector	Nationalized industries	Training
1979	17.9	1.9	7.5	1.9	–
1982	16.9	2.2	7.0	1.6	–
1985	17.8	2.6	6.6	1.1	0.2
1988	19.3	3.0	6.3	0.8	0.3
1990	20.9	3.3	6.0	0.7	0.4
1998	21.9	3.2	5.1	0.7	0.2

Source: *Economic Trends, Monthly Digest of Statistics* (London, HMSO, 1979–)

Registered unemployed people, 1937–98 (000)

Year		Year		Year	
1937	1 484	1957	312	1977	1 450
1938	1 791	1958	457	1978	1 381
1939	1 514	1959	475	1980	1 668
1940	963	1960	360	1982	2 809*
1941	350	1961	341	1985	3 149*
1942	123	1962	463	1986	3 289*
1943	82	1963	573	1987	2 953*
1944	75	1964	380	1988	2 370*
1945	137	1965	329	1989	1 798*
1946	374	1966	353	1990	1 664*
1947	480	1967	556	1991	2 291*
1948	310	1968	554	1992	2 607*
1949	308	1969	534	1993	2 992*
1950	314	1970	579	1994	2 790*
1951	253	1971	724	1995	n/a
1952	414	1972	899	1996	2 122*
1953	342	1973	575	1997	n/a
1954	285	1974	542	1998	1 820*
1955	232	1975	866		
1956	257	1976	1 322		

* Changes introduced in the method of recording unemployment statistics have removed significant numbers of people from unemployment totals.

Sources: B R Mitchell and P Deane, *Abstract of British Historical Statistics* (Cambridge University Press, 1962) p 66; B R Mitchell and H G Jones, *Second Abstract of British Historical Statistics* (Cambridge University Press, 1971) p 43; *Britain 1979* (London, HMSO, 1979) p 310; *Annual Abstract of Statistics* (London, HMSO, 1987) p 116; Central Statistical Office, *Key Data, 1992/3* (London, HMSO, 1993) p 17; *Pears Cyclopaedia 1998–1999* (London, Penguin, 1999)

6 TRANSPORT

Railway mileage, passengers and freight carried in the UK, 1940–97

	Railway track open (miles)	Passengers (million)	Freight (million tonnes)
1940	19 931	691.1	294.4
1945	19 863	1 055.7	266.4
1950	19 471	704.0	281.3
1955	19 061	730.2	274.2
1960	18 369	721.3	248.5
1965	14 920	580.5	228.5
1970	11 799	823.9	n/a
1977	11 169	702.0	156.0
1985	10 410	697.4	122.0
1993	10 300	745.0	32.0
1997	10 300	695.0	105.0

Sources: B R Mitchell and H G Jones, *Second Abstract of British Historical Statistics* (Cambridge University Press, 1971) p 104; *Britain 1994* (London, HMSO, 1994) p 253; *Britain 1999* (London, HMSO, 1998) p 369

Motor vehicles in use, 1939–97

	Private cars (000)	Goods vehicles (000)	All vehicles* (000)
1939	2 034	488	3 149
1945	1 487	473	2 553
1950	2 258	895	4 409
1955	3 526	1 109	6 465
1960	5 526	1 397	9 439
1965	8 917	1 602	12 940
1970	11 515	1 622	14 950
1978	14 069	2 216	17 654
1985	16 453	2 704	21 166
1992	20 700	2 637	24 800
1997	21 700	2 714	27 100

*'All vehicles' includes buses, trams, taxis and motor-cycles, as well as cars and goods vehicles.

Sources: B R Mitchell and P Deane, *Abstract of British Historical Statistics* (Cambridge University Press, 1962) p 230; B R Mitchell and H G Jones, *Second Abstract of British Historical Statistics* (Cambridge University Press, 1971) p 106; *Annual Abstract of Statistics* (London, HMSO, 1987) p 193; *Britain 1994* (London, HMSO, 1994); *Britain 1999* (London, HMSO, 1998) p 359

Air transport: passengers carried, 1938–97 (000)

1938	220[1]
1950	1 157[1]
1958	3 985[1]
1965	10 868[1]
1977	34 600
1988	71 400
1992	83 000
1997	132 200

[1] UK airlines only

Sources: B R Mitchell and H G Jones, *Second Abstract of British Historical Statistics* (Cambridge University Press, 1971) p 108; Central Statistical Office, *Key Data, 1992/3* (London, HMSO, 1993) p 55; *Pears Cyclopaedia 1998–1999* (London, Penguin, 1999)

Transport developments since 1945

1946 Civil Aviation Act reorganizes civil aviation into British Overseas Airways Corporation (BOAC), British European Airways (BEA) and British South American Airways (BSAA). Heathrow airport given to civil aviation authorities.

1947 Transport Act nationalizes railways, canals, docks, road haulage and London transport. British Transport Commission set up and six executive boards set up to administer different divisions.

1949 BSAA merged with BOAC.

1952 BOAC inaugurates first scheduled jet services with Comet aircraft. Development of Gatwick airport approved.

1953 Transport Act denationalizes road haulage.

1954 'Rationalization Plan' launched for railways, aiming to replace steam by diesel and electric power. £1,230 million allocated to electrification.

1958 Gatwick airport opened for full-scale air passenger traffic.

1959 Britain's first motorway, the M1, opened between London and Birmingham. British Rail plans for 230 stations to close.

1960 Dr Beeching appointed to study British Rail.

1963 'Beeching Plan' proposes huge cuts in railway services, mainly affecting branch lines.

1964 Mass closure of railway services adopted.

1966 British Airports Authority set up to run Heathrow, Gatwick, Stansted and Prestwick (Glasgow) airports. Breathalyser introduced to check alcohol levels in drivers.

1968 Manchester Ringway airport extended for international flights.

1969 Victoria underground line opened in London. New Heathrow terminal opened; Stansted opens first passenger terminal.

1971-2 Some of BOAC's routes allocated to British Caledonian.

1972 Road deaths reach highest post-war level at 7,700.

1974 Under the provisions of the Civil Aviation Act of 1971, BOAC and BEA merged to form British Airways.

1976 First scheduled flights by supersonic Concorde aircraft from Heathrow.

1981 British Rail announces work on new Advanced Passenger Train with a tilting mechanism which will permit higher speeds on existing track.

1985 500 millionth passenger travels through Heathrow.

1986 New Heathrow terminal opened.

1986-8 British Airways privatized by Thatcher government.

1987-9 British Airports Authority privatized.

1990 £110 million refurbishment of Heathrow Terminal Three completed. Advanced Passenger Train abandoned.

1991 New terminal opened at Stansted; second terminal opened at Birmingham; second runway authorized at Manchester.

1993 Building of Heathrow Express Link; second terminal opened at Manchester. Demonstrations against M3 extension at Twyford Down near Winchester. Protests also at M11 link road.

1994 Channel Tunnel opened. Government postpones inquiry into widening of M25 for a further year and cuts road programme for first time in ten years.

1995 Privatization of British Rail. Track and signalling to be run by Railtrack and services operated by franchises. Road deaths decline to 70-year low of 3,621.

1997 Election of Labour government with promise of 'new deal' for transport.

1998 Britain's first toll-motorway authorized, the North Birmingham link road. Virgin Trains announces major investment in West Coast route, utilizing Italian 'tilting train' technology.

1999 New extension to A30, Honiton to Exeter, opened in spite of earlier protests.

7 NATIONALIZATION AND PRIVATIZATION

Chronology of legislation and principal events

1946　Bank of England is taken into public ownership. Coal industry is nationalized by Coal Industry Nationalization Act 1946, which sets up National Coal Board. Civil aviation is reorganized by Civil Aviation Act 1946, covering British Overseas Airways Corporation (BOAC, set up in 1939), and two new corporations, British European Airways (BEA) and British South American Airways (BSAA).

1947　Electricity is fully nationalized by Electricity Act 1947, which sets up the British Electricity Authority.

1948　Railways, canals (and some other transport) are nationalized by Transport Act 1947. British Transport Commission is established and docks and inland waterways, hotels, railways, London transport, road haulage, and road passenger transport are to be administered by six executive boards. Gas is nationalized by Gas Act 1948, which establishes the Gas Council and twelve area gas boards.

1949　Iron and steel are nationalized by Iron and Steel Act 1949, which establishes Iron and Steel Corporation of Great Britain. The vesting date of the Act is 15 Feb. 1951. BSAA is merged with BOAC.

1953　Iron and Steel Act 1953 denationalizes the industry and sets up the Iron and Steel Board. Transport Act 1953 denationalizes road haulage industry.

1954　UK Atomic Energy Authority Act 1954 establishes UK Atomic Energy Authority.

1957　Electricity Act 1957 sets up Electricity Council and Central Electricity Generating Board; the twelve area boards remain financially autonomous.

1962　Transport Act 1962 reorganizes nationalized transport undertakings and provides for the establishment of separate boards for railways, London transport, docks and waterways, and for a Transport Holding Company, as successors to British Transport Commission.

1967　Iron and Steel Act 1967 renationalizes the industry as from 28 July.

1969　Post Office ceases to be a government department and becomes a public corporation.

1971–74 The Conservative government begins to 'hive off' some areas of nationalized industries.

1971 Rolls-Royce Ltd is established with government support following the company's bankruptcy.

1971–72 Some BOAC routes are allocated to British Caledonian.

1972 Gas Act 1972 establishes British Gas Corporation, replacing the Gas Council and twelve area boards.

1972–74 BOAC and BEA are merged to become British Airways (BA).

1973 Thomas Cook's travel agency and the Carlisle state breweries (which had been nationalized in 1916) are sold off to the private sector.

1975 British Leyland is established; the majority of the shares are acquired by the government. Industry Act 1975 establishes the National Enterprise Board (NEB).

1976 Petroleum and Submarine Pipelines Act 1975 establishes British National Oil Corporation. Rolls-Royce and British Leyland shares are vested in National Enterprise Board.

1977 Aircraft and Shipbuilding Act 1977 establishes British Aerospace and British Shipbuilders.

1979 Conservative government comes to power promising to privatize large segments of nationalized industry. Parts of BP, ICL and Suez Finance Co. are sold to private investors.

1980 Ferranti, Fairey, North Sea Oil Licences, British Aerospace, and smaller NEB holdings are sold.

1981 British Sugar, Cable and Wireless, Amersham International and the National Freight Consortium, and miscellaneous Crown Agent and Forestry holdings are to be sold.

1982 Parts of Britoil and Associated British Ports, BR Hotels, and more oil licences and stockpiles are sold.

1983 Further parts of Britoil, BP, and Cable and Wireless are sold.

1984–5 Enterprise Oil (British Gas's offshore oil assets), British Telecom, Royal Ordnance factories, Sealink, National Bus, Jaguar, Land Rover, Rolls-Royce, Unipart, British Nuclear Fuels, naval shipbuilding yards, and parts of British Steel and British Shipbuilders are to be sold.

1986–8 British Airways is sold.

1986 British Gas is sold.

1987–9 British Airorts Authority is sold.

1987 Rolls-Royce is sold; Royal Ordnance is sold.

1988 British Steel is sold; Rover Group is sold.

1989–92 Regional Water Authorities are sold.

1990 Regional Electricity Companies are sold; further sale of British Gas.

1991 Electricity Generating Companies are sold; further sale of British Telecommunications.

1993 Government seeks private bids for collieries to be closed under Coal Board closure plans.

1994 Government canvasses schemes for privatization of Royal Mail, but withdraws plan following back-bench pressure. Privatization of coal takes place (Dec.).

1995 Government White Paper proposes partial privatization of nuclear power industry.

1996 Labour party annual conference rejects a motion calling for the renationalization of the privatized utilities.

1997 Chancellor Brown announces the proposed privatization of the Tote, the Royal Mint, London Transport, the Commonwealth Development Corporation and air traffic control (June). Deputy Prime Minister Prescott persuades the Labour party annual conference not to demand the renationalization of the railways (Oct.).

1999 Labour government extends commercial freedom of the Post Office, ending speculation about possible full privatization, first raised under Mrs Thatcher. Plans announced for privatization of air traffic control.

Proceeds of privatization (£ million)

BP (1979–90)	5 273
National Freight Corporation (1981)	54
British Aerospace (1981, 1985)	390
Cable and Wireless (1981, 1983, 1985)	1 021
Amersham International (1982)	62
Britoil (1982, 1985)	962
British Ports (1983–85)	97
British Telecommunications (1984, 1991, 1993)	17 604
Jaguar (1984)	297
Enterprise Oil (1984)	382
Wytch Farm (1984)	149
British Airways (1986–88)	854
British Gas (1986, 1990)	7 793
British Airports Authority (1987–89)	1 332
Rolls-Royce (1987)	1 031
Royal Ordnance (1987)	186
British Steel (1988)	2 425
Rover Group (1988)	150
Regional Water Authorities (1989–92)	3 468
Regional Electricity Companies (1990)	7 997
Electricity Generating Companies (1991)	2 969

THE WIDER WORLD

1 THE EUROPEAN UNION

Chronology of principal events

1946

19 Sept.   Winston Churchill, in a speech at Zurich, urges Franco-German reconciliation with 'a kind of United States of Europe'.

1947

5 June   General Marshall proposes US aid to stimulate recovery in Europe.

29 Oct.   Creation of Benelux – economic union of Belgium, Luxembourg and the Netherlands.

1948

16 Apr.   Convention for European Economic Cooperation signed – the birth of OEEC.

1949

5 May   Statute of the Council of Europe signed by Belgium, Denmark, France, Ireland, Italy, Luxembourg, the Netherlands, Norway, Sweden and the United Kingdom.

1950

9 May   Robert Schuman makes his historic proposal to place French and German coal and steel under a common authority.

1951

18 Apr.   Treaty setting up the European Coal and Steel Community (ECSC) is signed in Paris by Belgium, France, Germany (Federal Republic of), Luxembourg, Italy and the Netherlands.

1953

10 Feb.   ECSC common market for coal, iron ore, and scrap is opened.

1 May   ECSC common market for steel is opened.

1955

1–3 June   Messina Conference: the Foreign Ministers of the ECSC's six member states propose further steps towards full integration in Europe.

1957

25 Mar.   Signing of the Rome Treaties setting up the European Economic Community (EEC) and the European Atomic Energy Community (Euratom). The Treaty of Rome was signed by Belgium, France, Germany (Federal Republic of), Luxembourg, Italy and the Netherlands.

1958

1 Jan.   Rome Treaties come into force: the EEC and Euratom are established.

19–21 Mar. First session of the European Parliament – Robert Schuman elected President.

1959

1 Jan.   First tariff reductions and quota enlargements in the EEC. Establishment of common market for nuclear materials.

20 Nov.   European Free Trade Association (EFTA) convention signed between Austria, Denmark, Norway, Portugal, Sweden, Switzerland and the UK.

1961

9 July   Greece signs association agreement with EEC (comes into force 1 Nov. 1962).

1 Aug.   Republic of Ireland applies for membership of EEC.

10 Aug.   UK and Denmark request negotiations aiming at membership of EEC.

8 Nov.   Negotiations with the UK open in Brussels.

15 Dec.   The three neutral countries (outside the NATO alliance) – Austria, Sweden and Switzerland – apply for association with EEC.

1962

30 Apr.   Norway requests negotiations for membership of EEC.

1963

14 Jan.   President de Gaulle declares that the UK is not ready for membership of EEC.

29 Jan.   UK negotiations with the EEC broken off.

1 July   Yaounde Convention is signed, associating eighteen independent states in Africa and Madagascar with the EEC for five years from 1 June 1964.

12 Sept.   Turkey signs association agreement with EEC (comes into force 1 Dec. 1964).

1964

15 Dec.   EEC adopts the Mansholt Plan for common prices for grains.

1965

31 Mar.   European Commission proposes that, as from 1 July 1967, all EEC countries' import duties and levies be paid into Community budget and that powers of European Parliament be increased.

8 Apr.   Six sign treaty merging the Community Executives.

31 May   European Commission publishes first memorandum proposing lines of Community policy for regional development.

1 July   Council fails to reach agreement by agreed deadline on financing common farm policy; French boycott of Community institutions begins seven-month crisis.

26 July   Council meets and conducts business without French representative present.

1966

17 Jan.   Six Foreign Ministers meet in Luxembourg without Commission present and agree to resume full Community activity.

10 Nov.   UK Prime Minister Harold Wilson announces plans for 'a high-level approach' to the Six with intention of entering EEC.

1967

11 May   United Kingdom lodges formal application for membership of the European Economic Community.

1968

16 May   Second de Gaulle veto on British application.

1969

25 Apr.   General de Gaulle resigns as President of France.

2 Dec.   At a Summit Conference at The Hague the Community formally agrees to open membership negotiations with the UK, Norway, Denmark and the Republic of Ireland on their applications of 1967.

1970

29 June   Talks begin in Luxembourg between the Six and the UK, Norway, Denmark and the Republic of Ireland.

1971

23 June   The Council of Ministers of the Community announces that agreement has been reached with the United Kingdom for the basis of the accession of the UK to the Communities.

11–13 July   At a ministerial-level negotiating session, agreement is reached on major outstanding issues: the transitional period for the UK, Commonwealth sugar, capital movements, and the common commercial policy.

28 Oct.   Vote in the House of Commons on the motion 'That this House approves Her Majesty's Government's decision of principle to join the European Communities on the basis of the arrangements which have been negotiated'. The voting figures in the House of Commons were 356 for, 244 against, majority of 112; in the House of Lords 451 for, 58 against, majority of 393.

1972

22 Jan.   Treaty of Accession was signed in Brussels between the European Communities (France, Belgium, Germany, Italy, Luxembourg and the Netherlands) on the one side and the United Kingdom, Denmark, Norway and the Republic of Ireland on the other.

22 July   EEC signs free trade agreements with Austria, Iceland, Portugal, Sweden and Switzerland.

26 Sept.   Rejection by Norway of full membership of EEC following a referendum.

31 Dec.   UK and Denmark withdraw from EFTA.

1973

1 Jan   UK, Republic of Ireland and Denmark join the EEC.

1974   Agreement that heads of government should meet three times a year under the title of the European Council.

1975   UK confirms membership of the EEC by referendum (see p 70). Greece applies for membership.

June   European Regional Development Fund set up.

1977   Portugal and Spain apply for membership of the EEC. Roy Jenkins appointed President of the Commission.

1979

May   European Monetary System introduced with a common European Currency Unit (ECU) linking the exchange rates of individual countries.

June   First direct elections held to the European Parliament, when 410 members (MEPs) are elected.

1980   'Crocodile Group' established by MEPs wishing to see radical reform of the Community.

1981

Jan.   Greece becomes tenth member of the EEC: entry to be phased over five years.

1983

June   Agreement at Stuttgart Summit on principle of budgetary reform and reform of Common Agricultural Policy (CAP); Common Fisheries Policy established.

1984

June   Fontainebleau Summit agrees principles of budgetary discipline and UK budget rebate.

1985   Spain and Portugal sign accession treaty to join the EC from 1 Jan. 1986. At summit meeting in Luxembourg heads of state draw up main principles of a 'single Europe' defining 1992 as date for completion of frontierless internal market within the EC with open frontiers, harmonization of regulations, free movement of labour and capital. These principles are contained in the Single European Act which also extends majority voting in the Council of Ministers.

1986

Feb.   Single European Act signed by member states and ratified by their parliaments. European flag adopted.

1988

Feb.   Delors reforms of the European budget agreed, putting controls on farm spending and expanding structural funds. Committee set up under Delors to prepare plans for European Monetary Union (EMU).

Sept.   Mrs Thatcher makes Bruges speech attacking attempts to create a European 'superstate'.

1989

June   Third direct elections to European Parliament. Madrid Summit receives three-stage Delors Plan for European Monetary Union.

Apr.   Agreement reached that first stage of EMU would begin on 1 July 1990 with all twelve members beginning to adhere to the EMS. Austria applies to join EEC.

1990

Oct.   Britain joins EMS.

Dec.	Inter-governmental Conference on EMU plans further development of EMU.

1991

Oct.	Luxembourg plan for inter-governmental conference at Maastricht turned down.
Dec.	Maastricht Summit gives Britain opt-out clauses over monetary union and social chapter.

1992 Several currencies (including sterling) forced to suspend membership of EMS following speculation. Conservative rebels stage first Maastricht rebellion (Nov.).

1993 British Parliament eventually passes Maastricht Bill (receives Royal Assent, July).

1994

Jan.	European Union comes into force.
Nov.	Conservative whip withdrawn from eight Euro rebels.

1995 Madrid summit confirms 1999 as the start of final move to monetary union and single currency.

1996

Mar.	Turin Summit begins inter-governmental conference to review Maastricht Treaty.
Apr.	Sir James Goldsmith announces he will run Referendum party candidates in forthcoming general election.
Nov.	Blair promises a future Labour government will hold referendum on a single currency.

1997

Oct.	Treaty of Amsterdam (new successor Union Treaty to Maastricht).
Nov.	EU Special Summit in Luxembourg to tackle unemployment.
Dec.	Luxembourg Summit decides on candidates for possible admission from Eastern Europe.

1998

Jan.	British EU presidency. EU begins ratification of Amsterdam Treaty.
May	Brussels Summit confirms founding members of single currency.

1999

Jan.	EMU formally launched (the euro is born).
May	Resignation of entire EU commission; Prodi eventually named as successor to Santer.

June   Elections to EU marked by widespread apathy and swing to the right (see p 70 for results in UK).

July   Santer finally leaves EU presidency. Fall of euro causes concern as it nears parity with the dollar. Chris Patten becomes new EU Commissioner.

2000

Feb.   Blair attacks 'opt-out mentality' in speech at Ghent.

Presidents of the European Commission

1958–66	Walter Hallstein (Federal Republic of Germany)
1966–70	Jean Rey (Belgium)
1970–72	Franco Malfatti (Italy)
1972–73	Sicco Mansholt (Netherlands)
1973–77	Francois-Xavier Ortoli (France)
1977–81	Roy Jenkins (UK)
1981–85	Gaston Thorn (Luxembourg)
1985–95	Jacques Delors (France)
1995–99	Jacques Santer (Luxembourg)
1999–	Romano Prodi (Italy)

Membership of the European Union, January 2000

Country	Date of Joining	Country	Date of Joining
Austria	Jan. 1995	Italy	1957
Belgium	1957	Luxembourg	1957
Denmark	Jan. 1973	Netherlands	1957
Finland	Jan. 1995	Portugal	Jan. 1986
France	1957	Spain	Jan. 1986
Germany*	1957	Sweden	Jan. 1995
Greece	Jan. 1981	United Kingdom	Jan. 1973
Ireland	Jan. 1973		

*As the Federal Republic of Germany (i.e. West Germany)

2 THE COMMONWEALTH

Chronology of principal events

1942 Cripps mission to India offers dominion status after the war; rejected by Indian nationalists. Japanese capture Singapore – a major blow to Britain's imperial prestige in Asia.

1946 North Borneo becomes a colony. Sarawak ceded. Full independence granted to Transjordan.

1947 Independence granted to India and Pakistan (the latter in Muslim majority areas).

1948 Ceylon and Burma become independent. State of Israel formed. Beginning of a conflict with communist guerrillas in Malaya.

1949 Eire withdraws from the Commonwealth and becomes Republic of Ireland.

1950 India becomes the first republic to belong to the Commonwealth.

1952 Beginning of Mau Mau rebellion in Kenya.

1953 Southern Rhodesia, Nyasaland and Northern Rhodesia are united in the Federation of Rhodesia and Nyasaland.

1956 Suez expedition. Mau Mau rebellion in Kenya suppressed.

1957 Ghana and the Malay states gain independence.

1958 West Indies Federation formed.

1960 Harold Macmillan's 'wind of change' speech presages African decolonization. Cyprus, Nigeria and British Somaliland gain independence.

1961 South Africa withdraws from the Commonwealth. Tanganyika, Sierra Leone and British Cameroons gain independence.

1962 West Indies Federation breaks up when Jamaica and Trinidad and Tobago become independent. Western Samoa and Uganda gain independence.

1963 Zanzibar and Kenya gain independence.

1964 Commonwealth Secretariat established. Malta gains independence. The Federation of Rhodesia and Nyasaland is dissolved; Nyasaland becomes the independent state of Malawi; Northern Rhodesia becomes Zambia.

1965 Southern Rhodesia unilaterally proclaims independence. Gambia becomes independent.

1966   Basutoland (Lesotho), Bechuanaland (Botswana), British Guiana (Guyana) and Barbados become independent.

1967   Aden gains independence.

1968   Mauritius and Swaziland gain independence.

1970   Fiji and Tonga gain independence.

1972   East Pakistan gains independence from Pakistan as Bangladesh.

1973   Bahamas gain independence.

1974   Grenada becomes independent.

1975   Papua New Guinea gains independence.

1976   Seychelles become independent.

1978   Dominica becomes independent.

1979   Rhodesian settlement reached; Britain and Patriotic Front conclude a ceasefire agreement; Kiribati (formerly known as the Gilbert Islands) becomes independent.

1980   Elections in Rhodesia, under supervision of monitoring force. Zimbabwe independent (Apr.). New Hebrides becomes independent state of Vanuatu (July).

1981   Belize becomes an independent republic.

1982   Argentine troops invade Falkland Islands and South Georgia (Apr.). British task force sent to recapture the islands (May–June) forces Argentine surrender. Maldive Islands gain independence.

1984   Brunei becomes independent. Sino-British agreement signed on the future of Hong Kong, guaranteeing its future as a capitalist system after its reversion to Chinese rule in 1997.

1985   Britain isolated among Commonwealth leaders over further sanctions against South Africa.

1987   Fiji leaves Commonwealth as a result of military coup.

1990   Independence of Namibia (formerly South-West Africa) recognized. Namibia becomes 50th member of the Commonwealth.

1994   After historic multiracial elections, South Africa rejoins Commonwealth.

1995   Mozambique (a former Portuguese colony, independent since 1975) joins Commonwealth. The first territory never part of the British Empire to join the Commonwealth. Cameroon also joins Commonwealth.

1997   Return of Hong Kong to China (1 July).

1998   Dependent Territories of Britain renamed United Kingdom Overseas Territories.

1999   Return of Nigeria to Commonwealth after period of suspension (29 May). Pakistan suspended after military coup (Oct.).

Major new nations of the Commonwealth

Bangladesh prior to 1947 part of British Indian Empire; 1947–71 known as East Pakistan.

Belize British Honduras until 1973, independent in 1981.

Botswana British Bechuanaland until 1966.

Brunei former British Protectorate in British Borneo.

Gambia formerly British Gambia, temporarily part of Confederation of Senegambia (with Senegal).

Ghana formerly British Gold Coast, including British Togoland, formerly German Togoland (to 1922).

Grenada formerly part of British Windward Islands.

Guyana formerly British Guiana.

India formerly part of the British Indian Empire, then including present-day Pakistan and Bangladesh.

Jamaica British colony of Jamaica until 1962.

Kenya formerly British colony of Kenya (to 1963), known as British East Africa prior to 1920.

Lesotho British protectorate of Basutoland until 1966.

Malawi formerly part of Federation of Rhodesia and Nyasaland (1953–64), previously British protectorate of Nyasaland.

Malaysia formerly the Federation of Malaya (to 1963) previously known as the Straits Settlements and the Federated Malay States.

Mozambique formerly Portuguese Mozambique. Independent after long independence struggle, 1975. Joined Commonwealth (1995) although never part of British Empire.

Namibia formerly South West Africa (to 1990), prior to 1920 German South-West Africa.

Nigeria formerly British protectorates of Northern and Southern Nigeria.

Pakistan prior to 1947 part of British Indian Empire.

Papua New Guinea formerly (1920–45) Australian mandated territory, thereafter Australian-governed to 1975. Prior to 1920 the area comprised German New Guinea and Australian-run Papua.

Sierra Leone British Sierra Leone until 1961.

Singapore British Crown Colony, then part of Malaysia 1963–65.

Sri Lanka British colony of Ceylon to independence in 1948; in 1972 changed name to Sri Lanka.

Tanzania formerly German East Africa (to 1918), then League of Nations mandated territory of Tanganyika under British control. Following independence in 1961, it joined with Zanzibar (independent in 1963) in 1964 to form Tanzania.

Trinidad and Tobago British colony of Trinidad and Tobago until 1962.

Uganda British protectorate until independence in 1962.

Zambia formerly known as Northern Rhodesia and a British protectorate; in 1953 combined with Southern Rhodesia and Nyasaland in a Federation, dissolved in 1963, becoming independent Republic of Zambia in 1964.

Zimbabwe formerly known as British Southern Rhodesia; in 1953 combined with Northern Rhodesia and Nyasaland in a Federation, dissolved in 1963, becoming British colony of Rhodesia. It declared independence in 1965 as Rhodesia, but following the war and agreement of 1979 became Zimbabwe.

Secretaries General of the Commonwealth

Arnold Smith (Canada)	1965–75
Sir Shridath S Ramphal (Guyana)	1975–89
Chief Emeka Anyaoku (Nigeria)	1989–

3 DEFENCE POLICY

Chronology of legislation and principal events

1945   Ministry of Defence created.

1947   National Service Act provides for continuation of compulsory military service; at first for twelve months; extended to two years in 1950. British withdrawal from India and Pakistan (Aug.).

1948   Britain signs Brussels Treaty with France and Benelux countries, committing itself to military assistance in the event of an attack on Europe; confirmed in North Atlantic Treaty Organization (NATO) Treaty of 1949. British Army of the Rhine (BAOR) henceforth to be part of the NATO forces in Germany. Independence of Burma (Jan.). British withdrawal from Palestine (May). State of emergency in Malaya. Commonwealth forces suppress communist insurgency, and state of emergency is ended July 1960.

1949   North Atlantic Treaty signed (4 Apr.) in Washington by Belgium, Canada, Denmark, France, Iceland, Italy, Luxembourg, the Netherlands, Norway, Portugal, the UK and the USA to provide for the collective defence and security of the western world. The treaty comes into force on 24 Aug. 1949. Greece and Turkey join 18 Feb. 1952, and the German Federal Republic on 5 May 1955.

1950   Outbreak of Korean war (June): forces from the UK, Canada, Australia, New Zealand and South Africa sent to support United Nations operations.

1951   Pacific security agreement signed by Australia, New Zealand and USA (ANZUS Pact) (Sept.).

1952   Britain tests its first atomic bomb (3 Oct.). State of emergency in Kenya: violence by Mau Mau suppressed, and state of emergency ended Jan. 1960.

1953   British forces intervene to overthrow government of British Guiana.

1954   Agreements reached on Indo-China at Geneva conference chaired jointly by Britain and the USSR (July). South-East Asia Defence Treaty signed in Manila by Britain, USA, Australia, New Zealand, France, Pakistan and the Philippines (Sept.).

1955   Britain signs the Baghdad Pact with Turkey and Iraq (Apr.): Pakistan and Iran joins in Sept. and Nov. Naval cooperation agreement between Britain and South Africa. Simonstown base is transferred to South African control, but the Royal Navy can continue to enjoy its facilities; the British and South African navies will work under the Royal Navy Commander-in-Chief South Atlantic (July).

1956 Suez crisis: Britain and France attack Egypt after the nationalization of the Suez Canal and Israel's invasion of Sinai (Oct.). Ceasefire call by the UN leads to an end of hostilities (6–7 Nov.).

1957 Agreement between Britain and the Maldive Islands on establishment of airfield on island of Gan (Jan.). Sultan of Muscat and Oman requests British aid after his forces are defeated by rebels (July). RAF begins operations, and involvement of land forces (6 Aug.) leads to collapse of the rebellion. First British hydrogen bomb is exploded near Christmas Island (Aug.). Independence of Malaya (Aug.): Britain commits itself to the defence of Malaya by a treaty (signed 12 Oct.). Trincomalee naval base and Katunayake air force station transferred to Ceylon (Oct.–Nov.). Decision announced to station an element of the strategic reserve in Kenya, available as reinforcement for either the Arabian peninsula or the Far East (Nov.). Defence White Paper envisages reduction in conventional armed forces and greater reliance upon nuclear deterrence and a strategic reserve stationed in the United Kingdom. Followed by large-scale amalgamation of existing regiments 1958–61.

1958 The first meeting of Campaign for Nuclear Disarmament (CND) is held in London (Feb.). British paratroopers sent to Jordan at the request of King Hussein (July).

1959 Singapore becomes a self-governing state within the Commonwealth (June).

1960 National Service abolished. Decision announced to move amphibious warfare squadron to Aden (Mar.).

1961 Ruler of newly independent Kuwait asks for British assistance in case of an Iraqi attack (June); the crisis passes and British troops are withdrawn (Sept.).

1962 After communist successes in Laos, SEATO (South East Asia Treaty Organization) (qv) forces from USA, Britain, Australia, New Zealand and the Philippines are sent to the support of Thailand (May). Agreement reached on Laos at Geneva Conference chaired jointly by Britain and the USSR (July). Brunei oil town, Seria, occupied by rebels (Dec.); the rebellion collapses after intervention by British troops. US President John F. Kennedy meets British Prime Minister Harold Macmillan at Nassau in the Bahamas and agrees to make US Polaris missiles available to Britain for use with British warheads.

1963 War Office, Admiralty and Air Ministry brought under the control of the Ministry of Defence. Defence Council set up under the secretary of state to exercise the powers previously wielded by each service. Federation of Malaysia established (Sept.): Commonwealth forces support Malaysia against Indonesian policy of 'confrontation' until June 1966.

1964 British troops called in by governments of Tanganyika, Uganda and Kenya to suppress army mutinies (Jan.). Last British troops leave Kenya (Dec.).

1965 Singapore separates from Malaysia (Aug.). Removal of population from Diego Garcia in Indian Ocean to prepare for military base.

1966 Defence review undertaken by Labour government states that Britain will not carry out major operations of war outside Europe without the cooperation of allies, or incur defence obligations unless the country in question is prepared to provide appropriate facilities; no defence facilities will be maintained in an independent country against its wishes. The base of Aden is to be abandoned by the end of 1968, but there is to be a small increase in forces in the Persian Gulf. The base at Singapore is to be retained as long as possible, and there are to be discussions about defence facilities in Australia. Britain's carrier force is to be phased out in the 1970s. At home, the Territorial Army (TA) is to be greatly reduced and replaced by a smaller Territorial and Army Volunteer Reserve (TAVR). In 1967 there are further amalgamations of regiments and brigades.

1967 Last British troops leave Borneo (Jan.); one battalion remains in Brunei. Negotiations between Britain and the Republic of South Africa result in a new agreement on the Simonstown base (Jan.). Britain withdraws the Commander-in-Chief South Atlantic and its remaining frigate from Simonstown, and defence of the Cape route becomes primarily the responsibility of the Republic of South Africa (Jan.). Agreement between Britain and USA on joint use of British Indian Ocean Territory for defence purposes (Apr.). British Supplementary Defence White Paper: British troops are to be withdrawn from South Arabia and Aden by Jan. 1968, though naval and air forces are to remain in the area. Further cuts in Malaysia and Singapore are to lead to complete withdrawal by the mid-1970s (July). British withdrawal from Aden completed (Nov.).

1968 New cuts in British defence expenditure announced: all British bases outside Europe and the Mediterranean, except Hong Kong, are to close by 1971. Britain is to remain a member of SEATO, but cease to commit forces to any SEATO plans, and negotiations would take place regarding Britain's defence responsibilities towards Malaysia and Singapore. Britain's Far East amphibious force is to be transferred to the Mediterranean. In the Persian Gulf the bases of Bahrain and Sharjah are to be given up, and defence agreements with the Persian Gulf and the adjacent sheikhdoms (the Trucial States under British protection) would be renegotiated (Jan.). Exchange of notes ending Anglo-Kuwaiti defence pact (Apr.). Conference at Kuala Lumpur between Britain, Australia, New

Zealand, Malaysia and Singapore agrees to set up an integrated air defence system covering Malaysia and Singapore. Britain announces that it will continue to train and exercise forces in the area after 1971 (June).

1969 A joint programme for the defence of Malaysia and Singapore is outlined at talks in Canberra between Britain, Australia, New Zealand, Malaysia and Singapore. An Australian is given command of the group's integrated air force, and joint naval exercises are held in local waters (June).

1970 At the SEATO ministerial meeting in Manila, Britain's new Conservative government announces that it will consult its Commonwealth partners about maintaining a force in Malaysia and Singapore after 1971 (July). In a supplementary statement on defence policy the British government outlines proposals for a continuing British presence 'East of Suez', including plans to contribute to Commonwealth defence arrangements for Malaysia and Singapore, and to continue discussions with local leaders in the Gulf about a British presence there (Oct.). Agreement between Britain and USA to begin building a naval communications station on Indian Ocean island of Diego Garcia (Dec.).

1971 Talks in Singapore between Britain, Australia, New Zealand, Malaysia and Singapore reach agreement on new five-power arrangements for the defence of Malaysia and Singapore (Jan.). Australia, New Zealand and Britain (ANZUK) are to maintain land and naval forces in Singapore, and Australia will also station air forces in Malaysia and Singapore; the ANZUK forces take over on 1 Nov. At five-power talks in London on the defence of Malaysia and Singapore it is agreed to set up a joint council for regular consultation (Apr.). Integrated air defence system under five-power agreement inaugurated at Butterworth, Malaysia (Sept.). Britain and Brunei sign a new defence agreement by which Britain will no longer assist in the event of internal, as opposed to external, aggression (Nov.). British forces leave the Persian Gulf, except for small rear parties (Dec.).

1973 Australia withdraws most of its land forces from the ANZUK force, but leaves its air forces as part of the integrated air defence system (Dec.).

1974 New cuts in British defence expenditure are announced (Dec.).

1975 Simonstown agreement between Britain and Republic of South Africa ends (June). SEATO Council agrees to disband the organization, but retain the treaty (Sept.).

1976 Britain withdraws its forces from Singapore, except for a small contribution to the integrated air defence system; New Zealand troops remain, along with Australian air forces in Malaysia (Mar.).

1982   Argentine invasion of Falkland Islands/Malvinas (Mar.). Dispatch of British task-force to reconquer islands (Apr.). Reconquest completed June (see p 211). Conservative government decides to replace Polaris submarines with new fleet of Trident II submarines (Mar.).

1983   First Cruise missiles arrive at Greenham Common (Nov.).

1989   Cruise missiles removed from Greenham Common (Aug.).

1990   Invasion of Kuwait by Iraq (Aug.). British forces join Allies to eject Iraqi invaders (see p 212).

1991   'Options for Change' programme of reducing and restructuring armed forces (modified in 1993).

1993   British troops sent to Bosnia as part of peacekeeping force in former Yugoslavia. First Trident submarine, HMS *Vanguard*, launched.

1994   British Army of the Rhine (BAOR) renamed United Kingdom Support Command – a 25,000-strong force to serve as a multinational rapid reaction force.

1995   Biggest reorganization of the British army since 1945 brings nearly 140,000 regular and part-time soldiers under a single Land Command based at Erskine barracks, Witton, Salisbury. Its commander is General Sir John Wilsey.

1998   Government defence review (July). Renewed crisis around Drumcree. Anglo-French Defence agreement at St Malo Summit (Dec.).

1999   British forces sent to Balkans during Kosovo crisis (see p 212). Defence Secretary George Robertson confirmed as next NATO Secretary General (Aug.).

Armed forces: personnel

	Royal Navy	Army	Royal Air Force
1945	852 600	3 007 300	1 124 400
1950	140 000	377 600	202 000
1960	97 800	264 300	163 500
1970	87 000	173 000	113 000
1979	72 900	163 681	90 000
1990	63 000	153 000	90 000
1997 (Apr.)	46 000	110 000	57 000

Armed forces: total expenditure (in £ million)

1950	740.7
1960	1 475.7
1970	2 266.0
1980	9 178.0
1990	20 755.0
1997	22 345.0

British defence reductions in the 1990s

	1990	1997
Army manpower	152 800	109 500
Navy	63 214	45 506
RAF	89 685	60 302
Armoured regiments	18	11
Infantry battalions	55	40
Destroyers/frigates	47	35
Nuclear submarines	22	16
Tornado air defence	128	100
Tornado ground attack	148	112

Defence spending (as % of GDP), 1990

Greece	5.6	Germany	2.9
US	5.5	Netherlands	2.7
Turkey	4.5	Belgium	2.5
UK	4.0	Italy	2.3
France	3.6	Spain	2.0
Norway	3.3	Denmark	2.0
Portugal	3.0	Canada	2.0

The British nuclear deterrent

1952   Britain tests first atomic bomb (3 Oct.).

1955   First V-bombers (delta-winged Vulcan strategic bombers armed with free-fall nuclear bombs).

1960   Planned Blue Streak missile (to replace V-bombers) dropped in favour of US submarine-launched Polaris missile.

1963   Macmillan and Kennedy agree Polaris deal.

1968   First Polaris submarine, HMS *Resolution*, goes on patrol.

1969   Ending of nuclear role of V-bombers.

1975   Labour secretly decides to fit Polaris missile with new Chevaline multiple warhead system.

1981   Thatcher government's decision to replace Polaris with US Trident missile (each armed with a maximum of eight warheads).

1994   First Trident submarine, HMS *Vanguard*, goes on patrol.

1996   Last Polaris submarine still in service, HMS *Repulse*, returns from final patrol.

1998   Launch of fourth (and final) Trident submarine, HMS *Vengeance* (all four Trident submarines to be operational in year 2000).

4 MAJOR CONFLICTS

Palestine 1945–48

A period of guerrilla warfare by Jewish Zionists against British mandate forces and the Arab population, to achieve an independent Jewish nation. On 22 July 1946 the King David Hotel in Jerusalem, housing the British headquarters, was blown up, with the loss of 91 lives. With the proclamation of the independence of Israel on 14 May 1948, Britain surrendered its League of Nations mandate over Palestine and withdrew its armed forces.

Malayan emergency 1948–60

The Federation of Malaya was proclaimed on 1 Feb. 1948. Communist guerrilla activity began, and on 16 June a State of Emergency was declared. In April 1950 General Sir Harold Briggs was appointed to coordinate anticommunist operations by Commonwealth forces. He inaugurated the Briggs Plan for resettling Chinese squatters in new villages to cut them off from the guerrillas. After the murder of the British High Commissioner, Sir Henry Gurney, on 6 Oct. 1951, General Sir Gerald Templer was appointed High Commissioner and director of military operations on 15 Jan. 1952; on 7 Feb. a new offensive was launched. On 8 Feb. 1954 British authorities announced that the Communist party's High Command in Malaya had withdrawn to Sumatra. The emergency was officially ended on 31 July 1960.

Berlin Blockade 1948–49

From July 1948 to May 1949 a major confrontation (the first real test of the west's determination in the Cold War) developed over Berlin between Russia and the western allies. Following the defeat of Germany, Berlin was divided into sectors under four-power control (as was the rest of Germany). Alleging that the west had not fulfilled its commitments on the status of Germany, the USSR attempted to force Britain, France and the United States out of their sectors of Berlin by blocking road and water transport into the city. A massive and continuous airlift was mounted to supply essential provisions to the city and eventually the Russians conceded that their tactics had failed.

Korean War 1950–53

North Korean troops invaded the South on 25 June 1950. The United Nations decided to intervene following an emergency session of its Security Council, which was being boycotted by the Soviet Union. The first US troops landed at Pusan airport on 1 July 1950. General MacArthur mounted an amphibious landing at Inchon on 15 Sept. 1950, and Seoul was recaptured on 26 Sept. The advance of the UN forces into North Korea on 1 Oct. 1950 led to the entry of China into the war on 25 Nov. 1950. Seoul fell to the Chinese on 4 Jan. 1951, but was retaken by UN forces on 14 Mar. 1951. General MacArthur was relieved of his command on 11 Apr. 1951 after expressing his desire to expand the war into China. Truce talks began on 10 July 1951, and an armistice was finally signed at Panmunjon on 27 July 1953. Casualties suffered by the British contribution to the UN force were 686 killed, 2,498 wounded and 1,102 missing.

Cyprus emergency 1952–59

Agitation for union with Greece ('enosis') by the Greek population of Cyprus led to terrorism and guerrilla warfare against British forces and the Turkish minority by EOKA, the militant wing of the enosis movement. It was led by Colonel Grivas, and supported by Archbishop Makarios, who was deported to the Seychelles in March 1956. A ceasefire came into effect on 13 Mar. 1959, prior to the establishment of the independent republic of Cyprus on 16 Aug. 1960.

Mau Mau revolt 1952–60

Violence by the Mau Mau, an African secret society in Kenya, led to a British declaration of a State of Emergency on 20 Oct. 1952. Leading Kikuyu nationalists were arrested and Jomo Kenyatta was given a seven-year prison sentence in Oct. 1953. A separate East African command consisting of Kenya, Uganda and Tanganyika was set up under General Sir George Erskine. In campaigns in the first half of 1955 some 4,000 terrorists in the Mount Kenya and Aberdare regions were dispersed. Britain began to reduce its forces in Sept. 1955; the State of Emergency in Kenya ended on 12 Jan. 1960.

Suez crisis 1956

Following Egyptian nationalization of the Suez Canal on 26 July 1956, Israel invaded Sinai on 29 Oct. When Egypt rejected a ceasefire ultimatum by France and Britain, French and British air forces began to attack Egyptian air bases on 31 Oct. On 5 Nov. Franco-British forces invaded the Canal Zone, capturing Port Said. Hostilities ended at midnight on 6–7 Nov., following a ceasefire call by the United Nations. Allied losses were 33 killed and 129 wounded.

Indonesia and Malaysia confrontation 1963–66

When the Federation of Malaysia was established on 16 Sept. 1963, President Sukarno of Indonesia announced a policy of 'confrontation', on the grounds that it was 'neo-colonialist'. There followed a campaign of propaganda, sabotage and guerrilla raids into Sarawak and Sabah. An agreement ending 'confrontation' was signed in Bangkok on 1 June 1966 (ratified 11 Aug.). In the conflict Commonwealth forces lost 114 killed and 181 wounded, and the Indonesians 590 killed, 222 wounded and 771 captured.

Aden 1964–67

On 18 Jan. 1963 Aden acceded to the South Arabian Federation. British troops were involved in frontier fighting with the Yemen, and in suppressing internal disorders in Aden. A large-scale security operation was launched in Jan. 1964 in the Radfan region, north of Aden. On 26 Nov. 1967 the People's Republic of South Yemen was proclaimed, and the British military withdrawal from Aden was completed on 29 Nov. In the period 1964–67 British security forces lost 57 killed and 651 wounded in Aden.

Northern Ireland civil insurgency 1969–94

In 1968 long-standing sectarian animosity between the Catholic and Protestant communities in Northern Ireland degenerated into violent conflict, sparked by the campaign for Catholic civil rights. British troops were deployed in Londonderry on 14 Aug. 1969 and Belfast on 15 Aug. at the request of the government of Northern Ireland. The first British soldier to be killed was shot by an Irish Republican Army (IRA) sniper in Belfast on 6 Feb. 1971. Internment without trial was introduced on 6 Aug. 1971, and direct rule from London was imposed on 30 Mar. 1972. On 'Bloody Sunday' (30 Jan. 1972) British troops opened fire on a Catholic civil rights march, and thirteen people were killed. At the peak, in Aug. 1972, there were 21,500 British soldiers in Northern Ireland, but this was reduced to 10,000 by the mid-1980s. Over 3,160 people had died in the conflict by the end of Aug. 1994, when the IRA called a 'complete cessation' of military operations. This was followed by a reciprocal offer from the loyalists (13 Oct. 1994). The worst single terrorist outrage was the Omagh bombing (see p 117).

Falkland Islands (Malvinas) 1982

Argentina maintained a long-standing claim to the sovereignty of the Falkland Islands and on 2 Apr. 1982 the Argentine dictatorship, under General Galtieri, launched a successful invasion of the islands, forcing its garrison of eighteen Royal Marines to surrender. Argentine forces also seized the island of South Georgia. On 5 Apr. a British task-force set sail to recapture the islands and on 7 Apr. an exclusion zone of 200 miles was declared around them. On 25 Apr. South Georgia was recaptured and on 1 May air attacks began on the Argentine garrison on the Falklands. The next day the Argentine cruiser *General Belgrano* was sunk by a British submarine and on 4 May HMS *Sheffield* was hit by an Exocet missile. On 21 May British troops went ashore at San Carlos. Two British frigates, the *Ardent* and *Antelope*, were sunk and others damaged by air attack, but British troops took Darwin and Goose Green by the end of May and on 11–14 June an attack on Port Stanley led to the surrender of the Argentine forces. During the conflict 255 British and 720 Argentine troops were killed. A large permanent garrison and modern airstrip have been placed on the islands for their future security.

211

Gulf War 1990

On 2 August 1990 Iraq invaded Kuwait. UN Resolution 660, condemning the invasion and calling for immediate and unconditional withdrawal, was passed the same day. The USA ordered naval forces to the Gulf on 3 Aug. and sent troops to Saudi Arabia on 7 Aug. (Operation 'Desert Shield'). UN Resolution 661, imposing economic sanctions on Iraq, was passed on 6 Aug. On 8 Aug. Iraq announced the annexation of Kuwait. On 29 Nov. UN Resolution 678 sanctioned the use of force if Iraq had not withdrawn by 15 Jan. 1991. Britain joined the Allied forces (led by the USA under General Norman Schwarzkopf), contributing land, sea and air forces. The Allied air offensive against Iraq (Operation 'Desert Storm') began shortly before midnight GMT on 16 Jan. The Allied ground offensive began on 24 Feb. Kuwait City was entered by the Allies on 26 Feb. With Kuwait liberated and the Iraqi army defeated, US President George Bush ordered a ceasefire, which came into effect on 28 Feb. During the conflict, Allied forces lost 166 killed, 207 wounded and 106 missing or captured. The Iraqi losses were estimated by some to be 200,000.

Balkan War 1999

Conflict in Kosovo, until 1989 an autonomous province in 'rump' Yugoslavia mainly inhabited by Kosovar Albanians, gradually intensified as Serbian forces embarked on a policy of ethnic cleansing. Yugoslav President Slobodan Milosevic ignored a series of NATO warnings during 1998. On 24 March 1999 NATO forces (including British aircraft) launched air strikes against Yugoslavia. Cruise missile attacks followed. Milosevic intensified his ethnic cleansing policy, producing a human tide of refugees into Macedonia and Albania. NATO air strikes were marked by a series of calamitous errors (including a missile attack on the Chinese embassy in Belgrade on 8 May) and a serious worsening of relations with Russia. Eventually air power (backed by the threat of a land offensive) caused Milosevic to sue for peace and a mainly NATO peacekeeping force (KFOR, with some Russian troops) was stationed in Kosovo.

5 TERRORISM INVOLVING BRITISH TARGETS

Chronology of principal events

1969

18 July   Bombs planted by Palestinians explode in Marks and Spencer store in London.

1971

15 Dec.   Zaid Rifai, Jordanian ambassador in London, is wounded when shots are fired at his car by Black September guerrillas.

1972

22 Feb.   A Provisional IRA bomb attack on the Officers' Mess of the Parachute Regiment in Aldershot kills seven soldiers.

21 July   Nine people are killed in Belfast in a coordinated series of at least 20 bombings by the Provisional IRA.

19 Sept.   Dr Arni Shachori, counsellor for agricultural affairs at the Israeli Embassy in London, is killed by a letter bomb sent from Amsterdam by Black September.

1973

8 Mar.   Car bombs in London outside the Old Bailey and the Army Recruiting Office near Trafalgar Square kill one man and injure some 200 other people.

18 Dec.   Two IRA car bombs and a parcel bomb injure some 60 people in London.

31 Dec.   Edward Sieff, president of Marks and Spencer, survives assassination attempt at his home in London by Carlos, the Venezuelan terrorist.

1974

3 Feb.   An IRA suitcase bomb hidden in the luggage compartment of a bus travelling through Yorkshire with soldiers and their families kills eleven people and wounds fourteen.

17 July   IRA bomb explosion in the armoury of the Tower of London kills one tourist and injures 36.

21 Nov.   Birmingham pub bombings by IRA kill 21 people and injure 120.

1975

5 Sept.   Two people are killed and 63 injured by an IRA bomb at the London Hilton Hotel.

23 Oct.   An explosion outside the Kensington home of a Conservative MP, Mr Hugh Fraser, kills a passer-by, Professor Gordon Hamilton Fairley, a renowned cancer specialist.

27 Nov.   Ross McWhirter, editor of the *Guinness Book of Records*, is shot dead by the IRA at his north London home after he establishes a reward fund for information leading to the arrest of terrorists.

12 Dec.   Four IRA gunmen surrender after a six-day siege in a flat in Balcombe Street in central London.

1976

4 Jan.   Five Catholics are murdered in Belfast.

5 Jan.   Ten Protestant workmen are shot dead by the IRA in Belfast.

21 July   Christopher Ewart-Biggs, British ambassador in Ireland, and his secretary, Judith Cooke, are killed by an IRA landmine as he is driving near his home in Dublin.

28 Oct.   Maire Drumm, former vice president of the Provisional Sinn Fein, is shot dead in a Belfast hospital, while recuperating from cataract treatment, by members of the Ulster Volunteer Force, a Protestant paramilitary group.

1977

10 Apr.   Palestinian terrorists assassinate the former Yemeni Prime Minister Abdullah al-Hejiri and his wife in London.

1978

4 Jan.   Said Hammami, representative of the Palestine Liberation Organization (PLO) in London, is shot dead in his office by Palestinians opposed to Yasser Arafat's policy of negotiating with Israel.

17 Feb.   Twelve people are killed and 30 injured in an IRA firebomb explosion at the Le Mon House restaurant in Belfast.

9 July   General al-Naif, former Premier of Iraq, is assassinated outside the Intercontinental Hotel in London.

20 Aug.   An attack on an El Al aircrew bus outside the Europa Hotel in London leaves one stewardess dead and nine other people injured.

11 Sept.   Georgi Markov, a Bulgarian exile working for the BBC, is murdered by an injection of a powerful poison in a London street.

1979

22 Mar.   Sir Richard Sykes, British ambassador to the Netherlands, is shot in The Hague by a member of the Provisional IRA.

30 Mar. Airey Neave, Conservative MP for Abingdon and Opposition spokesman on Northern Ireland, is killed by an INLA bomb in his car as he leaves the House of Commons garage in London.

27 Aug. Eighteen British soldiers are killed by a remote-controlled bomb at Warrenpoint, County Down.

27 Aug. Earl Mountbatten, his grandson, Nicholas Knatchbull, the Dowager Lady Brabourne, and a local boy, Paul Maxwell, are killed when an IRA bomb blows up their fishing boat off the coast of County Sligo.

1980

30 Apr. Gunmen demanding the release of political prisoners in Iran seize the Iranian Embassy in London and kill two hostages. The SAS storm the Embassy on 5 May; five terrorists are killed and one is arrested.

1981

21 Jan. Sir Norman Strange, former Stormont Speaker, and his son are shot dead by the IRA at their home in South Armagh.

19 May Five soldiers die in a landmine explosion in South Armagh.

17 Oct. Lieutenant-General Sir Steuart Pringle, Commandant-General of the Royal Marines, is severely injured when a bomb explodes beneath his car outside his home in Dulwich, South London.

19 Oct. An IRA nail-bomb attack on a bus carrying Irish Guards in London kills two passers-by and wounds 35 people.

13 Nov. Bomb explodes outside the home of the Attorney-General, Sir Michael Havers, in Wimbledon, south-west London.

1982

3 June Shlomo Argov, Israeli ambassador, is shot and critically wounded in London.

20 July Eleven soldiers are killed and over 50 people injured by IRA bombs in Hyde Park and beneath the bandstand in Regent's Park.

6 Dec. Seventeen people, including eleven soldiers, are killed in an explosion at a public house in Ballykelly.

1983

17 Dec. Six people are killed and 90 injured by an IRA car bomb outside Harrods store in London.

1984

17 Apr. Policewoman Yvonne Fletcher is killed by shots fired from the Libyan People's Bureau in London at anti-Gadaffi demonstrators; Libyan diplomats are expelled after a ten-day siege.

12 Oct. An IRA bomb planted in the Grand Hotel, Brighton, where Prime Minister Margaret Thatcher and members of her Cabinet are staying for the Conservative party conference, kills five people and injures 32.

1985

28 Feb. Eight policemen and one civilian are killed in an IRA mortar attack on Newry police station.

1987

25 Apr. Lord Justice Maurice Gibson and his wife are killed by a car bomb as they cross from the Irish Republic into Northern Ireland at Killen.

8 Nov. Bomb explosion at Remembrance Day service at Enniskillen kills eleven people and injures 31.

1988

16 Mar. Three people are killed and 50 injured in a grenade and pistol attack by a loyalist gunman at the funeral of three IRA members killed by the SAS in Gibraltar on 6 March.

1 May Three off-duty British soldiers die in two IRA attacks in the Netherlands.

15 June Six soldiers are killed when their van is blown up by the IRA at Lisburn.

1 Aug. One soldier is killed and nine injured by an IRA bomb at army barracks in Mill Hill, north London.

20 Aug. Eight British soldiers are killed when their coach is blown up by the IRA near Omagh, County Tyrone.

21 Dec. Pan Am Boeing 747, flying from London to New York, is blown up over Scotland, killing 259 passengers and crew, and eleven residents of Lockerbie.

1989

Feb. IRA bomb attacks on service bases in Europe, followed later in year by attacks in Osnabruck, Hanover and other places.

22 Sept. IRA bomb attack on Royal Marines barracks at Deal in Kent kills eleven bandsmen.

1990

20 Jan. IRA bomb kills a boy during 'Bloody Sunday' anniversary march.

4 Apr. Huge IRA bomb near Downpatrick kills four Ulster Defence Regiment (UDR) soldiers.

11 Apr. Teesside Customs seize parts of suspected 'supergun' destined for Iraq. Trucks carrying suspected parts are later seized in Greece and Turkey.

26 June IRA bombs Carlton Club in London's West End.

30 July Conservative MP Ian Gow assassinated by IRA car bomb at his Sussex home.

Aug. Attempts by IRA to murder Lord Armstrong, former head of the Civil Service (6th), and later Lieutenant-General Sir Anthony Farrar-Hockley (13th).

19 Sept. Sir Peter Terry, former Governor of Gibraltar, shot and severely wounded by IRA. He had authorized the SAS operation which led to the killing of three IRA terrorists in March 1988.

1991

7 Feb. IRA mortar bomb attack on British Cabinet at 10 Downing Street, London.

18 Feb. IRA bombs Paddington and Victoria railway stations, London. All London rail terminals temporarily closed.

2 Nov. IRA bombs Musgrave Park Hospital, Belfast. Two British soldiers are killed.

1992

5 Feb. Five Catholics are killed in Belfast betting shop. British government begins review of Protestant Ulster Defence Association (UDA) activities. UDA proscribed in August.

10 Apr. IRA bombs Baltic Exchange building in City of London; three people are killed and 80 injured.

14 Nov. IRA 'Bookmaker's Shop Massacre' in North Belfast. Three people are killed and twelve injured. IRA bombing also devastates centre of Coleraine.

1993

26 Feb. IRA bombs gas works in Warrington.

20 Mar. IRA strikes again in Warrington, where the two young civilian casualties cause outrage.

24 Apr. City of London bombed by IRA for second time (in Bishopsgate) leaving one person dead, 36 injured.

May £28 million damage by bombs in Belfast, Portadown and Magherafelt.

23 Oct. Ten die in Shankill bombing by IRA.

30 Oct. Greystead pub bombing by loyalists.

1994

Mar. Mortar attacks on Heathrow Airport by IRA.

18 June UVF attack on Loughinisland pub kills six.

July Car bomb attack outside Israeli embassy in London.

1996

Feb.   IRA bombing of Canary Wharf. Two killed, 100 injured.

1998

Jan.   Centre of Portadown devastated by car bomb.

Aug.   Worst-ever terrorist bombing in Northern Ireland leaves 28 dead and 220 injured in Omagh.

Section V

BIOGRAPHIES

Acland Sir Richard Thomas Dyke (1906–90): Liberal MP for Barnstaple 1935–42, then Common Wealth MP 1942–45. Espoused radical proposals for 'common ownership', publicized in a bestselling Penguin Special, *Unser Kampf* (1940), an answer to Hitler's *Mein Kampf*, he gave his Devon family estate to the National Trust. In 1942 he launched Common Wealth party to contest wartime by-elections against 'reactionary' candidates and in support of progressive policies. Three by-election victories against sitting Conservative MPs helped to establish the need for policies of social reform in the post-war settlement. When the party's 23 candidates were overwhelmed in the Labour victory of 1945, returning only a single MP, Acland joined the Labour party and served as MP for Gravesend 1947–55. He resigned his seat over Labour's decision to support the hydrogen bomb programme. A principled idealist, he continued to write on political and moral questions until the last months of his life.

Abbott Diane Julie (b. 1953): First black woman MP. Educated Harrow County Girls' Grammar School and Cambridge. Civil servant; National Council for Civil Liberties (NCCL) race relations officer; television researcher and reporter; trade union equality officer; press officer, Greater London and Lambeth Councils; Westminster City councillor, 1982–86. MP for Hackney North and Stoke Newington since 1987. Secretary, Campaign Group of Labour MPs since 1992.

Adams Gerry (b. 1948): Republican activist and president of Sinn Fein. Provisional Sinn Fein MP for West Belfast 1983–92 (though he had refused to take his seat at Westminster). Participated in unsuccessful secret talks with Home Secretary William Whitelaw in June 1972. Principal spokesman for the strategy of the 'ballot box in one hand and the Armalite in the other', but, following talks with John Hume, announced ceasefire on 31 Aug. 1994. Signatory to the 'Good Friday agreement' in 1998.

Ashdown (Jeremy John Durham) 'Paddy' (b. 1941): Liberal politician and leader of the Social and Liberal Democrats 1988–99; MP for Yeovil since 1983. Former Royal Marine, followed by career in business and two periods of unemployment. Defeated Alan Beith for the leadership of the new merged party which emerged from the Alliance. Energetically rebuilt the Liberal Democrats into a significant force in local politics and through a series of by-election victories before and after the 1992 general election, pursuing a more centrist position on defence, economic policy and Europe. Sought cooperation with Labour opposition on constitutional matters prior to the 1997 election. Secured the return of a record number of MPs in the 1997 election (46) and continued close cooperation with Labour on constitutional reform, including devolution and electoral reform. Voluntarily resigned as leader with effect from July 1999.

Attlee Clement Richard, 1st Earl Attlee (1883–1967): Labour MP for Limehouse Stepney 1922–50, and for West Walthamstow 1950–55. Parliamentary Private Secretary to Ramsay MacDonald 1922–24; Under-Secretary for War in 1924; Chancellor of the Duchy of Lancaster 1930–31;

Postmaster-General in 1931. He was elected leader of the Labour party in 1935. In the wartime Coalition government he took office as Lord Privy Seal 1940–42; Secretary for the Dominions 1942–43; Lord President of the Council 1943–45. He was Deputy Prime Minister 1942–45 and Prime Minister 1945–51. He was also Minister of Defence 1945–46. Leader of the Opposition 1951–55; created an earl in 1955. Attlee's rise to the leadership of the Labour party was facilitated by the disruption of the party in 1931. As Labour Prime Minister he presided over an active and able Cabinet which introduced the National Health Service and comprehensive social welfare, and nationalized many basic industries. With Bevin at the Foreign Office, he aligned Britain with the USA in the Cold War, entered NATO, and took the decision to build a British atomic bomb. A moderate socialist, he was one of Britain's most successful prime ministers.

Baker Kenneth Wilfred, Lord Baker (b. 1934): Conservative MP for St Marylebone 1974–83; Mole Valley 1983–97; Parliamentary Private Secretary to Edward Heath 1974–75; Secretary of State for Education 1986–89; Chancellor of the Duchy of Lancaster and chairman of the Conservative party 1989–90; Home Secretary 1990–92. He was responsible for introducing the National Curriculum and regular testing of schoolchildren in the Education Reform Act 1988, the introduction of City Technology Colleges, the freezing of student grants and the introduction of 'top-up' loans, and the removal of tenure from new university teachers. Once considered a possible contender for the succession to Thatcher, he retired to the back benches voicing opposition to the Maastricht Treaty.

Barber Anthony Perrinott Lysberg, Baron Barber (b. 1920): Conservative politician. Trained as a barrister; MP for Doncaster 1951–64; Altrincham and Sale 1965–74. Conservative Whip, 1955–58; Parliamentary Private Secretary to Prime Minister Macmillan 1958–59; Economic Secretary to Treasury 1959–62; Financial Secretary 1962–63; Minister of Health 1963–64; chairman of Conservative party 1967–70; Chancellor of the Duchy of Lancaster 1970; Chancellor of the Exchequer 1970–74. Involved in early negotiations to join the EEC, he became Chancellor in July 1970 following the sudden death of Macleod. He pursued tax-cutting and liberalizing policies, encouraging the 'Barber boom'. In Nov. 1972 he was forced to introduce a statutory prices and incomes policy to control inflation and introduced large-scale cuts in spending in 1973. Although he achieved his growth rates and a surge in output, the pay policy precipitated conflict with the miners which brought down Heath's government. He took a life peerage in 1974.

Beckett Margaret Mary (b. 1943): Party leader and Cabinet minister. Educated Notre Dame High School, Manchester, and Manchester University. Metallurgist; television researcher 1979–83. MP for Lincoln 1974–79; Derby South since 1983. Assistant government whip 1975–76. Parliamentary Secretary, Department of Education and Science 1976–79. Party NEC member 1980–81, 1985–86, 1988–. Opposition spokesperson on social security 1984–88; shadow Chief Secretary to the Treasury 1989–92. Deputy leader of the Opposition 1992–94; acting leader 1994. Shadow leader of the House of Commons and campaign coordinator 1992–94. Unsuccessful candidate for party leadership and deputy leadership 1994. Shadow Secretary of State for Health 1994–95; for Trade and Industry 1995–97. President of the Board of Trade 1997–98. Lord Privy Seal and Leader of the House 1998–.

Beith Alan (b. 1943): Liberal (then Liberal Democrat) politician. First elected for Berwick-on-Tweed 1973. Deputy Leader of the Liberal Party 1985–88. Unsuccessful contender for leadership of Liberal Democrats 1988. Subsequently Economics, then Home Affairs, spokesman.

Benn (Anthony Wedgwood) 'Tony' (b. 1925): Labour party politician and minister. Postmaster-General 1964–66; Minister of Technology 1966–70 (Minister of Power 1969–70); Secretary of State for Industry 1974–75; Secretary of State for Energy 1975–79. Labour MP for South-East Bristol from 1950, he lost his seat in the Commons in 1961, following his succession to his father's title, Viscount Stansgate. He supported the Peerage Act 1963 which allowed him to relinquish his title and resume his Bristol seat in the Commons until 1983, returning to the Commons at the Chesterfield by-election in 1984. An advocate in his earlier years of high technology including the Concorde programme, he was a leading opponent of Britain's entry into the EEC. As Industry Secretary he was responsible in 1975 for setting up the National Enterprise Board, seen as a major instrument of state direction of industry, and for obtaining funding for workers' cooperatives. Following Labour's defeat in the 1979 general election, he went to the back benches where he became the focus of attempts to widen the selection procedure for the party leadership, to force reselection of sitting MPs and greater control by the National Executive Committee over the party manifesto. Benn's influence in the party reached a peak in Oct. 1981 when he was defeated by the narrowest of margins for the deputy leadership of the party by Healey. Benn's candidature was widely seen as symbolic of the growing leftward shift in the party under Foot's leadership. He announced in 1998 that he would resign his seat at the next election.

Bevan Aneurin 'Nye' (1897–1960): Labour politician. Born Tredegar, South Wales, son of a miner. Became a miner himself, aged 13, rising through the South Wales Miners' Federation. Independent Labour party MP for Ebbw Vale 1929–31, then Labour party MP 1931–60. As Minister of Health in the Attlee government he introduced the National Health Service, securing the cooperation of the doctors and consultants. Minister of Labour in Jan. 1951, he resigned in April in protest against the introduction of prescription charges. Led the 'Bevanite Left' in opposition to Gaitskell, who defeated him in the contest for the Labour leadership in 1955. As chief spokesman for foreign affairs, he ultimately turned against the unilateralism with which he had been associated. Deputy leader of the party in 1959, his early death deprived the party of one of its best-loved figures and finest orators.

Beveridge William Henry, 1st Baron Beveridge (1879–1963): Economist and author of Beveridge Report on *Social Insurance and Allied Services* (1942) which became blueprint for Britain's welfare state. Particularly interested in unemployment from his early career, he was director of labour exchanges 1909–16; director of London School of Economics and Political Science 1919–37; master of University College, Oxford 1937–45. He transformed his 1942 investigation from a technical inquiry into the rationalization of existing insurance provision to a comprehensive scheme to provide support 'from the cradle to the grave'. In cooperation with Keynes he persuaded the Treasury that the costs were supportable and extensively publicized the results of his report. The radical gloss he gave to his proposals masked its foundation on the existing insurance principle of contributions from employee, employer and the state and an assumption that full employment would be possible after the war. His proposals were broadly accepted in a government White Paper in 1944 and implemented in the National Insurance Act 1946.

Bevin Ernest (1881–1951): Trade union leader, Labour politician and statesman. With only an elementary school education, Bevin worked as a carter in Bristol before becoming a full-time trade union official in the dockers' union in 1911. By 1918 the leading figure in the National Transport Workers' Federation (NTWF), he achieved prominence for his presentation of the workers' case before the Shaw Inquiry of 1920, where he earned the nickname 'the Dockers' KC'. He urged moderation on his union over Black Friday in 1921, against support for the Triple Alliance with the miners and railwaymen. In 1922 he formed the Transport and General Workers' Union (TGWU), soon to become Britain's largest union, and was its general secretary 1922–40. Following the General Strike he played a leading part with Walter Citrine in strengthening links with the Labour party, and through the TUC General Council had increasing influence on the direction of Labour policy, especially after the 1931 election débâcle. A fierce anti-communist, he maintained the pro-Labour stance of his union throughout the Depression. Minister of Labour in Churchill's wartime coalition 1940–45, he used his massive influence to ensure organized labour's cooperation with the war effort. As Foreign Secretary in the Attlee government he supported NATO and the development of nuclear weapons. A confirmed opponent of Soviet communism, he helped to align Britain with the USA in the Cold War. He resigned from the Foreign Office in 1951, occupying the post of Lord Privy Seal for the few weeks before his death. Tough and self-educated, he played a crucial role in Labour and trade union politics in the twentieth century.

Blair Anthony Charles Lynton (Tony) (b. 1953): Prime Minister and leading architect of 'New Labour'. Educated Fettes College and Oxford. Called to the Bar 1976. Lost deposit as unsuccessful candidate for Beaconsfield 1982. MP for Sedgefield since 1983. Opposition spokesperson on Treasury and economic affairs 1984–87; trade and industry 1987–88; energy 1988–89; employment 1989–92 (where he ended party support for the trade union closed shop and backed retention of Conservative legislation on strike ballots and secondary action); home affairs 1992–94 (where his slogan 'Tough on crime, tough on the causes of crime' undermined Conservative dominance over the issue). Party National Executive Committee member since 1992. Emerged as one of the party's leading 'modernizers'; frustrated at the slower pace of party reform under Smith's leadership 1992–94. Following withdrawal of Gordon Brown from the contest (with alleged souring of relations), elected Labour's youngest ever leader in 1994. As Opposition leader, continued reforms initiated by Kinnock to build a 'New Labour' capable of winning office; fundamentally revised Clause IV, 1995. While Labour benefited from his remarkable popularity, the vagueness of his policies (variously called the 'project', the 'stakeholder society' and the 'Third Way') led to him being described as Tony 'Blur'; the Labour left accused him of being 'tough on socialism, tough on the causes of socialism'. Prime Minister of a Labour government with an impregnable majority, he has also been accused of authoritarian tendencies; took leading role in securing the 'Good Friday agreement' in Northern Ireland in 1998 and strong advocate of the bombing of Serbia and sending forces to Kosovo in 1999. Has continued peace initiatives in Ireland in 1999.

Blunkett David (b. 1947): Cabinet minister and local government leader. Educated Sheffield University and Holly Bank College of Education. Clerk/typist; industrial relations lecturer. Deputy chairman, Association of Municipal Authorities 1984–87. Sheffield City councillor 1970–88; leader 1980–87. MP for Sheffield Brightside since 1987. Opposition spokesperson on the environment 1988–92; on health 1992–94; education 1994–95; education and employment 1995–97. Secretary of State for Education and Employment 1997–. Party National Executive member 1983–; chairman 1993–94. Among his jointly written publications are *Democracy in Crisis: The Town Halls Respond* (1987) and *On a Clear Day* (1995).

Boothroyd Betty (b. 1929): Labour MP since 1973 (West Bromwich 1973–74; West Bromwich West since 1974). Speaker of the House of Commons since May 1992, the first woman to be elected to the Speakership. Chancellor of the Open University since 1994.

Bottomley Arthur George, Baron Bottomley (1907–95): Labour MP for Chatham 1945–50; Rochester and Chatham 1950–59; Middlesbrough East 1962–74; Middlesbrough 1974–83. Parliamentary Under-Secretary of State for the Dominions 1946–47; Secretary for Overseas Trade, Board of Trade 1947–51; Secretary of State for Commonwealth Affairs 1964–66; Minister of Overseas Development 1966–67.

Bottomley Virginia (b. 1948): Conservative politician. MP for Surrey South West since May 1984. Secretary of State for Health 1992–95. National Heritage Secretary 1995–97. One of only two women in John Major's Cabinet.

Boyle Sir Edward Charles Gurney, Baron Boyle of Handsworth (1923–81): Conservative Cabinet Minister. MP for Birmingham Handsworth 1950–70.

Parliamentary Secretary to the Ministry of Supply 1954; Financial Secretary to the Treasury 1959–62; Minister of Education 1962–64; Opposition Spokesman on Education and Science 1964–69.

Brittan Sir Leon, Lord Britten (b. 1939): Conservative politician and European Commissioner. Conservative MP, Cleveland and Whitby (then Richmond) 1974–89. Secretary of State for Home Affairs 1983–85. Secretary of State for Trade and Industry 1985–86. EC Commissioner 1989–99 (Vice President from 1995 to 1999).

Brockway (Archibald) Fenner, Baron Brockway (1888–1988): Socialist, anti-colonial campaigner, and leading representative of the pacifist tradition within the twentieth-century Labour movement. A conscientious objector in the First World War and imprisoned for opposition to conscription. Thereafter chaired No More War Movement 1923–28. Served on inquiry into prison service 1920; wrote on prison conditions and an investigation of poverty and unemployment, *Hungry England* (1932). Early supporter of Indian independence. Labour MP, Leyton East, 1929–31, then active in Independent Labour party; general secretary ILP 1933–39. Rejoined Labour party 1946; Labour MP, Eton and Slough, 1950–64. Continued active involvement in colonial independence movement. President of British Peace in Vietnam movement from 1970.

Brooke Henry, Baron Brooke of Cumnor (1903–84): Conservative MP for Lewisham West 1938–45; Hampstead 1950–66. Financial Secretary to the Treasury 1954–57; Minister of Housing and Local Government and Minister for Welsh Affairs 1957–61; Chief Secretary to the Treasury and Paymaster-General 1961–62; Home Secretary 1962–64.

Brown George Alfred, Baron George-Brown (1914–85): Labour politician and key figure in the 1964 Wilson administration. Put in charge of new Department of Economic Affairs (DEA) to act as counterweight to the Treasury and encourage strategic view of the economy. His National Plan of Sept. 1965 envisaged a 25 per cent increase in national output by 1970 but was quickly overtaken by balance of payments problems and devaluation. Appointed Foreign Secretary in 1966, he resigned in 1968 and was appointed a life peer in 1970. Deputy leader of the Labour party 1960–70, and Wilson's rival for the leadership in 1963, his strong position was undermined by the failure of the DEA and his own maverick behaviour.

Brown (James) Gordon (b. 1951): Cabinet minister. Educated Kirkcaldy High School and Edinburgh University; PhD 1982. Lecturer 1975–80; head of Scottish TV current affairs 1980–83. MP for Dunfermline East since 1983. Member Scottish Labour Party executive 1977–83; chairman of the party's Scottish Council 1983–84; chairman, Labour party in Scotland 1987. Shadow Chief Secretary to the Treasury 1987–89. Shadow Trade and Industry spokesperson 1989–92. Shadow Chancellor 1992–97. As Chancellor from May 1997, he followed Labour's pledges in opposition to maintain the

Conservatives' budgetary targets and income tax rates for two years, but introduced a 'Windfall Tax' on public utility profits to fund Welfare-to-Work scheme and took major step on entering office of entrusting the Bank of England with setting interest rates.

Butler Richard Austen 'Rab', Baron Butler (1902–82): leading Conservative politician. As President of the Board of Education 1941–45, pushed through 'Butler' Education Act 1944, establishing free secondary education for all. On the liberal wing of the party, was instrumental in adjusting its policies after the 1945 election defeat to meet aspirations for improved housing and social welfare. His centrist, consensus policies as Chancellor of the Exchequer 1951–55 became dubbed Butskellism for similarity to those of Labour's Gaitskell. Butler filled every major office of state and as Deputy Prime Minister was seen by many as the natural successor to Macmillan in 1963. His failure to capitalize on his advantage and the choice of the more patrician Douglas-Home as Premier was a pivotal moment in post-war Conservative politics, followed by the narrow loss of the 1964 general election. He took a life peerage in 1965, effectively retiring from active politics.

Callaghan (Leonard) James, Baron Callaghan (b. 1912): Prime Minister in 1976, after defeating Foot for the Labour party leadership on the resignation of Wilson, who had led the party since 1963. Entered the House of Commons as Labour MP for Cardiff South 1945 and served in the Attlee government. Chancellor of the Exchequer 1964, but his career was blighted by devaluation in 1967 and by his opposition to membership of the EEC. Callaghan inherited a difficult position in 1976 with serious economic difficulties of strikes and inflation. He accepted restrictions on government policy in return for support from the International Monetary Fund in 1976, beginning a period of severe restraint on government spending and local authority finance which in some ways prefigured the early Thatcher years. Forced to seek support from the minority Liberal party in the Lib–Lab Pact 1977–78, many believed Callaghan had done sufficiently well to risk an election in the autumn of 1978. He delayed and the subsequent industrial strife of 1978–79, the 'Winter of Discontent', when he attempted to force a pay norm on the trade unions, fatally compromised his party's standing. In March 1979 his government fell on a vote of 'no confidence' as a result of the defection of Welsh and Scottish Nationalist support, and was defeated in the subsequent general election by the Conservatives led by Thatcher. Callaghan retired as leader of the party in 1980, making way for Foot. Associated throughout his career with the centre-right of the Labour party, he remained opposed to the leftward drift of the party after his retirement to the House of Lords.

Carrington Peter Alexander Rupert, 6th Baron Carrington (b. 1919): Conservative politician and Foreign Secretary in the 1979 Thatcher administration. First Lord of the Admiralty 1959–63; Defence Secretary 1970–74 and Energy Secretary 1974. In 1979 supervised Lancaster House conference which ended the guerrilla war in Rhodesia, paving the way to free elections and black majority rule. Resigned as Foreign Secretary in 1982 following the Argentine invasion of the Falkland Islands. Secretary-General of NATO 1984–88; in charge of European Community peacekeeping attempts in former Yugoslavia in 1991, a position from which he resigned in 1992.

Carr (Leonard) Robert, Baron Carr of Hadley (b. 1916): Conservative MP for Mitcham 1950–74; Carshalton 1974–76. Parliamentary Secretary, Ministry of Labour and National Service 1955–58; Secretary for Technical Cooperation 1963–64; Secretary of State for Employment 1970–72; Lord President of the Council and Leader of the House of Commons 1972; Secretary of State for Home Affairs (Home Secretary) 1972–74.

Castle Barbara Anne, née Betts, Baroness Castle of Blackburn (b. 1910): Labour politician and only female member of Wilson Cabinet of 1964 as Minister for Overseas Development 1964–65. As Transport Minister 1965–68, she introduced the breathalyser and a 70 mph speed limit; she worked on an abortive Transport Bill to distribute goods traffic between road and rail. Appointed to newly created Department of Employment and Productivity in April 1968 charged with enforcing prices and incomes legislation. Defeated by Trades Union Congress (TUC) and Cabinet pressure in attempts to back up industrial relations Bill, *In Place of Strife*, with penal sanctions to enforce strike ballots and a 'cooling-off' period for unofficial strikes. As Secretary of State for Social Services 1974–76, she ended private beds in National Health Service hospitals. She was removed from government following Callaghan's assumption of the leadership in April 1976. A dynamic figure on the left of the party, she relinquished her long tenure as MP for Blackburn 1945–79 for a seat in the European Parliament from 1979. She was vice-chairman of its Socialist Group 1979–84.

Charles (Philip Arthur George), Prince of Wales (b. 1948): Heir to the British throne as eldest son of Elizabeth II and Prince Philip. Noted for outspoken views on contemporary issues, opposing environmental pollution, criticizing modern architecture and supporting initiatives to ease inner-city problems. 'Fairy-tale' marriage to Lady Diana Spencer in July 1981 raised media interest in the Royal Family to new heights, subsequently blighted by the exposure of difficulties in their marriage and ultimate divorce in 1996. He has played a major role in rehabilitating the image of the Royal Family following widespread criticism of their reaction to the death of Princess Diana in August 1997.

Chichester-Clark James (b. 1923): Ulster Unionist politician; leader of the Ulster Unionist party and Prime Minister of Northern Ireland 1969–71. Elected over Faulkner by a majority of one in May 1969 after the resignation of O'Neill. Faced with an escalation of violence and competing demands from Unionists for repression and attempts by Westminster to conciliate, he was forced to resign in March 1971. He became Lord Mayola.

Churchill Sir Winston Leonard Spencer (1874–1965): Prime Minister and statesman. Son of Lord Randolph Churchill and his wife, Jennie Jerome. Served in the army and as war correspondent, in Sudan 1898 and Boer War. Entered Parliament as a Conservative in 1900, but became a Liberal in 1904 over tariff reform, holding various seats until 1922. Returned to Parliament as a Conservative in 1924; Under-Secretary at the Colonial Office 1906–08; President of the Board of Trade 1908–10; Home Secretary 1910–11, where he had to deal with industrial unrest in South Wales. First Lord of the Admiralty 1911–15; he resigned from the government after the failure of the Dardanelles Campaign, serving on the Western Front. Minister of Munitions 1917–19; Secretary for War and Air 1919–21; Colonial Secretary 1921–22. As Chancellor of the Exchequer 1924–29, he returned Britain to the Gold Standard and took a strong line during the General Strike. With fall of the Baldwin government in 1929 he became increasingly isolated over his opposition to Indian independence and his calls for rearmament as opposed to appeasement. Returning as First Lord of the Admiralty in 1939, he succeeded Chamberlain as Prime Minister in May 1940 forming an all-party War Cabinet. His vigour, determination and speeches inspired the country after Dunkirk and during the Battle of Britain. Forged a strong relationship with President Roosevelt, obtaining Lend-Lease agreements vital to the war effort. Took part in series of wartime conferences shaping post-war settlement, attempting to preserve the interests of the British Empire. He accepted wartime plans for social reform, but mismanaged the 1945 election campaign and was defeated by Attlee. A fervent anti-communist, he made the Iron Curtain speech at Fulton, Missouri, in 1946. Returned as Prime Minister in 1951, his government encouraging house-building and removing restrictions on the economy. His last years in office were affected by illness and old age; he finally gave way to Eden in 1955. He left Parliament only in 1964 and was given a state funeral on his death. Considered by many to be one of the greatest prime ministers ever.

Chuter-Ede See Ede.

Citrine Walter McLennan (1887–1983): Trade union leader; general secretary of the Trades Union Congress (TUC) 1926–46, playing crucial role in establishing trade union influence within the Labour party. Opposed cuts proposed by MacDonald's Labour Cabinet in August 1931, precipitating fall of the government, and responsible, with Bevin, for rallying bulk of the Labour party in opposition to the National government and securing MacDonald's expulsion. Increasingly asserted control of the trade union movement over Labour party policy from 1931 via the TUC-dominated National Joint Council. Cooperated with Bevin in pursuing strong anti-communist stance and opposition to fascism. Wholly supported war effort and chaired committee which led to setting up of national and local production boards in 1942. Presided over the nationalization of the electricity industry; Chairman of Central Electricity Authority 1947–57.

Clarke Kenneth Harry (b. 1940): Conservative MP for Rushcliffe since 1970. Parliamentary Private Secretary to Solicitor-General 1971–72; Assistant Government Whip 1972–74 (Whip for Europe 1973–74); Under-Secretary of State for Transport 1979–82; Minister for Health, Department of Health and Social Security, 1982–85; Paymaster-General and Minister for Employment 1985–87; Chancellor of Duchy of Lancaster and Minister for Trade and Industry (also policy coordinator on inner cities) 1987–88; Secretary of State for Health 1988–90; Secretary of State for Education and Science 1990–92; Home Secretary 1992–93; Chancellor of the Exchequer 1993–97. A successful Chancellor, securing low inflation and economic growth, he was a strong contender for the leadership in the party ballot in June 1997, heading the first two rounds before his ultimate defeat by Hague. His strong pro-Europeanism and opposition to him from Eurosceptics were widely blamed for him not being Major's natural successor.

Cook Robert Finlayson (Robin) (b. 1946): Cabinet minister. Educated Aberdeen Grammar School and Edinburgh University. Workers' Education Association (WEA) tutor-organizer 1970–74. Edinburgh Corporation member 1971–74. MP for Edinburgh Central 1974–83; Livingston since 1983. Opposition Treasury spokesperson 1980–83. Party leadership campaign manager for Kinnock 1983. Spokesperson on Europe 1983–84; Parliamentary Labour Party (PLP) campaign coordinator 1984–86. Spokesperson on trade 1986–87; health 1987–92. Party leadership campaign manager for Smith 1992. Spokesperson on trade and industry 1992–94; on foreign affairs 1994–97. Foreign Secretary 1997–.

Cripps Sir (Richard) Stafford (1889–1952): Labour politician and minister. Qualified as a barrister in 1913; Labour MP for Bristol East 1931–50 (independent MP 1939–45); Bristol South-East 1950. Solicitor-General in second Labour government 1930–31, but his left-wing views led to his expulsion from the Labour party in 1939. British Ambassador to the USSR 1940–42, where he helped to secure the Anglo-Soviet alliance against the Nazis. As Lord Privy Seal and Leader of the Commons, he joined the War Cabinet in Feb. 1942. In Apr. 1942 he made the unsuccessful 'Cripps Mission' to India to negotiate with Indian national leaders support for the war effort in return for an offer of self-government, serving thereafter from Nov. 1942 until May 1945 as Minister of Aircraft Production. Readmitted to the Labour party, he was President of the Board of Trade in the Attlee government from July 1945 and Chancellor of the Exchequer 1947–50. He became widely known as the public face of the post-war Labour government's austerity programme of continued rationing, strict controls, and government regulation. Forced to devalue the pound in Sept. 1949, he retired due to ill-health in Oct. 1950. High-principled and of impeccable moral stature, he was a widely respected and able member of Labour's post-war administration.

Crosland (Charles) Anthony Raven (1918–77): Labour politician and theorist. His highly influential book *The Future of Socialism* (1956) advocated improved economic performance to advance socialist policies of welfare provision. The emphasis on economic competence was seen as setting the agenda for the Wilson governments of the 1960s in which Crosland served as Minister of State at Economic Affairs 1964–65. As Secretary of State for Education and Science 1965–67, he played a major role in promoting comprehensive schools. As Secretary of State for the Environment 1974–76, he called a halt to local authority spending in the face of unresolved economic difficulties. Appointed Foreign Secretary in 1976, his death in office deprived Labour of one of its intellectual heavyweights.

Crossman Richard Howard Stafford (1907–74): Labour MP for Coventry East 1945–74. Minister of Housing and Local Government 1964–66; Lord President of the Council and Leader of the House of Commons 1966–68; Secretary of State for Social Services 1968–70. Editor of the *New Statesman* 1970–72. Major intellectual force in the first Wilson government and pursued active housing policy. Broke tradition of Cabinet secrecy with the publication of his *Diaries* (1975–77) after legal-political battle, paving the way for subsequent Cabinet memoirs to appear.

Cunningham John Anderson (Jack) (b. 1939): Cabinet minister. Educated Jarrow Grammar School, Durham University; PhD. Research chemist; teacher; trade union official. Chester-le-Street councillor 1969–74. MP for Whitehaven 1970–83; Copeland since 1983. Parliamentary Under-Secretary, Department of Energy, 1976–79. Opposition spokesperson on Industry 1979–83; Environment 1983–92; shadow Leader of the House of Commons and campaign coordinator 1989–92; Opposition spokesperson on foreign affairs 1992–94; on Trade and Industry 1994–97. Minister of Agriculture and Fisheries 1997–98. Chancellor of the Duchy of Lancaster 1998–99.

Dalton Hugh, Baron Dalton (1887–1962): Labour politician. MP for Peckham 1924–29, Bishop Auckland 1929–31 and 1935–59. One of the leading intellectual figures in Labour's revival from the late 1930s. Taught at the London School of Economics and Political Science between the wars and published works on public finance and planning. Entered the War Cabinet in 1940 as Minister of Economic Warfare; as President of Board of Trade from 1942 advocated nationalization of coal and power. Appointed Chancellor of the Exchequer in Attlee's Cabinet in 1945, he oversaw the nationalization of the Bank of England in 1946 and weathered the severe financial and fuel crisis of 1947. He was forced to resign after a premature leak of budget information in 1947; returned as Chancellor of the Duchy of Lancaster in 1948; Minister for Town and Country Planning 1950–51.

Davies Clement (1884–1962): Liberal politician and party leader 1945–56. Trained as a lawyer and became KC in 1926; MP for Montgomeryshire 1929–62. Accepted leadership after the defeat of Sir Archibald Sinclair in the 1945 general election and fended off Conservative offers of a Cabinet post and merger in order to maintain the Liberals as an independent force. He saw the party through the nadir of its fortunes when reduced to only six

MPs in the House of Commons in 1951 and witnessed the first signs of Liberal revival when the leadership passed on to Grimond in 1956.

Deakin Arthur (1890–1955): Trade union leader. General secretary of Transport and General Workers' Union (TGWU) 1946–55. Left school at 13 and worked in Warwickshire, South Wales and Flintshire. Became full-time TGWU organizer and acting general secretary 1940–45 in place of Bevin. A right-wing trade unionist and strong supporter of the Attlee government, he banned communists from holding union office and helped form a non-communist International Confederation of Free Trade Unions. Opposed the 'Bevanites' in the Labour party, providing TGWU support for moderate Labour policies. Seen as an authoritarian union boss in the tradition of Bevin.

Denning Alfred Thompson, Lord Denning (1899–1999): Judge. KC 1938; Lord Justice of Appeal 1948–57; Lord of Appeal in Ordinary 1957–62; Master of the Rolls 1962–82; conducted inquiry into the Profumo affair, producing best-selling Denning Report (1963). Outspoken defender of individual liberties and common law against state encroachment.

Dewar Donald Campbell (b. 1937): First Minister, Scottish Parliament since 1999. Educated Glasgow Academy and Glasgow University. MP, Aberdeen South 1966–70; Glasgow Garscadden since 1978. Opposition spokesman on Scottish affairs 1981–92; on Social Security 1992–95; Opposition Chief Whip 1995–97: Secretary of State for Scotland with responsibility for devolution campaign in 1997–98.

Devlin See McAliskey.

Douglas-Home Sir Alec (Alexander Frederick), Lord Home of the Hirsel (1903–95): Conservative politician and Prime Minister. Douglas-Home was styled Lord Dunglass 1918–51, succeeding as Earl of Home 1951. MP for Lanark 1931–45 and 1950–51, he renounced his title under the Peerage Act 1963 and served again as MP 1963–74, when he took a life peerage. His early career lay in foreign affairs, serving under Neville Chamberlain; at the Scottish Office 1951–55; Secretary for Commonwealth Relations 1955–60; Lord President of the Council 1957 and 1959–60; Leader of the House of Lords 1957–60. Between 1960 and 1963 he was Foreign Secretary under Macmillan, securing the Nassau agreement and the Test Ban Treaty. An unexpected choice as Prime Minister to succeed Macmillan in 1963, he was effectively a 'caretaker' Premier until the 1964 election. Contrasting unfavourably with Wilson's technocratic image, he was successful in containing the size of Labour's victory to four seats. He resigned as party leader in 1965 and was succeeded by Heath, returning as Foreign Secretary 1970–74 where he helped conduct the negotiations which led Britain into the EEC.

Ede James Chuter, Baron Chuter-Ede (1882–1965): Labour MP for Mitcham 1923–24; South Shields 1929–31, 1935–64. Parliamentary Secretary, Ministry of Education, 1940–45; Secretary of State for Home Affairs 1945–51.

Eden Sir (Robert) Anthony, 1st Earl of Avon (1897–1977): Conservative politician and Prime Minister. Conservative MP for Warwick and Leamington 1925–57. Parliamentary Private Secretary to Sir Austen Chamberlain (Foreign Secretary) 1926–29; Under-Secretary at Foreign Office 1931–33; Lord Privy Seal 1934–35; Minister without Portfolio with special responsibility for League of Nations Affairs 1935; Foreign Secretary 1935–38. In 1938 he resigned in protest at the government's policy of appeasement. He was Secretary for the Dominions 1939–40; Secretary for War 1940; Foreign Secretary 1940–45. He was also Leader of the Commons 1942–45. He returned to the Foreign Office 1951–55. In 1954 he was made a Knight of the Garter. He was Prime Minister 1955–57, resigning because of ill-health. In 1961 he was created Earl of Avon. Eden was an extremely experienced diplomat but he miscalculated domestic and world opinion when authorizing the ill-fated invasion of Suez in 1956.

Evans Gwynfor (b. 1912): Plaid Cymru MP for Carmarthen 1966–70; 1974–79. President of Plaid Cymru 1945–81; chairman, Union of Welsh Independents, 1954. Publications include *Plaid Cymru and Wales* (1950) and *Wales Can Win* (1973). Presided over the revival of Welsh nationalism from the mid-1960s through to the devolution referendum débâcle of 1978 when the people of Wales failed to vote for a devolved assembly.

Ewing Winifred (b. 1929). Scottish Nationalist politician. MP for Hamilton 1967–70; Moray and Nairn 1974–79; MEP for Highlands and Islands 1975 to 1999. Her victory at the Hamilton by-election marked the emergence of the Scottish Nationalists as a major force and made her the major celebrity of the Scottish Nationalist party (SNP). Subsequently built up a strong position as European Parliamentary representative, confirming her popularity at the direct elections in 1979, 1984, 1989 and 1994.

Falkender See Williams.

Faulkner Brian, Lord Faulkner (1921–77): Ulster Unionist politician; leader of Ulster Unionist party and Prime Minister of Northern Ireland 1971–72; chief executive in power-sharing administration 1974. Minister of Home Affairs 1959–63; Minister of Commerce 1963–69. Defeated IRA border campaign while at Home Affairs, but resigned as a minister in 1969 because of growing disagreement with O'Neill's policies. Defeated by one vote by Chichester-Clark for premiership the same year, but served as Minister of Development, carrying out reforms in local government and housing. Succeeded Chichester-Clark in 1971 and introduced internment, but lost his position when Westminster imposed direct rule in 1972. Eventually took his Unionist party into power-sharing executive in 1974, which he led, but saw that destroyed by a loyalist general strike, leading to the reimposition of direct rule. Retired from politics in 1976.

Feather Victor Grayson Hardie, Baron Feather (1908–76): Trade unionist; general secretary of Trades Union Congress (TUC) 1969–73. Started work at 14; served as trade union official in Shopworkers' Union; joined TUC in

1937, becoming assistant general secretary in 1960. As acting general secretary from March 1969 (confirmed Oct.) opposed Labour government's *In Place of Strife* legislation and proposals for legal restraints on trade union action, forcing acceptance of voluntary 'solemn and binding' undertaking in its place. Led campaign against Heath government's Industrial Relations Act 1971, persuading unions not to register and suspending those who did from the TUC. His retirement in 1973 left trade union reform at an impasse in which only voluntary agreements appeared possible.

Foot Michael (b. 1913): Labour politician, journalist and party leader. In his early years a follower and supporter of Bevan, he became a lifelong supporter of the Campaign for Nuclear Disarmament (CND) and a member of the Tribune Group. Elected leader of the Labour party in succession to Callaghan in Nov. 1980, his leadership saw the defection of the 'Gang of Four' and the formation of the Social Democratic party. A genuine left-wing leader of the party, he presided over a period of left-wing advance in the constituencies and party programme. Defeated by a crushing majority by Thatcher in June 1983, he stood down as leader shortly afterwards in favour of Kinnock. A cultivated figure of the intellectual left, he was pilloried in the press as being out of touch and lacking the qualities required to modernize the party. None the less he managed to restrict the right-wing breakaway in 1981 to a minority of MPs and see the party through one of its deepest crises.

Fowler Sir Norman (b. 1938): Conservative MP for Sutton Coldfield since 1970. Secretary of State for Transport 1979–81, for Social Services 1981–87 and for Employment 1987–90; chairman of the Conservative party 1992–94. Major force in reshaping social security benefits and pensions. Resignation as chairman widely expected in July 1994 because of the failures of Conservative party in council elections, by-elections and Euro-elections. Served on William Hague's first Shadow Cabinet.

Gaitskell Hugh Todd Naylor (1906–63): Labour MP for Leeds South 1945–63; Chancellor of the Exchequer 1950–51; Labour party leader 1955–63. Considered by some the outstanding representative of the social democratic tradition within the Labour party; clashed with Bevanites over Eden's Suez policy; sought unsuccessfully after 1959 election defeat to persuade party to drop socialist commitments. Died shortly after reuniting party on EEC issue and defeating unilateralists.

Gordon-Walker Patrick Chrestien, Baron Gordon-Walker (1907–80): Labour MP for Smethwick 1945–64; Leyton 1966–74. Parliamentary Under-Secretary of State for Commonwealth Relations 1947–50; Secretary of State for Commonwealth Relations 1950–51; Secretary of State for Foreign Affairs 1964–65; Minister without Portfolio 1966–67; Secretary of State for Education and Science 1967–68. His entry into the Wilson government of 1964 was disrupted by his failure to secure his seat in the 1964 election and his defeat in a subsequent by-election, forcing Stewart to take over as Foreign Secretary in 1965.

Grimond Joseph 'Jo', Baron Grimond (1913–93): Leader of the Liberal party 1956–67 and principal architect of its revival after 1956. Trained as a barrister; MP for Orkney and Shetland 1950–83. Took over the leadership from Davies at the nadir of the party's fortunes and gave it fresh vision and drive. His leadership saw the party achieve its first by-election success since 1928 at Torrington in 1958, further success at Orpington in 1962, and a doubling of its MPs from six in 1956 to twelve in 1966. His aim to create an effective, radical, non-socialist party of the left had achieved only partial success by the time of his resignation in 1967 with the Liberals still a minor parliamentary force. Succeeded by Thorpe, he served as interim leader in May–June 1976 after Thorpe's resignation. He became a life peer in 1983 and remained a respected elder statesman.

Hague William Jefferson (b. 1961): Conservative leader since 1997. MP for Richmond (Yorks.) since 1989. Comprehensive-educated, then Oxford University; management consultant 1983–88; Political Adviser, HM Treasury, 1983; Parliamentary Private Secretary to Chancellor of the Exchequer 1990–93; Parliamentary Under-Secretary of State, Department of Social Security, 1993–94; Minister for Social Security and Disabled 1994–95; Secretary of State for Wales 1995–97. Emerged as youthful compromise candidate to defeat front-runner Kenneth Clarke on third ballot in June 1997. Early criticism of his style and lack of personality were allayed by successes in the 1999 local and European elections; has tried to steer a moderately Eurosceptic line, seeking a ballot of members in 1998 to confirm the position on Europe.

Hattersley Roy, Lord Hattersley (b. 1932): Labour MP for Birmingham Sparkbrook 1964–97; Secretary of State for Prices and Consumer Protection 1976–79; deputy leader of Labour party 1983–92, forming with Neil Kinnock the so-called 'dream ticket'. Shadow Home Secretary 1987–92; announced in Feb. 1994 that he would retire from the Commons at the next election. Prominent centre-right figure in Labour party whose refusal to countenance defection to the Social Democratic party provided an important element in rebuilding the Labour party around more centrist policies.

Haughey Charles (b. 1925): Irish politician, Prime Minister of the Irish Republic 1979–81, 1982 and 1987–91. Leader of Fianna Fail 1979–91. Early career suffered from allegations of involvement in 'gun-running' scandal to assist the IRA for which he was dismissed from the government. None the less, he worked to improve the relationship with Britain under Thatcher, including the establishment of an 'Intergovernmental Council' in 1981 to review policy on Northern Ireland, a step on the road to the Anglo-Irish agreement 1985. In spite of attacks on British policy towards the hunger strikes of 1981, he cooperated with Britain within the framework set up in 1985 in his final period of office.

Healey Denis Winston, Baron Healey (b. 1917): Labour politician, Chancellor of the Exchequer and deputy leader, leading figure on the right of the party in the Wilson and Callaghan governments. First elected as MP for Leeds South East in 1952 and subsequently Leeds East, and appointed Defence Secretary under Wilson 1964–70, carrying out extensive retrenchment, including cancellation of TSR2 fighter-bomber and running down role 'East of Suez'. Opposition spokesman on Foreign Affairs 1970–72; Treasury Affairs 1972–74. Chancellor of the Exchequer 1974–79; forced in 1976 to use IMF loan and initiate major cuts in programmes because of economic crisis, but supervised gradual stabilization of the economy by 1978–79. Defeated in contest for Labour leadership by Callaghan in 1976 and by Foot in 1980, when he became deputy leader. Retained the deputy leadership by narrow margin against left-wing challenge of Benn in 1981, but stood down following the general election defeat in 1983. A consistent supporter of multilateralism, the EEC and social democracy, he was marginalized in the party's shift to the left in 1979–83. Considered by some the best leader the Labour party never had.

Heath Sir Edward Richard George (b. 1916): Conservative politician, Prime Minister 1970–74 and leader of the Conservative party 1965–75. The son of a carpenter, he has been Conservative MP for Bexley since 1950. In successive Conservative governments he was Government Chief Whip 1955–59; Minister of Labour 1959–60; Lord Privy Seal 1960–63; and Secretary of State for Industry and Trade 1963–64. He became Conservative leader in 1965, and Prime Minister following an unexpected victory in the 1970 general election. A strong supporter of Britain's entry into the European Economic Community, Heath signed the Treaty of Accession which gained Britain membership in Jan. 1973. His attempts to reform industrial relations produced confrontation with the Trades Union Congress and the miners leading to a 'State of Emergency' in 1972 and a 'three-day week' in the winter of 1973–74. Combined with the collapse of the economic boom of his Chancellor, Barber, this led to a narrow defeat by Labour in a snap election called in Feb. 1974, which was repeated in Oct. 1974. He was ousted from the leadership of the Conservative party by Thatcher in 1975. He has remained a persistent critic of Thatcherism and her stance on Europe.

Heathcoat-Amory Derick, 1st Viscount Amory (1899–1981): Conservative politician and Chancellor of the Exchequer under Macmillan. Minister for Pensions 1951–53, at Board of Trade 1953–54, and Agriculture and Food 1954–58; became Chancellor of the Exchequer in Jan. 1959, following the resignation of Thorneycroft. Introduced 'credit squeeze' in June 1960, but retired to the Lords the following month in Cabinet reshuffle.

Heseltine Michael (Ray Dibdin) (b. 1933): Conservative politician whose challenge for the leadership in autumn 1990 brought about the fall of Thatcher. A successful millionaire publisher, he was MP for Tavistock 1966–74, and Henley since 1974; Minister of Aerospace and Shipping under Heath 1972–74. Highly popular figure with Conservative conferences for his rousing speeches and blond good looks. Nicknamed 'Tarzan' by the media. Minister for the Environment 1979–83; Thatcher gave him special responsibility for Merseyside following the Toxteth riots 1981; he was instrumental in setting up inner-city initiatives. Appointed Defence Secretary 1983–86, his growing opposition to the Thatcher premiership led to his resignation over the Westland Affair in 1986. A long-expected challenge to the leadership came following the resignation of Howe in 1990, when Heseltine obtained sufficient votes to force a second-round ballot of MPs, precipitating Thatcher's withdrawal and effective resignation as party leader and Prime Minister. Defeated by Major in the second-round ballot, Heseltine returned as Minister of the Environment 1989–92, overseeing the replacement of the poll tax. President of the Board of Trade 1992–95. In July 1995 he was appointed Deputy Prime Minister and First Secretary of State following Major's success in the leadership election. Illness prevented him from playing a larger role when Major resigned following the 1997 election. Strongly pro-European, he is regarded as a major elder statesman of the party.

Home of the Hirsel See Douglas-Home.

Howard Michael (b. 1941): Conservative MP for Folkestone and Hythe since 1983; Secretary of State for Employment 1990–92; for the Environment 1992–93; Home Secretary 1993–97. Piloted much amended Criminal Justice Act through Parliament in 1994. Heavily criticized for failure to halt mounting crime wave as Home Secretary. Unsuccessful leadership contender June 1997; subsequently foreign affairs spokesman before announcing retirement from front-bench politics.

Howe Sir (Richard Edward) Geoffrey, Baron Howe (b. 1926): Conservative politician; senior figure under Thatcher as Chancellor of the Exchequer, Foreign Secretary and Deputy Prime Minister, whose resignation speech fatally undermined her leadership. Trained as a barrister, serving under Heath as Solicitor-General 1970–72; Minister of Trade and Consumer Affairs 1972–74. As Thatcher's Chancellor of the Exchequer 1979–83, presided over the application of monetarist policies to the economy, reducing inflation sharply at the price of a severe depression and the highest unemployment since the 1930s. As Foreign Secretary 1983–89, successfully negotiated the transfer of Hong Kong to Chinese control after 1997 with guarantees for maintenance of a western-style economic system. Increasingly discordant views with his Prime Minister over progress towards European unity led to his replacement as Foreign Secretary in July 1989, becoming Leader of the House of Commons and Deputy Prime Minister. Further clashes over Europe came to a head with his resignation from the government on 1 Nov. 1990, followed on the 13th with a devastating speech to the House of Commons directly attacking Thatcher's leadership and calling on others 'to consider their own response'. The following day Heseltine launched his long-anticipated leadership challenge which forced Thatcher's resignation as Conservative leader and Prime Minister. Howe was the butt of Denis Healey's famous remark, 'like being savaged by a dead sheep'.

Huddleston Most Revd (Ernest Urban) Trevor (1913–98): Chairman, International Defence and Aid Fund for Southern Africa after 1983. Vice-president of Anti-Apartheid Movement 1969–81; president after 1981. Leading campaigner against the apartheid regime in South Africa. Former Anglican Archbishop of the Indian Ocean.

Hume John (b. 1937): Northern Ireland Social Democratic and Labour party leader who played central part in the Northern Ireland peace process 1994–98. Educated St Patrick's College, Maynooth, and Queen's University, Belfast. Teacher and businessman; President of the Credit Union League of Ireland 1964–68. Northern Ireland Civil Rights Association activist. Co-founder and vice-chair Derry Citizens' Action Committee 1968. Elected Stormont MP for Foyle 1969. SDLP founder member 1970. SDLP member of Northern Ireland Assembly for Londonderry 1973–74. Minister of Commerce in power-sharing executive 1974. SDLP leader 1979. MEP from 1979. Talks with Sinn Fein culminated in the IRA ceasefires of 1994–96, 1997 and the 1998 peace agreement. Shared Nobel Peace Prize with David Trimble.

Hurd Douglas Richard, Lord Hurd (b. 1930): Conservative politician; Home Secretary and Foreign Secretary under Thatcher and a defeated contender for the premiership in Nov. 1990. Trained, and long career, as a diplomat 1952–66; political secretary to Prime Minister Heath 1970–74; entered Parliament in 1974 for Mid-Oxfordshire (for Witney 1983–97). Home Secretary 1983–84; Northern Ireland Minister 1984–85 in negotiations leading up to the Anglo-Irish agreement. Returned as Home Secretary in 1985; appointed Foreign Secretary in Oct. 1989 in reshuffle caused by Chancellor Lawson's resignation. Considered a traditional moderate Tory, he was, briefly, a favourite to succeed Thatcher, but failed to muster sufficient support to defeat Major. He retained his post as Foreign Secretary and was reappointed following the 1992 election. He retired in 1995.

Ismay General Sir Hastings Lionel Ismay, 1st Baron Ismay (1887–1965): Chief of Staff to Ministry of Defence under Churchill 1940–45; Deputy Secretary (Military), War Cabinet, 1940–45; Additional Secretary (Military) 1945; Chief of Staff to Viceroy of India 1947; Secretary of State for Commonwealth Relations 1951–52; Secretary General, North Atlantic Treaty Organization, 1952–57.

Jay Douglas Patrick, Lord Jay (1907–96): Labour MP for Battersea North 1946–83. Journalist on *The Times, The Economist* and *Daily Herald* 1929–40; civil servant with Ministry of Supply, Board of Trade and Prime Minister's Office 1940–46; Economic Secretary, Treasury, 1947–50; Financial Secretary 1950–51; President of Board of Trade 1964–67. Chairman, Common Market Safeguards Campaign, 1970–77. Major intellectual force in development of Labour party's programme of nationalization and economic regulation under Attlee.

Jenkins Roy, Baron Jenkins (b. 1920): Labour, then Social Democrat and Liberal Democrat politician, founder and first leader of Social Democratic party (SDP). Son of a Welsh miner, he entered Parliament in 1950. Home Secretary under Wilson 1965–67, overseeing liberalization of law on abortion and family planning. Took over as Chancellor of Exchequer on Callaghan's resignation in 1967 and through deflation in 1968–69 achieved trade and revenue surplus. His non-concessionary budget in April 1970 is often seen as playing a part in Labour's defeat in June. Returned as Home Secretary 1974–76, passing Anti-Terrorism Act. Defeated in 1976 Labour leadership election and became President of the Commission of the European Community 1977–81. At Dimbleby Lecture in Nov. 1979 launched campaign for a new centre party in Britain. In March 1981 founded SDP, becoming a leader, and formed Alliance with the Liberal party. Achieved a close result in safe Labour seat of Warrington in 1981, starting run of Alliance by-election victories, and won Glasgow Hillhead in March 1982. Named 'Prime Minister designate' in 1983 election campaign. Criticism of his performance led to his resignation as leader in favour of Owen in June 1983. A close ally of Liberal leader Steel, he advocated merger of the two parties, supporting the merged Social and Liberal Democrats after 1988. Charged with drawing up proposals for proportional representation at Westminster under terms of joint Labour and Liberal Democrat constitutional committee after 1997 election.

Joseph Sir Keith (Sinjohn), Baron Joseph (1918–94): Conservative MP for Leeds North-East 1956–87. Minister of State at Board of Trade 1961–62; Minister of Housing and Local Government and Minister for Welsh Affairs 1962–64; Secretary of State for Social Services 1970–74; for Industry 1979–81; for Education and Science 1981–86. Leading 'guru' of free-market and liberalizing policies in the early Thatcher government.

Kennedy Charles (b. 1959): Leader of Liberal Democrats since July 1999. MP for Ross, Cromarty and Skye for SDP 1983–88, and as Liberal Democrat 1988–97; Liberal Democrat for Ross, Skye and Inverness West since 1997. Educated at Glasgow University; spokesman on social security, Europe and East–West relations, trade and industry, amongst others, most recently, from 1997–99, on agriculture and rural affairs. Widely regarded as leading younger Liberal Democrat, likely to consolidate the party's success in the 1997 election.

Kennedy John Fitzgerald (1917–63): President of the United States 1961–63. Son of wartime US ambassador to Britain, Joseph Kennedy. In 1960 won Democratic presidential nomination, becoming the youngest US President ever elected. Inspirational figure whose behaviour in the Cuban Missile Crisis of 1962 and visit to the Berlin Wall in 1963 earned him widespread recognition as a strong President but also with genuine concerns for social welfare and civil rights. Forged a strong relationship with Macmillan, granting Britain use of the Polaris system of submarine-launched nuclear missiles under the Nassau agreement 1962 and working with him on the Test Ban Treaty 1963. His assassination on 22 Nov. 1963 was widely mourned in Britain.

Kenyatta Jomo (1897–1978): Leader of Kenyan independence and first President of Kenya 1964–78. Joined native Kenya Central Association in 1922, becoming general secretary in 1928. Defended Kikuyu people before Commission on Land Use in London in 1929, returning for fifteen years from 1931. Formed pan-African movement in 1945 with Nkrumah and returned to Kenya to head nationalist movement in 1946. Transformed the Kikuyu-based Kenya African Union into a national party. Imprisoned during the Mau Mau emergency 1952–61, though consistently denied involvement. In 1960 the newly formed Kenya African National Union named him President *in absentia*. After his release from prison, he became the first Prime Minister of self-governing Kenya in June 1963. A moderate nationalist, Kenyatta sustained tribal and racial harmony during his presidency from Dec. 1964, though his later years gave rise to accusations of corruption.

Keynes John Maynard, 1st Baron Keynes (1883–1946): Economist and pioneer of the theory of full employment. Worked in the Treasury during the First World War and chief Treasury representative at negotiations prior to the Treaty of Versailles 1919. He achieved recognition for criticism of reparation plans in *The Economic Consequences of the Peace* (1919). In the 1920s he developed radical proposals for dealing with mass unemployment by deficit financing and state intervention which influenced Lloyd George's election campaign of 1929 and Oswald Mosley's proposals to the second Labour government in 1930. His full theoretical position was published in *The General Theory of Employment, Interest and Money* (1936), which inspired the 'Keynesian Revolution' in economic thinking during and after the Second World War. This rejected the classical belief in the self-regulating economy, arguing the benefits of government expenditure and economic management by the state to maintain maximum output and full employment. He acted as an economic adviser in the Second World War and cooperated with Beveridge over the funding of the welfare state. He was the chief British delegate at the Bretton Woods Conference in 1944 and in the discussions leading to the creation of the International Monetary Fund and the World Bank. His economic ideas proved immensely influential until the rise of monetarism in the 1970s and the apparent inability of 'Keynesianism' to cope with the simultaneous onset of stagnation and inflation.

Kinnock Neil Gordon (b. 1942): Labour politician and party leader. Born in South Wales. MP for Bedwellty (subsequently Islwyn) 1970–95 and member of the National Executive Committee 1978–94. Elected leader of the party in 1983 in succession to Foot. Initially identified with the left of the party, his attacks upon Militant Tendency and extremist influence attempted to moderate the party's image after its crushing defeat in 1983. He promoted attempts to improve Labour party organization and mounted a highly professional and dynamic campaign in 1987. Another large election defeat prompted a wholesale policy review in which many existing policies were jettisoned or substantially altered. In spite of considerable modernization of the party's policies and image, Kinnock's fate as leader was sealed by his defeat in the general election in April 1992, after which he announced his resignation and return to the back benches. Kinnock has been seen as being in the traditional mould of Labour leaders who have come from the left of the party and moved it into the centre-ground. Since 1999 a Vice-President of the Commission.

Lamont Norman, Lord Lamont (b. 1942): Conservative politician. MP for Kingston-on-Thames from 1972 to 1997. Financial Secretary to the Treasury 1986–89. Chief Secretary to the Treasury 1989–90. Chancellor of the Exchequer 1990–93. A virulent opponent of John Major since his removal as Chancellor (earlier he had been Major's campaign manager when he became leader) and Redwood supporter in 1995.

Lawson Nigel, Baron Lawson of Blaby (b. 1932): Conservative politician and Chancellor of the Exchequer under Thatcher. MP for Blaby Feb. 1974–92. Financial Secretary to the Treasury 1979–81; Energy Minister 1981–85; Chancellor of the Exchequer 1985–89. Lawson eased the monetarist policy of his predecessor Howe, stimulating a rapid credit boom and high growth which contributed to the Conservative election victory in 1987. His reduction of income tax to 25p in the pound and of top tax rates to 40p in March 1988 was blamed for a rise in inflation and a worsening trade deficit, forcing increased interest rates and recession. Following disagreement with Thatcher and her economic adviser, Alan Walters, over membership of the European Monetary System, Lawson dramatically resigned in Oct. 1989. Has suffered a roller-coaster reputation, widely praised as author of Conservative victory in 1987 but held responsible for the deepening recession from 1989.

Lee Jennie, Baroness Lee (1904–88): Labour politician. Married to Nye Bevan. First elected (at age of 24) as MP for Lanark North 1929–31, then for Cannock 1945–70. First Minister for the Arts (1964) and founder of the Open University.

Livingstone Ken (b. 1945): Left-wing Labour politician. MP for Brent East since 1987. Best known for his leadership of the (now abolished) Greater London Council (GLC) from 1981 to 1986. Attempted to secure Labour nomination as candidate for elected Mayor of London, 1999–2000, in a bitter contest.

Lloyd (John) Selwyn Brooke, Baron Selwyn-Lloyd (1904–78): Conservative politician; Foreign Secretary under Eden and Macmillan and during Suez crisis. Minister of Supply 1954–55; Minister of Defence 1955; appointed to Foreign Office Dec. 1955. Agreed to secret collusion with Israelis to justify Anglo-French invasion. Survived the humiliation over Suez and as Foreign Secretary under Macmillan helped restore the 'special relationship' with the USA. Appointed Chancellor of Exchequer 1960; early fiscal relaxation had to be swiftly followed by deflation and a 'pay pause' in 1961. Involved in setting up National Economic Development Council (NEDC) 1962. One of seven ministers axed in Cabinet reshuffle of July 1962: 'the Night of the Long Knives'.

McAliskey Bernadette Josephine, neé Devlin (b. 1947): Irish Nationalist politician. MP for Mid-Ulster 1969–74. Took seat while a student at Queen's University, Belfast, aged 22. Imprisoned for involvement in civil violence in 1970. Physically attacked Home Secretary Maudling in House of Commons in 1972 over 'Bloody Sunday'. Stood in the European elections in 1979; she survived an assassination attempt in 1980. Has operated on the fringes of official politics since losing her parliamentary seat in 1974.

Macleod Iain Norman (1913–70): Conservative politician and leading exponent of liberal, 'one-nation' Toryism under Eden and Macmillan. Minister of Health 1952–55; Minister of Labour 1955–59. As Colonial Secretary 1959–61 implemented Macmillan's policy of accelerating independence of African colonies. Leader of the Commons 1961–63, he resigned on Douglas-Home's accession to the premiership. Returned as Chancellor of the Exchequer under Heath in 1970 but died suddenly in office.

Macmillan (Maurice) Harold, 1st Earl of Stockton (1894–1987): Conservative politician and Prime Minister. MP for Stockton-on-Tees 1924–29 and 1931–45; for Bromley 1945–64. Parliamentary Secretary to Ministry of Supply 1940–42; Under-Secretary to Colonial Office 1942; Minister Resident at Allied HQ in North-West Africa 1942–45; Secretary for Air 1945; Minister of Housing and Local Government 1951–54; Minister of Defence 1954–55; Foreign Secretary 1955; Chancellor of the Exchequer 1955–57; Prime Minister 1957–63. From the 1930s Macmillan advocated a Tory paternalism, flirting with interventionist ideas in *The Middle Way* (1938), a stance which assisted his rise in the new mood of post-war conservatism. As Housing Minister he surpassed election pledges to build 300,000 houses a year and his period as Prime Minister was seen as a high point of post-war prosperity. He devoted much time to foreign affairs, signing the Partial Test Ban Treaty, speeding up decolonization, and signing the Nassau Agreement in 1962 which secured British access to the US Polaris nuclear deterrent. His last years as Premier witnessed failure to gain admission to the EEC, growing balance of payments problems and the Profumo scandal. Although a skilled politician and publicist, famously dubbed 'Supermac', by the time of his retirement due to ill-health in Oct. 1963 he was criticized as a dated figure out of tune with a new decade. A liberal Conservative, who in his later years publicly criticized aspects of the Thatcher premiership as socially divisive, his premiership is often interpreted as one in which fundamental decisions on Britain's world role and economic performance were left unresolved. Famous quotations include his 'wind of change' speech (in South Africa) and his 1959 election slogan 'You've never had it so good'.

Major John (b. 1943): Conservative politician who succeeded Thatcher as leader of the Conservative party and Prime Minister in Nov. 1990. Major left school at 16 and worked in banking, before entering local government in south London. MP for Huntingdon since 1983; served in junior posts 1985–87; joining the Cabinet in 1987 as Chief Secretary to the Treasury in charge of public spending. Foreign Secretary July–Oct. 1989, then Chancellor of the Exchequer following Lawson's resignation. Took Britain into the European Exchange Rate Mechanism (ERM) in Oct. 1990. When Thatcher withdrew from the leadership contest in Nov. 1990, he obtained the largest number of votes on the second ballot. He earned praise for his conduct of the Gulf War and oversaw the replacement of the poll tax with a more acceptable system of local government taxation. His low-key, more consensual approach and 'classless' image were seen as important factors in his leading the Conservatives to a fourth consecutive election victory in April 1992 in spite of a deep economic recession. Major's authority was quickly shattered by the currency crisis of Sept. 1992 which forced Britain out of the ERM, hitherto the centrepiece of Major's economic policy. Deep divisions over the ratification of the Maastricht Treaty in 1993 brought the government to the brink of defeat and led to widespread speculation about Major's continued leadership. He entered 1994 as the most unpopular Prime Minister since opinion polls began, but the final passage of the Maastricht Bill and the sudden death of John Smith, the Labour leader, relieved pressure on his position. His attempts to secure a solution to the Northern Irish question in cooperation with the Irish Premier, Albert Reynolds, on the basis of the Downing Street declaration of Dec. 1993 appeared to have achieved a breakthrough with the declaration of an IRA ceasefire on 31 Aug. 1994. In June 1995 he resigned as party leader and sought re-election in an attempt to assert his authority. Defeated John Redwood, his only contestant, but failed to prevent schisms in the party over Europe. Heavily defeated in the May 1997 election, he resigned the leadership.

Makarios Archbishop Mihail Christodoulou Mouskos (1913–77): Head of the Greek Orthodox Church in Cyprus and Cypriot leader. Appointed Archbishop in 1950, but acting as political as well as spiritual leader of his people. Supported movement for 'enosis' (union) with Greece. Undertook negotiations with the British during Cyprus emergency but was deported to the Seychelles on suspicion of involvement with EOKA terrorist organization. Returned to Cyprus in 1959 and became first President of independent Cypriot republic in 1960. Survived assassination attempts by Greek extremist supporters of enosis but coup against him in 1974 forced him into temporary exile and precipitated a Turkish invasion and partition of the island. He returned in 1975 to head the Greek half of Cyprus until his death.

Mandelson Peter Benjamin (b. 1953): Minister and influential campaigns organizer. Educated Hendon Senior High School and Oxford. Chairman, British Youth Council, 1977–80; television producer 1982–85. Lambeth borough councillor 1979–82. Party director of campaigns and communications 1985–90; leading figure in the party's modernization. MP for Hartlepool since 1992. Minister without Portfolio 1997–98. Unsuccessful candidate for National Executive 1997; responsible for Millennium celebrations. Secretary of State for Trade and Industry 1998, but forced to resign over undisclosed loan from Paymaster-General Geoffrey Robinson. Appointed Secretary of State for Northern Ireland 1998. Widely seen as the *éminence grise* of 'New Labour' and close Blair confidant.

Marquis See Woolton.

Maudling Reginald (1917–79): Conservative politician, Chancellor of the Exchequer under Macmillan and Douglas-Home and unsuccessful candidate for leadership in 1965. A liberal Conservative, President of the Board of Trade 1959–61; Colonial Secretary 1961–62; Chancellor of the Exchequer in the wake of the major reshuffle of July 1962 and the departure of Lloyd. Maudling attempted to defeat rising unemployment through a policy of 'expansion without inflation' by tax cuts and concessions on investment spending. By early 1964 he was faced by severe balance-of-payments difficulties which were inherited by the incoming Labour government of Wilson. After Douglas-Home stepped down, he stood for the Conservative leadership in 1965 but was defeated by Heath. Home Secretary 1970–72; increasingly involved in dealing with security ramifications of Northern Ireland. Forced to resign from government in July 1972 over allegations that he had received money from John Poulson.

Maxwell (Ian) Robert (1923–91): Czech-born newspaper proprietor and media mogul. Chairman of Mirror Group Newspapers from 1984 and founder of Pergamon Press. A flamboyant self-made man, Maxwell was Labour MP for Buckingham 1964–70 and maintained the broadly pro-Labour stance of the Mirror Group after his takeover. Extended his activities into cable, satellite and other areas, rivalling those owned by Murdoch. His death revealed massive debts and abuse of pension funds for his own purposes.

Morris Bill (b. 1939): First black leader of major British trade union: general secretary of Transport and General Workers Union (TGWU) since March 1992. Born in Jamaica. Former car worker; shop steward; national TGWU secretary for passenger services 1979; deputy general secretary 1985–92. Opposed reform of Clause IV, 1995.

Morris William Richard, 1st Viscount Nuffield (1877–1963): Self-made millionaire motor manufacturer and philanthropist. Started work at 16 in bicycle shop, then set up own repair business and first car factory at Cowley, near Oxford, by 1914. Use of mass-production techniques allowed him to market cheap Morris cars within financial reach of the middle classes, selling over a million vehicles by 1939 and making him the biggest British car manufacturer. Absorbed the rival Austin Motor Company, forming in 1952 the British Motor Corporation, later British Leyland. One of the greatest philanthropists in British history, setting up the Nuffield Foundation for medical research with £10 million in 1943 and founding Nuffield College, Oxford, in 1937 for postgraduate research. He became a baronet in 1929 and was raised to the peerage in 1934.

Morrison Herbert Stanley, Baron Morrison of Lambeth (1888–1965): Labour politician and leading figure in wartime coalition and Attlee administration. Served political apprenticeship in the London County Council (LCC) from 1922, joining the Labour government as Minister of Transport 1929–31, where he created the London Transport Board. As leader of LCC 1934–40 he oversaw widespread development of London's housing, health, education and transport services. Lost his parliamentary seat in 1931 but returned in 1935. Appointed Minister of Supply in 1940 in wartime coalition, then Home Secretary and Minister of Home Security 1940–45 with responsibility for air-raid precautions and emergency services. Created the National Fire Brigade to coordinate services during the Blitz. Strong exponent and supporter of welfare programmes which assisted Labour victory in 1945. Deputy Prime Minister 1945–51, serving as Lord President of the Council 1945–47 and as Leader of the House of Commons 1947–51, he managed the passage of Labour's extensive legislative programme. Briefly Foreign Secretary in 1951, he was an unsuccessful rival to Gaitskell for the leadership in 1955.

Mountbatten Louis Francis Victor Albert Nicholas, 1st Earl Mountbatten of Burma (1900–79): Naval commander, later Admiral. A great-grandson of Queen Victoria, son of First Sea Lord Admiral Prince Louis of Battenberg (1854–1921) and uncle to Prince Philip. Served in battle cruisers in the First World War and was sunk in HMS *Kelly* off Crete in 1941 when commanding Fifth Destroyer Flotilla. Chief of Combined Operations in 1942 planning raids on St Nazaire and Dieppe. Supreme Allied Commander in South-East Asia from Oct. 1943, he took surrender of Japanese forces in 1945. Appointed last Viceroy of India on 20 Feb. 1947, he advised a speedy transfer of power and presided over partition and the independence of India and Pakistan. First Governor-General of India, Aug. 1947 to June 1948, later resuming naval career, becoming First Sea Lord 1955–59, then Chief of the Defence Staff 1959–65. He was assassinated by Irish terrorists in the Republic of Ireland in 1979. Widely admired for his overall conduct of operations in Burma in the war and his recognition of the need for a rapid transition to independence in the Indian sub-continent.

Mowlam Marjorie ('Mo') (b. 1949): Secretary of State for Northern Ireland 1997–99. Educated Durham University; MP Redcar since 1987; Opposition front-bench spokesperson on Northern Ireland 1988–89 and 1994–97; on city and corporate affairs 1989–92; member of shadow cabinet 1992–97. Took initiative of visiting prisoners in the Maze prison to break deadlock in Northern Ireland and played leading part in obtaining the 1998 'Good Friday' agreement. Has subsequently come under fierce loyalist attacks for being 'soft' on the IRA's obligations under the peace accords. Replaced by Peter Mandelson at Northern Ireland Office, 1999.

Murdoch (Keith) Rupert (b. 1931): Australian-born media magnate with worldwide newspaper and television interests. Chairman and owner of News International plc with leading popular newspapers in Britain including the

Sun, *Today* and *News of the World*; also acquired Times Newspapers in 1982, achieving unprecedented concentration of newspaper ownership. Successfully promoted populist tabloid journalism, which was used to support Thatcher in the 1979 election and her subsequent policies. Became a US citizen in 1985. Fought bitter but successful dispute with print unions in 1986 over introduction of new print technology at Wapping plant and launched first successful satellite TV company, Sky, in 1989. Widely seen as one of the first generation of global media moguls.

Nasser Colonel Gamal Abdel (1918–70): President of Egypt 1954–70, during Suez crisis. Led movement of army officers which expelled King Farouk in 1952 and replaced General Neguib as Prime Minister in 1954. Promoted domestic reform, including building of Aswan Dam, but when western loans were withdrawn announced the nationalization of the Suez Canal. This precipitated the Anglo-French invasion of Egypt in collaboration with the Israelis in 1956. Nasser's defiance of the west and the humiliating withdrawal of Anglo-French forces enormously enhanced his prestige and made him a symbol of Arab nationalism. His reputation was undermined by the failure of union with Syria in 1956–61 and the disastrous Six Day War with Israel in 1967, but he remained in office until his death. A 'hate' figure in Britain during the Suez crisis, he was the effective founder of the modern Egyptian state.

Nkrumah Kwame (Francis Nwia Kofi) (1909–72): First President of independent Ghana (former Gold Coast) 1950–66. The leading figure in movement for independence of African states from colonial rule and supporter of pan-Africanism. Educated by Catholic missionaries and trained as a teacher. Studied and taught in USA before reading law in London 1945–47. Active in West African Students' Union in Britain where he made contact with other leading African nationalists such as Kenyatta. Led United Gold Coast Convention (UGCC) on return to West Africa in 1947 but forced to resign in 1949 after leading campaign of civil disobedience. Launched his own mass Convention People's Party (CPP); imprisoned 1950–51. Following electoral victory of CPP he was released to become first Prime Minister of the Gold Coast's legislative assembly. Led the country after independence in 1957 and the adoption of the name Ghana, declaring Ghana a republic in 1960. In 1964 he named himself President for life and banned all other parties. He was deposed in 1966 while on a visit to Peking, having squandered much of his country's foreign exchange on prestige construction projects.

Nuffield See Morris.

O'Neill Terence, Baron O'Neill of the Maine (1914–90): Prime Minister of Northern Ireland 1963–69 who began process of conciliation of Catholics and reform which developed into the Ulster crisis. A Unionist MP from 1946, as Premier O'Neill sought to bridge the divide between the communities in Northern Ireland, visiting Catholic institutions and inviting the Republic of Ireland's Premier to Stormont. His initiatives stirred up Protestant opposition led by Ian Paisley, but also stimulated the Catholic civil rights movement. His offer of a package of local government reforms to the Catholics in 1968 could not prevent growing polarization and violence. Having failed to strengthen his position after an election held in Feb. 1969, which saw the break-up of the old Ulster Unionist party, he resigned in April in favour of Chichester-Clark. A liberal Unionist, he was tragically overtaken by sectarian rivalries.

Orwell George (1903–50): Pen-name for Eric Arthur Blair, political writer, novelist, best known for anti-totalitarian satires of the Cold War era, *Animal Farm* (1945) and *Nineteen Eighty-Four* (1949). Served in Burma police 1922–27, reflected in his first novel *Burmese Days* (1934). Worked at odd jobs in Paris and London, described in his *Down and Out in Paris and London* (1933), before becoming established as a novelist and political essayist. Semi-documentary study of unemployment, *The Road to Wigan Pier* (1937), published by the Left Book Club; fought and was wounded on Republican side in the Spanish Civil War, recorded in *Homage to Catalonia* (1938). A democratic socialist and patriot, Orwell displayed growing disillusionment with the totalitarian face of contemporary ideologies, brought to brilliant realization in his two famous political satires.

Owen Dr David Anthony Llewellyn, Baron Owen (b. 1938): Labour politician and leader of the Social Democratic party (SDP). Labour MP 1966–81, and for SDP 1981–92, for Plymouth Devonport. Foreign Secretary 1977–79 in the Callaghan government, his disillusion with the leftward drift of the party under Foot led to his co-founding the SDP with Roy Jenkins, William Rodgers and Shirley Williams. He became leader of the SDP during the 1983 election campaign and advocated distinct SDP views on defence and the 'social market' within the Liberal–SDP Alliance. Joint leader of the Alliance campaign (with David Steel) in the 1987 election, he opposed calls for a merger following the election and resigned the leadership of the SDP when a majority of its members showed in favour. He became leader of the 'continuing' SDP until its final demise in 1989 and was widely regarded as hindering the emergence of an effective 'third force'. He left the House of Commons in 1992 and was given a peerage by Major following possible discussion about a role in the Conservative party. He was appointed EU peace negotiator in the former Yugoslavia from 1992, resigning in 1995 after working tirelessly for a settlement.

Paisley Revd Ian Richard Kyle (b. 1926): Ulster Unionist politician. Founder and head of the fundamentalist Free Presbyterian Church. Attracted populist support for ultra-loyalist Ulster Defence Committee from 1960 and founded breakaway Democratic Unionist Party (DUP) in 1971. MP for North Antrim since 1970, he helped to organize the United Ulster Unionist Council (UUUC) which won eleven out of twelve Ulster seats in 1974. Supported the Ulster Workers' Council strike of May 1974 which brought down the power-sharing executive. Bitter opponent of the Anglo-Irish agreement of 1985, forming an electoral pact with the Ulster Unionist party

(UUP) to oppose it and to some extent healing the rift in unionist politics present since 1971. He has been a dominant voice of Ulster loyalism since the early 1970s.

Patten Christopher (b. 1944): Conservative politician and colonial governor. Secretary of State for the Environment 1989–90. Chairman of the Conservative Party 1990–92. Lost his Bath constituency in 1992 general election. Subsequently appointed Governor of Hong Kong as the colony prepared for its return to China in 1997. Returned to Britain after successful handover; produced Patten Report on the future of the Royal Ulster Constabulary; appointed European Commissioner in 1999.

Philby 'Kim' (Harold Adrian Russell) (1911–88): British Foreign Office official and 'Third Man' in the Burgess–Maclean spy scandal. Won over to communism at Cambridge in the 1930s, he conducted espionage at the centre of British government until 1951. That year he was forced to resign over suspected but unproved communist associations, but only after warning Burgess and Maclean to make their escape. He became a journalist, but went missing in Beirut in 1963, finally reappearing in Moscow where he was made an honorary Colonel in the KGB. He remained a committed communist until his death.

Portillo Michael (b. 1953): Conservative politician. MP Enfield Southgate 1984–97. Served as Chief Secretary to the Treasury, Secretary of State for Employment and from 1995 to 1997 as Defence Secretary. Seen by many as a possible future leader, he did not stand in the 1995 leadership contest and the shock loss of his seat removed him from the running for Major's position in 1997. Announced (Sept. 1999) he would seek to return to Westminster for Kensington and Chelsea after having revealed a homosexual phase in his life while at Cambridge. Appointed Shadow Chancellor of the Exchequer, Feb. 2000, following return to Commons.

Powell (John) Enoch (1912–98): Conservative and Unionist politician. Regarded as one of the most controversial politicians of the post-war era because of his outspoken views on 'coloured' immigration. Professor of Classics, he was Conservative MP for Wolverhampton South-West 1950–74, serving as Minister of Health 1960–63. His speeches against continued immigration in 1967 and 1968, one of which prophesied 'rivers of blood', and his calls for repatriation of 'coloured' immigrants, earned him considerable notoriety and led to his expulsion by Heath from the Conservative shadow cabinet. His views, however, were reflected in the tightening of the rules against Commonwealth immigration under both Conservative and Labour governments. Powell also campaigned against Britain's entry to the EEC, isolating himself from the Conservative party by advising voters in 1974 to support anti-European Labour candidates. He was Unionist MP for South Down 1974–87, opposing concessions of sovereignty over Ulster. A radical in economic affairs, he has been seen as a pre-Thatcherite, but detached from the Conservative party after 1974. He remained a staunch opponent of the erosion of British sovereignty within the European Union.

Prescott John Leslie (b. 1938): Party deputy leader and Cabinet minister. Educated Ellesmere Port Secondary Modern, Ruskin College, Hull University. Trainee chef 1953–55; steward in merchant navy 1955–63. General and Municipal Workers' Union (GMWU) official 1965; National Union of Seamen official 1968–70. MP for Kingston upon Hull East 1970–83; Hull East since 1983. Parliamentary Private Secretary to Secretary of State for Trade 1974–76. Opposition spokesperson on regional affairs and development 1981–83; on transport 1983–84, 1988; employment 1984–87; energy 1987–88. Council of Europe member 1972–75. Member of the European Parliament 1975–79; leader of the Labour Group 1976–79. Party National Executive member 1989–. Stood unsuccessfully for deputy Labour party leadership 1988. Deputy leader 1994. Deputy Prime Minister and Secretary of State for the Environment, Transport and the Regions 1997–.

Profumo John Dennis (b. 1915): Conservative MP for Kettering 1940–45; Stratford-on-Avon 1950–63. Joint Parliamentary Secretary, Ministry of Transport and Civil Aviation, 1952–57; Minister of State for Foreign Affairs 1959–60; Secretary of State for War 1960–63. Forced to resign after admitting that he had misled the House of Commons over security risks in the 'Profumo affair'.

Pym Francis Leslie, Baron Pym (b. 1922): Conservative MP for Cambridgeshire 1961–83; Cambridgeshire South 1983–87. Secretary of State for Northern Ireland 1973–74; Secretary of State for Defence 1979–81; Chancellor of the Duchy of Lancaster, Paymaster-General and Leader of the House of Commons 1981; Secretary of State for Foreign and Commonwealth Affairs 1982–83. Leading figure in Thatcher's Cabinet and seen by many as a potential future leader, he was unceremoniously removed from office by her following his apparent lack of enthusiasm for a large majority in the 1983 election campaign.

Redwood John (b. 1951): Conservative politician. MP for Wokingham since 1987. Head of Thatcher's Policy Unit 1983–85. Resigned as Secretary of State for Wales, 26 June 1995, to contest the leadership against John Major. His candidature, though unsuccessful, further established his reputation as an heir to the Thatcherite tradition. Also contested the 1997 leadership, unsuccessfully. Dropped by Hague from Shadow Cabinet, Feb. 2000.

Rees Merlyn, Lord Rees (b. 1920): Labour politician, serving as Secretary of State for Northern Ireland 1974–76 and Home Secretary 1976–79. Sent to Northern Ireland in March 1974 and met immediate challenge to the 'power-sharing' executive set up on 1 Jan. 1974 under Faulkner from a general strike organized by the Protestant Ulster Workers' Council. With Faulkner's resignation in May, Rees was forced to reimpose direct rule from Westminster. Set up an elected Constitutional Convention in 1974 to consider further initiatives for devolved government, but progress blocked by its Protestant majority's demand for a return to a Stormont-type government. Ended internment without trial by end of 1975 and increased use of Diplock courts. As Home Secretary, brought in troops during firemen's strike in 1977–78 and was faced with mass picketing in Grunwick dispute. Shadow Home Secretary 1979–80 and Opposition spokesman on Energy 1980–83. Supported cause of those wrongly convicted for Birmingham bombing in 1974. A moderate Labour figure who was unable to break the deadlock of sectarian distrust in Ulster.

Ridley Nicholas, Lord Ridley (1929–93): Conservative MP for Cirencester and Tewkesbury 1959–92; Secretary of State for Transport 1983–86, for the Environment 1986–89, and for Trade and Industry 1989–90. Strong supporter of Thatcher and opponent of European Union; forced to resign from the Cabinet in July 1990 following a *Spectator* interview in which he claimed the Germans were aiming to 'take over the whole of Europe'.

Rifkind Sir Malcolm (b. 1946): Conservative politician. MP for Edinburgh Pentlands from 1974 to 1997. Secretary of State for Scotland 1986–90, for Transport 1990–92 and for Defence 1992–95. Replaced Douglas Hurd as Foreign Secretary, July 1995.

Rodgers William Thomas, Baron Rodgers of Quarry Bank (b. 1928): Social and Liberal Democrat politician. Former Labour MP (for Stockton South from 1962) who was one of the founding 'Gang of Four' of the SDP. He lost his seat in the 1983 general election and his political influence declined somewhat, although he became leader of the Liberal Democrats in the Lords.

Russell Bertrand Arthur William, 3rd Earl Russell (1872–1970): Philosopher and peace campaigner. Grandson of Liberal peer Lord John Russell. Work at Cambridge on mathematical logic, *Principles of Mathematics* (1903) and *Principia Mathematica* (1910–13) (with A N Whitehead), established his reputation. Became widely known through his numerous books and broadcasts, winning the Nobel Prize for Literature in 1950. An opponent of nuclear weapons, he was co-founder of the Campaign for Nuclear Disarmament (CND) in 1958 and its first president.

Scargill Arthur (b. 1938): Trade union leader who advocated industrial action for political objectives in 1970s and 1980s. Educated secondary school and Leeds University. Miner 1953; National Union of Mineworkers (NUM) branch official 1960. Young Communist League (YCL) member 1955–62; Co-operative party member 1963; joined Labour party 1966. NUM national executive member 1972; led successful 'flying pickets' during 1972 miners' strike. Yorkshire NUM president 1973. Critic of the unions' 'social contract' with the 1974–79 Labour government. NUM president 1981–. Led unsuccessful miners' strike which divided the Labour party and trade union movement 1984–85. Member, TUC general council, 1986–88. Founded Socialist Labour party 1996.

Selwyn-Lloyd See Lloyd.

Shephard Gillian (b. 1940): Conservative politician. MP for Norfolk South-West since 1987. A close ally of John Major. Secretary of State for Employment 1992–93; Minister of Agriculture, Fisheries and Food 1993–94; Secretary of State for Education 1994–97 (Education and Employment after July 1995).

Smith Ian Douglas (b. 1919): Rhodesian, then Zimbabwean, politician; former RAF pilot who entered politics in 1948. Founded white supremacist Rhodesian Front party in 1961, becoming Prime Minister of Rhodesia 1964. Issued unilateral declaration of independence (UDI) in 1965 to frustrate movement towards black majority rule. Held inconclusive talks with Wilson and maintained regime against economic sanctions and growing guerrilla war led by forces of Joshua Nkomo and Robert Mugabe. In 1979 forced to accept an interim black government led by Bishop Muzorewa, and after the Lancaster House agreement in August agreed to free elections, leading to Mugabe's victory in 1980. Thereafter led white Conservative Alliance of Zimbabwe with guaranteed seats in the Zimbabwe parliament.

Smith John (1938–94): Labour MP for Lanarkshire North 1970–83; Monklands East 1983–94. Secretary of State for Trade 1978–79; shadow Chancellor 1989–92; leader of the Labour party 1992–94. Used his authority to secure reform of trade union block vote in Labour party (one member, one vote) and built up a commanding position as anticipated next Prime Minister in the face of Major's leadership difficulties in 1993–94. His sudden death on 12 May 1994 was widely mourned across the political spectrum. As leader, he continued the work of Kinnock in building a more moderate and modernized Labour party.

Steel Sir David Martin Scott, Lord Steel (b. 1938): Liberal politician; Liberal MP (for Roxburgh, Selkirk and Peebles) 1965–97 and leader of the Liberal party 1976–88. Helped party to recover from the Thorpe era and negotiated Lib–Lab Pact of 1977–78 to maintain the Labour government during the devolution referendum campaigns. Supported the formation of the Alliance with the newly founded Social Democratic party (SDP) in 1981 and helped achieve almost a quarter of the popular vote in 1983 general election. Jointly led the Alliance campaign in the 1987 general election with SDP leader David Owen, but immediately afterwards called for a merger of the two parties, precipitating a prolonged merger negotiation and a split in the SDP. He did not put himself forward for the leadership of the newly formed Social and Liberal Democrats in 1988 but became foreign affairs spokesman. A committed internationalist, Steel was also responsible for sponsoring the legalization of abortion in 1967. Stood down from Parliament at 1997 election, but became first Presiding Officer (Speaker) of the new Scottish Parliament after May 1999.

Stewart (Robert) Michael Maitland, Baron Stewart (1906–90): Labour politician; appointed Minister of Education in Wilson government of 1964 but replaced Gordon-Walker as Foreign Secretary 1965–66 and defended government's support for US involvement in the Vietnam War. First Secretary of State 1966 with responsibility for Economic Affairs until its abolition in Aug. 1967. Returned to the Foreign Office in 1968–70 where he attempted mediation in Nigerian civil war and in Rhodesian dispute. Supported entry to the EEC and served as leader of Labour group in European Parliament 1975–76. Retired from politics 1979. A Labour moderate closely involved in the first Wilson government and associated with its indifferent record in foreign affairs.

Stockton See Macmillan.

Straw, John Whitaker (Jack) (b. 1946): Cabinet minister. Educated Brentwood School and Leeds University. President, National Union of Students, 1969–71. Called to the Bar 1972. Islington borough councillor 1971–78. ILEA deputy leader 1973–74. Political adviser to Secretary of State for Social Services 1973–74; to Secretary of State for the Environment 1976–77. MP for Blackburn since 1979. Opposition spokesperson on Treasury and economic affairs 1981–83; on the environment 1983–87; education 1987–91; environment and local government 1992–93; local government 1993–94; home affairs 1994–97. Home Secretary 1997.

Tebbit Norman Beresford, Lord Tebbit (b. 1931): Conservative MP for Chingford 1970–92. Secretary of State for Employment 1981–83, for Trade and Industry 1983–85; Chancellor of the Duchy of Lancaster and chairman of Conservative party 1985–87. Leading exponent of hardline Thatcherite policies, though proceeded cautiously as Secretary for Employment. Injured in Brighton bombing in 1984 which also critically injured his wife Margaret. Took party to third successive victory though disagreed with Lord Young over conduct of campaign. Effectively faded away from leadership contention thereafter, though provided fierce opposition to the Maastricht Bill and one of the chief focuses of opposition to pro-European elements in the party. Known for his exhortation to the unemployed to get 'on your bike'.

Thatcher Margaret Hilda (née Roberts), Baroness Thatcher of Kesteven (b. 1925): Conservative leader and Prime Minister. Conservative MP for Finchley 1959–92. Parliamentary Secretary to the Ministry of Pensions and National Insurance 1961–64; Secretary of State for Education and Science 1970–74. In 1975 she was elected leader of the Conservative party. Between 1975 and 1979 she led the party away from the centrist policies of Heath and adopted a monetarist stance on economic problems and a tough line on law and order, defence and immigration. In May 1979 she became Britain's first woman Prime Minister, following her election victory. In spite of considerable unpopularity and very high unemployment, Thatcher's conduct of the Falklands War and Labour's disarray led to a landslide victory at the polls in 1983. Thatcher's second term was marked by the defeat of a year-long miners' strike and growing emphasis on liberalizing the economy, especially the privatization of major public concerns. In 1987 she achieved a record third term of office with a majority of over 100. Weakened by the resignation of her Chancellor, Lawson, and by the unpopularity of the poll tax, her intransigent attitude towards Europe led to the resignation of her deputy leader Howe in 1990. This precipitated a leadership challenge in which she failed to secure a convincing majority and withdrew from the contest, resigning as Prime Minister in Dec. 1990. She has remained an outspoken critic of European integration.

Thorpe (John) Jeremy (b. 1929): Liberal politician. MP for North Devon 1959–79. Leader of the Liberal party 1967–76. His leadership ended with the 'Thorpe affair', allegations of his relationship with male model Norman Scott and a series of bizarre accusations. He was acquitted of conspiracy to murder in 1979.

Trimble (William) David (b. 1944): Leader of Ulster Unionist party since 1995; educated Bangor Grammar School and Queen's University; called to Bar 1969; Senior Lecturer in Law; MP Upper Bann since 1990. Signed 'Good Friday' agreement 1998 and elected First Minister, Northern Ireland Assembly, 1998. Headed historic power-sharing executive (until its suspension, Feb. 2000).

Waddington David Charles, Lord Waddington (b. 1929): Conservative MP for Ribble Valley 1979–90. Government Chief Whip 1987–89; Home Secretary 1989–90; Leader of the House of Lords 1990–92.

Walters Alan (b. 1926): Economist. Thatcherite proponent of monetarism. Cassel Professor of Economics, London School of Economics, 1968–76. Professor of Economics, Johns Hopkins University, 1976–91. Personal Economic Adviser to the Prime Minister, 1981–84, 1989. His celebrated clashes with Nigel Lawson precipitated Lawson's resignation.

Whitelaw William Stephen Ian, Viscount Whitelaw (1918–99): Conservative MP for Penrith and the Border 1955–83. Lord President of the Council and Leader of the Commons 1970–72; Secretary of State for Northern Ireland 1972–73 and for Employment 1973–74; Home Secretary 1979–83 and trusted lieutenant of Thatcher in her first administration. Given, exceptionally, a hereditary peerage, he continued to serve as Lord President of the Council and Leader of the House of Lords 1983–88.

Williams Marcia Matilda, Baroness Falkender (b. 1932): Private secretary to Harold Wilson 1956–64; political secretary to Wilson and head of his Political Office 1964–76. Principal figure in Wilson's 'Kitchen Cabinet' at No. 10 Downing Street; criticized by opponents for exercising undue influence on Labour party policy. She was given a life peerage in 1974.

Williams Shirley Vivien Teresa Brittain (née Catlin), Baroness Williams (b. 1930): Labour MP 1964–79; SDP MP 1981–83. Daughter of Vera Brittain. Labour Secretary of State for Prices and Consumer Protection 1974–76, and for Education and Science 1976–79. Served on the National Executive Committee of the Labour party 1970–81. One of the 'Gang of Four' who co-founded the Social Democratic party (SDP) in 1981 and won sensational by-election victory for the SDP at Crosby. President of the SDP 1982–88, joining the merged Social and Liberal Democrats in 1988. Although now living in the USA, she has remained a forceful voice for realignment on the left of centre of British politics.

Wilson Sir (James) Harold, Baron Wilson of Rievaulx (1916–95): Labour politician and Prime Minister. Born of modest background, Wilson was director of economics and statistics at the Ministry of Fuel and Power 1943–44, then Labour MP for Ormskirk 1945–50 and for Huyton 1950–83. Parliamentary Secretary to the Ministry of Works 1945–47; Secretary of Overseas Trade 1947; President of the Board of Trade 1947–51. In 1951 he resigned in protest at the government's decision to impose prescription charges in the National Health Service. In 1963 he was elected leader of the Labour party. He became Prime Minister in 1964 with a majority of four, inaugurating attempts to devise a National Plan, and promote housing and other reforms. He secured a large election victory in 1966, but his government was increasingly beset by economic problems, forcing devaluation in 1967. He proved unable to end the unilateral declaration of independence (UDI) in Rhodesia and in 1969 was forced to withdraw a proposed Bill to curb unofficial strikes. Important social reforms included the expansion of higher education and the founding of the Open University, as well as reforms of the law on abortion, homosexuality and divorce. In 1970 he was defeated but returned in Feb. 1974 with a minority government which remained in power after a further election in Oct. 1974. He renegotiated British terms for entry to the EEC and conducted a referendum in June 1975 which returned a majority in favour of continuing membership. Sex Discrimination and Equal Pay Acts were passed in late 1975 but the government faced serious economic difficulties, having to seek a loan of £975 million from the International Monetary Fund. He resigned in March 1976 and was succeeded by Callaghan as Premier. A controversial figure whose governments were criticized on the Left for failing to carry out socialist policies, including bitter criticism over his support for the US involvement in the Vietnam War and the retention of nuclear weapons, and, more generally, for failing to tackle fundamental problems in the economy and the trade unions. These perceived failures of the 'Wilson years' have often overshadowed their substantial social advances.

Woolton 1st Baron (Sir Frederick James Marquis) (1883–1964): Wartime Minister of Food, Conservative politician and businessman. Served on several advisory bodies to government from 1928 and became director-general of the Ministry of Supply in 1939. Appointed Minister of Food by Churchill in 1940 because of long experience in retailing and became familiar wartime face of rationing. Minister of Reconstruction 1943–45 before joining the Conservative party in 1945. Served as party chairman 1946–55 and conducted the negotiations which brought the Liberal Nationals into the Conservative party in 1948. A strong influence on rebuilding the party's organization after 1945 and its acceptance of consensus policies. Served in the Churchill Cabinets 1951–55. A key figure in the history of the Conservative party and its response to defeat in 1945.

GLOSSARY OF TERMS

ABCA See Army Bureau of Current Affairs.

ABC trial Two journalists (Crispin Aubrey and Duncan Campbell) and a former signals intelligence corporal (John Berry) were charged under the Official Secrets Act (qv) over an article which appeared in the magazine *Time Out* in 1976 on electronic surveillance activity at GCHQ, the Government Communications Headquarters (qv) in Cheltenham. The case was dismissed in Sept. 1978 but another magazine, *Peace News*, was fined £500 under the Official Secrets Act for publishing the name of a security officer who gave evidence at the ABC trial. See also Zircon affair.

Aberfan A mining village near Merthyr Tydfil in South Wales in which a coal tip collapsed on 21 Oct. 1966, killing 28 adults and 116 children, who were buried in their school.

ACAS See Advisory Conciliation and Arbitration Service.

Accession, Treaty of Signed in Brussels on 22 Jan. 1972 setting out the conditions of Britain's entry to the European Economic Community (EEC), Euratom, and the European Coal and Steel Community (ECSC), and detailing the transitional arrangements. Britain joined the EEC on 1 Jan. 1973.

Adam Smith Institute Right-wing think tank whose economic policies were of major significance in the Thatcher era in the 1980s. Named after the economist Adam Smith.

Advisory Conciliation and Arbitration Service (ACAS) A statutory body established by the Labour government in 1975 with the power to intervene in and attempt to prevent industrial disputes and to encourage wider agreement between employers and trade unions.

age of affluence The period in Britain from 1951 to 1964 of low unemployment, a 50 per cent rise in real living standards, and the increased spread of consumer goods. From *The Affluent Society* (1958) by the US economist J K Galbraith.

Albany Trust The educational and counselling wing of the Homosexual Law Reform Society, established in 1958 to campaign for the implementation by legislation of the Wolfenden Report (qv), which had recommended the decriminalization of male adult homosexuality. The law was changed by the Sexual Offences Act 1967. See also Campaign for Homosexual Equality.

Aldermaston march Annual anti-nuclear weapons march mounted at Easter by the Campaign for Nuclear Disarmament (qv) from the Atomic Weapons Research Centre at Aldermaston to a rally in Trafalgar Square in central London; this drew large support from 1958 to 1964.

Aldershot bombing Seven people were killed and fifteen injured when a bomb exploded at the headquarters of the Parachute Brigade on 22 Feb. 1972. The bombing, which was in revenge for 'Bloody Sunday' (qv), narrowly missed killing many officers. The Official IRA, which was responsible for the bombing, gave up armed action shortly afterwards. See also Irish Republican Army.

Alliance The cooperation of the Liberal and Social Democratic parties from Sept. 1981 until the formal merging of the two parties (see p. 85). See also Ettrick Bridge.

alternative vote System by which a voter states a first and second preference among candidates. A candidate gaining an absolute majority of first preference votes wins. If no candidate achieves this then second preference votes are added to the total and the candidate with an absolute majority then wins. The Jenkins Commission on Electoral Reform proposed an alternative vote top-up system.

Alton Bill Bill introduced by Liberal MP David Alton in 1987–88 to limit abortion by reducing the final date of termination of a pregnancy from 28 to 18 weeks. With Alton and his supporters refusing to accept any compromise, the Bill ran out of time in Parliament.

Amethyst incident British frigate HMS *Amethyst* was fired on by communist Chinese guns on 20 Apr. 1949 while carrying supplies in the Yangtze-kiang river (an international waterway) to the British community in Nanking. Seventeen crew were killed and the ship was trapped for fourteen weeks before sailing 140 miles down-river to the sea on the night of 30–31 July.

Amnesty International London-based organization founded in 1961 which campaigns internationally for non-violent political prisoners, gives aid to their families, attempts to improve the conditions of political prisoners, and investigates and exposes torture and ill-treatment.

Anglo-Irish agreement Agreement on Northern Ireland reached by British Prime Minister Margaret Thatcher and Irish Prime Minister Garret Fitzgerald on 15 Nov. 1985. The agreement recognized the right of the Northern Irish population to decide its own destiny but created an Inter-governmental Conference to discuss political, security and legal matters, with the Irish government having a consultative role in the province's affairs. The agreement was angrily received by the Protestant community and Unionist MPs boycotted the House of Commons until 1987 in protest. See also Maryfield.

Angry Brigade Anarchist terrorist group active from 1968 to 1971 which bombed and mounted gun attacks on government buildings, banks, embassies and the home of Employment Secretary Robert Carr. Of eight alleged members tried in 1972, four were found guilty and imprisoned.

ANL See Anti-Nazi League.

Anti-Nazi League (ANL) The leading left-wing pressure group opposing the activities of fascist and racist groups in Britain, originally founded in the late 1970s in response to the activities of the National Front. It was relaunched in

Jan. 1992 to challenge the revival of the British National party (see p. 88), the rise of neo-Nazism in Europe, and the increase in racial attacks in Britain. Labour supporters dominated the ANL's 50,000 members, but the Socialist Workers' party (SWP), which founded the original ANL, was strongly represented.

Apostles Intellectual elite society centred on King's College, Cambridge, founded in the eighteenth century. The society achieved notoriety with the post-war revelation that among its members were the communist spies Anthony Blunt, Guy Burgess, Kim Philby and Donald Maclean, recruited by Soviet agents in the 1930s. See also Blunt affair, Burgess–Maclean scandal, Philby case.

Armalite and the ballot box The slogan setting out the strategy of the Provisional IRA and its political wing Provisional Sinn Fein, combining anti-British terrorist violence with electoral politics in the nationalist areas of Northern Ireland. See also Sinn Fein.

Army Bureau of Current Affairs (ABCA) Credited, probably unjustifiably, with helping Labour to victory in the 1945 general election by influencing troops to vote against the Conservatives. Established in June 1941, ABCA organized compulsory weekly discussions on current affairs and post-war reconstruction, prompting fears among many senior officers (and the Prime Minister, Winston Churchill) of politicization of the miltary rank-and-file.

Back to Basics Attempt by Prime Minister John Major at the 1993 Conservative party conference to inject ideological coherence into his drifting government. Apparently involving a return to 'old standards', the slogan was open to many interpretations. One was that it included an element of morality, with attacks, for example, on single mothers. But revelations of adultery and other sexual activities of some ministers led to the policy's collapse in ridicule in early 1994. See also Majorism.

Bank of Credit and Commerce International (BCCI) Established in 1972, the bank's British branches had a large proportion of Asian small business account-holders. Following increasing concern about the bank's activities, including the alleged involvement of officials in drug money laundering in Oct. 1990, the Bank of England ordered an end to BCCI's operations in Britain on 5 July 1991. Thousands of account-holders were left with minimal compensation for their subsequent losses.

bank rate The rate at which the Bank of England is prepared to lend to the clearing banks. When raised, it has the immediate effect of raising the rate of discount on Treasury Bills. Known as the Minimum Lending Rate (MLR) from October 1972 to August 1981. The Labour government elected in 1997 gave the Bank of England power to determine interest rates.

BAOR See British Army of the Rhine.

Barber Boom A period of economic prosperity in Britain in 1972–73 during a 'dash for growth' attempted by the Chancellor of the Exchequer Anthony Barber. Barber, who was subsequently blamed for the inflation which resulted, had reputedly been reluctant to be so expansive but Prime Minister Edward Heath was determined on the policy.

Basildon Parliamentary constituency in Essex with a predominance of C2s (qv) which usually makes the earliest declaration in general elections. The victory of the Conservative candidate in the 1992 general election made it clear that Labour, despite its growing hopes of winning back former support-ers, had lost the election. See also Essex Man.

BCCI See Bank of Credit and Commerce International.

Belgrano See *General Belgrano.*

Bennite Supporter of Tony Benn (b. 1925), a minister in the 1966–70 and 1974–79 Labour governments. He argued, particularly after the 1979 Conservative victory, for greater influence of activists in the formulation of party policy and for a more fundamentalist socialist approach. Although he narrowly missed election as deputy party leader in 1980, Benn's influence gradually weakened following the election of Kinnock as leader in 1983, the defeat of the 1984–85 miners' strike, and the third Conservative election vic-tory in 1987.

Bevanites Labour party members who supported Aneurin 'Nye' Bevan (1897–1960) on defence and a more 'socialist' emphasis in the early 1950s. Bevan resigned as Minister of Health in Apr. 1951 (with two other ministers) in protest against the imposition of prescription charges to help meet defence costs. In May 1952, 57 Labour MPs supported Bevan against the Labour leadership's backing of Conservative defence policy. Bevan retained much support in the constituencies and among left-wing and pacifist MPs in subsequent conflicts over nuclear weapons. But in 1957, following his appointment as shadow Foreign Secretary, he retracted his opposition to Britain's retention of nuclear weapons and effectively abandoned the 'Bevanites'. See also Gaitskellites.

Beveridge Report The *Report on Social Insurance and Allied Services* produced by the economist and academic William Beveridge (1879–1963) in 1942. The report was the foundation for the policies and institutions of the welfare state, promising support 'from the cradle to the grave' through children's allowances, a comprehensive health service, unemployment benefit and pensions financed through a national insurance system. It was broadly accepted in a government White Paper in 1944 and implemented in the National Insurance Act 1946.

Bevin Boys Men who were conscripted to work in the mining industry rather than the armed forces in the 1940s. They were named after Ernest Bevin (1881–1951), Minister of Labour from 1940–45.

Big Bang Major changes in the organization of the London Stock Exchange introduced on 27 Oct. 1986. The changes recognized that the Stock Exchange was part of a global financial market and altered the structure and ownership of firms, removed restrictions on charging for financial services, and introduced new forms of regulation in addition to new means of computerized trading.

Big Five Term used during the first years of the Attlee administration after 1945 to describe the key figures in the government – Attlee himself, Bevin, Cripps, Dalton and Morrison. The enforced resignation of Dalton following a budget leak in 1947 reduced the number to four.

Bingham Report (1) Report issued in Sept. 1978 following an inquiry under Thomas Bingham QC on the alleged breaking of sanctions (qv) against the white rebel regime in Southern Rhodesia after its unilateral declaration of independence (qv). The report suggested that the Labour government under Harold Wilson, despite its denials, was aware that oil was being supplied by Shell-BP and Total. (2) Report issued in 1992 by Mr Justice Bingham on the collapse of the Bank of Credit and Commerce International (qv). The report cleared the Bank of England of failing to act promptly enough to stop BCCI's operations.

Birmingham Six Six Irishmen (Hugh Callaghan, Patrick Hill, Gerry Hunter, Richard McIlKenny, William Power and John Walker) imprisoned for life in July 1975 for allegedly planting bombs in Birmingham public houses in Nov. 1974 which killed 21 people and injured 162. The six, together with many prominent supporters, continued to protest their innocence. On 14 Mar. 1991 they were released following the Director of Public Prosecutions' acceptance in the Court of Appeal that police and forensic evidence in the case was unsafe to rely upon. See also Guildford Four, Prevention of Terrorism Act.

Black Monday Term applied to the collapse of the New York Stock Exchange on 19 Oct. 1987, when the Dow Jones Industrial Average fell by 22.6 per cent, bringing major falls in other markets around the world. It was the worst fall since 1929.

black sections Organization in the Labour party restricted to black and Asian members advocated in the 1980s to strengthen ethnic minority voices in policy-making. The proposal was overwhelmingly rejected at the 1984 and 1986 Labour party conferences but 35 constituency parties nevertheless formed black sections. In 1993 the Black Socialist Society was formed as an alternative party grouping to black sections.

Black Wednesday Speculative selling of the pound on the money markets prompted the raising of the base rate twice on 16 Sept. 1992 to 15 per cent. When this failed to preserve sterling's value relative to the Deutschmark, Chancellor of the Exchequer Norman Lamont withdrew Britain from the Exchange Rate Mechanism (qv), effectively a devaluation (qv) of the pound. The crisis, and underlying impression of drifting and weak leadership, threatened the position of Lamont and of the Prime Minister, John Major. See also European Monetary System.

blanket protest Protest mounted by Irish republican prisoners in the Maze Prison from 1980 demanding political status. Prisoners refused to wear prison clothes, wrapping themselves in blankets. The campaign escalated into a 'dirty protest' in which prisoners soiled their cells, and then into a hunger strike in which ten died before the protest was ended in return for limited concessions.

block vote The allocation of votes at Labour party conferences (and at party constituency level) based on the total membership of affiliated organizations, for example trade unions and socialist societies. The most controversial aspect of the block vote was the influence over party policy exerted by leaders of the larger trade unions through their mass membership. Major objections to the block vote were that union members often had no voice in the decision and that the vote – cast by union officials in a show of hands or with voting cards – was monolithic, with no allowance for a dissenting opinion. One member, one vote (OMOV), introduced at the 1993 party conference, went some way to meet these objections.

Bloody Friday On 21 July 1972, following abortive negotiations with the British government, the Provisional IRA exploded 26 bombs within 75 minutes in shopping centres, bus and railway stations in the centre of Belfast, killing eleven people and seriously injuring 130.

Bloody Sunday Shooting by soldiers of the 1st Battalion Parachute Regiment in Londonderry on 30 Jan. 1972 of thirteen unarmed Roman Catholic civilians on a peaceful civil rights demonstration. The army claimed it was responding to IRA fire. A Tribunal of Inquiry conducted by Lord Widgery exonerated British troops but the events intensified the bitterness felt by sections of the Catholic community against Britain and encouraged support for the Irish Republican Army (qv). The Labour government elected in 1997 established the Saville Inquiry in January 1998 to re-examine the events of 'Bloody Sunday'.

Blue Streak British solid-fuelled surface-to-surface rocket intended to carry a nuclear warhead. Its development for the British independent nuclear deterrent was abandoned in 1959. Britain opted in 1962 for the submarine-based Polaris (qv) missile provided by the USA.

Blunt affair Sir Anthony Blunt (1907–83), the Queen's personal adviser on art (1945–72), previously a British intelligence officer (1940–45), confessed in 1964 (in exchange for immunity from prosecution) to having been a Soviet agent since the 1930s and to having been the 'fourth man' in the Burgess–Maclean scandal (qv). Revelation in a book published in 1979 forced an official admission of his role by Margaret Thatcher on 15 Nov. Blunt's knighthood was annulled by the Queen on the following day. See also Apostles, Philby case.

boat people Refugees from Vietnam, thousands of whom left by boat following the reunification of the country in 1975. Although some were allowed eventual entry into Britain, many more remained incarcerated in camps in Hong Kong. Britain entered into an agreement with Vietnam to arrange the forced repatriation from Hong Kong of large numbers of the refugees.

'bonfire of controls' The abolition by President of the Board of Trade Harold Wilson of controls over business, announced on 5 Nov. 1948. Within a few months, the Labour government scrapped the requirement for licences and permits relating to consumer goods and industrial equipment and for imports. Although the intention was to meet popular criticisms of a burgeoning bureaucracy, sections of the Labour left argued that the government was abandoning the basic elements of socialist planning.

Bow Group Pressure group formed in the late 1950s to encourage fresh thinking across the left and right of the Conservative party, particularly intended to encourage a greater emphasis on free-market economics. The first meetings were held in Bow in east London, whence the group takes its name.

Brighton bombing Provisional IRA bombing at the Grand Hotel, Brighton, on 12 Oct. 1984 during the Conservative party conference, which killed five people, including a Conservative MP. Margaret Thatcher, the Prime Minister, was among those who narrowly escaped death.

British Army of the Rhine (BAOR) The German based post-1945 British occupation force. Following recognition of West German sovereignty in 1955, BAOR became part of the NATO defence against potential Soviet attack. From 1994 it formed part of a new multinational rapid response force based in the reunited Germany. See also North Atlantic Treaty Organization.

British disease The alleged cause of Britain's post-war relative economic decline and persistently low industrial productivity reputedly categorized by weak management, strike-prone workers, and over-strong unions.

Brixton riots Rioting broke out on 11 Apr. 1981 following a week-long 'Operation Swamp' mounted by police to reduce street crime. The local black population saw the operation as unnecessarily provocative. During three days of rioting white and black youths fought the police, burnt buildings and vehicles and looted shops. Further riots broke out in Toxteth, Southall, Handsworth, Moss Side and other inner-city areas in July. There was further rioting in Brixton on 28 Sept. 1985, following the accidental shooting of a black woman by police. See also Broadwater Farm, Scarman Report.

Broadwater Farm A council estate in Tottenham, north London, the scene of rioting on 6 Oct. 1985 at which a police officer, Keith Blakelock, was killed. The three black youths who were imprisoned for the murder were released in 1991 following successful appeals. See also Brixton riots.

Bruges Group Group formed following Margaret Thatcher's speech in Bruges on 20 Sept. 1988. The group supported her view of restricting European cooperation to a relationship between separate sovereign nations rather than thoroughgoing federal unity. It now concentrates on publishing research papers.

B-Specials Protestant-dominated part-time armed police in Northern Ireland, seen by the Roman Catholic community as a symbol of Protestant oppression. They were disbanded in 1969 and replaced by the Ulster Defence Regiment (qv), which was intended to be a non-denominational force which would secure their support against terrorism of the Catholic community. See also Royal Ulster Constabulary.

Burgess–Maclean scandal Guy Burgess (1910–63), second secretary at the British Embassy in Washington, and Donald Maclean (1913–83), head of the US Department at the Foreign Office – both involved in high-level security work – disappeared on 25 May 1951. They reappeared in the Soviet Union confirming they had been long-term communist agents. Kim Philby (1911–88) was later revealed to be the 'third man' who had warned them to leave before they were revealed as spies. A 'fourth man', Sir Anthony Blunt (1907–83), and a 'fifth man', John Cairncross, were later exposed, bringing British intelligence into even greater disrepute. See also Apostles, Blunt affair, Philby case.

Butskellism The broad post-war political consensus between Labour and the Conservatives on the mixed economy, full employment and the welfare state, combining the names of R A 'Rab' Butler, Conservative Chancellor of the Exchequer (1951–55), and Hugh Gaitskell, Labour Chancellor of the Exchequer (1950–51) and party leader (1955–63).

butter mountain Late 1970s phenomenon in Europe resulting from the Common Agricultural Policy (qv) which, by subsidizing agricultural producers to protect their interests, encouraged unsellable surpluses of butter and grain 'mountains' and milk and wine 'lakes'. It was criticized as an inevitable result of 'feather-bedding' European farmers, and attempts were made to cut back on subsidies and to reduce production.

by-election Election held to fill a parliamentary or local council vacancy following the resignation or death of an MP or councillor during the normal term of office. For famous by-elections, see pp 63–5.

C2s Skilled manual and clerical workers who were traditionally Labour voters but whose shift towards the Conservative party from 1979 – reputedly because of council house sales and promised income tax reductions – provided significant electoral support for Margaret Thatcher, largely in the Midlands and south of England. See also Basildon, class definition, Essex Man.

CAFE See under Conservatives Against a Federal Europe.

Campaign for Democratic Socialism (CDS) Right-wing group in the Labour party formed (allegedly with the help of US Central Intelligence Agency funds) following the victory for unilateralism (qv) at the Oct. 1960 Labour party conference. Supporters of party leader Hugh Gaitskell (1906–63), the CDS successfully undermined left-wing influence in constituency parties and the trade unions and reversed the unilateral decision in 1961.

Campaign for Homosexual Equality (CHE) Pressure group formed in 1969 when the North-Western Committee of the Homosexual Law Reform Society (see Albany Trust) became the Committee for Homosexual Equality. In 1971 CHE was renamed the Campaign for Homosexual Equality and within a short period became the biggest gay organization in Britain. In the same year the Campaign founded its own counselling division, Friend (Fellowship for the Relief of the Isolated and in Need and Distress). It was very active until the late 1970s, when it was overtaken by other organizations such as the Gay Community Organization, OLGA and Stonewall. CHE had two main roles: to encourage further legal reform (e.g. equalizing the age of consent for homosexuals and heterosexuals) and influence public opinion in favour of reform, and to act as a national body in support of local groups throughout the country.

Campaign for an Independent Britain A cross-party organization aiming at repeal of the 1972 European Communities Act, through which United Kingdom law can be overruled by European Union directives. The organization took its present title in 1989. It developed from anti-Common Market campaigners in the 1975 referendum on the issue, becoming the Safeguard Britain Campaign in 1976, renaming itself the British anti-Common Market Campaign in 1983. Relatively small in numbers, the Campaign publishes a newsletter, *Independence*.

Campaign for Labour Party Democracy (CLPD) Labour pressure group founded in 1973 to make the parliamentary party respond more to the wishes of constituency activists.

Campaign for Nuclear Disarmament (CND) Launched on 17 Feb. 1958, demanding a unilateral British abandonment of nuclear weapons and a reduction in arms expenditure. Mounted an annual Aldermaston march (qv) between 1958 and 1964 and its influence was such that in 1960 the Labour party conference passed a unilateralist resolution. From 1961 to 1979 support fell away but membership rose again with the deployment of Cruise missiles (qv) in western Europe. This renewed surge brought membership to over 100,000 in 1984. With the end of the Cold War, and successfully negotiated multilateral nuclear disarmament, support once more declined rapidly. Membership by the end of the 1990s was down to 45,000. See also Committee of 100, European Nuclear Disarmament, Holy Loch, unilateralism.

Campaign Group Section of the Labour Left in Parliament which broke away from the Tribune Group (qv) in 1984. Its supporters favoured a defence of fundamentalist socialism in the face of the policy changes being made under the leadership of Neil Kinnock. See also Hard Left.

CAP See Common Agricultural Policy.

cardboard cities Shanty settlements of homeless and unemployed people which appeared in the centres of British towns and cities (along with increased numbers of beggars) from the late 1980s, particularly in London, largely because of deepening economic recession and the withdrawal of social security benefits from 16 and 17 year olds.

Cathays Park The building where the Welsh Office is situated in Cardiff.

CBI See Confederation of British Industry.

Central African Federation Unification of the African territories of Nyasaland, Northern and Southern Rhodesia on 3 Sept. 1953 to promote economic development and defend the interests of the white minority. Deeply unpopular with the majority African population, the federation collapsed in 1961.

Central Office Headquarters since 1958 of the Conservative party, situated in Smith Square (qv), central London.

Centre for Policy Studies Right-wing research institute founded in 1974 by Sir Keith Joseph (1918–94).

Centre Forward Anti-Thatcherite group formed among Conservative backbenchers in 1983 by Francis Pym (b. 1922) after he had been dismissed as Foreign Secretary following the general election. (Pym had said in the campaign that a large Conservative majority was ill advised.) The group soon faded into insignificance. See also Thatcherite.

Charter 87 Organization launched in 1987 to campaign for the human and legal rights of asylum-seekers in the United Kingdom, and as a response to stricter Home Office policy regarding the treatment of such refugees and their applications for asylum. It seeks to enshrine in law a charter endorsing the principles of the 1951 UN Convention Relating to the Status of Refugees.

Charter 88 A political pressure group formed in 1988 advocating a written constitution, proportional representation and a Bill of Rights, transforming the British from subjects to citizens. Despite the tastelessness of naming itself after Czech dissidents who were genuinely and courageously active against Stalinist dictatorship (Charter 77), the ideas put forward by Charter 88 became increasingly influential.

Cheltenham Site of the Government Communications Headquarters (qv).

Chequers The official country residence of prime ministers, near Princes Risborough, Bucks. First occupied by Lloyd George in 1921, Chequers was acquired by Viscount Lee of Fareham in 1909 and provided by him as a weekend retreat in 1917.

Child Poverty Action Group (CPAG) Pressure group founded in 1965 to campaign for the relief of poverty among children, particularly by ensuring that families on low income with children receive their full statutory entitlement of income benefits.

Chiltern Hundreds An ancient royal sinecure office, application to hold which enables MPs (who are debarred from holding an 'office of profit' under the Crown) to resign their seats.

Christian Action Pressure group founded in 1949 to encourage involvement of Christians in social and political affairs. One of its offshoots was the Defence and Aid Fund, established in the 1950s as a 'treason fund' for defendants accused of treason in South Africa.

Citizen's Charter Attempt to make public services more responsive to consumers' wishes, announced by John Major on 22 July 1991. Among the most prominent of individual charters were those for the health service and education, with pledges of guaranteed performance targets and greater information for consumers.

class definition Shorthand used in politics, the media and advertising to differentiate social classes. A: upper-middle class; B: professional middle class; C1: white-collar lower-middle class; C2: skilled manual and clerical; D: unskilled working class; E: subsistence, for example pensioners, lone parents and long-term unemployed or sick people dependent on state benefits. See also C2s.

Clause IV The clause in the 1918 Labour party constitution which embodied the party's objective to 'secure for the workers by hand or by brain the full fruits of their industry and the most equitable distribution thereof that may be possible upon the basis of common ownership of the means of production, distribution, and exchange, and the best obtainable system of popular administration and control of each industry or service'. Labour leader Hugh Gaitskell came into conflict with the left by attempting to remove it in the 1950s (see Gaitskellites), but the party under Neil Kinnock effectively abandoned the clause, though it remained in the party's constitution. In 1994 Tony Blair urged a new constitution, with the clause amended. This came about at the April 1995 party conference with a vote of 65.2 to 34.7 in favour of rewording the clause.

Clause 28 A section (originally Clause 27) of the Local Government Act 1988 inserted by Conservative back-benchers which banned local authorities from promoting the acceptability of homosexuality and from allowing schools to teach that a family with two gay or lesbian parents was a legitimate unit. The clause was ostensibly provoked by the antics of 'Loony Left' (qv) Labour councils, but was seen by many lesbians and gay men as an attack on their legal rights. Labour is now (2000) committed to its repeal.

Clay Cross revolt Labour opposition to the Housing Finance Act 1972 – which aimed to force local authorities to charge a market rent for council housing – led to a refusal to implement the legislation by left-wing councillors in the Derbyshire mining community of Clay Cross. The councillors were surcharged and barred from office by the District Auditor.

closed shop Compulsory trade union membership for all employees in a particular workplace. Criticized as an infringement of individual choice, it is defended by unions arguing that all workers sharing gains made in negotiations should contribute to maintaining the union machinery. The closed shop was effectively ended by post-1980 Conservative employment legislation and 'New Labour' has no plans to change this.

CND See Campaign for Nuclear Disarmament.

Cod War Dispute between Britain and Iceland from Sept. 1972 to June 1976 over Iceland's unilateral extension from 12 to 50 miles of territorial waters limit in which foreign trawlers were allowed to fish. Icelandic gunboats attempted to intercept British trawlers and Royal Navy frigates intervened. A compromise agreement allowed a maximum of 24 British trawlers into the area.

Cold War The term was first used in the US Congress to describe deteriorating relations between the United States and the USSR. It describes the period of tension between 1946 and the early 1970s and the accompanying crises (Greek Civil War, Berlin, Cuba). The divisions were formalized by the creation of NATO (1949–50) and the Warsaw Pact (1955). With the advent of Gorbachev in the USSR, and the fall of communist regimes in eastern Europe after 1989, it was effectively over in its old form (though tensions with Russia have resurfaced as over Kosovo). It was formally ended by the signing of the Conference on Security and Cooperation in Europe (CSCE) on 19 November 1990.

Commission on Social Justice Established under the chairmanship of Sir Gordon Borrie by the Labour leader John Smith (1938–94) in 1992, the Commission was intended to conduct a fundamental re-examination of the party's welfare and benefits policies. In a final report issued in 1994, the Commission made a number of recommendations for a future Labour government, including a commitment to full employment, a minimum wage, subsidies for employers to assist the long-term unemployed, restoration of benefits to 16 and 17 year olds, higher child benefit, guaranteed nursery education for 3–5 year olds, and an increased top rate of income tax. Although the report was shelved, some of the recommended policies were carried through by the Labour government elected in 1997.

Committee of 100 Militant section of the Campaign for Nuclear Disarmament (qv) formed in Oct. 1960 by the philosopher Bertrand Russell (1872–1970) and supported by many theatrical and literary personalities, which advocated civil disobedience rather than constitutional action to achieve unilateral nuclear disarmament.

Common Agricultural Policy (CAP) This dictated farming and other primary production of EEC member states by allocating subsidies to encourage or discourage the production of certain goods. See also butter mountain, European Union.

Common Market Popular name for the European Community or EEC (qqv). Now used of the European Union.

Commonwealth A grouping of states, numbering 54 in 2000, which evolved from the former territories of the British Empire. The Statute of Westminster (31 Dec. 1931) defined the structure of the British Commonwealth and recognized the dominions as 'autonomous communities'. The organization works to improve economic collaboration and other forms of cooperation between member states. Not all former territories of the British Empire are members. Burma (Myanmar) never joined. The Republic of Ireland is not a member. South Africa left in 1961, rejoining in 1994. Pakistan left in 1972 and rejoined in 1989, but left again after the military coup in 1999. A recent member (1995) is the former Portuguese colony of Mozambique.

Community, The See European Union.

community charge Also known as the poll tax, local government taxation introduced to replace rates in Scotland on 1 Apr. 1989 and in England and Wales on 1 Apr. 1990. The charge caused widespread protests and refusals to pay, largely because it was levied on individuals and took little account of ability to pay. In 1991 the Conservative government announced the tax's abandonment, replacing it with the council tax (qv) in 1993. See also Trafalgar Square riot, Wandsworth.

community politics Political activity developed by the Liberal party in the 1970s on the basis that voters are more concerned with immediate local issues – the condition of pavements, rubbish collection, education and medical services – than with wider national issues. The success, albeit limited and temporary, of the tactic encouraged rival parties to give more serious attention to local issues.

comprehensives System of schooling favoured by progressive educationalists which took pupils without any form of selection (unlike the traditional grammar schools, which were attacked as elitist and divisive). The first purpose-built comprehensive was at Kidbrooke in 1954. Controversy over 'comprehensive education' has raged for several decades.

Confederation of British Industry (CBI) The leading employers' organization formed in 1965 by the merger of the British Employers' Federation, Federation of British Industry, and the National Association of British Manufacturers.

Confederation of Indian Organizations A body established in 1975 by a number of groups concerned with discrimination against the Asian community, which acts as the national umbrella body for Indian organizations throughout the UK. It works as a lobbying group, and campaigns through the media and by means of research and conferences for equal opportunities for Asian citizens.

confrontation Military conflict between Indonesia and the Malaysian Federation which began with the latter's establishment in Sept. 1963 and continued until a peace agreement on 1 June 1966. See p 210.

271

Congress House Headquarters of the Trades Union Congress (qv) in Great Russell Street, London.

conscription Compulsory military service in Britain was introduced by the National Service Act of February 1916 which remained effective until 1920. In April 1939, a new National Service Act conscripted men aged 20 to 41; this was extended in September 1939 to men between the ages of 19 and 41 and in December 1941 to men aged between 18 and 41 and single women of 20 to 30. When peace returned women were exempted and the period of service for men reduced to eighteen months (two years during the Korean War of 1950–53). Conscription was ended in Britain in 1960.

Conservatives Against a Federal Europe (CAFE) Influential Eurosceptic pressure group (mainly but not exclusively of Conservative party members). Its presidents are Lord Pearson of Rannoch (a prominent Tory sceptic) and Lord McAlpine (a former Conservative party treasurer who switched to the Referendum party). Its chairman is former Conservative Chancellor Lord Lamont. Launched in 1995, the organization claimed 4,000 members in 1999. No less than eleven of William Hague's front-bench team are claimed as members.

Control Commission The administrative authority in the British zone of Germany 1945–48 (the other occupying powers – France, the USA and the USSR – had similar commissions). The four military commanders acted together as a supreme Control Council.

Council of Europe Grouping of European states established in May 1948, based in Strasbourg, and which concentrates on cultural and human rights issues. Following the collapse of communism in 1989, former Czechoslovakia, Hungary and Poland were admitted as members of the Council. They have been followed by the Baltic states and such Balkan countries as Bulgaria, Albania and Romania.

council tax Local tax replacing the deeply unpopular community charge (qv), announced by Environment Secretary Michael Heseltine on 21 Mar. 1991 and introduced on 1 Apr. 1993. The council tax attempted to introduce an element of fairness by being levied on the value of the property rather than, as with the community charge, on an individual resident.

County Hall The headquarters (on the South Bank of the Thames) of London's local government (post-war generally under Labour party control): the London County Council (LCC) from the building's completion in 1933 until 1965, and the Greater London Council (GLC) from 1965 until the GLC's abolition by the Conservative government on 31 Mar. 1986. The building, following an unsuccessful acquisition attempt by the London School of Economics and Political Science in 1992, was eventually bought by a Japanese company for conversion into a hotel. See also Greater London Council.

Crabb affair Royal Navy frogman Commander Lionel 'Buster' Crabb disappeared while searching the underside of the Soviet cruiser *Ordjonikidze* in Portsmouth Harbour in May 1956. The cruiser had carried Soviet leaders Khrushchev and Bulganin on a visit to Britain. The British government denied any knowledge of Crabb's activities and the incident – and Crabb's fate – remained a mystery. Rumours suggested that Crabb had defected, been drowned, or that he had been killed by British intelligence because of the possible political embarrassment that his action might cause.

Crichel Down Affair arising from the Ministry of Agriculture's refusal to allow the three owners of 725 acres of Dorset farmland, compulsorily purchased to build an airfield in 1938, to buy it back after the war. The ministry argued that it could be farmed more effectively as a single unit but an inquiry under Sir Arthur Clark QC publicly criticized named civil servants for a faulty decision. The minister, Sir Thomas Dugdale, took responsibility and resigned in July 1954.

cross-bencher A member of the House of Lords who remains politically neutral and does not take the whip (qv) of any of the main parties.

Cruise missiles Accurate intermediate-range ground- or air-launched missiles deployed in western Europe from 1983 in response to the Soviet SS-20A, encouraging a growth in anti-nuclear agitation, particularly in Britain, the Netherlands and West Germany. In Britain the missiles were sited at Molesworth and Greenham Common (qv). Their withdrawal was negotiated in 1987 and removal of Cruise from Britain began in 1989.

Cunningham amendment An amendment to the Scottish Devolution Bill tabled by Labour MP George Cunningham in January 1978 and passed by 166 votes to 151 which had the effect of eventually negating the government's policy. The amendment invalidated a Scottish vote in support of devolution unless at least 40 per cent of registered voters declared in favour. In the referendum held in March 1979, although the devolution case won a majority, only 32.9 per cent of registered voters supported devolution.

DEA See Department of Economic Affairs.

Death on the Rock Television documentary on the shooting on 6 Mar. 1988 of three IRA members by soldiers from the SAS (see Special Air Service) while allegedly preparing a bombing action in Gibraltar (qv). The programme caused controversy by claiming that the victims were not resisting and questioning evidence that they were on a terrorist mission. Shown by Thames Television, the programme encouraged Conservative antagonism towards independent television rather than solely, as in the past, the BBC.

decimalization The introduction of decimal currency on 15 Feb. 1971, replacing the 20 shilling pound with the 100 pence pound.

decommissioning The giving up of weapons and bomb-making materials by paramilitaries in Northern Ireland, an important element of the April 1998

273

Good Friday agreement (qv). Under the agreement, political groupings said they would use their influence to persuade paramilitary forces to which they were connected to disarm. However, the refusal of the Provisional IRA to do so, on the grounds that disarming would be construed as surrender, proved an obstacle to the peace process. In July 1999 the British and Irish governments proposed decommissioning under a timetable produced by an independent commission headed by General John de Chatelain. Continuing difficulties led to the Ulster Unionists refusing to sit in the Northern Ireland Executive with Sinn Fein until the IRA provided definite evidence of disarming. It was lack of progress on decommissioning that led to the crisis of Feb. 2000.

Delors Plan Plan for European political and monetary union drawn up by a committee formed in 1988 and headed by Jacques Delors (b. 1925), President of the Commission of the European Community 1985–95. It involved the creation of a European Monetary System (qv), the formation of a system of central banks to exert greater influence on national monetary policies and eventual central control over monetary policies, budget deficits and exchange rates. The plan was accepted in 1989 as the basis for future planning of European Monetary Union but some aspects aroused resistance, notably from the British government headed by Margaret Thatcher.

Democracy Movement Grouping established to mobilize the anti-Euro vote when the Labour government's promise of a referendum on the entry into the single European currency takes place. The movement, chaired by Paul Sykes (who provided finance for anti-Euro Conservative candidates in the 1997 general election), is in practice a successor to the Referendum party (qv) and campaigns on the slogan 'Give a pound to save the pound'.

Democratic Left Name adopted by what remained of the Communist party of Great Britain in 1991 following the collapse of the USSR.

denationalization The return of nationalized industries to private ownership, a policy first put forward by the Conservatives following their return to power in 1951 when they undid the Labour government's nationalization (qv) of the steel and road haulage industries. Overtaken in the 1980s by the term privatization (qv).

Denning Report Report of an inquiry under Lord Denning, Master of the Rolls, in 1963 into the security implications of the Profumo affair (qv). The report, which was a phenomenal best-seller, concluded that War Minister Profumo's relationship with the prostitute Christine Keeler had not threatened national security and that the rumours of sexual impropriety among other ministers were unfounded.

Department of Economic Affairs (DEA) Department set up by the Labour government in 1964, ostensibly as a counterweight to the restricting influence of the Treasury in economic policy. Under its first minister George Brown, the DEA published a five-year National Plan in 1965 aiming at an annual expansion in domestic output of 4 per cent. Balance of payments crises and devaluation in 1967 prevented this being achieved. Increasingly less influential, the DEA was wound up in 1969.

deselection The withdrawal of support by constituency Labour parties from sitting MPs to be replaced by new candidates for the next election. Although there were few cases of deselection following Labour's reselection (qv) reform, perhaps ironically in view of the left's support for the policy, the earliest victims were two left-wing MPs who were replaced by black candidates. Among prominent Conservative victims of deselection was Sir George Gardiner, Eurosceptic MP for Reigate, in 1997.

devaluation Reduction in the value of a country's currency relative to that of other countries, aiming at cutting the price of exports and increasing the price of imports to ease balance of payments deficits. Britain devalued the pound under Labour governments in 1949 and 1967 (see July Measures). The Conservative government effectively devalued in 1992 on 'Black Wednesday' (qv).

devolution Decentralization of political power to a region, usually referring to Scotland and Wales in Britain. In a referendum (qv) held on 1 Mar. 1979 only 32.85 per cent voted in support of a Scottish Assembly. In Wales 11.9 per cent supported Welsh devolution and 46.9 per cent opposed it. Scottish devolution returned as a major issue in the 1997 general election, with Labour committed to a Scottish Parliament and Welsh Assembly. After referenda in 1997 (see pp 120 and 122) these became operational in 1999.

Diplock courts Trials of terrorist suspects held in Northern Ireland by a judge sitting alone without a jury. They were introduced in 1973 because of the alleged reluctance of juries to convict and witnesses to give evidence for fear of intimidation. Named after Lord Diplock.

direct rule Term used for the direct administration and government of Northern Ireland from Westminster rather than by the devolved Northern Ireland assembly at Stormont (Stormont was suspended and direct rule introduced in March 1972).

disestablishment Removing the Church of England's privileged role as the established state church, with the sovereign as supreme head. Although both the Labour and Liberal parties favoured disestablishment, it remained a relatively dead issue in British post-war politics until the separation of the Prince and Princess of Wales in Dec. 1992 posed questions about the position of Prince Charles as a potentially divorced king. The Prince of Wales has appeared sympathetic to disestablishment as an acknowledgement of Britain's multicultural community. Some senior Anglicans are now in favour of disestablishment.

D-Notice Defence Notice: a request issued by the Defence, Press and Broadcasting Committee (the D-Notice Committee whose secretary is a Ministry of Defence official) to media editors not to publish or to broadcast on subjects which might lead to breaches of security. The system, introduced in 1911, is not legally binding but acts as a form of voluntary self-censorship.

Donovan Commission Royal Commission on Trade Unions and Employers' Associations chaired by Lord Donovan, which was appointed in Apr. 1965 and reported in June 1968. The commission's report recognized the increased decentralization of pay bargaining and the growing influence of shop stewards in industrial relations but rejected legal or penal sanctions to discourage strikes, preferring instead voluntary reform.

Downing Street declaration Agreement announced on 15 Dec. 1993 between British Prime Minister John Major and Irish Prime Minister Albert Reynolds in an attempt to open the way to peace in Northern Ireland. The declaration offered Sinn Fein (qv) participation in multi-party talks on Ireland's future within three months of a ceasefire. Although the loyalist veto on unification remained, Britain adopted a near-neutral position on the possibility. The declaration followed meetings between Sinn Fein president Gerry Adams and SDLP leader John Hume and the revelation in Nov. 1993 that the British government had held secret talks with Sinn Fein in Feb. 1993. Hopes of immediate peace were disappointed but the IRA announced a ceasefire on 31 Aug. 1994.

dream ticket Political leadership combination which promises the best hope of party unity and electoral victory. Used of election of Neil Kinnock and Roy Hattersley to Labour leadership and deputy leadership in 1983, balancing the left and right of the Labour party. They went on to lose the 1987 and 1992 general elections.

Dries Conservative party members favouring a policy of strict monetarism (qv), reduced public expenditure, increased privatization (qv), strong defences, and a curtailing of trade union power. Prominent among the post-1979 Dries were Margaret Thatcher, Norman Tebbit and Sir Geoffrey Howe. See also Wets.

Dunkirk, Treaty of Fifty-year agreement signed by Britain and France on 4 Mar. 1947 for mutual assistance against any future German aggression and to consult over economic relations.

Ebbw Vale The South Wales constituency represented by left-wing Labour MP Aneurin Bevan (1897–1960). He was succeeded by Michael Foot, Labour party leader 1980–83.

EC European Community; see European Union.

EEA See European Economic Area.

EEC European Economic Community; see European Union.

EFTA See European Free Trade Association.

Eire Name by which the Republic of Ireland was known when it was a dominion within the Commonwealth (qv) 1937–48.

Electoral Reform Society Pressure group founded in 1884 as the Proportional Representation Society. The association aims to promote the use of the single transferable vote form of proportional representation, especially in the UK, in parliamentary and local government elections. In 1959 the present name was adopted.

EMS See European Monetary System.

END See European Nuclear Disarmament.

entryism Tactic, adopted by Trotskyist groupings, of joining the Labour party and capturing positions to subvert the party and force it to take a more left-wing stance. Prominent post-war entryists have been the Socialist Labour League (later the Workers' Revolutionary party) which captured the Young Socialist movement in the 1960s, forcing its abandonment by the Labour party, and the Militant Tendency. Militant supporters won control of Liverpool city council and secured the election of four MPs. Individuals who were identified as members were purged from the Labour party in 1985. Militant later set up a separate party, the Militant Labour party.

EOKA (Ethniki Orgánosis Kypriakoú Agónos/National Organization of Cypriot Struggle) Armed movement for the union of Cyprus with Greece (enosis) led by Colonel George Grivas (1898–1974) which began a guerrilla campaign against British forces in Cyprus in Apr. 1955, forcing the declaration of a state of emergency on 27 Nov. When a ceasefire came into effect on 13 Mar. 1959, British military and civilian casualties were 142 dead and 684 wounded, with almost 1,000 Greek and Turkish Cypriots killed or injured. Cyprus became independent under Archbishop Makarios (1913–77) as President on 16 Aug. 1960 without 'enosis'. EOKA continued its campaign and Makarios was ousted by EOKA members of the Cyprus National Guard, provoking the 1974 Turkish invasion and partition of the island.

ERM See Exchange Rate Mechanism.

Essex Man Archetypal south-east of England Conservative voter and Thatcher supporter in the 1980s, stereotypically seen as a vulgar, materialist racist. The expression (together with the sexist archetype Essex Girl) – although first coined by Conservative political columnist Simon Heffer – was used with superior disdain by liberal middle-class members of the media or who worked in the public services threatened by Conservative attack. See also Basildon, C2s.

Ettrick Bridge The home in the Scottish borders of Liberal party leader David Steel (b. 1938) where, on 29 May 1983, Steel replaced SDP leader (and Prime Minister designate) Roy Jenkins (b. 1920) as the main Alliance (qv) figure in the general election campaign then taking place. This followed Liberal criticisms that Jenkins, despite his political experience, was an ineffective campaigner.

EU See European Union.

Euratom European Atomic Energy Community, established by the Treaty of Rome in March 1957, which came into existence on 1 Jan. 1958. Its original members were Belgium, France, Italy, Luxembourg, the Netherlands and West Germany. Member states are pledged to cooperation in the development and application of nuclear power for peaceful purposes.

European Assembly See European Union.

European Defence Community Plan to create a European defence force by a treaty signed on 27 May 1952 between Belgium, France, Italy, Luxembourg, the Netherlands and West Germany. The French National Assembly refused to ratify the treaty on 30 Aug. 1954. At a conference held in London (28 Sept.–3 Oct. 1954) Italy and West Germany were invited to accede to the 1948 Treaty of Brussels; the Western European Union (qv) was inaugurated on 6 May 1955.

European Economic Area (EEA) Economic agreement which came into effect on 1 Jan. 1994 between the European Union (qv) and the remaining members of the European Free Trade Association (qv) as a preliminary to the latter's eventual membership of the EU.

European Economic Community See European Union.

European Free Trade Association (EFTA) Founded on British initiative in opposition to the European Economic Community in Jan. 1960 following the Stockholm Convention of 1959 to establish free trade in industrial products and promote trade in agricultural products between member countries. The original members were Austria, Denmark, Norway, Portugal, Sweden, Switzerland and the UK (the 'outer seven'). Finland became an associate member in 1960 and Ireland joined in 1970. By the end of 1966 all customs duties and quotas on industrial trade between EFTA members had been abolished. When Denmark, Britain and Ireland left to join the EEC, the remaining EFTA members negotiated free trade agreements with the EEC. By 1992 the majority of EFTA members had either joined or were applying to join the European Community. See also European Economic Area, European Union.

European Monetary System (EMS) Attempt to stabilize European currencies developed from 1979 by which members of the European Community coordinate exchange rates through the Exchange Rate Mechanism (qv). Rates are fixed in relation to the European Currency Unit at regular meetings of finance ministers. Between meetings members support the agreed value of each other's currencies by drawing from the European Monetary Cooperation Fund. All EC members were to have entered the EMS by 1992. Britain joined in Oct. 1990 but left 'temporarily' following 'Black Wednesday' (qv) in Sept. 1992, with apparently beneficial results for its economy. See also Delors Plan.

European Movement The leading pro-European pressure group. The UK Council of the European Movement was established in July 1948 under the chairmanship of the Liberal peer Lord Layton, in succession to Winston Churchill's United Europe Movement. The function of the council was to coordinate the activities of British organizations, or British sections of international organizations, working for the cause of European unity. In 1969 the UK Council merged with a sister organization, Britain in Europe.

European Nuclear Disarmament (END) British-based movement formed in 1980 to secure the removal of nuclear weapons from Europe and the creation of a united Europe free from both Soviet and US control. See also Campaign for Nuclear Disarmament.

European Union (EU) The Common Market set up by the Treaty of Rome signed in 1957 by France, Germany, Italy, Belgium, the Netherlands and Luxembourg ('the Six'). Britain applied to join in 1961 and 1967 but its entry was vetoed by France under de Gaulle. Negotiations which began in 1971 led to the membership of Britain, Ireland and Denmark in 1973 (see 'the Nine'). British membership was confirmed by a referendum (qv). The treaty established a common internal market and external tariff and aimed at establishing a Common Agricultural Policy (qv) and eliminating barriers to the free movement of capital, labour and transport and to coordinate economic policies. Executive powers were vested in a Council of Ministers and a Commission comprising two members from each of the larger states and one from each of the smaller states. The European Assembly – initially nominated but directly elected since 1979 – exercises general control. The EEC became the European Community (EC) in 1980 and then, on 1 Jan. 1994, the European Union (EU). There are currently (1 Jan. 2000) fifteen members. See also European Free Trade Association.

Eurosceptics Conservative party members who oppose further moves towards European political and economic integration. The group, which emerged after the replacement in 1990 of Margaret Thatcher as leader by John Major, came within three votes of defeating the government over the ratification of the Maastricht Treaty (qv) in Nov. 1992, almost bringing Major's administration down. Under the leadership of William Hague after 1997 the party has adopted an increasingly Eurosceptic tone (as in its policy towards the euro).

Exchange Rate Mechanism (ERM) Coordination of the currencies of members of the European Union. The ERM requires member states to keep their exchange rates within narrow bands and to adopt domestic monetary policies to achieve this. Disagreement over Britain's entry to the ERM between Prime Minister Margaret Thatcher (who feared a weakening of national sovereignty) and her Chancellor, Nigel Lawson (who believed it would curb inflationary tendencies in the economy), was largely responsible for Lawson's resignation in Oct. 1989. See also Black Wednesday, European Monetary System.

Fabian Member of a strand in Labour party politics deriving from the largely middle-class group established in 1884 to spread socialist ideas in Britain.

The Fabian Society later acted as a research body attached to the party. The term Fabian was subsequently applied to an advocate of gradual rather than radical social reform.

Falklands Factor Britain's success in the Falklands War (qv) reputedly gave Margaret Thatcher, hitherto one of the most deeply unpopular prime ministers ever, victory in the 1983 general election and consolidated her power in the Conservative party until 1990.

Falklands War Aimed to restore the 2,000-population Falkland Islands (Malvinas) to British control following the Argentine invasion of 2 Apr. 1982. A 6,000-strong naval and military task-force landed on 21 May and captured the capital Port Stanley on 14 June. See also Falklands Factor, Franks Report, *General Belgrano*, Ponting case, Special Air Service.

fellow-traveller A person who supports the policies of a political party without taking out formal membership; used most frequently of Communist party sympathizers.

Finchley North London constituency represented (1959–92) by Margaret Thatcher (b. 1925), Conservative leader (1975–90) and Prime Minister (1979–90).

first past the post Voting system by which the candidate who gains more votes than the next most supported candidate wins, even if the winning candidate has taken only a minority of the overall number of votes cast.

flying pickets Technique during a strike of transporting pickets to concentrate on vulnerable points. It was developed by Yorkshire miners in an unofficial dispute in 1969 but was seen to its fullest effect in the 1972 national miners' strike. Pickets of up to 1,000 strong were dispatched all over Yorkshire and as far afield as Ipswich, where they succeeded in closing down the port. See also miners' strikes, Saltley.

Fontainebleau agreement Agreement reached by European Community members on 25 June 1984 over Britain's rebate on its net contribution to the EC budget, demanded vociferously by Margaret Thatcher over the previous five years. Britain was to have a rebate of 66 per cent of the difference between what it paid in and what it received.

Footsie *Financial Times* Shares Index of the leading 100 companies in Britain. Its movement, which reflects buying and selling of shares and is reported daily, is seen as an indicator of the City of London's confidence in the economy.

Franks Report Report on an inquiry conducted by privy councillors under Lord Franks on whether the Conservative government was responsible for the Falklands War (qv) because it had been lax in not realizing that Argentina was planning to invade the islands in 1982. The report found that the government could not be held responsible for Argentina's 'unprovoked aggression'. It did, however, note that the Foreign Secretary, Lord

Carrington, had vainly urged the Defence Secretary, John Nott, not to proceed with the withdrawal of the patrol ship *Endurance* as the Argentine government might view it as a sign of weakness. Former Labour Prime Minister James Callaghan had made a similar request to Margaret Thatcher, who replied that she agreed with Mr Nott that 'other claims on the defence budget should have greater priority'.

Friends of the Earth Environmental pressure group founded in 1971.

Gaitskellites Labour party members who supported the social democratic tradition of moderate reformism advocated by Hugh Gaitskell (1906–63), party leader 1955–63. Argument with the more left-wing Bevanites (qv) also involved unilateral versus multilateral nuclear disarmament. Following the 1959 general election defeat, Gaitskell attempted to alter Labour's image by suggesting the abandonment of the socialist Clause IV (qv) but this was rejected after intense argument.

Gang of Four Labour politicians – Roy Jenkins, David Owen, William Rodgers and Shirley Williams – who, in response to increased left-wing influence in the party, formed a Council for Social Democracy with the 'Limehouse declaration' (qv) on 25 Jan. 1981. Although not ostensibly intended to constitute a breakaway from the Labour party, the Council was the forerunner of a new party, the Social Democratic party (SDP), which was launched on 26 Mar. 1981.

GCHQ See Government Communications Headquarters.

General Belgrano Argentine battleship sunk during the Falklands War (qv) by a British submarine on 2 May 1982 with the death of 323 of her 1,040 crew, leading to controversy over whether she genuinely posed a threat to the British task-force and to accusations that the sinking may have scuppered possible peace negotiations. See also Ponting case.

gerrymandering The drawing of electoral boundaries to give one section of the population or a political party an unfair advantage. The Unionist government in Northern Ireland traditionally used this method to give the Protestant community an even greater preponderance of seats in the parliament at Stormont than their numbers merited. This ended when direct rule was imposed in 1972.

Gibraltar British territory in southern Spain. Spain renewed its claim to Gibraltar after the Second World War but in Sept. 1967 the population voted to remain British by 12,438 votes to 44. In response, Spain closed the land frontier in May 1968 and sea links from Spain in June. The frontier was reopened following talks in Jan. 1985 but Spain still claims the territory. See also *Death on the Rock*, Special Air Service.

Gleneagles agreement Agreement reached by the Commonwealth heads of government at the Gleneagles Hotel in Scotland in 1977 banning official sporting links with South Africa as long as apartheid remained in effect.

Good Friday agreement A stage in the Northern Ireland peace process, the agreement was signed on 10 April 1998 and contained sections on the internal structure of Northern Ireland (including an elected Assembly and power-sharing), the North's relations with the Republic of Ireland (including a number of North–South bodies), and relations between the Republic and the United Kingdom (which included a Council of the British Isles). There were additional sections on constitutional and human rights, decommissioning of weapons, security, policing and prisoners. The agreement was put to a referendum in Northern Ireland and the Republic on 22 May 1998. Of those who voted, 94.39 per cent supported the agreement in the Republic and 71.12 per cent in the North. Lack of progress over decommissioning threatened the agreement in Feb. 2000.

Government Communications Headquarters (GCHQ) Based in Cheltenham, an installation for collecting signals intelligence, coordinating a worldwide network of listening posts. The Conservative government banned GCHQ workers from union membership on 25 Jan. 1984 following the allegedly disruptive effects of a civil service strike in 1981. Workers who refused to give up union membership were dismissed. The ban was overturned in May 1997 by the newly elected Labour government. See also ABC trial.

Grassroots Alliance Centre-left grouping (its full title is the Centre Left Grassroots Alliance) in the Labour party formed to contest the party's National Executive Committee (NEC) elections against the leadership's preferred Members First. Grassroots Alliance candidates took four of the six constituency places in the 1997 NEC elections and three out of six in 1998. While not overtly 'Old Labour', the Grassroots Alliance tends to reflect the position of members who do not completely support the party establishment.

Greater London Authority (GLA) A strategic authority for London, partly a replacement for the Greater London Council abolished by the Conservative government in 1986. The 1998 Greater London Authority Act provided for an elected mayor and a 25-member GLA covering the 32 London boroughs (both ratified in a referendum held in May 1998). The GLA has a £3 billion annual budget and has responsibility for transport, the environment, planning, the police, fire services and economic regeneration. The first elections for mayor and GLA members were set for May 2000.

Greater London Council (GLC) Formed in 1963 as an enlarged London County Council (LCC) to include the suburbs, intended – according to the Labour party – to create a built-in Conservative majority. In practice Labour held the GLC for most of its existence. The GLC had strategic authority over housing and planning, later taking over London Transport. Led by Ken Livingstone from 1981, the authority took an increasingly anti-government stance, as well as introducing radical equal opportunities and transport policies. The GLC was abolished in 1986, but a new authority for London has been created by the Blair government. See also County Hall, Inner London Education Authority, Loony Left.

Greenham Common Base at which Cruise missiles (qv) were deployed in 1983. Women protesting at their deployment began a vigil on the base perimeter on 12 Dec. 1982 before their arrival and a 'peace camp' of protesters remained there until the missiles were withdrawn in 1989. The camp became a significant symbol of anti-nuclear protest and growing feminist consciousness.

Greenpeace Environmental pressure group founded in 1971 to protect the environment through peaceful direct action on land and sea. It has been prominent in its efforts to prevent whaling, nuclear power and industrial pollution.

Grosvenor Square London square where the US Embassy is situated, the scene of anti-Vietnam War demonstrations in the late 1960s, most notably in March and Oct. 1968.

Groundnuts scheme Attempt to use areas of unproductive land in Tanganyika (now Tanzania) to grow groundnuts, instituted by the Labour government in 1947. Hurriedly introduced and ill planned, the scheme was abandoned three years later, having lost £30 million. The expression was regularly used by opponents as an example of Labour's economic incompetence.

Grunwick A photo-processing plant in north London, the scene of a bitter struggle for trade union recognition in 1977. Mass picketing, particularly on 11 July when 18,000 pickets clashed with police and there were 70 arrests, encouraged anti-union publicity. The employer, George Ward, succeeded in preventing unionization among his workforce.

Guildford Four Four people (Patrick Armstrong, Gerald Conlon, Paul Hill and Carole Richardson) arrested in Dec. 1974 for alleged involvement in the IRA bombings of public houses in Guildford and Woolwich in which a total of eight people were killed and 59 injured. They were said to have confessed but withdrew their confessions at their trial in Sept. 1975. They were jailed for life and, though their appeals were rejected, continued to protest their innocence, gradually gaining influential support. Following a fresh police investigation which began in Aug. 1987, new evidence was referred to the Court of Appeal in Jan. 1989 and the four were released when the Director of Public Prosecutions announced that he would not seek to sustain the convictions. See also Birmingham Six.

Gulf War See p 212.

handbagging Allegedly, and humorously, the tactic used by Prime Minister Margaret Thatcher to persuade those who disagreed with her in Cabinet and outside to accept her view. Reputedly first coined by dissident Conservative MP Julian Critchley. See also Iron Lady.

Hansard The official report of parliamentary debates, named after the Hansard family who took over publishing regular reports in 1812.

Hard Left Section of the Labour party (particularly in the 1980s while the party was under Neil Kinnock's modernizing leadership) which argued for adherence to what it claimed was socialist fundamentalism. Its most prominent parliamentary figures were Tony Benn, Eric Heffer and Dennis Skinner. The Campaign Group of Labour MPs was formed by the Hard Left. In local government, it was particularly strong in inner London (in areas such as Lambeth). Its influence declined in the 1980s with the Kinnock leadership and the miners' defeat. See also Soft Left.

Hola Camp scandal Hola Camp was a detention centre in Kenya holding suspects during the anti-British Mau Mau (qv) campaign which began in 1952. Eleven detainees died in 1959 and a subsequent inquiry revealed that they had been beaten to death. The infamous incident caused a political outcry in Britain and undermined the policy of the government towards the Mau Mau revolt.

Holy Loch Area of the Firth of Clyde near Glasgow, the British base for US Polaris (qv) submarines (1961–92). Scene of many anti-nuclear protests by the Campaign for Nuclear Disarmament (qv) and Scottish nationalists.

House Church Movement Loosely organized groups of charismatic Christians, often fundamentalist evangelical Protestants operating outside the traditional confines of the Church of England, which grew in support through the 1980s.

hung parliament A parliament in which no single party has gained sufficient seats to form a majority government.

Huyton Liverpool parliamentary constituency (1950–83) of Harold Wilson (1916–95), Labour leader (1963–76) and Prime Minister (1964–70 and 1974–76).

hypothecation Liberal Democratic party policy of informing taxpayers what proportions of their taxes would be allocated to what areas of government expenditure. An initial example came in the 1992 general election when the Liberal Democrats proposed a penny increase in income tax to go specifically towards education.

identity cards Cards introduced in Britain during the Second World War which every citizen had to carry. They were abolished by the Conservative government in 1952. Their reintroduction has been regularly suggested by Conservative party members (and in 1988 by the Metropolitan Police Commissioner Sir Peter Imbert) as a way of combating crime and terrorism.

IEA See Institute of Economic Affairs.

ILEA See Inner London Education Authority.

Indian Workers Association (IWA) The leading organization representing the interests of people from the Indian sub-continent settled in Britain, established in 1956. The IWA provides advice on education, housing, immigration and race relations and promotes cultural activities.

Information Research Department Section within the Foreign Office, established secretly by the Labour government in 1948 to undertake propaganda against Communist-controlled eastern Europe. The department, which was linked with the security services and was outside parliamentary control because of its secrecy, used journalists and trade union officials, as well as politicians, to influence public opinion against Communism.

INLA See Irish National Liberation Army.

Inner London Education Authority (ILEA) The elected body (generally Labour-controlled) responsible for administering the capital's education from 1965 until its abolition by the Conservative government in 1990. See also Greater London Council.

Institute of Economic Affairs (IEA) Institute founded in 1957 by Sir Antony Fisher, under the inspiration of Professor Friedrich von Hayek. It has campaigned to promote the causes of monetarism (qv) and free market economics, under such persons as Arthur Seldon and Lord Harris of High Cross.

Institute for Public Policy Research (IPPR) Left-wing think tank, established by the businessman Clive Hollick in conjunction with Neil Kinnock's office in 1988. The IPPR has been responsible for running the Commission on Social Justice, set up by John Smith.

International Socialist Group (ISG) See p 96.

internment Imprisonment without trial, introduced in Northern Ireland on 9 Aug. 1971 in an attempt to reduce terrorism by mass arrests of Republican and Protestant suspects against whom there was no hard evidence. In fact the action increased unrest and support in the Catholic community for the Irish Republican Army (qv) and the policy was suspended in Dec. 1975.

IPPR See Institute for Public Policy Research.

IRA See Irish Republican Army.

Irish Dimension, The Title of a White Paper published in 1973 by the Northern Ireland Secretary William Whitelaw which represented a move – deeply resented by the Protestant community – towards the involvement of the government of the Republic of Ireland in Northern Ireland affairs.

Irish National Liberation Army (INLA) Terrorist group formed in 1975 by members of the Official IRA dissatisfied with its abandonment of violence. The INLA acted as the armed wing of the Irish Republican Socialist party. INLA members were responsible for the death of Conservative shadow Northern Ireland Secretary Airey Neave in a bombing at the House of Commons car park on 3 Mar. 1979. It declared a ceasefire in August 1999. It has the reputation even among republican militants of being extreme.

Irish Republican Army (IRA) Organized as the military wing of Sinn Fein (qv) to fight for a 32-county Irish Republic from the remnants of the Irish

Republican Brotherhood following the defeated Easter Rising in 1916. The IRA was defeated in the Irish Civil War and was outlawed by both the Irish and British governments before the Second World War. It did, however, continue to carry out sporadic bombing attacks and raids on military armouries. The IRA re-emerged as a significant, if initially disorganized, force during the 1969 Protestant attacks on the Catholic community in Northern Ireland which came in the wake of a civil rights campaign. Dissatisfaction with the ill-preparedness of the existing IRA led in 1971 to a division between the Marxist-inclined Official IRA and the more militant and violent Provisional IRA. The Official IRA abandoned armed action after the Aldershot bombing (qv) in 1972. See also Bloody Sunday, internment, Noraid.

Iron Lady Title bestowed on Conservative Opposition leader Margaret Thatcher (Prime Minister 1979–90) by the Soviet Army newspaper *Red Star* on 23 Jan. 1976 because of her uncompromising position on defence and international relations. Mrs Thatcher took the title with pride. See also handbagging.

Jenkins Commission A commission on electoral reform chaired by former Labour deputy leader and SDP founder Lord Jenkins, appointed in 1997 and which issued a report in October 1998. Jenkins proposed an alternative vote top-up system intended to ensure fairer representation. Each elector would have two votes, one going to the constituency candidate and the other to top-up candidates. A constituency candidate winning half the vote would take the seat but if no candidate reached 50 per cent the votes won by the least popular candidate would be redistributed until a victor emerged. The second vote would be used to give unrepresented parties in a county or city a top-up member. The House of Commons – which would be reduced from 659 members to a maximum of 560 – would consist of 80–85 per cent constituency members and 15–20 per cent top-up members.

July Measures Announced by Labour government on 20 July 1966 to support sterling in the face of a projected rise in the balance of payments deficit from £100 million to £350 million. The measures included a six-month freeze on prices and wages, stricter hire-purchase controls, higher duties on alcohol, tobacco and petrol, and increased purchase tax. Britain was nevertheless forced into devaluation (qv) in Nov. 1967.

Keep Left Group Left-wing Labour group formed in Nov. 1946, largely because of criticisms of Foreign Secretary Ernest Bevin's 'Cold War' policies towards the Soviet Union. The group – whose leading figures included Michael Foot, Richard Crossman and Ian Mikardo – advocated a 'third force', a European socialist alliance taking a middle position between the USA and the Soviet Union, and sought greater British independence from the USA. The term Keep Left came from a British road sign.

Kenyan Asians British citizens living in Kenya who lost their businesses and livelihoods as a result of an 'Africanization' policy. Labour Home Secretary James Callaghan announced on 22 Feb. 1968 that 7,000 had entered Britain in the previous three months and the following day introduced a Bill placing controls on passport holders who had 'no substantial connections' with Britain. A voucher system was introduced from 1 March restricting entry to 1,500 voucher holders annually. Conservative Home Secretary Reginald Maudling increased this figure in 1971. See also Ugandan Asians.

Kilbrandon Report Report of a Royal Commission on the Constitution chaired by Lord Kilbrandon following growing electoral success of Scottish and Welsh Nationalist candidates. The report (published Oct. 1973) recommended the setting up of elected assemblies in Scotland and Wales. A referendum (qv) held on the issue in Scotland and in Wales on 1 Mar. 1979 required a minimum of 40 per cent support of all eligible voters for the proposal. The proposal was narrowly rejected in Scotland, overwhelmingly so in Wales.

Kitchen Table Conservatism William Hague announced in March 1999 that Conservative party policies would be formulated with the kitchen table in mind, focusing on such everyday issues as crime, the public services, taxes, the care of elderly people and genetically modified food. Mr Hague arranged for a five-foot long table to be placed in the Conservative Central Office foyer as a symbol for party workers. The inspiration for the idea allegedly came from a visit Mr Hague made earlier in the year to the Texas governor and Republican presidential hopeful, George Bush Jr. Little more was heard of Kitchen Table Conservatism as the party shifted – in the wake of successes in the 1999 European parliamentary elections – towards growing opposition to the euro and European unity.

Labour Coordinating Committee A 'hard left' body in the Labour party set up in 1978 to press for constitutional reform which would strengthen the position of overwhelmingly left-wing constituency activists and demonstrate a greater commitment to extra-parliamentary activity. However, following the electoral disaster of 1983, members developed a 'soft left' position which supported the modernizing party leadership of Neil Kinnock.

Lady Chatterley's Lover Sexually explicit novel by D H Lawrence (1885–1930), banned from publication in its unexpurgated form in Britain from 1929 until 1960, when it was the subject of a celebrated trial for obscenity. The trial's result symbolized the opening of an era of greater liberalization in the arts and in general social attitudes. See also permissive society.

Lancaster House Scene in London of talks on the independence of Southern Rhodesia which began on 10 Sept. 1979. A treaty was signed at Lancaster House on 21 Dec. and the territory became independent as the state of Zimbabwe on 18 Apr. 1980. See also unilateral declaration of independence.

Lawrence Report The report of a committee chaired by Sir William Macpherson examining the Metropolitan Police investigation of the murder in 1993 of black teenager Stephen Lawrence, published in February 1999. The report criticized the police investigation as being marked by 'professional incompetence, institutional racism and a failure of leadership by senior officers'. Acknowledging that institutional racism was not confined to the police, the report made 70 recommendations. Among these were improvements in police race awareness training, racism to be punishable by dismissal, and independent investigation into police complaints. More controversial were suggestions to criminalize the use of racist language and for retrials of acquitted people where new evidence came to light.

Liberation Pressure group formerly known as the Movement for Colonial Freedom. Liberation was founded in 1954 to campaign for self-determination for colonial peoples. Its original constituents were the British branch of the Congress against Imperialism, the Central Africa Committee, the Kenya Committee, and the Seretse Khama Defence Committee. It adopted its current name in 1970. It continues to press for the application of the UN Declaration of Human Rights throughout the world and for the economic liberation of newly independent states from neo-colonialism.

Liberty Pressure group formerly known as the National Council for Civil Liberties (NCCL) which was established in 1934. It works to promote the rights of the individual and to oppose racial, political, religious or other forms of discrimination and abuses of power. NCCL was prominent in the 1930s in opposing fascism and anti-semitism in the UK. Its level of activity declined somewhat during the 1950s, but has revived since the late 1960s.

Lib–Lab Pact Period of cooperation between the Liberal and Labour parties to keep James Callaghan's Labour government in office. By Jan. 1977 Labour's parliamentary majority had fallen to one. In March the Conservatives threatened a 'no confidence' motion. Labour was guaranteed support in the House of Commons in return for allowing the Liberals to veto proposed legislation before it went to Cabinet. The Liberals withdrew from the pact in the autumn of 1978. With the election of the 1997 Labour government, the Liberal Democrats entered into a form of limited cooperation, sitting on a Cabinet committee to discuss constitutional reform.

life peer Under the Life Peerages Act 1958, the sovereign can appoint men (and, for the first time, women in their own right) to the House of Lords with a title which lasts for their lifetime and cannot be inherited by their children. The purpose was to meet the need for greater political balance in the House of Lords. Recommendations for life peerages are made by the Prime Minister and Opposition party leaders.

Limehouse declaration Statement issued on 25 Jan. 1981 by the Gang of Four (qv) proposing the formation of a Council for Social Democracy as a protest against the Labour party's newly introduced method of selecting a leader, and more generally against the party's shift to the left. 'We believe', the declaration said, 'that the need for a realignment of British politics must now be faced.' One of the Gang, Dr David Owen, lived in Limehouse, east London.

Lockerbie A Pan Am Boeing 747 flying from London to New York was blown up by a terrorist bomb over Lockerbie in Scotland on 21 Dec. 1988, killing 259 passengers and crew and eleven residents on the ground. Libya persistently refused to hand over those who some believed to be responsible for the explosion until 1999, when they were flown to face trial in the Netherlands.

London County Council See Greater London Council.

London Labour Briefing An initially influential organization of the Labour left in London formed in February 1980 under Lambeth Council leader Ted Knight, Jeremy Corbyn and Ken Livingstone. The group met with an early success when Livingstone ousted a moderate to become Greater London Council (GLC) leader following Labour's electoral victory in 1981. The next phase, entitled Target 82, was less triumphant as Labour-controlled local authorities either failed to meet pledges to confront the Conservative government or where they did so (as in the case of Lambeth and the GLC) achieved nothing.

Loony Left Term used in the 1980s to describe left-wing Labour councils – notably Lambeth, Brent, Haringey and the Greater London Council (qv) – castigated in the right-wing media for their alleged obsession with feminism, gay rights, and positive action in favour of ethnic minorities. The councils held power in the most hard-pressed inner-city areas. In the GLC's case in particular a motive behind the policies was in part to produce a 'rainbow coalition' to replace the declining manual working class vote. See also Clause 28, Wandsworth.

Low Pay Commission The body established by the Labour government in June 1997 to determine the level at which the proposed national minimum wage should be set. Chaired by Professor George Bain of the London Business School, it eventually set a rate of £3.60 per hour (much to the disappointment of many trade unionists) which was effective from April 1999.

loyalist A member of the majority Protestant community who wishes Northern Ireland to remain part of the United Kingdom rather than become part of a united Ireland or become a separate independent state.

Loyalist Volunteer Force (LVF) Protestant paramilitary in Northern Ireland formed by loyalists dissatisfied with the position taken by other loyalist groupings. In March 1998 the LVF warned Protestants not to become involved in the Northern Ireland peace process but in May the organization declared a ceasefire to enable it to campaign for a 'No' vote in the Good Friday agreement referendum. The group's leader, Billy Wright, was murdered in the Maze Prison in December 1998 by members of the Irish National Liberation Army.

Lynskey Tribunal Set up in 1948 under Mr Justice Lynskey to investigate allegations that Board of Trade ministers and civil servants had accepted bribes.

The leading witness, Polish-born Sydney Stanley, was revealed to be a confidence trickster. However, cases of misjudgement were found and junior Trade Minister John Belcher was forced to resign and George Gibson, a trade union nominated Bank of England director, was reprimanded.

Maastricht Treaty Signed on 10 Dec. 1991 following a summit of European leaders which set out agreements reached on the Treaty of European Union. Leading a party deeply divided on Britain's relationship with Europe, Conservative Prime Minister John Major obtained opt-out clauses on a single currency and the social chapter (qv) on the grounds of the defence of British national interests. The treaty was ratified by Parliament, despite a vigorous campaign for a referendum on the issue led in the House of Lords by Mr Major's predecessor, Baroness Thatcher. See also Eurosceptics.

Majorism Journalistic attempt to define the policies of John Major (b. 1943) when he replaced Margaret Thatcher as Conservative party leader and Prime Minister in Nov. 1990 which included suggestions that Major would be more 'caring', less dogmatically opposed to the public services and show greater willingness to listen to different views. See also Back to Basics, Citizen's Charter.

Manifesto Group Labour party group formed by centre-right MPs in 1974–75 to combat Tribune Group (qv) demands for the Labour government to adopt a more left-wing stance.

Marshall Aid Plan US plan for post-war European economic recovery, named after Secretary of State General George C. Marshall (1880–1959). An Organization for European Economic Cooperation was established to administer the aid in Apr. 1948. Some $17,000 million was provided by the USA to Europe between 1948 and 1952, though aid to Britain ended in Dec. 1950.

Maryfield Site in Belfast of the secretariat of the Anglo-Irish Conference, established under the Anglo-Irish agreement (qv), which operated joint consultation between Irish and British officials on Northern Ireland's affairs.

Matrix-Churchill A Coventry machine tool company, three of whose executives were charged with breaking an embargo imposed in the Iraq–Iran War 1980–88 on arms trading with Iraq illegally. The evidence of a former minister, Alan Clark, proved crucial; the judge also found that four documents which ministers had not wanted the court to see proved that the defendants had acted with government approval. They were acquitted in Nov. 1992. One of the executives was in addition a British intelligence agent. The case caused uproar, not least because of ministers' apparent willingness to see the men imprisoned rather than admit that policy had changed. A judicial inquiry under Lord Justice Scott investigated the affair.

Mau Mau Anti-European terrorist movement among the Kikuyu tribe in Kenya which began action on 20 Oct. 1952, leading to a state of emergency and the arrest of Jomo Kenyatta as its leader. The security forces killed

11,000 Mau Mau members and 2,000 people were killed by Mau Mau before the movement was virtually extinguished by late 1954. See also Hola Camp scandal.

Militant Originally formed as the Revolutionary Socialist League, Militant became the main Trotskyist group. Its newspaper was *Militant Tendency*. Through its policy of entryism, it penetrated deep into the Labour party in areas such as Liverpool. Two Militant supporters were elected to Parliament (Terry Fields and David Nellist). Bitterly attacked by the Labour leadership after 1982, its leaders were expelled from the Labour party and its influence rapidly declined. In January 1997 it relaunched itself as the Socialist party. See entryism, p 277.

Millwall Ward in the London Borough of Tower Hamlets (an area with a high Bangladeshi population) in which a member of the right-wing racist British National party, Derek Beacon, was elected as a councillor at a by-election in Nov. 1993. Although he subsequently lost the seat in the May 1994 council elections, Beacon increased his vote.

miners' strikes There had been no national miners' strike since 1926 when in 1972 the National Union of Mineworkers (NUM) challenged the Conservative government's pay guidelines and demanded a £5 per week increase for coalface workers and £8 for surface workers. They were offered £2. The NUM won a dispute which included the use of 'flying pickets' (qv), secondary picketing (qv) and the Saltley (qv) battle; the Wilberforce Inquiry awarded them approximately what they had asked. The 1973–74 dispute – in which the NUM sought a 35 per cent increase – came against the background of the oil crisis caused by the 1973 Arab–Israeli War. An overtime ban forced a 40 per cent reduction in coal supplies and the Conservative government imposed a three-day week (qv) on industry. Prime Minister Edward Heath called a 'Who governs Britain?' election in Feb. 1974, was surprisingly defeated and replaced by a minority Labour government which quickly settled on terms, favourable to the miners, set by the Pay Board (qv). The third and most bitter of the disputes was in 1984–85 and was seen in part as the Conservative party's revenge for 1974. The NUM under its president Arthur Scargill took action against what he claimed was a plan for massive pit closures. The NUM refused to hold a national ballot and this lost the support of the wider trade union leadership, as well as opening the way for a breakaway Union of Democratic Mineworkers (qv) to continue working. Tactically, the miners suffered from opening their strike in the spring when coal stocks (prepared for just this eventuality) were high. The dispute was harshly fought, with much hardship among miners' families. The Labour party, led by Neil Kinnock, though sympathetic to the miners, distanced itself from the dispute for fear of the impact on its electoral prospects. The miners' eventual defeat was followed by a closure programme far worse than that Scargill had warned of. By 1994 the mining workforce had been reduced to 10,000 men. See also Orgreave.

Mods Youth sub-culture in the 1960s, mainly among semi-skilled and clerical workers in London and the south-east of England, marked by a fastidious smartness in dress and appearance and, often, ownership of a motor scooter. Mods were in marked contrast to the more working-class Rockers (qv), with whom the Mods fought at regular seaside clashes.

Monday Club Right-wing pressure group in the Conservative party formed in 1961 by, among others, Julian Amery and the Marquess of Salisbury. The name came from its Monday lunchtime meetings. Its objective was to place the party on a right-wing course.

monetarism Economic theory influential in the 1970s and 1980s which argued that the money supply was the main factor in economic activity and that government should control its rate of growth, tying expansion to the potential growth in gross domestic product. Monetary targets were set by the International Monetary Fund as a condition of granting credits to the Labour government in 1976. The policy was adopted enthusiastically by the Conservative government in 1979, leading to major public spending reductions and greater reliance on market forces, in an attempt to reduce inflation. The policy was relaxed after 1983, with less emphasis attached to formal monetary targets. See also Dries, Institute of Economic Affairs.

multilateralism The policy, usually connected with nuclear weapons, of negotiating disarmament on the basis that all powers possessing weapons should agree to reduce or withdraw the weapons simultaneously. See also unilateralism.

Nassau agreement Agreement reached on 18 Dec. 1962 after negotiations in Nassau between British Prime Minister Harold Macmillan (1894–1986) and US President John F Kennedy (1917–63) that the USA would supply Polaris (qv) missiles for use on Royal Navy submarines operating under NATO command. The agreement strengthened the Anglo-American relationship but led to the vetoing by French President Charles de Gaulle (1890–1970) of Britain's application to join the European Economic Community (see European Union) on the grounds that Britain was closer to the USA than to Europe. See also North Atlantic Treaty Organization.

National Abortion Campaign Pressure group set up in 1975 whose aim, to build a mass campaign to oppose all legislation restricting a woman's right to terminate a pregnancy, has been largely organized around each successive parliamentary Bill on abortion (e.g. Benyon Bill 1977; Corrie Bill 1979).

National Board for Prices and Incomes Formed by the Labour government in 1965 (and abolished by the Conservatives in 1972), the board had no statutory powers but the government could delay proposed price or income changes by referring them for its report.

National Council for Civil Liberties See Liberty.

National Economic Development Council (NEDC) Popularly known as 'Neddy', the NEDC was formed in 1962 as a discussion forum between government, employers and the unions to examine methods of increasing the national growth rate to 4 per cent a year. 'Little Neddies' were set up in individual industries and services in 1964.

National Enterprise Board Created by the Labour government in 1975 to extend public ownership of industry, with powers to purchase a controlling interest in private companies or to lend money for investment.

National Executive Committee (NEC) The ruling body of the Labour party, elected each year at the party conference. Prior to 1997 it comprised the leader and deputy leader and representatives of the trade union section, the constituency Labour parties (CLPs), the socialist societies, the women's section, and the party treasurer. The composition and method of election of the NEC were greatly transformed when the 1997 party conference adopted *Partnership into Power*. The women's section was to be abolished and trade union representation reduced from seventeen to twelve (although six of these were to be women). Three places were reserved for members of the government (nominated by the Prime Minister), three for MPs (elected by the Parliamentary Labour Party) and one for the leader of the Labour Group in the European Parliament. Six were set aside for representatives elected by postal ballot of all members.

National Front See p 91.

nationalization State ownership of an enterprise or the exercise of control by the government taking a majority shareholding. Between 1945 and 1951 the Labour government nationalized the Bank of England, civil aviation, coal, electricity, gas, iron and steel. These nationalized industries were arranged around a centralized hierarchy of management. There was no form of workers' participation. See also privatization, Tribune Group.

NATO See North Atlantic Treaty Organization.

Neddy See National Economic Development Council.

Neill Report Report on the funding of political parties issued by the Committee on Standards in Public Life, chaired by Lord Neill of Buxton, in 1998. The Committee – established in 1994 – had been asked to include party funding as part of its examination of conduct in public life in 1997. The report made a hundred recommendations, including maximum general election expenditure of £20 million for each party, full disclosure of all donations of over £5,000, an end to acceptance of donations from abroad, tax relief on individual donations up to £500 and procedures to allay concerns that large donors had been able to 'buy' honours. The Labour government introduced draft legislation based on Neill's proposals in July 1999.

New Labour The project of Tony Blair (born 1953, party leader from 1994, Prime Minister from 1997) to modernize the Labour party and win middle-class support through what has also been described as the 'Third Way'. New Labour largely accepted the terms of the Thatcherite revolution, sought closer links with the private sector and the inculcation of 'enterprise' culture in the public sector. The party leadership attempted to distance itself from 'Old Labour' (which it blamed for successive electoral defeats) by revising Clause IV, moving away from the trade unions, encouraging labour flexibility and a reformed welfare system. Although successful in securing victory in the 1997 general election, strains within the party over the pace of modernization became increasingly evident.

Night of the Long Knives The dismissal by Conservative Prime Minister Harold Macmillan in July 1962 of one-third of his Cabinet – including the Chancellor of the Exchequer, the Ministers of Defence, Education and Housing, the Secretary of State for Scotland and the Lord Chancellor – following growing Liberal electoral successes, notably at Orpington (qv). The event prompted Liberal leader Jeremy Thorpe's remark, 'Greater love hath no man than this, that he lays down his friends for his life.'

Nine, the Membership of the European Economic Community (qv) between 1973 – when Britain, Ireland and Denmark joined the original six members France, Germany, Belgium, the Netherlands, Italy and Luxembourg – and 1982, when Greece became the tenth member.

1922 Committee Tory back-bench MPs' group, named after a meeting on 19 Oct. 1922 at the Carlton Club where Conservative back-benchers forced their leaders to withdraw from Lloyd George's Coalition government.

Nolan Committee The Committee on Standards in Public Life set up in 1994 under the chairmanship of Lord Nolan following a series of 'sleaze' events. One of its recommendations was the establishment of the office of Parliamentary Commissioner for Standards.

Noraid The Northern Aid Committee, which channels funds from sympathizers in the USA to the Provisional IRA. See also Irish Republican Army.

North Atlantic Treaty Organization (NATO) Formed for the collective defence and security of the western world against feared Soviet aggression, and more cynically described as a means of 'keeping the Americans in and the Germans down'. The North Atlantic Treaty was signed on 4 Apr. 1949 by Belgium, Canada, Denmark, France, Iceland, Luxembourg, the Netherlands, Norway, Portugal, the United Kingdom and the USA, coming into force on 24 Aug. 1949. Greece and Turkey joined on 18 Feb. 1952, the German Federal Republic on 5 May 1955, and Spain on 30 May 1982. In March 1999, following the fall of Communism, NATO was expanded to include Hungary, the Czech Republic and Poland. See also British Army of the Rhine, Nassau agreement.

north–south divide Expression used in the 1980s (as in the 1930s) to describe concern about the increasing economic disparity between the declining industrial areas of the north of England and Scotland and the expansion in technological and financial activity in the south of England, particularly in the 1981–82 recession. It was widely referred to in the 1987 general election, but with the recession which began in 1990 and affected the service and finance industries in the south, the expression lost much of its force. See also Two Nations.

Notting Hill Area in west London which was the scene of racial disturbances, primarily of attacks by white youths on West Indian immigrants, in Aug. 1958. It was the site of Peter Rachman's slum property empire (see Rachmanism). The Notting Hill Carnival celebrates West Indian culture annually in August.

Official IRA See Irish Republican Army.

Official Secrets Act Enacted in 1911, Section 1 dealt with espionage while Section 2, which aroused increasing criticism during the 1960s and 1970s, was intended to prevent civil servants revealing information about their work which governments felt was not in the national interest, although publication could be justified if it was demonstrated that it was in the national interest. The Ponting case (qv) effectively undermined Section 2. The Official Secrets Act 1989, introduced by the government following disquiet arising from the Ponting trial (and a Private Member's Bill introduced by Conservative back bencher Richard Shepherd), made some changes but effectively removed the public interest defence. See also ABC trial.

Ombudsman The Parliamentary Commissioner for Administration was first appointed in 1965 to investigate complaints about maladministration by government departments. A complaint from a member of the public must be referred through an MP and if the complaint is found justified the Ombudsman informs both parties and publicizes the findings. There is also an Ombudsman for local government. Ombudsmen have been appointed by, for example, banks, building societies and insurance companies. The name comes from the Swedish term for legal representative.

One member, one vote (OMOV) A key part of the attempt at internal reform in the Labour party which culminated in the 1993 party conference. Supporters of the principle of OMOV argued that at constituency level, the system would allow the wider membership to participate more effectively in the selection of candidates, voting for the party leadership, etc. A consequence of this would, very likely, be a weakening of the left and further pressure on the trade unions to abandon the block vote (qv) at party conference.

One Nation Group Conservative party group formed in 1950 by MPs Cuthbert Alport and Angus Maude, the membership of which included Enoch Powell, Iain Macleod and Edward Heath. Taking its name from Benjamin Disraeli's novel *Sybil, or The Two Nations* (1845), the group advocated the encouragement of individual opportunity underpinned by an adequate welfare state. Alport resigned the Conservative whip (qv) in the House of Lords in 1984 in protest against the government's injection of market forces into the National Health Service. See also Two Nations.

Open University The pioneering venture begun in 1969 by Harold Wilson's Labour government. It opened up part-time degrees to those without a background of formal academic qualifications. Based at Milton Keynes, it has been one of the great successes of 'access' in education, teaching via correspondence and TV programmes.

Operation Motorman British army operation in July 1972 to end the IRA control of 'no go' areas of Londonderry and west Belfast which police and troops had refrained from entering. Fearing bloodshed, the army announced the operation in advance, giving IRA members the opportunity to leave, then 1,250 troops with armoured cars, bulldozers and tanks were deployed and met no resistance.

opting out Right of a school to leave local education authority control if a majority of parents and governors vote to do so. The school is then directly funded by central government and the governing body is responsible for spending and performance. Opting out was introduced in the Education Reform Act 1988.

Options for Change The title of a 1991 White Paper on Britain's future defence needs in the wake of the collapse of the threat posed by the Soviet Union. There were protests at the suggested disbandment of a number of infantry regiments. *Options for Change*, together with further White Papers in the years following, proposed overall cuts in service personnel of 20 per cent. See also Peace Dividend.

Orangemen Members of the Orange Order, a society formed in Ulster in 1795 to preserve Protestantism in Ireland, named after William III, former Prince of Orange. The Order formed the backbone of the Unionist party which ruled Northern Ireland from 1921 to 1972 and has offshoots in the Protestant areas of Glasgow and Liverpool. Orange marches have been at the centre of confrontations in the 1990s (as at Drumcree).

Orgreave Scene of one of the crucial confrontations during the 1984–85 miners' strike. Thousands of Yorkshire miners attempted to force the closure of the British Steel coking plant near Sheffield in a series of clashes on 29 and 30 May, 1 and 18 June 1984. There were large numbers of arrests and injuries and complaints of police violence. Charges of riot and unlawful assembly against fourteen miners were dropped a year after their arrest. See also miners' strikes, Saltley.

Orpington The suburban north-west Kent scene of a remarkable Liberal by-election victory on 14 March 1962 at which Eric Lubbock (later Lord Avebury) transformed a Conservative majority of 14,760 into a 7,855 Liberal majority. Although the seat was held until 1970, the long-awaited Liberal revival failed to follow Lubbock's victory. The result led also to the coining of the phrase 'Orpington man', describing the typical suburban commuter's disenchantment with the Conservative government. See also Night of the Long Knives.

outing Tactic used by radical gay pressure groups, such as OutRage, to 'name' or 'out' those in public life (such as MPs or churchmen) who, they claim, are guilty of hypocrisy in their own private lives.

Parkinson scandal After a long affair with Trade and Industry Secretary Cecil (later Lord) Parkinson, Sara Keays, his former secretary, became pregnant in 1983. Parkinson, as Conservative party chairman, had been instrumental in the party's landslide general election victory in May. With Margaret Thatcher's support, Parkinson attempted to stay in office but further revelations forced his resignation at the party conference in October. Parkinson, who remained with his wife, returned to office as Energy Secretary in 1987, later becoming Transport Secretary. He left the government on Mrs Thatcher's resignation in 1990. He was surprisingly recalled as party chairman by William Hague in 1997.

Parliament Act 1949 Legislation introduced by the Labour government which reduced the power of the House of Lords to delay legislation already agreed by the House of Commons from two years to one year.

Patten Report The report of the Patten Commission (chaired by former Hong Kong Governor Chris Patten) on the future of policing in Northern Ireland. Published in September 1999, it recommended sweeping changes to the Royal Ulster Constabulary, including renaming it the Police Service of Northern Ireland.

Pay Board Established by the Conservative government in 1972 to administer wage control and to monitor Stages 1, 2 and 3 of the government's counter-inflation policy. It was abolished by the Labour government in 1974. See also miners' strikes, Price Commission, Social Contract.

pay pause Euphemism used by the Chancellor of the Exchequer, Selwyn Lloyd, to describe the freezing of public sector wages introduced in July 1961.

peace camps See Greenham Common.

Peace Dividend The reduction of government expenditure on arms – and the increase on, for example, education and social services – that was expected to follow the end of the Cold War after the collapse of the Warsaw Pact and of the Soviet and East European regimes at the end of the 1980s. See also *Options for Change.*

peace people Group founded in Northern Ireland in 1976 by Mairead Corrigan and Betty Williams in an attempt to rouse popular feeling against sectarian violence. The movement appeared successful, with rallies against loyalist and republican terrorism and the award of the Nobel Peace Prize in 1977. But internal divisions weakened its activities and the movement declined.

Pearce Commission Inquiry chaired by Lord Pearce to test whether the terms of an agreement on possible independence between rebel Southern

Rhodesian Premier Ian Smith and British Foreign Secretary Lord Home were acceptable. A report published on 23 May 1972 showed that the majority of the population were not in favour.

permissive society Weakening of cultural and moral authoritarianism in the 1960s, signified by the Labour government's encouragement of reform in the laws on abortion, divorce and homosexuality, and the end of theatre censorship. Conservative politicians on the right of the party (notably Norman Tebbit) later blamed the permissive society for a range of ills from Britain's economic weakness to the onset of AIDS. See also *Lady Chatterley's Lover*.

Philby case Harold 'Kim' Philby (1911–88), a leading British intelligence official, resigned after admitting communist associations in July 1951. He became a journalist but disappeared in Beirut in March 1963, resurfacing behind the Iron Curtain. In 1967 it was admitted that Philby had also been a Soviet KGB agent and suspicions that he had been the 'third man' in the Burgess–Maclean scandal (qv) were confirmed. See also Apostles, Blunt affair.

Plaid Cymru See p 92.

Plant Commission Labour party inquiry appointed in 1991 under Raymond Plant, Professor of Politics at Southampton University, to examine the arguments for and against proportional representation. It reported in 1994.

Polaris A submarine-based missile system which replaced Britain's V-bomber force as an independent nuclear deterrent in the mid-1960s (see pp 207–8). Polaris was provided by the USA following the Nassau agreement (qv) of 18 Dec. 1962 and continued to be developed until its replacement by Trident (qv) in the 1990s. See also Blue Streak, Holy Loch.

poll tax See community charge.

Ponting case Defence Ministry civil servant Clive Ponting was acquitted at the Old Bailey, London, in March 1985 of breaching the Official Secrets Act (qv) after leaking classified papers to Labour MP Tam Dalyell suggesting ministers had lied to Parliament about the sinking of the Argentine battleship *General Belgrano* (qv) in 1982 during the Falklands War (qv). Ponting had leaked the information when it became clear that Defence Minister Michael Heseltine intended to continue with the original story that the battleship was sunk because of the danger it posed to British ships. His acquittal ended the previous assumption that the interests of the state and the interests of the government were synonymous.

Powellite Supporter of Conservative (later Ulster Unionist) MP Enoch Powell (1912–98), particularly one who favoured the nationalism of his anti-European federalist stance and the anti-immigrant sentiments he expressed in the notorious 'rivers of blood' speech that he delivered in Birmingham in April 1968. For a short period Powell appeared the possible leader of a new right in Britain. Many of his supporters would have been unaware of, or incapable of understanding, his economic views on monetarism (qv).

Prevention of Terrorism Act Introduced by the Labour government in 1974 following the IRA bombings in Birmingham, the Act was described by Home Secretary Roy Jenkins as 'draconian'. The Act allows detention without trial of terrorist suspects for up to seven days, the denial of the right to silence, and allows for a form of internal exile by restricting suspects to live in Great Britain or Northern Ireland. The Act has been regularly renewed. See also Birmingham Six.

Price Commission Established by the Conservative government in 1972 to control prices, with civil servants having the power to prevent increases. It was retained by the Labour government in 1974 but wound up in 1979. See also Pay Board.

Private Finance Initiative (PFI) A system introduced by the Conservative government under John Major by which public sector projects, for example, schools and hospitals, were constructed by private companies and leased back by the government for up to 35 years. The purpose was to remove the cost of construction from the Public Sector Borrowing Requirement. Although criticized by the Labour party in opposition, the Labour government elected in 1997 continued with the practice. A major criticism is that as the private companies make a profit, the taxpayer ultimately ends up paying more for projects financed by PFI than by the government directly.

privatization Selling of nationalized industries and other public sector activities to private businesses and individuals, encouraged by the Conservative government from 1979 to 1997 as part of its free market policies and to reduce the role of the state. Among the industries partly or wholly sold off were British Aerospace and Britoil (1983), British Telecom (1984) and British Gas (1986). Among others were British Airways, Jaguar and the Trustee Savings Bank. A further aspect of privatization was the requirement to contract out local authority activities to private companies and to introduce 'internal markets' in the National Health Service. Since 1997 Labour has not reversed this policy in any major way and has even extended it (e.g. to air traffic control). See pp 186–8. See also denationalization, Dries, nationalization.

Profumo affair Political scandal involving Conservative War Minister John Profumo (b. 1915). He denied having had an affair with Christine Keeler (b. 1942), a prostitute who was also involved with the Soviet naval attaché. The revelation that he was lying forced his resignation on 4 June 1963. The Denning Report (qv) claimed that national security had not been put in jeopardy by the affair. The scandal, which coincided with a growing popularity of political satire, undermined an already unpopular government in a pre-election year. See also Rachmanism.

proportional representation System of voting designed to ensure that the legislature accurately reflects the strength of support for the various parties among the electorate. Minority parties receive a fair number of seats in the legislature so that a vote for a small party is not a 'wasted' vote. Proportional representation may take several forms. In October 1997, the Labour government announced proposals to introduce proportional representation for European parliamentary elections and in December appointed an Electoral Reform Commission chaired by former Labour minister Lord Jenkins to devise a system for Westminster elections in preparation for a referendum on the issue. A partial proportional representation system was introduced by Labour for the elections to the Scottish Parliament and Welsh Assembly in May 1999.

Proscribed list A list of political organizations, the bulk of them fronts for the Communist party, membership of which was deemed incompatible with Labour party membership, introduced in 1947. The abolition of the list in 1973 made it easier for Trotskyist organizations, including Militant Tendency, to work inside the Labour party. The list was replaced with a requirement that Labour party members could not also be members of bodies which fielded candidates against Labour at elections.

Provisional IRA See Irish Republican Army.

Provisional Sinn Fein See Sinn Fein.

Public Order Act 1986 The Act created a new range of public order offences by extending police powers over marches and demonstrations and creating for the first time statutory controls over open-air meetings and picketing during industrial disputes. The Act made trespass a criminal offence, enabling the police to be used against squatting and workplace occupations.

Punks Youth sub-culture which emerged in Britain in the mid-1970s with anarchic undertones but a cultural and sartorial style posing as an antithesis to what was seen as the soft self-indulgence of the 1960s Hippies.

quango Quasi-autonomous non-governmental organization: a government-appointed body that has the power to spend public money but is not directly answerable to Parliament. Although the Conservative government elected in 1979 was pledged to reduce their number, even more were created during its period in office.

Rachmanism Term used to denote ruthless landlordism, derived from Peter Rachman (1919–62), a Polish immigrant and owner of a slum property empire in the Notting Hill (qv) area of West London who became notorious for the methods he used to evict tenants paying low rents to replace them with West Indian immigrants willing to pay higher rents. His activities were exposed during the Profumo affair (qv) and prompted legislation giving some protection to private tenants.

ratecapping Legislation introduced in 1984 to reduce local authority spending by empowering the government to prevent councils making up reductions in central grants by increasing rates. In 1985–86, eighteen councils were ratecapped for exceeding spending targets. See also Wandsworth.

rationing First introduced in 1917, rationing was reintroduced in the Second World War. In January 1940 bacon, butter and sugar were rationed. The list was rapidly extended. Non-food goods included petrol, clothing and coal for domestic use. In the post-war austerity years, bread (July 1946) and potatoes (December 1947) were rationed. From April 1948, restrictions were gradually lifted. Some rationing however lasted into the 1950s (butter and meat rationing continued until 1954, coal until 1958).

Ravenscraig Steelworks outside Glasgow in Motherwell which was closed down in June 1992 following a six-year campaign to keep it open by Scottish Nationalists and opponents of the Conservative government's policy of allowing the decline in traditional industries. The works had been built with grants from the Macmillan government during the 1960s.

Real IRA Paramilitary grouping which broke away from the Provisional Irish Republican Army (IRA) and Provisional Sinn Fein in disagreement with the latter's involvement in the peace process which culminated in the 1998 Good Friday agreement. The Real IRA, which declared in May 1998 that it was in a state of war with the British government, was responsible for a number of terrorist actions, including the August 1998 Omagh bombing. The body's political wing describes itself as the 32 County Sovereignty Movement. Other republican groups opposed to the peace process included the Continuity IRA (linked to Republican Sinn Fein) and the Irish National Liberation Army (linked to the Irish Republican Socialist party).

Red Lion Square Square in central London, the scene of a violent anti-National Front demonstration in 1974 at which Kevin Gateley, an anti-fascist student, died.

referendum Reference of a specific political issue to the electorate for a direct decision by popular vote. Referenda have been held in Britain on continued membership of the European Economic Community in 1975 (the result was that retaining membership was supported) and on devolution (qv) proposals for Scotland and Wales in 1979, when the proposals were rejected. Referenda on the devolution question were held again in 1997. On this occasion, both Scotland and Wales (narrowly) voted yes. See also European Union, Kilbrandon Report.

reselection The mandatory reselection of sitting Labour MPs by their constituency parties became Labour policy at the party conference held 29 Sept.–3 Oct. 1980. Behind it lay a desire on the left to have the opportunity to remove MPs whom they saw as being too moderate or right-wing. See also deselection.

Ribble Valley A sensational Liberal Democrat by-election victory on 7 March 1991 at which the Conservatives lost a hitherto safe seat, largely because of the unpopularity of the poll tax or community charge (qv). The by-election sounded the end of the poll tax.

Robbins Report Report by Lord Robbins on higher education delivered in Sept. 1963. Robbins recommended an expansion in higher education provision, with a guaranteed place for every young person who would benefit. The Conservative government pledged funding for six new universities.

Rockers Sub-culture in the 1960s among working-class youth with a uniform of leather jacket and jeans and a motorcycle. Their aggressive scruffiness was in stark contrast to the Mods (qv), with whom their violent clashes at seaside resorts were a regular feature of the mid-1960s.

Royal Ulster Constabulary (RUC) The armed force responsible for policing in Northern Ireland. The RUC was established in 1921 and replaced the Royal Irish Constabulary. Throughout its existence the RUC's membership has been predominantly Protestant and seen by the minority population as an anti-Catholic force. An inquiry into its future role, chaired by Chris Patten, was held in 1998. It recommended sweeping changes. See also Stalker affair.

RUC See Royal Ulster Constabulary.

Saatchi and Saatchi Advertising agency whose campaigns for the Conservative party reputedly won the party the 1979, 1983, 1987 and 1992 general elections. Its 1979 'Labour isn't working' poster is perhaps the best remembered. Founded in 1970 by the brothers Charles (b. 1943) and Maurice (b. 1946), it became by the late 1980s one of the world's largest advertising companies. The company was rent by internal splits in 1994.

Salads Nickname, often used derisively, of the Social and Liberal Democrats formed on 3 Mar. 1988 following votes in favour of merging the two parties by the Social Democratic party (SDP) on 31 Aug. 1987 and the Liberal party on 17 Sept. 1987.

Salisbury convention A House of Lords convention – dating from the 1945–51 Labour governments and named after the Conservative leader of the House of Lords, the Marquess of Salisbury – that peers do not oppose legislation which the government had included in its general election manifesto and which has received House of Commons approval.

Saltley A coke depot in Birmingham, the successful closure of which by mass picketing in 1972 because of police fears of violence (the 'Battle of Saltley Gate') symbolized the victory of the National Union of Mineworkers in their strike and established the Yorkshire miners' leader Arthur Scargill as a leading trade union figure. See also flying pickets, miners' strikes, Orgreave.

Sanctions An economic boycott was imposed on Southern Rhodesia by Britain and the United Nations following the unilateral declaration of independence (qv) in Nov. 1965. The ban on trade was intended to bring the government down within weeks but evasion by individual companies – with the assistance of South Africa – made the policy ineffective. More recently, sanctions have been imposed on such states as Libya and Iraq. See also Bingham Report.

SAS See Special Air Service.

Satanic Verses Title of a novel by Salman Rushdie (b. 1947) published in 1988, the allegedly blasphemous anti-Islamic nature of which antagonized Ayatollah Khomeini's Iranian regime. The Ayatollah pronounced a *fatwa* sentencing Rushdie to death and there were worldwide demonstrations against the book. Rushdie remained in hiding under armed guard for many years. One effect of the *fatwa* was a further deterioration in Britain's relations with Iran.

Scarman Report Lord Scarman was appointed by the Conservative government to investigate the causes of the April 1981 Brixton riots (qv). His report said little not already suggested in reports on the 1960s inner-city riots in the USA. He defended the measures that the police had used to contain the disturbances. He pointed to the need for more ethnic minority police officers, for the screening of recruits for racist attitudes and the dismissal of proven racist officers, greater consultation with local communities, more police on the beat, and regulation of police search powers. Scarman also stressed the need to confront underlying social issues: the essential regeneration of the inner cities and the prevention of racial discrimination in employment, education and housing.

SEATO (South East Asia Treaty Organisation) A defence agreement signed in Manila on 8 September 1954 by Great Britain, the USA, France, Australia, New Zealand, Pakistan, the Philippines and Thailand. It established a collective defence system and pledged the signatories to form a united front against communism. The headquarters were in Bangkok. SEATO was formally dissolved in 1977.

secondary picketing Picketing by strikers of places not directly involved in their dispute. In the 1972 miners' strike, pickets of mineworkers were able, for example, to close Ipswich docks to prevent coal imports weakening the effectiveness of their industrial action. Secondary picketing was outlawed in the Conservative government's trade union reforms in the 1980s. See also miners' strikes.

Selsdon Man Term used by Labour Prime Minister Harold Wilson to describe what he alleged were new 'uncaring' Conservative policies during the run-up to the 1970 general election. The expression came from the Selsdon Park Hotel, Croydon, South London, where the shadow cabinet held a policy-making meeting on 30 Jan.–1 Feb. 1970 out of which appeared to emerge a break with the post-war consensus.

shadow cabinet Alternative government-in-waiting formed by the parliamentary Opposition party. A spokesperson on, for example, foreign affairs 'shadows' the Foreign Secretary. The first Conservative shadow cabinet was formed following the 1906 general election defeat. The Labour party's shadow cabinet consists of twelve House of Commons members elected annually to the Parliamentary Committee together with other members appointed directly by the Leader of the Opposition.

Shares Index See Footsie.

Shelter Pressure group launched in 1966 as the National Campaign for the Homeless. One of its first directors was the Liberal politician Des Wilson. Shelter has played a prominent part in formulating new strategies to solve the housing crisis in Britain.

Simonstown agreement Agreement with South Africa allowing the Royal Navy access to the Simonstown naval base, near Cape Town. The agreement, which also involved joint naval manoeuvres with South Africa, was much criticized by opponents of apartheid and was terminated by the Labour government in the late 1970s.

Sinn Fein (Gaelic, 'we ourselves') Irish nationalist movement founded in 1905. Following an upsurge of activity in the late 1960s and early 1970s, Sinn Fein split into the Official and Provisional movements. Official Sinn Fein stepped back from support for armed action and transformed itself into a socialist workers' party, concentrating on electoral politics and the attempt to appeal to Catholics and Protestants on a class basis. Traditional militant nationalism re-emerged in the form of Provisional Sinn Fein, the political wing of the Provisional Irish Republican Army. In the 1980s Provisional Sinn Fein turned to a combined electoral-armed campaign. Growing electoral success in the Catholic community – Provisional Sinn Fein MPs were elected but refused to take their seats in Parliament – concerned the British government and attempts were made to deny the organization publicity. Sinn Fein's electoral appeal grew during the 1990s and it was a partner in the Good Friday agreement (qv). See also Armalite and the ballot box, Downing Street declaration, Irish Republican Army, Sinn Fein ban.

Sinn Fein ban Order issued by the Home Secretary Douglas Hurd on 19 Oct. 1988 preventing the broadcasting of direct statements by representatives of Sinn Fein (qv), the Ulster Defence Association (qv) and other organizations allegedly linked with terrorism. Actors were, however, allowed to read transcripts of their remarks, making the ban ineffective. The ban was lifted in Sept. 1994.

Six Counties The counties of Northern Ireland – Antrim, Armagh, Down, Fermanagh, Londonderry and Tyrone – which remained part of the United Kingdom after the Treaty of London in 1921. They were formerly part of the nine-county province of Ulster with Cavan, Donegal and Monaghan.

Skinheads Youth sub-culture which emerged in the late 1960s, partly derived from the Mods (qv). Skinheads, some of whom were involved in racist attacks on ethnic minorities and attracted to far-right political organizations, wore an aggressively pseudo-proletarian uniform of cropped hair, rolled-up jeans, braces and heavy 'Doc Marten' boots.

sleaze A contributory factor in the Conservatives' 1997 general election defeat, the issue of sleaze first arose in 1994 with allegations that Tory junior ministers Neil Hamilton and Tim Smith had asked questions in the Commons in 1985–90 in return for undeclared payments. Both resigned and the Nolan Committee on Standards in Public Life (and, later, a Parliamentary Commissioner for Standards) was set up in response to general concern over the issue. The financial questions became interlinked in the public mind with a series of sexual scandals involving Tory MPs. Mr Hamilton continued to deny any impropriety but lost his seat at the general election. Sleaze returned as an issue under the Labour government with suggestions that Treasury minister Geoffrey Robinson had used offshore investments to avoid tax. After the setting up of a Department of Trade and Industry investigation into Mr Robinson in 1998, it emerged that he had lent DTI minister Peter Mandelson £373,000 to buy a house while Labour was in opposition. Mr Mandelson had not declared the loan and resigned in December, followed by Mr Robinson.

Smethwick West Midlands constituency which, in the Oct. 1964 general election, elected Conservative candidate Peter Griffiths after he had fought an allegedly racist campaign, defeating the leading Labour figure Patrick Gordon-Walker. Prime Minister Harold Wilson said in the House of Commons on 3 Nov. that Griffiths would 'serve his time here as a Parliamentary leper'.

Smith Square Central London square housing the Conservative party's Central Office (qv). The Labour party also had its headquarters there, in Transport House (qv), from 1928 to 1980, when it moved to Walworth Road (qv).

social chapter Section of the Treaty of European Union rejected by the Thatcher and Major governments. The seven articles of the chapter include: the improvement of living standards within the context of economic competitiveness; encouragement of health and safety at work; equality for women and consultation of workers by employers; promotion of management–worker consultation by the European Commission; contractual relations between management and workers; European coordination of social policy; equal pay for men and women; regular reporting by the European Commission on the chapter's progress. Following its 1997 election victory, the new Labour government announced it would sign the social chapter. See also Maastricht Treaty.

social contract Agreement between the Labour government elected in 1974 and the Trades Union Congress by which the unions accepted measures to control inflation in return for the repeal of the Industrial Relations Act 1971, the abolition of the Pay Board (qv), and the acknowledgement of the concept of a 'social wage' through increased public spending. The government promised food subsidies, price controls and increased pensions. Both sides broke the agreement in 1977, effectively ending the contract. The expression had first been used in this context by James Callaghan at the Labour party conference in Oct. 1972. Left-wing opponents dubbed it the 'social con-trick'.

Socialist Charter Labour party activists' grouping formed in 1968 against a background of growing dissatisfaction with the Wilson government to place constituency pressure on the parliamentary party and to organize a stronger non-parliamentary left. Although Socialist Charter claimed the backing of almost 200 constituency and trade union bodies by 1969, its existence was short-lived as fundamental differences between the parliamentary and extra-parliamentary strands emerged.

Socialist Workers' Party See p 96.

Soft Left A section of the Labour party in the mid-1980s which, although it wanted to retain Clause IV (qv) socialism as the party's objective, was willing to support Neil Kinnock's attempt to modernize the party to improve its chances of gaining electoral support. See also Hard Left.

Solidarity Labour party grouping formed in 1981 by centre and right MPs who, while opposing the activities of the left within the party, would not go as far as leaving to support the recently formed Social Democratic Party (SDP). Among leading members of the group were John Smith (Labour leader 1992–94) and Roy Hattersley (deputy leader 1983–92).

Southall Suburb in west London with a high Asian minority population, the scene of a violent anti-National Front demonstration on 23 Apr. 1979 in which a teacher, Blair Peach, died from a blow to his head from a truncheon. There were allegations that he was killed by a Metropolitan Police Special Patrol Group officer (who was named in the left-wing press) but demands for a public inquiry were rejected.

Special Air Service (SAS) An elite specialized British army unit deployed on anti-terrorist and clandestine activities. Developing out of the Second World War Long Range Desert Patrol Group, the SAS uses unorthodox tactics and deliberately encourages an air of secrecy. The regiment came into public prominence when it stormed the Iranian Embassy in April 1980 and killed six gunmen who were holding hostages. SAS members were active in the 1982 Falklands War (qv) and the 1990–91 Gulf War (qv) and have conducted operations in Northern Ireland. They were involved in the controversial shooting of three Provisional IRA members in Gibraltar (qv) in 1988 (see *Death on the Rock*).

special relationship Term used to describe a relationship between Britain and the United States allegedly built on historical and sentimental links of culture and kinship rather than merely diplomatic expediency. It was briefly rekindled in the Thatcher–Reagan era, and resurfaced in the close alliance of Bill Clinton and Tony Blair after 1997.

spin doctor A party official employed to ensure that the presentation of policies and the reaction to criticism works in the party's interests. The Labour party's spin doctors (sometimes described as 'media manipulators') have been given some credit for the party's 1997 general election victory, but with the party in government there has been growing public cynicism about the triumph of presentation over substance.

Spycatcher The title of the autobiography of former MI5 member Peter Wright (1917–95) which contained details of abuses by the agency, including a plan to overthrow the Labour government in the 1970s. Margaret Thatcher attempted to ban its publication and the government fought a celebrated case in the Supreme Court of New South Wales, where Wright was living. It was during this trial that the Cabinet Secretary Sir Robert Armstrong admitted he had been 'economical with the truth'. The government lost the Australian case on 2 June 1988. Publication of *Spycatcher* was prevented in Britain until 13 Oct. 1988 when the House of Lords ruled against the government.

Stalker affair On 30 May 1986 the Deputy Chief Constable of Greater Manchester, John Stalker, was removed from duty over allegations of misconduct in his relationship with a Manchester businessman. Mr Stalker had been appointed in 1984 to head an inquiry into a 'shoot-to-kill' policy that the Royal Ulster Constabulary (qv) was allegedly operating against Irish Republican terrorists. RUC officers had shot six IRA suspects in three incidents in 1982. In 1985 Mr Stalker's interim report recommended the prosecution of eleven officers. Mr Stalker was replaced on the inquiry by West Yorkshire Chief Constable Colin Sampson. Neither his nor Mr Stalker's report was ever made public. Mr Stalker, vindicated on the misconduct allegations, resigned from the police.

stalking horse A candidate (particularly in party leadership elections) who – while having no chance of winning – puts his or her name forward to test how vulnerable the leader would be to a challenge from a more serious candidate.

Stormont The building in Belfast housing the Northern Ireland Parliament until 1972, when direct rule from London was imposed. Since then, it has been the location of the Northern Ireland Office and, in 1973–74, and again after 1998, of the Northern Ireland Assembly.

Suez crisis See p 210.

Sunningdale agreement Agreement on a Protestant–Catholic powersharing assembly and the creation of a Council of Ireland reached at the Civil Service College at Sunningdale, Surrey, following a conference on Northern Ireland 6–9 Dec. 1973.

Supermac Harold Macmillan (1894–1986), Conservative Prime Minister (1957–63). A cartoon by Vicky in the *Daily Express* on 6 Nov. 1958 portrayed him ironically as Supermac because of his deft political touch. The sobriquet, which became a central part of Macmillan's image, rebounded as his government drifted into crisis in 1962–63.

tactical voting A decision made by the voter based on support for a candidate who appears to have the best prospect of defeating a less preferred candidate rather than on party loyalty.

Tartan Tories Labour party description of the Scottish National party (SNP) as it made electoral progress in the 1970s, winning 30 per cent of the Scottish vote and eleven seats at the October 1974 election. As the strongest party in Scotland, Labour felt it had most to fear from an SNP advance. Used by the SNP in the 1992 general election to describe the Labour party for its advocacy of devolution (qv) rather than independence.

Teddy Boys The first post-war youth sub-culture, connected with the emergence of rock and roll in the 1950s. They were predominantly working-class, with a uniform of Edwardian (hence 'Teddy') style jackets, drainpipe trousers, and crepe-soled shoes.

Television Act 1954 Set up the Independent Television Authority (later the Independent Broadcasting Authority) and gave birth to commercial television with rigorous rules controlling the relationship between advertisers and programme makers.

Terence Higgins Trust The trust was named in memory of the first person known to have died of AIDS in the UK. It was founded in 1982 and was the first national voluntary organization concerned with AIDS.

Test Ban Treaty British, US and Soviet agreement concluded on 5 Aug. 1963 following five years of negotiations, ending nuclear weapons tests in the atmosphere, in space or under water. Underground testing was allowed to continue. France and China refused to sign the treaty but over 90 states signed in the course of the following two years.

Thatcherite Supporter of the radical right-wing economic, defence, and foreign policies of Margaret Thatcher (b. 1925), leader of the Conservative party (1975–90) and Prime Minister (1979–90). See also Centre Forward, Wandsworth.

Think Tank The Central Policy Review Staff established by Conservative Prime Minister Edward Heath in 1971. It was intended to meet a need for the Cabinet to reach outside the Civil Service for information and policy formulation. The Think Tank continued to function during the 1974–79 Labour governments but was abolished by Margaret Thatcher in 1983.

Think Twice Campaign Conservative opponents of devolution in Scotland during the run-up to the referendum on the issue held in Sept. 1997. The title derived from the two questions facing voters, on setting up a Scottish Parliament and on exercising tax-raising powers, both of which the campaign opposed. The body was weakened by the fact that a number of the most influential anti-devolution Conservatives had lost their Commons seats in the 1997 general election defeat. Led by former Conservative solicitor-general Lord Fraser of Carmyllie and lawyer Donald Findlay, Think Twice was unsuccessful.

Third Way A somewhat vague expression of the ideology associated with New Labour (qv) and the Blair administration after 1997. It was seen as a philosophy that was neither socialism nor the strident capitalism of the Thatcher era. Leading academics who talk in these terms include Anthony Giddens, Director of the London School of Economics since 1997. His book *The Third Way* was published in 1998.

thirty-year rule The rule which does not allow government papers to be seen by the public at the Public Record Office until 30 years have elapsed, introduced by the Labour government in 1968. Until then, the period was 50 years. However, the government retains the right to hold sensitive documents back for a longer period. Hence government documents on sensitive issues (such as the abdication crisis of the 1930s) have still not been released, to the dismay of historians.

three-day week In late 1973, as a result of the Arab–Israeli War, oil prices rose and supplies were reduced. In November the National Union of Mineworkers banned overtime working in support of a pay claim. With fuel supplies running low, the government declared a state of emergency on 13 Nov. On 1 Jan. 1974 the government announced that electricity could be supplied to most industries only on three specified days, meaning that many people could work only those three days. A snap general election called on 28 Feb. resulted on 4 March in a minority Labour administration which ended the three-day week on 9 March. See also miners' strikes.

Tiger talks Meeting off Gibraltar on the cruiser HMS *Tiger* in Dec. 1966 between Labour Prime Minister Harold Wilson and the rebel Southern Rhodesian Premier Ian Smith to reach a settlement of the Rhodesian unilateral declaration of independence (qv). The talks failed, as did a second round on HMS *Fearless* in Oct. 1968, because of Smith's unwillingness to accept the principle of unimpeded progress towards black majority rule.

Trades Union Congress (TUC) Federation of some 72 British trade unions founded in 1868, whose basic function is to coordinate union action by means of annual conferences of union representatives where matters of common concern are discussed.

Trafalgar Square riot Violent demonstration against the widely unpopular poll tax or community charge (qv) on 31 Mar. 1990, the culmination of prolonged nationwide protests. Over 130 were injured, including 57 police, and 341 were arrested in fighting and looting which spread throughout the centre of London. Prime Minister Margaret Thatcher – who was deeply committed to the poll tax – was replaced as Conservative leader in the autumn; plans to replace the poll tax were announced a year after the riot.

Transport House Headquarters in London's Smith Square (qv) of the Transport and General Workers' Union (TGWU) from 1928, of the Trades Union Congress (1928–60), and of the Labour party (1928–80). Built by influential

TGWU leader Ernest Bevin (1881–1951), the sharing of the property symbolized the close links between the trade unions and the Labour party.

Treaty of European Union See Maastricht Treaty.

Tribune Group Left-wing group in the Labour party named after the weekly magazine *Tribune*. The 'Tribunites' argued for wider nationalization (qv) and unilateral nuclear disarmament, and opposed entry to the European Economic Community. In the 1950s the most prominent figure was Aneurin Bevan (1897–1960) and the group provided the core of opposition to the party leader Hugh Gaitskell. It remained active, if less influential, with the splitting off of the Campaign Group (qv) in 1982. See also Manifesto Group.

Trident US-designed submarine-launched missile which the Conservative government announced in 1980 it would purchase to replace the ageing Polaris (qv) at a cost of £7.5 billion over fifteen years. The missile contained eight warheads of 100 kilotons each.

Troubles, the Euphemism for the violence arising from Catholic resentment at the British presence in Ireland, initially referring to the period 1916–21, but later in Northern Ireland from 1968 onwards.

TUC See Trades Union Congress.

Two Nations Phrase – originally from the novel *Sybil, or The Two Nations* (1845) by Conservative politician Benjamin Disraeli (1804–81) – describing a society with a gulf between rich and poor. Used in the 1980s to encapsulate the division between the depressed north of England and Scotland, with collapsing industries and unemployment, and the more prosperous south of England. See also north–south divide, One Nation Group.

Twyford Down The scene in Hampshire of bitter demonstrations against the building of an extension of the M3 motorway finally completed in the autumn of 1994. The road crossed the Down and an ancient burial site; protests against its construction encouraged other direct action against the M11 link road in east London and the Swainswick bypass near Bath. It marked an important stage in the growth of the anti-road lobby.

UDA See Ulster Defence Association.

UDI See unilateral declaration of independence.

UDM See Union of Democratic Mineworkers.

UDR See Ulster Defence Regiment.

UFF See Ulster Freedom Fighters.

Ugandan Asians In Aug. 1972 President Idi Amin (b. 1925) announced the expulsion of Asians, all of whom were British passport holders, from Uganda. The Conservative government announced that it had a legal and moral duty to allow them entry. Although 50,000–60,000 were expected, negotiations with India, Canada and other countries reduced the number who eventually came to 28,000. The National Front and the Monday Club (qv) mounted a campaign against their entry but the Conservative party conference in Oct. 1972 supported the policy by a two to one majority, despite a bitter attack by Enoch Powell. See also Kenyan Asians.

Ulster Defence Association (UDA) A Protestant paramilitary organization formed by the amalgamation of a number of small defence and vigilante groups in 1971 in response to growing nationalist and IRA activity. Some of its members have allegedly been responsible for attacks on members of the Catholic community under the name of the Ulster Freedom Fighters (qv). At one time it was the largest loyalist paramilitary grouping (with 40,000 members in 1972). It called a ceasefire in 1994. See also Sinn Fein ban.

Ulster Defence Regiment (UDR) A part-time military force in Northern Ireland which replaced the RUC B-Specials (qv) when they were disbanded on 1 Apr. 1970. The creation of the UDR was an attempt to break away from the Protestant dominance of the former RUC B-Specials, but although initially 17 per cent of its members were Catholics, by the end of 1971 this had fallen to 5 per cent. The UDR was amalgamated into the Royal Irish Regiment in June 1992.

Ulster Freedom Fighters (UFF) A Protestant terrorist organization which has been responsible for the deaths of a number of Catholics. The UFF is the military wing of the Ulster Defence Association (qv).

Ulster Volunteer Force (UVF) Protestant paramilitary organization formed in 1966 to oppose what was seen as an increasingly liberal unionism, named after the army set up by Sir Edward Carson in 1912 to fight for preservation of the Union with Britain. Until it announced a ceasefire in 1994, the UVF (with an estimated membership of a few hundred) was involved in political assassinations and the sectarian murder of Catholics. The UVF is linked with the Progressive Unionist party, which won two seats in elections to the Northern Ireland assembly.

unilateral declaration of independence (UDI) The declaration by Southern Rhodesia on 11 Nov. 1965 under Ian Smith's (b. 1919) Rhodesian Front government was prompted by white objections to sharing power with the African majority and a refusal to concede eventual majority rule. UDI was rejected by Britain and condemned by the United Nations but the regime survived sanctions (qv) on trade and an oil embargo until 1980 when, weakened by guerrilla war, a settlement was reached at Lancaster House (qv) which led to elections and an African majority government under Robert Mugabe. See also *Tiger* talks.

unilateralism Normally used in the context of nuclear weapons, the policy of abandoning possession of nuclear weapons regardless of their continued possession by other states. The issue has often divided the Labour party. The 1960 party conference adopted unilateralism, but reversed the decision in

311

1961. The policy was effectively adopted in 1980 and then abandoned at the 1989 party conference. See also Campaign for Nuclear Disarmament, multilateralism.

Union of Democratic Mineworkers (UDM) Breakaway organization formed by members of the National Union of Mineworkers in Nottinghamshire on 18 Oct. 1985. They had refused to support the 1984–85 miners' strike and continued to work throughout the dispute. Miners in the area had formed a similar organization in the 1926 General Strike, the Miners' Industrial Union. See also miners' strikes.

UVF See Ulster Volunteer Force.

Walworth Road Thoroughfare in south London where the Labour party relocated its headquarters in 1980, when it moved from Smith Square (qv). The headquarters were named John Smith House in memory of the party's leader from 1992 until his sudden death in 1994. In 1997 much of the administrative machinery of the party was moved to Millbank Tower (more conveniently situated for Westminster).

Wandsworth The Conservative-controlled local authority in southwest London which provided a model for Conservative boroughs in the 1980s by pioneering the reduction and contracting-out to private business of council services. Known as the 'flagship' authority because of its exemplary Thatcherite (qv) policies, Wandsworth was also unique in setting a nil level of community charge (qv) thanks to substantial central government grants. Wandsworth was always compared favourably (by Conservatives) with neighbouring Lambeth, controlled by the Labour 'Loony Left' (qv). See also ratecapping.

Wapping The east London former docklands site of the editorial offices and printing works of Rupert Murdoch's (b. 1931) News International, publishers of *The Times* and the *Sun*. News International's sudden move there from Fleet Street destroyed the power of the print unions and allowed the rapid introduction of new technology into newspaper production. Wapping was the scene of heavy picketing and of a particularly violent mass demonstration in Jan. 1987 which resulted in complaints about indiscriminate police violence.

Warrenpoint Coastal resort in County Down, Northern Ireland, the scene of the killing of eighteen soldiers by a double IRA bombing on 27 Aug. 1979. A few hours earlier the IRA had killed Lord Mountbatten by blowing up his boat in the Republic of Ireland.

welfare state Term for the system of comprehensive social welfare provision proposed by the Beveridge Report and introduced after 1945 by the Attlee government. It was widely seen as being undermined by Conservative policies (on, for example, the National Health Service) under Thatcher and Major. The 1997 Labour government initiated a debate on the future of the welfare state.

Welsh Office See Cathays Park.

Western European Union Grouping of countries (originally Britain, France, the Netherlands, Belgium and Luxembourg) for collaboration in economic, social and cultural matters and for collective self-defence. They signed a 50-year treaty in March 1948. Most defence functions were taken over by NATO. The WEU played an increasing role as a forum for ideas (e.g. for collaboration with the countries of the former Eastern bloc). The original members have been joined by, among others, Germany, Greece, Italy, Portugal and Spain.

West Lothian Question A key argument (named after the anti-devolution Labour MP Tam Dalyell, who represented West Lothian) in the debates of the 1970s on devolution. In essence, Dalyell asked why an MP for a Scottish constituency could vote at Westminster on English issues, but an MP for an English constituency could not vote on Scottish issues. In the 1990s, devolution went ahead but the question was never satisfactorily answered.

Westland affair A government crisis which almost forced Margaret Thatcher's resignation as Prime Minister in 1986. On 13 Nov. 1985 the ailing Westland Helicopters announced a rescue deal involving a US–Italian consortium. Defence Secretary Michael Heseltine favoured a deal with a European company. On 6 Jan. 1986 a letter written to Mr Heseltine by Solicitor-General Sir Patrick Mayhew, warning him about the position he was taking, was leaked to the press. In protest, Mr Heseltine resigned dramatically by walking out of a Cabinet meeting on 9 Jan. On 24 Jan. Trade and Industry Secretary Leon Brittan resigned amid allegations of his involvement in the leak. Poor handling of a debate in the House of Commons by Opposition leader Neil Kinnock prevented responsibility being attached to Mrs Thatcher. Mr Brittan was later knighted and appointed a Commissioner in Europe. Mr Heseltine remained a loyal but threatening back-bench figure until he stood against Mrs Thatcher as leader in 1990, rejoining the government after her fall.

Wets Members of the Conservative party during the period of Margaret Thatcher's leadership who were less than fervent supporters of her more radical policies, used as a term of abuse by her followers, the 'Dries' (qv). Wets favoured a more traditionalist and centrist economic line and were concerned with the social implications of policies which involved reduced public spending, particularly mass unemployment. Mrs Thatcher inherited a large number of Wets from her predecessor Edward Heath, but had removed most of them by 1983.

whip An MP who acts as a parliamentary party manager, with the dual role of gauging back-bench opinion on controversial issues and enforcing voting support. The number of lines marked under an instruction to vote denotes its importance to the party leadership. See also cross-bencher.

wind of change Expression used by Prime Minister Harold Macmillan (1894–1986) in a speech to the South African parliament on 3 Feb. 1960. He was describing growing national and anti-colonial consciousness among black Africans throughout the continent and implicitly warning South Africa about its apartheid policies.

Winter of Discontent Wave of public and private sector strikes in the winter of 1978–79 against the Labour government's attempt to impose a 5 per cent ceiling on pay increases. The disruption, caused particularly by local government manual workers, together with scenes of violence on picket lines, played a significant part in Labour's defeat at the 1979 general election. Repetition of the phrase continued to undermine Labour in successive general elections.

Wolfenden Report Report of a committee, chaired by Sir John Wolfenden (Aug. 1954 to Aug. 1957), which recommended reform of the law on homosexuality, the practice of which had been a criminal offence for many years. Reform did not take place until the election of a Labour government in the 1960s. See also Albany Trust.

Workers' Revolutionary party See p 97.

Yesterday's Men Title of a BBC programme critical of Labour Opposition leaders televised a year after Labour's defeat in the 1970 general election which led to loud protests from Labour in the House of Commons and a long-drawn-out argument on the role of the governors of the BBC and the professional ethics of television journalists. The controversy encouraged documentary makers to weaken their criticism of politicians.

Zircon affair In Jan. 1987 the BBC banned – under government pressure – the broadcast of a television documentary on the Zircon spy satellite, the existence and £5 million cost of which the programme said had been concealed. Prior to its banning, the offices of BBC Scotland and the *New Statesman* (where Duncan Campbell, the journalist responsible for the documentary, worked) were raided by Special Branch officers seeking tapes of the programme. Although it was eventually broadcast in Sept. 1988, the raids were seen as evidence of the government's increasing authoritarianism. See also ABC trial.

TOPIC BIBLIOGRAPHY

Abbreviations

AmHR	*American Historical Review*
BJPS	*British Journal of Political Science*
CR	*Contemporary Record*
EHR	*English Historical Review*
GO	*Government and Opposition*
HJ	*Historical Journal*
H	*History*
HT	*History Today*
JCH	*Journal of Contemporary History*
JICH	*Journal of Imperial and Commonwealth History*
JMH	*Journal of Modern History*
NLR	*New Left Review*
PAff	*Parliamentary Affairs*
PQ	*Political Quarterly*
PSQ	*Political Science Quarterly*
Pol S	*Political Studies*
Pol R	*Politics Review*
PA	*Public Administration*
PBA	*Proceedings of the British Academy*
SSR	*Social Studies Review*
TRHS	*Transactions of the Royal Historical Society*
TCBH	*Twentieth Century British History*

Introductory note

This bibliography is arranged in rough chronological order and is intended to represent a fair selection of the major topics in British history and politics since 1945. The essay titles are merely intended to focus attention on some of the most commonly raised issues, but by no means exhaust the range of possibilities on each subject. The reading is deliberately greater than would be required for an average essay, but does reflect the wealth of bibliographical material now available for most of these subjects and allows a degree of specialization on particular aspects of a topic. Similarly, the article literature mentioned, while not an exhaustive list, is intended as a guide to some of the most important material from which a selection can be made according to preference.

1. General texts

Very general texts which include the post-war period are J Ramsden and G Williams, *Ruling Britannia: A Political History of Britain, 1688–1988* (1990); and G Alderman, *Modern Britain, 1700–1983* (1986). Two works which take their starting-point as the late nineteenth century and cover the post-war period are K Robbins, *The Eclipse of a Great Power, Modern Britain, 1870–1975* (1983) and M Pugh, *State and Society: British Political and Social History, 1870–1992* (1994). More exclusively concerned with the twentieth century are P Clarke, *Hope and Glory: Britain, 1900–1990* (1996); A Marwick, *A History of the Modern British Isles: 1914–1999* (2000); and R Blake, *The Decline of Power, 1915–1964* (1985). For exclusive focus on post-1945, see A Sked and C Cook, *Post-War Britain: A Political History* (4th edn, 1993); D Childs, *Britain since 1945* (3rd edn, 1992); K O Morgan, *The People's Peace: British History, 1945–1990* (1990); P Hennessy and A Seldon (eds) *Ruling Performance: British Governments from Attlee to Thatcher* (1987). A collection of value on a number of issues is T Gourvish and A O'Day (eds) *Britain since 1945* (1991).

For Scotland see C Harvie, *No Gods and Precious Few Heroes: Scotland, 1914–1997* (3rd edn, 1998); T C Smout, *A Century of the Scottish People, 1830–1950* (1986). For Wales see G A Williams, *When Was Wales? A History of the Welsh* (1985); K O Morgan, *Rebirth of a Nation: Wales, 1880–1980* (1982). Ireland is excellently served by R F Foster, *Modern Ireland, 1600–1972* (1988), which can be helpfully supplemented by J J Lee, *Ireland, 1912–1985: Politics and Society* (1989) and by the documents in the later sections of A O'Day and J Stevenson (eds) *Irish Historical Documents since 1800* (1982).

For the economic history of the period, see R Floud and D McCloskey (eds) *The Economic History of Britain since 1700* (2 vols, 1981); C More, *The Industrial Age: Economy and Society in Britain, 1750–1985* (1989); S Pollard, *The Development of the British Economy, 1914–1980* (1983). The social history of the period is treated as part of a continuum in E Royle, *Modern Britain: A Social History, 1750–1985* (1987) and F Bedarida, *A Social History of England, 1851–1975* (1976), while A Marwick, *British Society since 1945* (1982) and

318

R Lowe, *The Welfare State in Britain since 1945* (1993) deal exclusively with the post-war period.

For reference, see D E and G Butler, *British Political Facts, 1900–1994* (1994); F W S Craig (ed) *British Electoral Facts, 1832–1987* (1989) and on social history A H Halsey (ed) *British Social Trends since 1900* (1988). For research students, the archival sources are given in the 2-volume *Longman Guide to Sources in Contemporary British History* (ed. C Cook *et al*) (1993, 1994). The Nuffield General Election series, authored or coauthored since 1951 by D E Butler, provides an analysis of each of the post-war elections.

2. Britain and the Second World War

Essay topics

Why did the Labour party win the general election of 1945?

Assess the impact of the Second World War on British politics and society.

Secondary works

Of the general studies, A Marwick, *Britain in the Century of Total War: War, Peace and Social Change, 1900–1967* (1968) and A J P Taylor, *English History, 1914–45* (1965) have relevant sections. P Addison, *The Road to 1945: British Politics and the Second World War* (1975) has a brilliant analysis of wartime politics. See also H Pelling, *Britain and the Second World War* (1970) and the essays by P Addison and A Marwick in A Sked and C Cook (eds), *Crisis and Controversy: Essays in Honour of A J P Taylor* (1976). For Churchill see K Robbins, *Churchill* (1992); R Rhodes James, *Churchill: A Study in Failure* (1973); H Pelling, *Winston Churchill* (1977); R Blake, *The Conservative Party from Peel to Thatcher* (1985). For the Labour party see H Pelling, *A Short History of the Labour Party* (8th edn, 1985); A. Thorpe, *A History of the British Labour Party* (1997); and S Brooke, *Labour's War* (1992). Major personalities of the period are covered in J Harris, *William Beveridge: A Biography* (1977); A Bullock, *The Life and Times of Ernest Bevin*, vol I (1967); B Donoughue and G W Jones, *Herbert Morrison* (1973). A Calder, *The People's War* (1969) discusses the war from the point of view of the civilian population. The effects of the war on social policy and politics are surveyed in H L Smith (ed) *War and Social Change* (1987); D Fraser, *The Evolution of the British Welfare State* (1973); J MacNicol, 'Family allowances and less eligibility' in P Thane (ed) *Origins of British Social Policy* (1978); J Harris, 'Social planning in wartime: some aspects of the Beveridge Report' in J M Winter (ed) *War and Economic Development* (1975). C Barnett, *The Audit of War* (1986) is a major critique of the war effort and its long-term effects, but see also A Booth, *British Economic Policy, 1931–49* (1989) and J Tomlinson, *Employment Policy: The Crucial Years, 1939–51* (1987).

The 1945 general election is discussed in R B McCallum and A Readman, *The British General Election of 1945* (1947). The Attlee governments have received excellent treatment in K O Morgan, *Labour in Power, 1945–1951* (1983); H Pelling, *The Labour Governments, 1945–51* (1984); M Sissons and

319

P French (eds) *The Age of Austerity* (1963); N Tiratsoo (ed) *The Attlee Years* (1992) and P Hennessy, *Never Again: Britain 1945–51* (1992).

Biographies of the major Labour politicians can be consulted in K Harris, *Attlee* (1982); B Pimlott, *Hugh Dalton* (1984); A Bullock, *Ernest Bevin: Foreign Secretary* (1982); M Foot, *Aneurin Bevan, 1945–60* (1975); J Campbell, *Nye Bevan* (1987). The performance of the Labour governments has been reviewed in the essays by Addison and Hennessy in P Hennessy and A Seldon (eds) *Ruling Performance: British Governments from Attlee to Thatcher* (1987). A crucial aspect of the post-war period, economic survival, has been the subject of debate, see Barnett (above), but has received fuller treatment in A Cairncross, *Years of Recovery: British Economic Policy, 1945–51* (1985) and S Howson, *British Monetary Policy, 1945–51* (1993). Foreign policy is discussed in V Rothwell, *Britain and the Cold War, 1941–47* (1983); R Ovendale, *The Foreign Policy of the British Labour Governments, 1945–51* (1984), and A Bullock, *Ernest Bevin: Foreign Secretary* (1982).

Of the large literature on post-war decolonization, most relevant here are J Darwin, *Britain and Decolonization: The Retreat from Empire in the Post-War World* (1987); M E Chamberlain, *Decolonisation: The Fall of the European Empires* (1985); D Judd and P Slinn, *The Evolution of the Modern Commonwealth, 1902–80* (1982). On India see B R Tomlinson, *The Political Economy of the Raj, 1914–47* (1979); R J Moore, *Escape from Empire: The Attlee Government and the Indian Problem* (1987). The decision to pursue a nuclear future is discussed in M Gowing and L Arnold, *Independence and Deterrence: Britain and Atomic Energy, 1945–51* (1974).

For the Conservative response to the post-war situation, see R Blake, *The Conservative Party from Peel to Thatcher* (1985); B Schwartz, 'The tide of history, the reconstruction of conservatism, 1945–51' in N Tiratsoo (ed) *The Attlee Years* (1992); J D Hoffmann, *The Conservative Party in Opposition, 1945–51* (1964); J Ramsden, *The Conservative Party and the Making of Conservative Party Policy: The Conservative Research Department since 1929* (1980).

Articles

The general acceptance of 'consensus' and its ramifications are examined in R Lowe, 'The Second World War, consensus, and the foundation of the Welfare State', *TCBH* (1990); J C Hess, 'The social policy of the Attlee government' in W J Mommsen (ed) *The Emergence of the Welfare State in Britain and Germany* (1981); B Pimlott, 'Is postwar consensus a myth?', *CR* (1989). On politics see I Zweiniger-Bargielowska, 'Rationing, austerity and the Conservative party recovery after 1945', *HJ* (1994); H Pelling, 'The 1945 Election Reconsidered', *HJ* (1980) and J Ramsden, '"A party for owners or a party for earners?" The Conservative party after 1945', *TRHS* (1987). On social policy see A Marwick, 'The Labour party and the Welfare State in Britain, 1900–48', *AmHR* (1967); J Tomlinson, 'Welfare and the economy: the economic impact of the welfare state', *TCBH* (1995); C Webster, 'Conflict and consensus: explaining the British Health Service', *TCBH* (1990) and I Zweiniger-Bargielowska, 'Bread rationing in Britain, 1946–8',

TCBH (1993). On foreign policy see R Ovendale, 'Britain, the U.S.A. and the European Cold War, 1945–48', *H* (1982).

3. Decolonization and foreign policy, 1945–64

Essay topics

Why did Britain grant independence to so many of its colonies after 1945?

What was the significance of the Suez crisis for the conduct of British foreign policy in the post-war period?

Secondary works

General studies of foreign affairs include D Reynolds, *Britannia Overruled: British Policy and World Power in the Twentieth Century* (1991); C M Woodhouse, *British Foreign Policy since the Second World War* (1961); F S Northedge, *British Foreign Policy, The Process of Readjustment, 1945–1961* (1962) and *Descent from Power: British Foreign Policy, 1945–73* (1974); W N Medlicott, *British Foreign Policy since Versailles, 1919–63* (1968).

For the Empire, see J Brown, *The Oxford History of the British Empire, Volume IV: The Twentieth Century* (1999) and B Porter, *The Lion's Share: A Short History of British Imperialism, 1850–1970* (1975). C Cross, *The Fall of the British Empire 1918–1968* (1968) is an outline of decolonization; see also J Darwin, *Britain and Decolonization: The Retreat from Empire in the Post-war World* (1987); D C Watt, *Personalities and Policies* (1965), M E Chamberlain, *Decolonisation: The Fall of the European Empires* (1985), and D Judd and P Slinn, *The Evolution of the Modern Commonwealth* (1982) are good studies. Other features of British policy are considered in P S Gupta, *Imperialism and the British Labour Movement, 1914–64* (1975); P Darby, *British Defence Policy East of Suez 1947–1968* (1973); P M Kennedy, *The Rise and Fall of British Naval Mastery* (1976); C J Bartlett, *The Long Retreat: A Short History of British Defence Policy, 1945–70* (1972); M Gowing and L Arnold, *Independence and Deterrence: Britain and Atomic Energy, 1945–51* (1974).

The immediate post-war period is discussed in M A Fitzsimmons, *The Foreign Policy of the British Labour Government, 1945–51* (1953); A Bullock, *Ernest Bevin: Foreign Secretary* (1982); M Edwards, *The Last Years of British India* (1963); M Zinkin and T Zinkin, *Britain and India: Requiem for Empire* (1964); B R Tomlinson, *The Political Economy of the Raj, 1914–47* (1979); R J Moore, *Escape from Empire* (1987). For the returning Conservative government, see A Seldon, *Churchill's Indian Summer, 1951–5* (1981) and J. Ramsden, *The Age of Churchill and Eden, 1940–57* (1995).

The background to the Suez affair can be found in E Monroe, *Britain's Moment in the Middle East, 1914–56* (1963). On the crisis itself, see K Kyle, *Suez* (1991); H Thomas, *The Suez Affair* (rev. edn, 1970); S Lloyd, *Suez 1956: A Personal Account* (1978): A Nutting, *No End of a Lesson* (1967). Eden's role is discussed in D Carlton, *Eden* (1981); R Rhodes James, *Anthony Eden* (1986). Also see D Carlton, *Britain and the Suez Crisis* (1989); R Louis and R Owen (eds) *Suez 1956: The Crisis and its Consequences* (1992).

On attitudes to Europe, see J Young, *Britain and European Unity 1945–1992* (1993); E Barker, *Britain and a Divided Europe, 1945–70* (1971); R B Manderson-Jones, *The Special Relationship: Anglo-American Relations and Western European Unity, 1947–56* (1972); M Camps, *European Unification in the Sixties* (1967); U Kitzinger, *The Second Try: Labour and the EEC* (1973) and *Diplomacy and Persuasion: How Britain Joined the Common Market* (1973). J Young, *Britain, France and the Unity of Europe, 1945–51* (1984) and J Young, 'The parting of the ways: The 1955 Messina Conference' in M Dockrill and J Young, *British Foreign Policy, 1945–56* (1989) discuss early turning points.

Articles

J Darwin, 'The fear of falling: British politics and imperial decline since 1900', *TRHS* (1986) and 'British decolonization after 1945: a pattern or a puzzle', *JICH* (1992); R Ovendale, 'Macmillan and the wind of change in Africa, 1957–60', *HJ* (1995); R Butt, 'The Common Market and the Conservative party, 1960–61', *GO* (1967); S George, 'Britain in the EEC', *CR* (1992).

4. The domestic policy of the Conservative governments, 1951–64

Essay topics

Were the 'thirteen wasted years' really wasted?

Why did the Conservatives rather than Labour enjoy the support of the electorate between 1951 and 1964?

Secondary works

On the Conservative administrations see R Blake, *The Conservative Party from Peel to Thatcher* (1985); V Bogdanor and R Skidelsky (eds) *The Age of Affluence* (1970) chs 2–4; J Ramsden, *The Age of Churchill and Eden, 1940–57* (1995); P Addison, *Churchill on the Home Front 1900–1955* (1992) ch 12. On a crucial election see D E Butler and R Rose, *The British General Election of 1959* (1960) chs 2–5; on 1951–55 see A Seldon, *Churchill's Indian Summer: The Conservative Government 1951–5* (1981). For the Eden and Macmillan premierships, see D Carlton, *Eden* (1981); R Rhodes James, *Anthony Eden* (1986); A Horne, *Macmillan* (2 vols, 1987–88); J Turner, *Macmillan* (1994); A Howard, *RAB: The Life of R A Butler* (1987) chs 11–16. More generally see K Middlemas, *Power, Competition and the State*, I (1986) chs 7–11; P Hennessy and A Seldon, *Ruling Performance: British Governments from Attlee to Thatcher* (1987); S Ball and A Seldon (eds) *The Conservative Century, 1900–1994* (1994).

On the Labour party in this period, see the sections in H Pelling, *A Short History of the Labour Party* (8th edn, 1985) and C Cook and I Taylor (eds) *The Labour Party* (1980). Discussion of Labour figures can be found in P Williams, *Hugh Gaitskell* (1979); M Foot, *Aneurin Bevan, 1945–60* (1973); J Campbell, *Nye Bevan* (1987); shorter profiles are in K O Morgan, *Labour People* (1986). S Haseler, *The Gaitskellites* (1969) examines an important group. J Cronin, *Labour and Society in Britain, 1918–1979* (1980) chs 8–10 examines the unions' role. Some of the dissident forces are examined by

D Howell, *British Social Democracy* (1976) chs 6–8; E Shaw, *Discipline and Discord in the Labour Party* (1992) chs 2–5; F Parkin, *Middle Class Radicalism* (1968) ch 6.

Articles

See B Pimlott, 'Is the "post-war consensus" a myth?', *CR* (1989); D Dutton, 'Anthony Eden and the judgment of history', *CR* (1991).

5. The Labour government of 1964–70

Essay topic

Did the social achievements of the Labour government of 1964–70 outweigh its economic failures?

Secondary works

For the general course of events see A Sked and C Cook, *Post-War Britain: A Political History* (4th edn, 1993) chs 8 and 9; K O Morgan, *The People's Peace: British History, 1945–1990* (1990); P Hennessy and A Seldon (eds) *Ruling Performance: British Governments from Attlee to Thatcher* (1987). Outstanding sets of memoirs are available for the period: R H Crossman, *The Diaries of a Cabinet Minister, 1961–70* (1975–77), most easily consulted in the condensed version ed. A Howard, *The Crossman Diaries* (1979); B Castle, *The Castle Diaries, 1964–1976* (1980–84), available in one volume, *The Castle Diaries, 1964–1976* (1990) and the first two volumes of T Benn, *Diaries* (5 vols, 1987–93). For analysis of the period see D McKie and C Cook (eds) *The Decade of Disillusion: British Politics in the 1960s* (1972); R Coopey, S Fielding and N Tiratsoo (eds), *The Wilson Governments, 1964–70* (1993); B Pimlott, *Harold Wilson* (1992); P Ziegler, *Harold Wilson* (1993); B Donoughue, *Prime Minister: The Conduct of Policy under Harold Wilson and James Callaghan* (1987). C Ponting, *Breach of Promise: Labour in Power, 1964–70* (1989) is a useful account. On the central issue of the management of the economy, see S Pollard, *The Development of the British Economy, 1914–1980* (3rd edn, 1983); D W E Alford, *British Economic Performance since 1945* (1986). The broader context of decline is considered in A Sked, *Britain's Decline: Problems and Perspectives* (1987); A Gamble, *Britain in Decline: Economic Policy, Political Strategy and the British State* (1985).

For the major social developments of the period, see A Marwick, *British Society since 1945* (1982); J Weeks, *Sex, Politics and Society* (1991); P Foot, *Immigration and Race in British Politics* (1965); A H Halsey, *Change in British Society* (1978); J Burnett, *A Social History of Housing* (1992); H Jones, *Health and Society since 1900* (1993).

Articles

P Anderson, 'Origins of the present crisis', *NLR* (1964); A H Albu, J Bray and R Prentice, 'Lessons of the Labour government', *PQ* (1970); W B Gwyn, 'The Labour party and the threat of bureaucracy', *Pol S* (1971).

6. The trade unions and British governments since 1945

Essay topics

To what extent can the trade unions be described as 'an integral part of the governing system' since 1945?

Was the alliance between the trade unions and the Labour party of value to either partner in the years after 1945?

Secondary works

See H Clegg, *A History of British Trade Unions since 1889: volume III, 1934–51* (1994); H Pelling, *A History of British Trade Unionism* (4th edn, 1987) chs 11–14; C J Wrigley (ed) *A History of British Industrial Relations* (1982); B Pimlott and C Cook (eds) *Trade Unions in British Politics* (2nd edn, 1991) chs 7–9, 12; A Fox, *History and Heritage: The Social Origins of the British Industrial Relations System* (1985) chs 7–9; K Middlemas, *Politics in Industrial Society: The Experience of the British System since 1911* (1979) chs 10, 13–15; E H Phelps Brown, *The Origins of Trade Union Power* (1983) chs 5–6. On the political impact of the trade unions see K O Morgan, *Labour in Power, 1945–1951* (1984) chs 8–9; R Taylor, *The Trade Union Question in British Politics; Government and Unions since 1945* (1993) and his *Fifth Estate: British Unions in the Modern World* (1978); J E Cronin, *Labour and Society in Britain, 1918–1979* (1984); L Minkin, *The Contentious Alliance: Trade Unions and the Labour Party* (1991); G A Dorfman, *Government versus Trade Unionism in British Politics since 1968* (1979); R Currie, *Industrial Politics* (1979) chs 5–6. For attempts to reform the trade unions, see D Barnes and E Reid, *Government and the Trade Unions: The British Experience, 1964–1979* (1980); C Ponting, *Breach of Promise: Labour in Power, 1964–1970* (1989) ch 22; M Moran, *The Politics of Industrial Relations: The Industrial Relations Act of 1971* (1977). For the Thatcher period, see the section in D Kavanagh and A Seldon (eds) *The Thatcher Effect: A Decade of Change* (1989); D Marsh, *The New Politics of British Trade Unions: Union Power and the Thatcher Legacy* (1992). On the NUM see M Crick, *Scargill and the Miners* (1985).

Articles

R Taylor, 'Thatcher's impact on the TUC', *CR* (1992); F Blackaby and A Dean, 'The dismal history of the Social Contract', *New Society* 13 Feb. 1975; 'The strange death of a social contract', *New Statesman* 26 Jan. 1979; see also the symposium: 'The Winter of Discontent', *CR* (1987).

7. Welsh and Scottish nationalism

Essay topics

Account for the fluctuating fortunes of Welsh and Scottish nationalism after 1945.

Why did devolution become an issue in British politics during the 1970s?

Why did devolution fail in the 1970s but succeed in the 1990s?

Secondary works

For the early history see R Coupland, *Welsh and Scottish Nationalism: A Study* (1954); A Butt Philip, *The Welsh Question: Nationalism in Welsh Politics, 1945–1970* (1975); H J Hanham, *Scottish Nationalism* (1969); C Harvie, *Scotland and Nationalism: Scottish Society and Politics, 1707–1997* (3rd edn, 1998). T Nairn, *The Break-up of Britain* (1977) was an influential analysis of the pressures on the British state in the 1970s, while V Bogdanor, *Devolution* (1979) examines the devolution issue. J Brand, *The National Movement in Scotland* (1992), G Webb, *The Growth of Nationalism in Scotland* (1992) and R Levy, *Scottish Nationalism at the Crossroads* (1992) discuss the issue of Scottish nationalism. Wales is examined in K O Morgan, *Rebirth of a Nation: Wales, 1880–1980* (1982) chs 3, 9, 13. T Gallagher (ed) *Nationalism in the Nineties* (1992) examines the fortunes of nationalism at the end of the century; see also A Marr, *The Battle for Scotland* (1992); A Midwinter, M Keating and J Mitchell, *Politics and Public Policy in Scotland* (1991); J Mitchell, *Strategies for Self-Government* (1996) and K Wright, *The People say Yes* (1997).

Articles

I. Green, 'Rational nationalists', *PolS* (1987); R Levy, 'The tartanization of the Labour party', *PAff* (1989).

8. The 1970s

Essay topics

To what extent was Britain 'ungovernable' in the 1970s?

Did either Heath or Callaghan have any answer to Britain's industrial decline?

Secondary works

For the Heath government see P Hennessy and A Seldon (eds) *Ruling Performance: British Governments from Attlee to Thatcher* (1989); R Blake, *The Conservative Party from Peel to Thatcher* (1985). On Heath himself, see J Campbell, *Edward Heath* (1993). For the ill-fated Industrial Relations Act see M Moran, *The Politics of the Industrial Relations Act of 1971* (1977). For union reactions see C Wrigley, 'Trade unions, the government and the economy' in T Gourvish and A O'Day (eds) *Britain since 1945* (1991); G Dorfman, *Government versus Trade Unionism in British Politics since 1968* (1979); R Taylor, *The Trade Union Question in British Politics: Government and Unions since 1945* (1993). See also B Pimlott and C Cook (eds) *Trade Unions in British Politics* (2nd edn, 1991).

For the Wilson and Callaghan administrations, see A Thorpe, *A History of the British Labour Party* (1997); M Holmes, *The Labour Government, 1974–79* (1985); P Hennessy and A Seldon (eds) *Ruling Performance* (1989); B Donoughue, *Prime Minister: The Conduct of Policy under Wilson and Callaghan* (1987); and D Kavanagh and P Morris, *Consensus Politics from Attlee to Thatcher* (1989). For the 'social contract', see G Dorfman, *Government versus Trade*

Unionism in British Politics since 1968 (1979); W J Fishbein, *Wage Restraint by Consensus* (1984). For a leading figure in the union influence on Labour, see J Jones, *Union Man: The Autobiography of Jack Jones* (1986). B Castle, *The Castle Diaries, 1974–76* (1980) offers an internal account, as do T Benn, *Diaries* (1987–93), D Healey, *The Time of my Life* (1989), J Callaghan, *Time and Chance* (1987), and R Jenkins, *A Life at the Centre* (1991). A major study of the economic crisis of 1976 is K Burk and A Cairncross, *Goodbye, Great Britain: The 1976 IMF Crisis* (1991) and of Callaghan's rise is P Kellner and C Hitchens, *Callaghan: The Road to Number 10* (1976).

On the rise of the left, see J Callaghan, *The Far Left in British Politics* (1987); P Seyd, *The Rise and Fall of the Labour Left* (1987); H Wainwright, *Labour: A Tale of Two Parties* (1987); A MacIntyre, 'The strange death of social-democratic England' in D Widgery (ed) *The Left in Britain, 1956–1968* (1976).

The rise of fascist, racist politics is discussed in M Walker, *The National Front* (1977); R Thurlow, *Fascism in Britain* (1987) chs 10–12; Z Layton-Henry, *The Politics of Race and Race Relations since 1945* (1992).

Articles

On the left, see R Samuel, 'The lost world of British communism', *NLR* (1985–86); see also the symposium: 'The Winter of Discontent', *CR* (1987).

9. The Northern Ireland crisis

Essay topic

What was the 'Irish question' after 1960 and why did successive British governments fail to solve it?

Secondary works

For documents on developments in Northern Ireland, see A O'Day and J Stevenson, *Irish Historical Documents since 1800* (1992) pt 8. For a general account see D Boyce, *The Irish Question and British Politics, 1968–1988* (1988); P Arthur and K Jeffery, *Northern Ireland since 1968* (1988); J J Lee, *Ireland 1912–1985: Politics and Society* (1989); and P Bew, P Gibbon and H Patterson, *Northern Ireland, 1921–94* (1995). On British policy towards Ireland, see M J Cunningham, *British Government Policy in Northern Ireland 1969–89: Its Nature and Execution* (1991); A Kenny, *The Road to Hillsborough: The Shaping of the Anglo-Irish Agreement* (1986). A useful collection on the background to the crisis is J Darby (ed) *Northern Ireland: The Background to the Conflict* (1983). Another perspective is given by R Rose, *Governing without Consensus: An Irish Perspective* (1971). Key personalities in the evolution of the conflict are examined in J Campbell, *Edward Heath* (1993) chs 22, 29.

On the security issue, see C Townshend, *Political Violence in Ireland: Government and Resistance since 1848* (1983); P Bew and H Patterson, *The British State and the Ulster Crisis from Wilson to Thatcher* (1985); C Townshend, *Britain's Civil Wars: Counter-insurgency in the Twentieth Century* (1986) ch 2; P Bishop and E Mallie, *The Provisional IRA* (1987); R Thurlow, *The Secret State* (1994).

Article

A Liphart, 'The Northern Ireland problem', *BJPS* (1975).

10. Third party politics and electoral reform since 1945

Essay topics

To what extent did this period see a revival of three-party politics?

Why did the Liberal–Social Democratic Alliance fail to 'break the mould' of British politics?

Why has proportional representation failed to attract more support in post-war Britain?

Secondary works

For the electoral system see M Pugh, *The Evolution of the British Electoral System, 1832–1987* (1988); V Bogdanor, *The People and the Party System: The Referendum and Electoral Reform in British Politics* (1981); D E Butler, *The Electoral System in Britain, 1918–51* (2nd edn, 1963) and *British General Elections since 1945* (1990).

For the history of the Liberal party, see C Cook, *A Short History of the Liberal Party 1900–97* (1998). For the third party position in general, see J Stevenson, *Third Party Politics in Britain since 1945* (1992); V Bogdanor, *Liberal Party Politics* (1983). The origins of the SDP are considered in I Bradley, *Breaking the Mould? The Birth and Prospects of the SDP* (1981); H Stephenson, *Claret and Chips: The Rise of the SDP* (1982); R Jenkins, 'Dimbleby Lecture' in W Kenner (ed) *The Rebirth of Britain* (1982). The definitive account of the SDP is now I Crewe and A King, *SDP: The Birth, Life and Death of the Social Democratic Party* (1995). For the accounts of participants see R Jenkins, *A Life at the Centre* (1991); D Steel, *Against Goliath* (1992); D Owen, *Time to Declare* (1991).

11. Women's history and the feminist movement

Essay topics

Why did a women's movement arise in Britain from the 1960s and what has it achieved so far?

How significant has gender been as the major determinant of life chances in Britain since 1945?

Secondary works

General studies of women's history include S Rowbotham, *Hidden from History* (1977); J M Mitchell and A Oakley (eds) *The Rights and Wrongs of Women* (1976); M Hartmann and L Banner (eds) *Clio's Consciousness Raised* (1974). Detailed studies which examine women's issues are J Lewis, *Women in Britain since 1945* (1991), E Roberts, *Women and Families: an Oral History, 1940–1970* (1994), J R Gillis, *For Better, For Worse: British Marriages 1600 to the*

Present Day (1986); E Wilson, *Only Halfway to Paradise: Women in Postwar Britain, 1945–1968* (1980). The development of attitudes towards sexuality is the subject of J Weeks, *Sex, Politics and Society since 1800* (2nd edn, 1992); see also L Bland, 'Purity, motherhood, pleasures or threats? Definitions of female sexuality, 1900–1970' in S Cartledge and J Ryan (eds) *Sex and Love* (1983).

Women's role in trade unionism can be traced in S Lewenhak, *Women and Trade Unions* (1977); N C Soldon, *Women in British Trade Unions, 1874–1976* (1978); S Boston, *Women Workers and the Trade Union Movement* (1980).

Articles

Useful general interpretations can be found in 'What is women's history?', *HT* (1985); E Richards, 'Women in the British economy since about 1700: an interpretation', *H* (1974).

12. Foreign policy and defence since 1964

Essay topics

Why has the European Community been such a divisive issue in British politics since 1964?

Was Britain anything other than a bit-part player in world affairs after 1964?

Secondary works

D Reynolds, *Britannia Overruled: British Policy and World Power in the Twentieth Century* (1991) is the most up-to-date overall assessment; see also D Sanders, *Losing an Empire, Finding a Role: British Foreign Policy since 1945* (1990). Britain's imperial position is examined in J Brown, *The Oxford History of the British Empire, Volume IV: The Twentieth Century* (1999); B Porter, *The Lion's Share: A Short History of British Imperialism, 1850–1983* (2nd edn, 1984); and P J Cain and A G Hopkins, *British Imperialism: Crisis and Deconstruction, 1914–1990* (1993). The economic position of Britain is discussed in B W E Alford, *Britain in the World Economy since 1880* (1995) and *British Economic Performance since 1945* (1986); A Sked, *Britain's Decline: Problems and Perspectives* (1987).

The important Anglo-American connection is considered in C J Bartlett, *'The Special Relationship': A Political History of Anglo-American Relations since 1945* (1992); W Louis and H Bull, *The Special Relationship: Anglo-American Relations since 1945* (1986). The retreat from East of Suez is examined in P Darby, *British Defence Policy East of Suez, 1947–1968* (1973); C J Bartlett, *The Long Retreat: A Short History of British Defence Policy 1945–70* (1972).

On early attitudes to Europe see E Barker, *Britain and a Divided Europe, 1945–70* (1971); M Camps, *European Unification in the Sixties* (1967); U Kitzinger, *The Second Try: Labour and the EEC* (1973) and *Diplomacy and Persuasion: How Britain joined the Common Market* (1973). The major overview now is J Young, *Britain and European Unity, 1945–1992* (1993). Key figures in the early attempts to join the European Community are considered in A Horne, *Macmillan, Vol II* (1991) especially chs 14–15; B Pimlott, *Harold Wilson* (1992); J Campbell, *Edward Heath* (1992). The pressure for entry is considered in R J Lieber, *British Politics and European Unity: Parties, Elites and Pressure Groups* (1970) and the 1975 referendum in A King, *Britain Says Yes; The 1975 Referendum* (1977). For notable opponents see P Cosgrave, *The Lives of Enoch Powell* (1989); M Foot, *Loyalists and Loners* (1986). For a pro-European perspective see R Jenkins, *A Life at the Centre* (1991) and *European Diary, 1977–81* (1989).

Other accounts of the European dimension include S George, *An Awkward Partner: Britain and the European Community* (1990), his shorter *Britain and European Integration since 1945* (1991), and the collection S George (ed) *Britain and the European Community: The Politics of Semi-detachment* (1992). See also S Bulmer, S George and A Scott, *United Kingdom and EC Membership Evaluated* (1992); N Nugent in P Dunleavy, A Gamble, I Holliday and G Peele (eds) *Developments in British Politics 4* (1994).

Margaret Thatcher's foreign policy impact can be examined in D Kavanagh and A Seldon (eds) *The Thatcher Effect* (1989); P Byrd (ed) *British Foreign Policy under Thatcher* (1988). The Falklands conflict is examined in L Freedman, *Britain and the Falklands War* (1988) and her Irish policy in A Kenny, *The Road to Hillsborough* (1985).

Articles

On Europe see R Butt, 'The Common Market and the Conservative party, 1960–61', *GO* (1967); S George, 'Britain and the EEC', *CR* (1992); on the Falklands, L Freedman and H Norpoth, 'The Falklands Factor', *CR* (1987–88).

13. The Thatcher era and after

Essay topics

Was Mrs Thatcher a Conservative?

To what extent did the Thatcher premiership mark a decisive shift in the conduct of British politics?

Secondary works

The Thatcher era is put into longer-term perspective in R Blake, *The Conservative Party from Peel to Thatcher* (1985); S Ball and A Seldon (eds) *The Conservative Century 1900–94* (1994). P Riddell, *The Thatcher Government* (1989) and the section in P Hennessy and A Seldon (eds) *Ruling Performance* (1987) offer an analysis of her premiership, though not of the last phase. For an analysis of 'Thatcherism' see D Kavanagh, *Thatcherism and British Politics* (1987); R Skidelsky (ed) *Thatcherism* (1988); and S R Letwin, *The Anatomy of Thatcherism* (1992). On specific aspects of policy, see A Gamble, *The Free Economy and the Strong State* (1988); W Keegan, *Mrs Thatcher's Economic Experiment* (1984) and *Mr Lawson's Gamble* (1989); D Smith, *From*

Boom to Bust: Trial and Error in British Economic Policy (1993); N M Healy (ed) *Britain's Economic Miracle: Myth or Reality?* (1993); P Byrd (ed) *British Foreign Policy under Thatcher* (1988); H Butcher, I Law, R Leach and M Mullard, *Local Government and Thatcherism* (1990); the essays in D Marsh and R Rhodes (eds) *Thatcherism: Audit of an Era* (1992). For biographies, see H Young, *One of Us: A Biography of Margaret Thatcher* (rev. edn, 1991) and K Harris, *Thatcher* (1988). M Thatcher, *The Downing Street Years* (1993), N Lawson, *The View from No. 11* (1992) and G Howe, *Conflict of Loyalty* (1994) are important views from insiders.

Opposition to Thatcher's government from within is considered in I Gilmour, *Inside Right* (1987) and for her final period in N Lawson, *The View from No. 11* (1992). The Labour Opposition is examined in P Seyd, *The Rise and Fall of the Labour Left* (1987). For Labour's leaders in the period see K O Morgan, *Labour People* (1987). G Elliott, *Labourism and the English Genius: The Strange Death of Labour England?* (1993) and P Seyd, 'Labour: the great transformation' in A King (ed) *Britain at the Polls, 1992* (1993) examine the later developments. For the growth of the Alliance and Liberal support, see C Cook, *A Short History of the Liberal Party, 1900–1997* (1998); J Stevenson, *Third Party Politics since 1945* (1992). For the Greens, see J Porritt and D Winner, *The Coming of the Greens* (1988); M Robinson, *The Greening of British Party Politics* (1992). The poll tax is considered in D Butler, A Adonis, and T Travers, *Failure in British Government: The Politics of the Poll Tax* (1994).

For the Major period, see A King (ed) *Britain at the Polls, 1992* (1992); E Pearce, *The Quiet Rise of John Major* (1992); B Anderson, *John Major* (1992); P Dunleavy, A Gamble, I Holliday and G Peele (eds) *Developments in British Politics 4* (1994); I Budge and D McKay, *The Developing British Political System: The 1990s* (3rd edn, 1994). Memoirs of the Major era now include J Major, *The Autobiography* (1999) and N Lamont, *In Office* (1999).

For the Labour Party under Smith and Blair, see S Fielding, *The Labour Party: 'Socialism' and Society since 1951* (1997), chs. 6 and 7; A Thorpe, *A History of the British Labour Party* (1997), and A Marwick, *A History of the Modern British Isles, 1914–1999* (2000), ch. 6.

Articles

M Wickham-Jones and D Shell, 'What went wrong? The fall of Mrs Thatcher', *CR* (1991); I Crewe, 'Why Mrs Thatcher was returned with a landslide', *SSR* (1987); 'Why did Labour lose (yet again)?' *Pol R* (1992).

Section VIII

MAPS

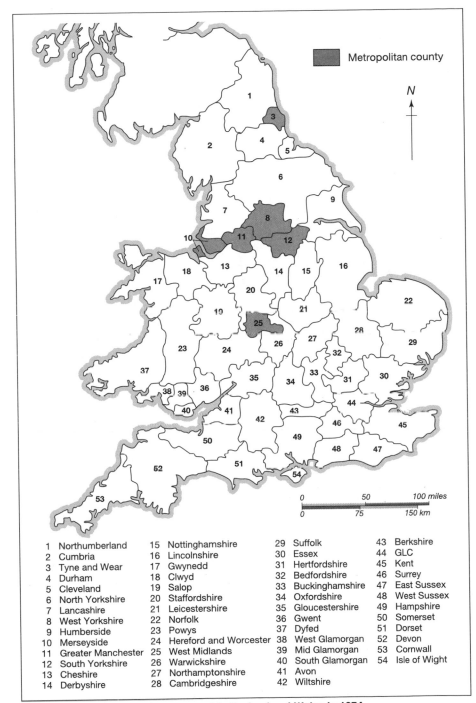

1	Northumberland	15	Nottinghamshire	29	Suffolk
2	Cumbria	16	Lincolnshire	30	Essex
3	Tyne and Wear	17	Gwynedd	31	Hertfordshire
4	Durham	18	Clwyd	32	Bedfordshire
5	Cleveland	19	Salop	33	Buckinghamshire
6	North Yorkshire	20	Staffordshire	34	Oxfordshire
7	Lancashire	21	Leicestershire	35	Gloucestershire
8	West Yorkshire	22	Norfolk	36	Gwent
9	Humberside	23	Powys	37	Dyfed
10	Merseyside	24	Hereford and Worcester	38	West Glamorgan
11	Greater Manchester	25	West Midlands	39	Mid Glamorgan
12	South Yorkshire	26	Warwickshire	40	South Glamorgan
13	Cheshire	27	Northamptonshire	41	Avon
14	Derbyshire	28	Cambridgeshire	42	Wiltshire

43	Berkshire
44	GLC
45	Kent
46	Surrey
47	East Sussex
48	West Sussex
49	Hampshire
50	Somerset
51	Dorset
52	Devon
53	Cornwall
54	Isle of Wight

Map 1: The reform of local government in England and Wales in 1974

333

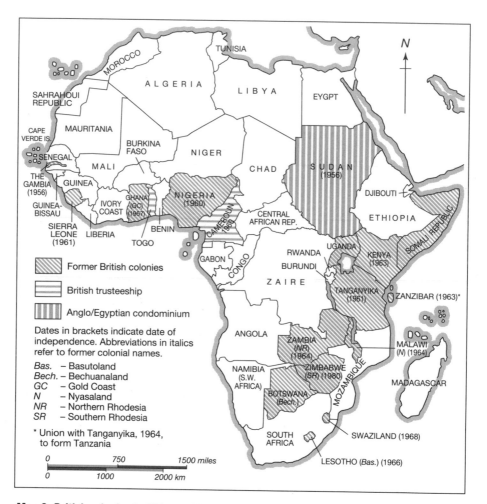

Map 2: British colonies in Africa and independence

INDEX